SALMON AND TROUT:

A resource, its ecology, conservation and management

Frontispiece   P<small>LATE</small> I

Salmon parr (*top*); Brown trout—juvenile (*middle*);
Brook trout (*foot*).

Artist: Christopher Lee

SALMON AND TROUT:

A resource, its ecology, conservation and management

DEREK MILLS M.Sc. Ph.D.

Department of Forestry and Natural Resources
University of Edinburgh

171

OLIVER & BOYD

EDINBURGH

OLIVER AND BOYD

Tweeddale Court, 14 High Street
Edinburgh EH1 1YL

A Division of Longman Group Ltd.

First published 1971

ISBN 0 05 002350 0

Printed in Great Britain by
Richard Clay (The Chaucer Press) Ltd,
Bungay, Suffolk

TO
FLORENCE
RICHARD and JENNY

PREFACE

The Atlantic salmon (*Salmo salar*), the trout (*S. trutta*), and other members of the salmon family, have a wide distribution in temperate regions and the conditions affecting their future as an important fishery resource are varied in the extreme. To produce sound plans for their future conservation and management it is necessary to review their history, value and method of exploitation and consider the ecology of the individuals forming the resource.

This book has been written to meet the needs of students in ecology, fishery management and regional planning. It is also hoped that it will be of use to fishery proprietors, river authorities, district fishery boards, estate managers, angling associations and civil engineers; and be of general interest to anglers. Because I endeavour to meet the requirements of individuals from a number of disciplines it is unavoidable that certain sections of the book may be irrelevant to the needs of some. For example, most of those directly concerned with salmon and trout should already be familiar with the life cycle of the salmon, although more than one angler and commercial fisherman have shown surprise when told that a grilse is a salmon which returns to freshwater to spawn the year after that in which it entered the sea as a smolt. This is a fact which many would consider general knowledge to those closely associated with salmon. However, those who are using the book for guidance in regional planning, for example, may not have appreciated the rather specialised habitat needs of salmon and trout. Furthermore, those who are to manage or conserve a renewable resource efficiently must know something of the biology and ecology of the fish concerned. Finally, those who own or rent fisheries may wish to improve their waters and the knowledge estate managers and angling clubs may require to carry out these improvements is dealt with in some detail.

This book is not meant to be an exhaustive account of the subject and in many sections I have given only a few examples to illustrate certain points. For example, aspects of legislation and pollution mainly concern the position in the British Isles.

I have only dealt briefly with 'other members of the salmon family' and, as the title of the book indicates, have concerned myself mainly with salmon and trout. However, I felt for the sake of completeness that these other fish should be mentioned as they live in close association with the two principal characters in this book. If I had tried to include any more detail the book would have become unwieldy. For this reason I hope that those whose work or area has not been mentioned will understand.

Finally, in defending the need for conservation and sound management of salmon and trout, I can do no better than quote the words of Dr Eggeling, Director of the Nature Conservancy (Scotland):

> Conservation basically implies looking after and making the best possible use of a resource, and particularly of a renewable resource – that is of something which through suitable management can produce a yield in perpetuity. Conservation must of necessity involve both fundamental research on all the many resources concerned and conservation research on their intelligent manipulation. Further, conservation seeks the positive information to say: 'Do this, do that, manage it thus, conserve it so, make use of it wisely for man.'

I am greatly indebted to Mr W. J. M. Menzies, at one time Inspector of Salmon Fisheries for Scotland, and Mr E. D. Le Cren, officer-in-charge of the River Laboratory of the Freshwater Biological Association of the United Kingdom, for so kindly reading through the manuscript of this book and for making a number of most valuable suggestions for its improvement.

I am also most grateful to Professor J. N. Black of the Department of Forestry and Natural Resources in the University of Edinburgh for his helpful comments.

The book has benefited immensely from my many discussions with: Mr P. L. Aitken, North of Scotland Hydro-electric Board; Mr R. N. Campbell, Nature Conservancy; Mr R. W. Covill, Lothians River Purification Board; Dr W. B. Currie (at one time editor of *Rod and Line*); Mr K. R. Elson, Marine Laboratory, Aberdeen; Mr A. V. Holden, Freshwater Fisheries Laboratory, Pitlochry; Mr K. A. Pyefinch, Freshwater Fisheries Laboratory, Pitlochry; Col. R. M. Ryan, Superintendent to the River Tweed Commissioners; Mr S. D. Sedgewick, Inspector of Salmon Fisheries for Scotland and Dr Isabel Smith, Department of Bacteriology, University of Edinburgh.

I greatly appreciate the work which the two artists, Mr Christopher Lee (Frontispiece and Plate II) and Mr Stanley Clement-Smith (Figs. 16, 59, 60, 63 and 64), put into their illustrations. I am also most grateful for the photographs supplied by Mr R. Balharry (Plate 14); Mr F. Howie (Plates 2, 3, 20, 28 and 33 to 37); Mr A. D. S. Macpherson (Plate 1); the North of Scotland Hydro-electric Board (Plates 17 and 18), and Planair (Plate 19).

My acknowledgements are also due to the following for so kindly allowing me to reproduce some of their material:

Edward Arnold (Publishers) Ltd. (Figs. 11 and 12); Association of River Authorities (Fig. 55); Atlantic Salmon Association (Fig. 13); Dr M. Berg (Fig. 15 and Plates 8, 9 and 10); Blackwell Scientific Publications Ltd. (Figs. 37, 61, 68 and 69); Butterworths Ltd. (Table 20); Cambridge University Press (Fig. 8); Mr R. N. Campbell (Fig. 49, Table 16 and Plate 11); Dr B. Carlin (Figs. 17, 18 and 44); Collins Ltd. (Figs. 23, 24, 26, 27 and 35 and Table 15); Controller of Her Majesty's Stationery Office (Figs. 20, 22, 25, 29, 30, 33 and 58 and Tables 8, 11, 12, 21, 22, 27 and 28 and Plates 12 and 13); Council of the Institute of Civil Engineers (Figs. 42, 43 and Tables 25 and 26); Dr N. O. Cronland; Dept. of Fisheries and Forestry, Canada (Plates 4 and 30); Mr T. B. Fraser (Table 32); Mr G. D. F. Hadoke (Table 6); Dr J. M. Hellawell (Figs. 5 and 6); Professor M. Huet (Table 17); Dr R. Hunt (Fig. 53 and Plates 25, 26 and 27); International Biological Programme (Figs. 61, 68 and 69); Dr A. Lindroth (Figs. 9 and 10); The Maccaferri River and Sea Gabions (London) Ltd. (Figs. 50, 51 and 52 and Plates 23 and 24); Professor J. T. McFadden (Fig. 28); Mersey and Weaver River Authority (Table 24); Mr W. R. Munro (Figs. 45 and 46); Thomas Nelson and Sons (Plates 6 and 7); *New Scientist* (Fig. 14); Dr E. Odum (Fig. 36); Mr G. C. S. Oliver (Table 30); Mr L. Rosseland (Fig. 7); The Salmon Net Fishing Association of Scotland (Figs. 1, 21 and 54); W. B. Saunders Company (Fig. 36); *Scottish Sunday Express* (Plate 13); *The Scotsman* (Table 7); Mr W. M. Shearer (Fig. 14); Dr H. D. Slack (Fig. 34); Societas Internationalis Limnologiae (Figs. 45 and 46); Trent River Authority (Table 23a); Miss E. Twomey (Figs. 47 and 48), Dr Ph. Wolf (Fig. 38) and M. F. Woodiwiss (Table 23b).

DEREK MILLS

Edinburgh
October, 1970

CONTENTS

PART I

MAN AND THE RESOURCE: EXPLOITATION

PART II

THE BIOLOGY OF THE RESOURCE

PART III

THE ENVIRONMENT, THE RESOURCE AND MAN

PART IV

CONSERVATION AND MANAGEMENT OF THE RESOURCE

PART V

THE FUTURE

ILLUSTRATIONS

COLOUR PLATES

BLACK AND WHITE PLATES

TEXT FIGURES

LIST OF TABLES

PART I

MAN AND THE RESOURCE: EXPLOITATION

B

Chapter 1

THE SALMON

1.1 The salmon as a natural resource. 1.2 Methods of commercial salmon fishing. 1.3 The sport fishery. 1.4 Private or common property resource. 1.5 The size and economic value of the fisheries. 1.6 Trends and fluctuations in the fisheries.

1.1 The salmon as a natural resource

The salmon has been a commercially valuable fish for centuries and its popularity probably dates from Roman times. During the Middle Ages it was an important item of domestic as well as international trade. We have records of Rhine salmon being shipped long distances and fetching high prices. Norway developed a thriving trade in salmon with neighbouring countries and the kings of Norway derived considerable revenue from taxes on the fish. In Norway records of exploitation of salmon fisheries go as far back as the third century A.D.

Salted salmon was a staple of Scottish exports by the thirteenth century, and by this date Aberdeen, Perth, Berwick and Glasgow were centres of the trade and merchants came from other countries to purchase the fish. Russel (1864) mentions evidence of a considerable export of Scotch salmon (pickled), chiefly to Flanders and France, as early as 1380; and a municipal order at Rheims, of that date, contains regulations for its sale. At the time of its prosperity, in the days of New France, salmon was the object of regular trading in Quebec and up to Montreal. Maheux (1956) makes numerous references to barrels of salted salmon purchased by the oldest inhabitants of learning in Canada.

Although England had many salmon rivers it is apparent that even from the late 1600s the supply could not meet the demand, and the first settlers in Nova Scotia were shipping schooner loads of salted salmon to the English market.

In many countries today the salmon is still an important item of commerce and in numerous areas it is very important in the general economy of the people who obtain a living directly or indirectly from it. It is important in that it supports commercial fisheries and provides a sport fishery on which is centred a large tourist industry.

1.2 Methods of commercial salmon fishing

The main commercial salmon fisheries are centred on the eastern seaboard of North America, the west coast of Greenland, Iceland, Ireland, the United Kingdom, Norway, Sweden and Denmark and, to a lesser extent, other countries bordering the Baltic Sea, and France.

Although in some countries there is offshore fishing for salmon using drift nets, the majority of the salmon fisheries are concentrated along the coasts and estuaries in order to catch the fish returning to their parent rivers to spawn. Fish moving along the coast are caught in a variety of fixed nets set out from the shore, while those ascending the rivers are taken at

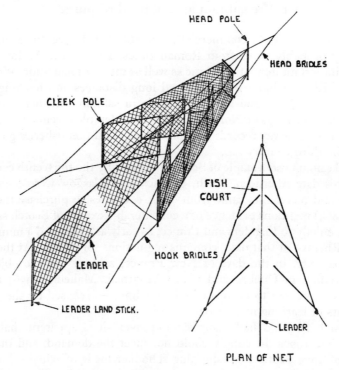

FIG. 1.   Diagram of a bag net (from Hector, 1966).

weirs or cruives, in beach seines or draft nets or by a variety of nets and traps peculiar to particular countries.

Scotland. In Scotland the principal fixed engines are the bag net and the fly net. The bag net (Fig. 1) is commonly used on rocky coasts and consists essentially of a trap made of netting to which fish are directed by a leader, that is a line of netting placed across the route the salmon usually follow as they move along the coast. The salmon swim towards the leader but cannot get through and instinctively turn seawards. Swimming along the leader they are led into the mouth of the net and through a succession of compartments into a final chamber or fish court.

A good description of the history, construction and operation of the bag net is given by Hector (1966). In describing the operation of fishing this type of net he says:

> The best time to fish a net is either at high water or low water when the tide is on the turn, and therefore at its slackest. The boat approaches the side from which the tide is flowing. The head pole is seized by means of a boat hook, and the rope untied at the top. This removes the rigidity of the net and the bottom floats towards the surface and the net now lies along the side of the boat. The crew grasp the net and by means of two ropes the bottom is brought to meet the top rope. The boat now crosses the net by the man grasping the meshes of the cover and the bottom. As a result of the flowing tide the netting forms a bulge and the salmon are imprisoned in this section. At the centre of the side is a lacing, which, when undone, allows the salmon to be removed and killed. The net is put in fishing order again by fixing the head pole in its original position, restoring the rigidity of the net. Once a week each net is replaced by a clean one to allow it to be repaired and the sea growth removed by exposure to the sun.

This method of obtaining fish must necessitate relatively calm seas and such a net is very susceptible to storm damage.

Stake nets, known as fly nets or 'jumpers' depending on their construction, are used on sandy shores and consist of walls of netting erected on stakes in the sea-bed which act as leaders to approaching salmon. At intervals pockets or traps are inserted to take the fish that are directed along the leader. Unlike bag nets, they are not floating but are fixed to the ground throughout their length. Fish taken by these nets and the bag net are trapped, and not caught in the meshes, and are usually alive when removed.

Another type of fixed net used in Scotland is the poke net. Poke nets are used exclusively on the Scottish side of the Solway Firth. They are mounted in lines on rows of poles and consist of a series of pockets of net in which fish are trapped and enmeshed.

Two other types of net used for catching salmon in the Solway Firth are the haaf net and the whammel net. Haaf nets (Plate 1) are mounted on a wooden frame (about 16 feet by 4 feet) with a handle in the middle of the long side. The fisherman stands in the tide with the middle stick over his shoulder and the net streaming behind him. When he feels a fish strike he lifts the lower lip to prevent its escape. The fisherman must place himself within a few yards of the probable course of moving fish. It is customary for a number of men to fish together. They stand side by side facing the current of the tide and as the tide rises the outermost man in turn transfers himself to the inner end. The procedure is repeated in the reverse order as the tide recedes. A whammel net is a small type of drift net only used to a limited extent, but from the decision of a Scottish court in 1962 it appears that the use of whammel nets on the Scottish side of the main channel in the Solway Firth is illegal.

The net and coble is the only method of net fishing which is legal inside estuary limits throughout Scotland. The net is loaded on the coble and attached to it is a rope held by a fisherman on the shore, who, once the operation begins, must keep the rope in motion by his own exertions. The coble moves across the estuary or river, shooting the net as it goes. Its course is roughly a semicircle finishing on the shore from which the boat started out. The ends of the net are then hauled in (Plate 2) and the fish removed. It is an essential part of the net and coble fishing that the net is hauled through the water continuously and kept in motion by the exertions of the fishermen, who are in some areas assisted by powered winches. The net must not be allowed to remain stationary or drift with the tide, as the fish taken in the net are guided to the landing ground, but not enmeshed in it. The central and deeper part of the net is generally bag-shaped and the fishermen drive the fish towards the bag by splashing the ropes as the net is being pulled in.

Among other catching devices at one time used in the rivers, *but now illegal*, were cruives, stell nets and cairn nets. Cruives consisted of weirs in which were incorporated boxes or traps. These are still present on some rivers (Plate 3) (e.g. the Conon and Beauly) but are no longer operational.

The stell net is rowed into the river in a semi-circular shape. A rope attached to one end of it is held by the fishermen on the shore, and to the other end is attached an anchor, which is cast and secured to the bed of the river. The fishermen in the boat then go near to the centre of the net on the outside of it, and take hold of it, and when they either feel fish strike against the net, or see them approach within its reach, they warn the men on the shore, and while the latter haul in their end of the net, the men in the boat hoist the anchor, release the net, and bring it to the shore.

A cairn net was a short net fastened to the outer end of a short pier, known as a cairn or putt which ran out two or three yards into the river, particularly the Tweed, causing an eddy or backwater. The net was allowed to swing down with the stream, so forming a barrier parallel between the eddy and the main current, and leaving a good chance of intercepting all fish that turned out to pass outwards from their resting place. Cairn and stell nets were made illegal by the Tweed Act of 1857.

One type of trap still in operation is the yair net, unique to the Galloway Dee. A yair consists of two converging fences or leaders made of stakes interwoven with saplings to form a coarse wicker work. In the apex of the V formed by the converging leaders is a rectangular opening, across the top of which is a platform on which the fisherman sits on a box. The actual net is a deep bag. The fisherman lowers it into the opening, so that the water flows through it, and sits, holding a system of lines leading from the end of the bag. If a fish touches the end of the bag, he feels the impact through the lines, and immediately hauls up the mouth of the net, thus securing it.

An interesting type of moving net was the shoulder net used on the Galloway Dee and described by King-Webster (1969):

> Shoulder nets were used in small pools among the rocks, some of which were reached by a system of wooden catwalks. The gear consisted of a 24 ft. shaft with a 6 to 7 ft. wooden cross-piece at the end, kept square by two rope stays. The triangle formed by cross-piece and stays supported the mouth of a deep bag of netting. Before making a cast, the fisherman flaked the net on top of the shaft, and rested the shaft on a wooden shoe fitted to his shoulder. The cast was made by shooting the net forward, so that the shaft slid over the shoe and the net fell beyond the fish. The net was then drawn in through the pool, the shaft sliding back over the shoe. Shoulder netting required great strength and skill, as fishing was done only at night, and the stance was often precarious and slippery.

Brief mention should also be made of a drift net fishery which developed off the east coast of Scotland in 1960. This drift net fishing was a new technique which had no parallel in Scotland and until the Prohibition Order became effective on 15 September, 1962, drift net fishing for salmon was lawful outside the three-mile limit. The development and description of this fishery is described fully in the First Report of the Hunter Committee, *Scottish Salmon and Trout Fisheries* (H.M.S.O. 1963). The drift nets consisted of sections of netting about 10 feet in depth suspended from a corked head rope and were either not weighted at all at the bottom or only very lightly. Each section of net measured about 100 yards in length. The sections were divided into two fleets, each consisting of about 1,000 yards of netting. The nets were shot by casting them over the side a few feet at a time in a straight line. Some skippers joined their two fleets of nets together and lay at one end of them while others preferred to let each fleet drift independently with the boat taking up station between them. The best results were obtained at night in breezy weather from wind force 3 to wind force 5 when the surface of the water was disturbed.

England and Wales. Fixed engines, which are the principal method of sea fishing for salmon in Scotland, are with a few exceptions, forbidden in England and Wales. One type of fixed engine used on the Northumberland coast is the T net which is very similar to the Norwegian kilenot. Its advantage over the Scottish stake and bag nets is its portability and frequently the net is moved inshore as the tide advances. Probably most salmon are taken with seine, draft or draw nets. Most of these are operated from a boat but in Carmarthen Bay and Norfolk a boat is not used and the net is shot by a man wading into the water while his companion holds the shore end.

Another common method of fishing in England and Wales is by drift nets. They consist of a wall of netting (approximately 24 feet deep) shot from a boat across the current and allowed to drift freely. One end of the net is attached to a floating buoy and the other remains fixed to the boat. The head rope is corked and the foot rope leaded, to keep the net upright. These nets are used in the Bristol Channel, the Ribble and the Lune estuaries, the Solway, and off the north-east coast from Filey to Berwick-on-Tweed.[1] These drift nets gill the fish, that is, their heads pass through the meshes of netting. The mesh sizes vary according to the size of fish expected to be caught. The salmon are generally meshed on the south side of the nets, and the best catches are made in the top ten meshes. In the estuary of the Cheshire Dee, the drift nets are trammels. Trammels consist of either two or three sheets of netting. One sheet, the middle one if there are three, is of standard mesh and is sometimes called the lint. The others are of much bigger mesh and are known as armouring. A fish striking the lint may, or may not, be gilled as it drives a pocket of this netting through a mesh of the armouring and is trapped.

The Welsh coracle net is used as a drift net and has one sheet of armouring. Coracle netting differs from drift netting, however, in that two coracles are used with the net between them, travelling downstream, armoured side foremost.

Other methods for catching salmon in England and Wales include: (1) types of landing nets going under the name of bow or click nets (Humber

---

[1] The actual limit is south of the legal mouth of the Tweed as defined in Section 4 of the Tweed Fisheries Amendment Act, 1859 (i.e. 7 miles south of Berwick).

PLATE I. Haaf netters in operation on the Solway Firth. As the tide rises the outer fisher is compelled by the deepening water to vacate his position and takes up his post on the landward end of the line.

PLATE 2. Beach seine or sweep net in operation on the River Tweed at Berwick.

area), lave nets (Severn) and haaf or heave nets (between the Lune and Eden). (2) Nets operated from a boat anchored across the current. These are known as stop nets (Wye) or compass nets (Cleddau). (3) Fixed weirs situated between tide marks. These may be of stone, or of stone surmounted by netting or of stakes and wattles. They consist of two arms set to form a V pointing in the direction of the ebbing tide. (4) Putchers, which consist of a wooden framework into which are inserted tiers of trumpet-shaped basket traps. These are used in the estuaries of the Severn, Wye, Parrett and the Bristol Channel. (5) Crib or coop, which is essentially a weir with a gap in it. Gratings are set at an angle pointing upstream from each of the downstream corners of the gap, so set that the space between the gratings is only just sufficient to allow a salmon to pass through. The rush of water through the gap entices salmon to pass between these gratings, but their egress to the river above the weir is stopped by another grating set across the gap and they are trapped.

Ireland. The methods which are or have been used for catching salmon in Ireland have been admirably described by Went (1964a). He divides the methods into four categories: (A) man-power engines (other than nets) which include spears or leisters; strokehauls; gaffs; snares and tailers. (B) Fixed engines such as head weirs; stake nets; bag nets; riverine weirs; cudjail nets, and baskets for smolts. (C) Nets (other than fixed engines) which are numerous and include draft nets; drift nets; snap; pole and hoop nets. (D) Other methods such as poisoning and explosives.

The methods in the first category are common to many countries and salmon spearing or leistering was a method used in Scotland and eastern Canada and abolished in both countries around 1857. The head weirs, under B, are similar to those used in England, while the riverine weirs have cruives as their counterpart in Scotland. Cudjail nets consisted of a stout wire frame to which netting was attached. The net was fixed in gaps in the navigation weirs on the River Barrow and the salmon moving upstream were trapped and eventually drowned. Went says that there is no documentary evidence that baskets for smolts were used in Ireland but there is much local tradition on the subject. Any suitable gap in an artificial or natural obstruction would be useful for this purpose and during the smolt run would provide quantities of small fish. The beach seine, or draft net, is fished in the same way as in the United Kingdom and accounts for more salmon in Ireland than all the other methods put together.

Drift nets as used in Ireland are of two types (1) Estuarine or bag drift nets and (2) Open sea drift nets. The latter are shot just before dark and in the biggest boats are normally only hauled at dawn. The smaller boats, with comparatively small nets, usually haul the nets several times a night.

The most favourable weather conditions are dark stormy nights, for on calm nights the fish do not mesh themselves. Generally salmon swim near the water surface and they normally become enmeshed in the upper three feet of the net. A survey of the open sea drift-net fishing for the years 1925 to 1954 has been described by Went (1956).

One of the traditional methods of taking salmon in Ireland is with the snap net. Snap nets require two boats, often called cots, to operate them. The net is suspended between the two cots which then drift downstream. The net is therefore fished in much the same way as in the Welsh coracle fishery, although the snap net is a single sheet of netting in which the fish is trapped rather than enmeshed. Two other types of net used in Ireland are the pole net, which is a type of landing net with which fish were actively hunted when they showed themselves at weirs or falls or in pools. The other net is the Swilly 'loop' net which is of unusual design to overcome fishing in the deep soft muddy conditions occurring in the River Swilly estuary.

The last two methods of catching salmon given in Went's list are prohibited by statute and they are: (1) poisoning – The poison used for killing fish in some parts of Ireland was from crushed roots of the giant spurge (*Euphorbia hiberna*). The roots were dug, allowed to decay and then crushed. The crushed mass was then put into bags and trodden into the water. The poisonous juices from the roots mixed with the water and the fish were soon killed and taken out by hand. (2) Explosives – like poisoning, explosives kill young as well as adult salmon and fortunately are prohibited.

The Baltic Countries. The countries bordering the Baltic, particularly Denmark and Sweden, fish for salmon in the open sea with drift nets and floating long-lines known as 'drift hooks' baited with herring. The floating long-line consists of a main line to which a nylon line, 52 feet to 66 feet long and baited with hooks, is attached. Netboy (1968a) describes the fishing procedure: "The operation begins with the placing of a buoy in the water, followed by other buoys at intervals of every 80 hooks, the whole forming a procession up to 18 miles long, marked by 25 or more buoys. Every buoy carried a numbered flag and usually a battery-charged lamp".

A similar method is used in the recently developed floating long-line fishery off the Faroes (Munro, 1969):

> The lines are made up in sets of 50–60 hooks with 2-fathoms mono-filament snoods mounted 8 fathoms apart on a light synthetic line. Yellow painted corks ($2\frac{3}{4}$ in. × 1 in.) are positioned on the line at the mid-point between the snoods. The snoods are mounted on the main line by means of a swivel, are weighted at their mid-point by a barrel lead incorporating a swivel and terminated in a No. 3/0 hollow point

'Mustad' hook. In use, these short lengths of line are joined into a continuous line with a 'Dhan' buoy between each set of hooks.

The lines are baited with sprats. According to Christensen (personal communication) before the Second World War the Danish salmon fishing was carried on by means of drift nets and 'fixed hooks' exclusively around the island of Bornholm. In 1947 'drift hooks' were introduced and in a few years dominated the salmon fishery. At the same time the Danish annual catches increased to a level of 1,000 tons, from around 100 tons before the war. In the season 1961/62 only 20% of the Danish salmon catches were made by means of drift nets. This percentage increased in the following seasons to 40%. As a consequence of the introduction of synthetic fibres in net manufacture the percentage of the catch by drift nets rose to 70–75% in the seasons 1964/65 and 1965/66. 'Drift hooks' are now mainly used for a few months in the winter time. The use of 'drift hooks' is, however, influenced by the success of the summer fishing in the North Sea. If the yield is poor, many fishermen from West Jutland will try their luck in the salmon fishery in the Baltic in the following winter, and of course they will only invest in the cheapest gear, which is 'drift hooks'.

Thurow (1968) has made a study of the catches of Baltic salmon by various gear. In referring to the feeding of the salmon in the Baltic he mentions that shoals of sprat may act as a powerful appeal and even baited hooks may do so. He has demonstrated the efficiency of long-lines as compared with nets by showing the number of hooks necessary to catch a number of salmon which is equal to the number caught by 100 drift nets. As an average for the three seasons between 1960–1962 the number of hooks were:

Oct./Nov.	997
Dec./Jan.	641
Feb./Mar.	1211

From these figures he pointed out that hooks were most efficient in winter when the amount of food available is at its lowest.

He also showed that the long-line catches were better with wind of a strength of more than 5 Beaufort than with light winds below 5 Beaufort. As an average over five seasons the catch per 1,000 hooks in the Danziger Tief amounted to:

9·2 salmon with no wind
12·4 salmon with wind < 5 Beaufort
17·9 salmon with wind > 5 Beaufort

The catches by drift nets tended to show the opposite pattern with greater catches when there was little wind.

The Swedish coastal fishery employs fixed engines similar to the Scottish stake nets. There are also sweep- or seine-net fisheries in the large northern rivers. One type of trap in use in the rivers, particularly the Torn Älv, the river separating Sweden from Finland, is the karsinapatorna. In some of the rivers in southern Sweden, such as the Murramsö, traps used to be set to catch seaward migrating smolts for feeding to pigs, this is of course now illegal.

Canada. Inshore drift nets are used in the Ungava fishery in northern Canada while offshore drift nets are used in the Maritime Provinces where drift-net fisheries are centred on Port Aux Basques, Newfoundland; Escuminac, New Brunswick, and the upper part of the Bay of Fundy and Nova Scotia. Trap or shore nets are used on the coast of the Gaspé Peninsula and on the north shore of the St Lawrence. Along the coast of New Brunswick gill nets, trap nets, pound nets and weirs are also used.

France and Spain. Commercial salmon fishing in France is carried out mainly with seine or draft nets, while in Spain all nets have been banned from salmon rivers and their estuaries since 1942. Spain is the only country which has handed over the salmon resource to the sport fisherman.

Greenland. A recent fishery to develop is that off the west coast of Greenland where fish are caught mainly in fixed hang nets. Braided nylon with a mesh of 2–3 inches knot to knot seems to be used exclusively. Nets are about 75 yards long and 10 yards deep. However, other engines, such as the kilenot, are being tried and consequently the principal method of fishing may eventually change. It is understood that floating seaweed makes fishing difficult and large amounts of *Laminaria* are found floating as far as 10 miles offshore. Because of this the gill net is set so that the headrope is some distance below the surface. Fishing begins in August and goes on until mid-November.

Iceland. The only commercial fishing for salmon in Iceland is that carried out in glacial rivers by means of stake nets as the salmon was declared a freshwater fish by law in 1930 and netting in the sea in territorial waters was prohibited.

Norway. The bag net or kilenot is the most important gear for taking salmon in the sea in Norway and this net has been in use in northern Norway for over a hundred years. About 88% of the salmon in north Norway are caught in the sea, mostly in bag nets. There is an intensive bag-net fishery in the fjords of northern Norway and Finnmark, particularly in Varanger, Tana, Porsanger and Alta fjords into which some of the best salmon rivers flow.

Although some drift-net fishing has been carried on for at least seventy years, offshore drift netting using long nets only began in 1960 and this latest fishery is similar to the one which started in Scotland at about that time. A complete ban on drift netting for salmon is under consideration.

Other types of net used in Norway include the flakenot and crooknet. The flakenot is shaped rather like a kilenot and has a number of compartments which may be closed or pursued separately. A white board is placed at the entrance to the net and as fish are seen passing over the board into the net the compartments can be closed. The crook net is set jutting out from the shore and is similar to the English fixed weirs.

One type of trap found on some Norwegian rivers, such as the Driva, is built like a box with a wooden fence leading up to it, the latter guides the fish through a V-shaped entrance into a single holding chamber.

While salmon spearing is illegal in the British Isles and Canada it is allowed in Norway on the Aura River at Eikesdalsvatn, but this is the only river in Norway where it is permissible and future legislation may make it illegal.

Russia. According to Kozhin (1964), the Atlantic salmon is taken in Russia with drift nets, bag nets and seines. Unfortunately no detailed information concerning their fisheries appears to be available.

1.3 The sport fishery

When fish are sought after for sport they are fished or angled for with the aid of a rod and line. Sport fishing is an ancient pastime, archaeologists have found fish hooks believed to be 5,000 years old and the earliest known picture of a rod fisherman dates from about 2000 B.C. There is a record from Roman writing that anglers were fishing with artificial flies more than seventeen centuries ago.

The main ways of luring salmon are with artificial flies and fish or with natural bait such as live earthworms, or preserved fish and prawns. The development of fishing tackle has increased rapidly in recent years. In the past salmon rods were long (up to 20 feet) and heavy, being built of green-heart or split-cane, and reels were of brass making them heavy and cumbersome. The lures were of a size in keeping with the rod, and flies were heavily dressed on large hooks or 'irons'. In recent years the rods have become shorter and, with the introduction of fibre glass, hollow or solid glass rods are to some extent replacing the more expensive split-cane rods. Brass has been replaced by light alloys in reel manufacture and the development of the fixed spool and multiplier spinning reels has produced an efficient piece of equipment which enables the novice to achieve a high standard of casting in a very short time. Synthetic fibres such as nylon and terylene have replaced the more expensive plaited silk lines in some branches of angling. This development has not stopped at rods, reels and lines but is seen also among the flies and lures. The flies tend to be smaller and hair has to some extent replaced the more expensive and exotic feathers used in fly dressing in the past. Artificial minnows are giving way to pieces of metal called spoons. The trend has been towards less elaborate tackle and more efficient methods of fishing. With increasing affluence and leisure, fishing is becoming more and more accessible to everyone. However, salmon angling remains on the whole an expensive sport because of the high rents salmon rivers can demand and sport fishing is a valuable asset to many salmon countries.

The sport fishery is a valuable resource and has been well-developed as a tourist attraction, although in some areas it is for commercial gain and the catch is sent direct to the market. The popularity of salmon angling is difficult to assess, particularly in Scotland where no licence is required. However, in countries where licences are issued this is possible. Went (1964b) indicated the present attraction of salmon angling in Ireland when he revealed that in 26 of the 32 counties in Ireland in 1961 the total number of licences issued for salmon rods was 9,820. In countries such as Canada, Norway and Scotland many of the salmon rivers run through sparsely populated country and the sport fishery centred on them helps to bring employment and money into remote areas. Because of their sporting value salmon have also been introduced to other countries such as Tasmania and New Zealand.

In some countries, such as Scotland, many of the better salmon rivers are only available to the more wealthy anglers who can afford to pay the large rents demanded when they are fortunate enough to get the opportunity of obtaining a lease. High prices have been paid for the better beats of the first-class salmon rivers, for example £40,000 ($112,000) have been paid for stretches of the Aberdeenshire Dee and Ness while £98,000 was paid for $2\frac{1}{2}$ miles of fishing on the Tweed at Boleside where the annual catch of salmon is in the region of 300. Rivers such as the Findhorn, Tweed, Tay, Spey and Aberdeenshire Dee have only small stretches upon which the average angler can fish. These stretches are usually leased from large estates as a concession to the local angling clubs or associations. These bodies then manage the rented water and make it available to the local and visiting angler on a ticket basis. In some districts there are some very good stretches of water running through towns such as Grantown-on-Spey, Inverness, Peebles and Perth which are available to the public at a nominal fee. However, this results in the rivers being overcrowded with anglers during the best parts of the season and as this sometimes happens on other ticket waters as well anglers may frequently be seen fishing practically shoulder to shoulder. Other rivers, particularly in the north and west of Scotland, are frequently owned or rented by hotels who keep their fishing for hotel guests. Beats on some of these, such as the Thurso, Oykell and Ewe, are therefore available to the holiday angler. Some Scottish rivers, which have been harnessed for power, have been purchased by the North of Scotland Hydro-electric Board and leased out to tenants through a sporting agent. Parts of these rivers are available to local angling clubs or individuals thus making salmon fishing accessible to the angler with a more modest income and this is the position on the rivers Blackwater and Conon. Most estates, tenants and hotels employ keepers or ghillies who look after the water and tend to the anglers' needs.

Lastly, mention should be made of fishing instruction holidays. These are held at a few angling resorts on good salmon or sea trout rivers.

Salmon rivers are frequently divided into beats and all of the bigger rivers have their pools named and some of these pools have become famous because of the number of salmon taken from them. Calderwood (1909), in his book *The Salmon Rivers and Lochs of Scotland* gives maps of some of the major salmon rivers with all the beats named.

The position in *Ireland* is similar to that in Scotland and many hotels own or rent fisheries on some of the famous rivers such as the Bandon, Laune and Newport; while the more private fishing is to be found on the Boyne, Slaney, Moy and Cork Blackwater. The estimated 'export' value of sport fishing inclusive of actual value of salmon exports is given in Fig. 2. The estimated number of anglers visiting Ireland to fish for brown trout, coarse fish and sea fish as well as salmon and sea trout for the years 1960–1967 is given in Fig. 3, and the estimated revenue from angling visitors for this period is shown in Fig. 4.

The exclusive and expensive nature of salmon angling is common to many countries. In *England* this is particularly true on rivers such as the Hampshire Avon, Eden, Lune and Wye. For example a 1,000-yards stretch on one bank of the Lune was sold for £30,000. In *Norway* the bigger the purse the better the fishing and the rent on good beats may be as much as £1,000 a fortnight per rod. Even so there is a shortage of available fishing places on the famous Norwegian rivers like the Laerddalsalven, Namsen and Aurlandsalven. Cheaper fishing is, however, available on rivers such as the Rauma, Driva and Gula. Berg (1964a), in his book on North Norwegian salmon rivers, mentions there being rod fishing in North Norway for the 'man in the street'. In Finnmark fishing licences may be bought for most of the rivers, while in Nordland and Troms many rivers are private.

Netboy (1968a) reviews the history of angling in Norway and refers to the rapid rise in the value of the Norwegian salmon sport fishery:

In the first decade of the twentieth century 80 rivers were leased

wholly or in part to sportsmen, with rentals totalling 300,000 kroner.
In 1951 rentals aggregated 450,000 kroner; ten years later they had
more than doubled: some 94 rivers were leased for a total of 1,150,000

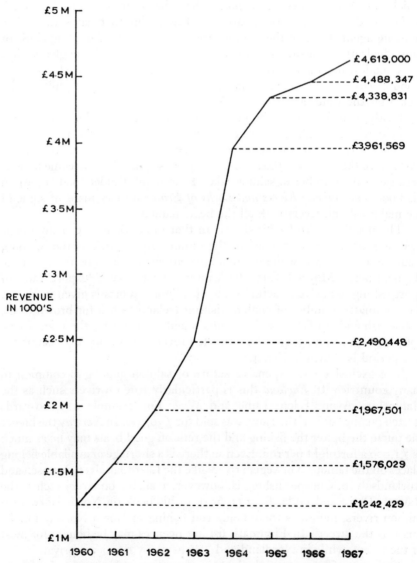

FIG. 2. Estimated 'export' value of sport fishing in Ireland exclusive of
actual value of salmon exports. (Source – Department of Agriculture and
Fisheries, Ireland, from data supplied by Bord Failte Eireann.)

kroner. In 1964 one river, the Alta, was leased to an American millionaire for 250,000 kroner ($35,000) for the period June 24 to July 24.

Norway, like Scotland, offers salmon fishing holidays. These can be very expensive and an all-inclusive 14-day salmon fishing tour may cost almost £426 ($1,020).

In *Sweden* salmon angling is not extensive because in the northern rivers salmon are not prone to take an angler's lure. There are only three or four rivers where anglers fish for salmon, one of these is the famous Morrumsö.

Salmon fishing in eastern *Canada* is a very popular, albeit exclusive,

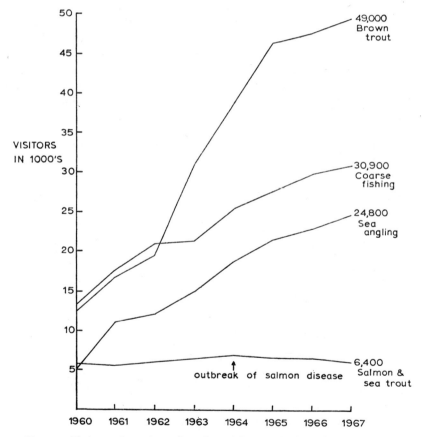

FIG. 3.   Estimated number of angling visitors to Ireland for years 1960–1967. (Source – Department of Agriculture and Fisheries, Ireland, from data supplied by Bord Failte Eireann.)

sport in the provinces of Quebec and New Brunswick. In New Brunswick it attracts annually some four or five thousand non-residents, almost exclusively from the United States. Many of these have formed angling clubs on the main salmon rivers such as the Miramichi, Restigouche and Tobique. Some others own their own luxury camps on the rivers. Most, however, use accommodation offered by 'outfitters' and self-employed guides licensed by the Province. Several hundred people find employment for a part of the year as outfitters, guides and camp helpers. A few companies own fishing lodges to entertain their guests and executives.

In New Brunswick, inland waters can be divided into four groups from the viewpoint of ownership and accessibility for anglers. (1) Private waters belonging to individuals or organisations who possess exclusive angling rights, subject to protective regulations limiting the amount of the catch. (2) Public waters leased for ten years to individuals or organisations by public auction, subject to protective regulations. (3) Crown reserved waters (about 86 miles on the Restigouche, Upsalquitch, Northwest Miramichi and north and south branch of the Big Sevogle River) are available to a limited number of licensed anglers per day. (4) The major part of public waters is open for angling, subject to usual protective restrictions.

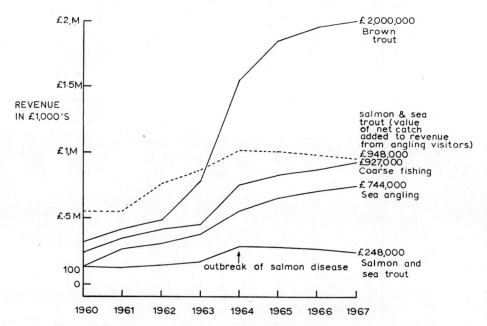

FIG. 4.   Estimated revenue from angling visitors to Ireland for years 1960–1967. (Source – Department of Agriculture and Fisheries, Ireland, from data supplied by Bord Failte Eireann.)

In Quebec most of the fishing is run by licensed clubs which are incorporated and kept up without pecuniary gain for salmon fishing in areas leased from the Province. Other methods of exploitation take the form of private fishing grounds where salmon are fished for pleasure by the owners; licensed outfitters, who exploit for profit an area leased from the Province, and Crown Salmon preserves, organised and operated by the Department of Game and Fisheries. Quebec rivers such as the St Jean, Grand Cascapedia and Little Cascapedia are very exclusive, while on the Matane River there are no restrictions on the number of anglers who may fish and no exclusive areas are reserved. Carter (1964) and Tétreault (1967) give good accounts of the present position of Quebec salmon rivers. In Quebec approximately 80% of the total received from the salmon revenue goes to the residents of Quebec in personal income.

In Nova Scotia and Newfoundland, in contrast to Quebec and New Brunswick, there are no private angling clubs and no privately owned or leased waters. Consequently all salmon rivers and streams are open to the public during the fishing season. However, a very great deal of the angling is done without guides, while in New Brunswick non-residents are almost without exception required to employ guides. The principal river systems of Nova Scotia are depicted in a paper by Morse (1965) on *The Economic Value of the Atlantic Salmon Fishery in Nova Scotia*, while the salmon rivers of Newfoundland are described by Palmer (1928) in a book with that title.

Salmon angling has only become popular among the people of *Iceland* since the Second World War. Prior to that few Icelanders fished for sport. Icelandic rivers are short and fast flowing but some sixty-five rivers contain Atlantic salmon. The larger rivers are in the south and west of the country and probably the best known is the Ellioaar, which flows close to Reykjavik. A few miles north is the Laxa and further up the western coast is the Ölfusa Hvitá system. The owners of the land adjoining the river have the fishing rights and often several owners band together in associations which control the rivers and let the fishing rights to angling groups or to individual anglers and these rents are now very high. The associations build accommodation, employ guardians and generally manage the rivers well. Fishing is controlled by regulations issued by the Ministry of Fisheries. In recent years the cost of salmon angling in Iceland has risen dramatically and the rent on one river, which in 1936 was £75, is now £10,000.

In *Spain* most of the salmon fishing on the better beats is under the control of the Government and accommodation has been built to attract anglers. Three of the best rivers, the Eo, Narcea and Deva-cares, were designated as national fishing preserves managed by the State Tourist Bureau. The rivers are divided into restricted zones, called 'cotos', and free areas. In the latter anybody who has a licence can fish during the season; on the cotos one must have a special permit specifying the dates on which he can fish. According to Netboy (1965) only seven salmon streams of any consequence remain in Spain: the Sella, Deva-Cares, Narcea, Navia, Eo and Ulla, and even their future is in jeopardy.

1.4 Private or common property resource[1]

Some mention has already been made of the ownership of the salmon fisheries but this section of the chapter describes the position of ownership in various countries in more detail.

In *Scotland* the salmon fisheries are a separate heritable estate. This means that the title, or right of ownership, of salmon fisheries does not go automatically with ownership of the land adjoining the fisheries, but is quite separate from it. The result is that it is not infrequent for one party to own the land on the banks of a river and another to own the right of salmon fishing in it. This situation arose due to the legal position of the salmon fisheries in the feudal era when most of the land titles were first granted. Originally all land in Scotland, as well as the salmon fisheries, was the property of the Crown. When the land was granted by Charter to persons other than the Crown, because of the great value of the salmon fisheries, the grant did not carry the salmon fisheries with it, unless the Charter specifically said so. Thus, long after most of the land had been granted by Charter to subjects, the Crown retained ownership of many of the salmon fisheries. This is still the case and a great stretch of the sea coast is still Crown property in so far as salmon fisheries are concerned and is administered by the Crown. Only a limited amount of freshwater is now so held as many grants of salmon fishing rights have been made. All salmon fisheries not alienated to a subject by the Crown, or to which no one can lay legal claim, still belong to the Crown. If, by the opening up of some waterfall or obstruction to the ascent of salmon, new fisheries are created, these must necessarily be, at the outset, in the possession of the Crown. The right of salmon fishing in the seas surrounding the coasts is vested in the Crown or in those to whom the Crown had made grants. Under Scottish Law salmon fishing rights in Scotland stretch to the extent of territorial waters. Orkney and Shetland are exceptions to this in that much of the land in these islands is held under Udal (Norse) Law; under this, salmon fisheries are a pertinent of the land as are ordinary freshwater fisheries elsewhere in Scotland. On

[1] Crutchfield and Pontecorvo (1969) use the term 'open access resources' instead of common property resource as they point out that the term 'common property', as it has been used by economists, is incorrect in a strictly legal sense. If a resource is not owned it is not property.

the mainland of Scotland it is the practice of the Crown Estate Commissioners to invite tenders for leasing their fisheries and in only one case, a net and coble fishery on the Spey, do the Commissioners themselves operate the fishery.

One result of this system of ownership is that it is legally impossible to have a public salmon fishery in Scotland, even on the coast within territorial waters. Although there are fisheries over which the owner does not trouble to exert his rights and which have therefore come to be regarded as common property, there is always a legal owner, either private or the Crown, and no length of public usage can extinguish this right. A Crown fishing on the coast is very frequently *ex adverso* the estate of a proprietor who has no interest in the salmon fishing. The tenant of a fishery must, however, have access to his fishery. In the same way, if a river flows through the estate of a proprietor who has no right of salmon fishing, the owner of the fishing rights has liberty to be upon the river banks to exercise his rights. In net fishing in a river it has in the same way to be decided that if the owner of the right has no property on either bank, he or his tenant may haul his net on either bank and may dry and mend his nets.

As at Common Law fish are animals *ferae naturae*, the owner of a salmon fishery does not own the fish but only the right to catch them.

In *England, Ireland* and *Wales*, apart from a small number of special cases, the ownership of land adjoining a river normally carries with it the ownership of the salmon fisheries, unless these have been specifically separated by some legal act. Commercial salmon fishing in England and Wales is mainly carried on in waters where the right of fishing is public. In coastal waters and in public navigable estuaries, generally speaking, all Her Majesty's subjects are equally entitled to fish and no one has an exclusive right. There are exceptions to this rule and private fisheries exist in several estuaries, the most notable being in the Severn and Wye. In practice, the full effect of the law is modified by the fact that in nearly all salmon rivers the fishermen have to be licensed and river authorities have power, which many of them have exercised, to limit the number of licences they issue.

Ownership of salmon fisheries is still largely controlled by Common Law, but several statutes have been created in both England and Scotland instituting regulatory measures. These statutes are separate, the English ones applying to England and Wales and the Scottish ones exclusively to Scotland.

The position of ownership in *Sweden* is similar to that existing in Scotland. Originally the rights to fish in the rivers belonged to the Crown and was granted by the King to various subjects for services rendered. Now they are either owned by the Government or by individuals whose titles are derived by descent from the original grantees or by purchase from their descendants or from the Crown. There are peasant holdings of fishing rights which have been handed down from generation to generation for 400 years. In the nineteenth century the usual arrangement was joint ownership of seines or traps by several farms, and the catch was divided up according to an ancient custom; by the number of people in each household.

In *Norway* and *Iceland*, as has already been mentioned (page 19) the owners of the land that adjoins the river, usually farmers, have the fishing rights. Often a fishery may be run by a group of people.

The British North America Act of 1867 placed the coastal and inland fisheries under federal jurisdiction. The coastal and tidal waters are the property of the *Canadian* Government. Salmon net fishing on these waters is conditional upon obtaining a licence for which a nominal fee is collected. Licences may be granted only to bona-fide owners of a boat who have been actively engaged in salmon fishing during the immediately preceding five years. The Provinces have property rights in the non-tidal fisheries and have been delegated certain administrative responsibilities.

In *France* the fishing rights on 90% of the rivers are privately owned while on 10% they belong to the state.

The position in *Spain* has already been described (pages 19–20).

While mentioning the question of ownership it is perhaps worth noting the views of Fletcher (1965) who discusses the property right in free-swimming fish:

> It (the property right) has an ancient heritage, going back at least to the time when the King asserted his right to the game in the forest. In the early *American* development of the law concerning game, it was very easy to substitute the state for the King, saying that the state now owns the game; and, to suit our ideas of the function of government, it was said that the state must act with respect to this game as a sort of trustee for the benefit of all the people.
>
> This makes some sense if used with restraint. It expresses the state's deep interest in the exploitation of natural resources and should be guided by the best judgement it can exercise. The state should measure the need to be served by the state, weigh it against the imposition on the individual, and enact legislation that best accommodates these conflicting considerations. But the use of 'property' in game should be confined to this limited setting.

1.5 The size and economic value of the fisheries

Details of the landings of Atlantic salmon for the years 1955 to 1968 are

TABLE I

Landed weight of Atlantic Salmon in thousand metric tons (1 metric ton = 2,204 lb)
Source: *FAO Yearbooks of Fishery Statistics*

	1955	1956	1957	1958	1959	1960	1961	1962	1963	1964	1965	1966	1967	1968
Canada	6·0	7·0	8·0	9·0	9·0	8·0	9·0	11·0	11·0	14·0	12·0	12·0	15·0	13·0
Greenland[c]	1·2	1·2	1·4	1·6	1·8	1·6	1·6	1·7	1·8	2·1	2·2	2·4	2·8	2·2
United States	—	—	—	—	—	—	—	—	—	—	—	—	—	0·6
Denmark[c]	0·6	1·0	0·9	1·1	1·1	1·1	1·7	1·5	1·2	1·7	2·0	1·7	2·1	2·5
Faroe Islands[c]	—	—	—	—	—	—	—	—	—	—	—	—	—	0·1
Finland[a]	0·0	0·0	0·0	0·3	0·3	0·3	0·6	0·5	0·5	0·6	0·5	0·5	0·5	0·6
France	0·2	0·3	0·4	0·2	0·3	0·2	0·4	0·3	0·2	0·3	0·2	0·2	0·2	0·0
Germany, Fed. Rep.[a]	—	—	—	—	—	—	0·2	0·1	0·2	0·3	0·2	—	0·2	0·2
Iceland	—	—	—	—	—	—	0·6	1·3	1·3	1·4	1·3	1·1	1·5	1·4
Ireland	0·6	0·7	0·9	0·8	0·8	0·6	0·0	0·0	0·0	0·0	0·0	0·0	0·0	0·0
Netherlands	0·0	0·0	0·0	0·0	0·0	0·0	0·0	0·0	0·0	0·0	0·0	0·0	0·0	0·0
Norway[a]	1·3	1·2	1·4	1·2	1·2	1·2	1·3	1·7	1·8	1·9	1·7	1·6	1·8	1·7
Poland	0·0	0·2	0·2	0·2	0·2	0·2	0·1	0·3	0·3	0·4	0·2	0·1	0·1	0·2
Portugal	0·0	0·0	0·0	0·0	0·0	0·0	0·0	0·0	0·0	0·0	0·0	0·0	0·0	0·0
Spain	0·0	0·0	0·0	0·0	0·1	0·0	0·6	0·4	—	0·6	0·5	0·4	0·5	0·7
Sweden	0·3	0·6	0·4	0·3	0·4	0·4	0·6	0·4	0·4	0·6	0·5	0·4	0·5	0·7
United Kingdom[b]	2·0	2·0	2·0	2·0	2·0	2·3	—	—	—	—	—	—	—	—
U.K. (England Wales)[b][c]	—	—	—	—	—	—	0·0	0·1	0·0	0·1	0·1	0·1	0·1	—
U.K. (Scotland)	—	—	—	—	—	—	1·3	2·1	1·7	1·9	1·3	1·3	1·8	1·3
U.K. (Northern Ireland)	—	—	—	—	—	—	0·2	0·6	0·5	0·6	0·4	0·4	0·5	0·3
U.S.S.R.	—	—	—	1·3	2·0	—	0·0	—	0·2	0·9	0·8	0·8	1·0	1·0

— Not available (mainly because unobtainable or included in another figure).

[a] Includes sea trout.

[b] Includes trout, char and smelt.

[c] Marine Fisheries.

0·0 Insignificant amount.

given in Table 1. The five countries with the heaviest landings are Canada, Denmark, Ireland, Norway and Scotland. All Danish salmon are caught in the sea, while the landings in the other four countries include fish taken in freshwater by rod and line. In Scotland, during the period 1952 to 1969 the average annual proportion of the salmon (and grilse) catch taken by rod and line was 24% and 4% respectively (Table 33). One development in the world salmon fisheries during this period has been the establishment and rapid expansion of a coastal and offshore fishery for salmon off the west coast of Greenland. The quantities of salmon exported from Greenland from 1957 to 1966 are given in Table 2a and the total catch of salmon, onshore and offshore, in Table 2b.

The 1964 figure of 1,400 metric tons is equivalent to approximately 20% of the total world's catch of Atlantic salmon, a figure which approximately equals the catch made by Danish fishermen in the Baltic, and that of the salmon fisheries in Scotland as a whole.

The total catch of salmon in neighbouring Iceland is much smaller, being only about 120 metric tons on the average for the period 1957–1968.

In the Baltic area the average annual catch over the period 1950 to 1960 (Table 3) was 2,640 metric tons with the Danes accounting for approximately 40% of the total. Although Sweden supplies about 60% of all the juvenile salmon entering the sea, the remainder coming from Finland,

TABLE 2a

Exports of salmon from Greenland expressed in metric tons (gutted weight)

1957	1958	1959	1960	1961	1962	1963	1964	1965	1966
2	4·2	13	55	115	290	420	1,400	857	1,200

TABLE 2b

Onshore and offshore catches of salmon off West Greenland

	Catch (metric tons)		
	Onshore	Offshore	Total
1961	127	—	127
1962	244	—	244
1963	466	—	466
1964	1539	—	1539
1965	825	36	861
1966	1251	119	1370
1967	1283	305	1588
1968	579	548	1127
1969	940[a]	1170[a]	2110[a]

[a] Provisional.

PLATE 3

The Cruive Dyke on the River Beauly, Inverness-shire. This is the largest structure of its kind in Scotland. There are several boxes or traps, four in one arm of the V and three in the other. These are no longer fished.

PLATE 4

Lamprey feeding on a Lake trout.

Poland and Russia, her share of the total sea catch is only 24·5%. It has been a sore point with some of the Baltic countries that although Denmark has no salmon rivers it lands the largest weight of salmon, all of which have originated from other countries.

The values of landings of Atlantic salmon for 1961–68 are given in Table 4, and the market value of salmon and sea trout captured in southern Ireland are given in Table 5. While these figures give a true picture in terms of direct value to each country, in some instances the figures do not represent the actual value. For example in Scotland, as in other countries with a large sport fishery for salmon, the benefit to income and employment of a rod-caught salmon is much greater than is represented by the price which the fish fetches when sold. Good salmon angling can command a high rent, as has already been mentioned (1.3), a fact that may be of import-ance to the owners of estates who are also proprietors of salmon fishing, and to local authorities. The availability of salmon angling contributes directly to the revenue of the tourist industry. Many Scottish hotels rely on angling visitors, particularly in the early spring and late autumn. A few may rely on anglers to such an extent that they would have to seek an entirely new type of customer if angling fell away, while others, but for angling, would have a shorter season and offer a shorter period of employment to most of their staff. This example of the value of rod-caught salmon being worth more than the price which the fish fetches when sold is further borne out by Maheux (1956). Maheux showed that the combined rod and net fishing for salmon in Quebec brings each year to the residents of the Province, in

TABLE 3

Weight of salmon caught in the Baltic area, 1950–1960
(metric tons)

	Sweden[1]	Denmark	Total for all Baltic countries
1950	1,339	1,317	4,118
1951	1,077	1,096	3,126
1952	791	1,350	3,080
1953	422	753	1,914
1954	484	962	2,184
1955	296	609	1,497
1956	670	961	2,585
1957	340	893	2,104
1958	288	892	1,766
1959	358	933	1,868
1960	425	1,096	2,152
Average	647(24·5%)	1,086(41·1%)	2,639

[1] Excluding river catches.
Source: Alm, 1958 and Netboy, 1968a.

TABLE 4

Values of landings of Atlantic Salmon in national currency[1]
(Source: *FAO Yearbooks of Fishery Statistics*)

	1961	1962	1963	1964	1965	1966	1967	1968
Canada (thousand Canadian dollars)	1,417	1,752	1,833	2,146	2,222	2,542	3,090	2,308
Greenland (thousand Danish kroner)ᶜ	—	970	1,305	7,907	2,894	6,753	6,320	4,007
United States (thousand U.S. dollars)	0	0	0	0	0	0	0	0
Denmark (thousand Danish kroner)ᶜ	18,106	20,106	17,745	26,449	24,396	25,778	28,120	33,847
Finland (ten thousand new Finnish markkas)	198	319	359	543	452	521	512	713
France (ten thousand new francs)	38	28	31	23	28	71	87	40
Germany Fed. Rep. (thousand Deutsche marks)	2,912	2,132	2,172	3,431	2,338	2,260	2,053	2,270
Iceland (thousand Icelandic kroner)	—	—	—	—	—	—	—	—
Ireland (thousand Irish pounds)	410	621	703	789	712	685	767	818
Netherlands (thousand guilders)	8	7	7	—	—	—	—	—
Norwayᵃ (thousand Norwegian kroner)	16,841	21,511	22,134	24,219	24,209	24,408	27,957	27,000
Poland (thousand zlotys)	—	—	—	—	—	—	—	—
Portugal (million escudos)	0	0	0	0	0	0	0	0
Sweden (thousand Swedish kroner)	6,085	3,874	4,298	6,890	5,354	5,509	6,230	6,476
U.K. (England and Wales)ᵇ andᶜ (thousand pounds sterling)	46	46	37	43	49	45	55	—
U.K. (England and Wales) (Inland Fisheries)	—	—	—	—	—	—	—	—
U.K. (Scotland) (thousand pounds sterling)ᶜ	1,132	1,563	1,268	1,654	1,129	1,231	1,524	1,323
U.K. (Northern Ireland)ᵇ (thousand pounds sterling)	148	271	271	328	198	228	229	193

[1] For conversion factors see Appendix 1.
o Denotes insignificant amount.
— Not available (mainly because unobtainable or included in another figure).
ᵃ includes sea trout.
ᵇ includes smelt.
ᶜ Marine fisheries.

personal income, $2,085,850 or 80% of the total received from the salmon resource. Of this sum, the 12,000 fish caught by rod and line (less than one-fifth of the commercial catch) contributed nearly 75%.

Detailed studies of the economic value of Atlantic salmon to the provinces of Quebec, New Brunswick and Nova Scotia have been made by Maheux (1956), Grasberg (1956) and Morse (1965) respectively. In the surveys by Maheux and Grasberg emphasis was placed on studies of the economic aspects or revenue channels of salmon fishing which was divided into sport fishing, commercial fishing, federal expenditure and personal income of residents. Each source of revenue was reviewed, then the elements composing each source were analysed. The studies are too large to permit a satisfactory summary and the reader is advised to refer to the original works. One paragraph of interest in the survey by Maheux is that concerning the cost of salmon angling to licensed clubs in Quebec:

> If we compare the $1,245,000 and the 7,000 salmon caught by the club members and their guests, we realize that the salmon is truly a luxury fish. Each salmon would come to about $175.00; and as the average weight of each fish is not far from 12 pounds, the price per pound of salmon would be $14.60. This is proof that we are dealing with a sport, that is to say a pastime, which has no price tag attached to it. It is also proof that, in this Province, the clubs constitute an important economic factor, since goods, for which the commercial fisherman received 40 cents, have, in the hands of the angler, a value 36 times as great. The net result of the activity of the clubs is to obtain higher incomes for a great number of people. Salmon angling is thus becoming an appreciable element of prosperity in those regions favoured by this fish, as well as an important factor of conservation.

It was impossible in Nova Scotia for Morse to estimate the values as has been done in Quebec and New Brunswick owing to the institutional arrangements in the Province and to the open and diffuse nature of the sport fishery. However, by using questionnaires Morse found that the average expenditure per salmon angler in Nova Scotia in 1964 was between $100 and $160 and the expenditures of 959 anglers who responded to the

TABLE 5

Market value of all salmon and sea trout captured in southern Ireland for years 1960–1967

Revenue in £1,000's for years							
1960	1961	1962	1963	1964	1965	1966	1967
410	410	620	710	800	720	705	700

questionnaire was $376,368. On an assumption (based on a list of known anglers) that there was a total of 3000 anglers the estimated minimum and maximum level of aggregated expenditures was $300,000 and $480,000. The landed value of the commercial fishery was $164,300.

Hadoke (1967) estimated the cost of salmon angling in the Foyle area in Northern Ireland from completed questionnaires returned by anglers. He found that the angling effort in the Foyle area compares favourably with that in Nova Scotia, but the cost to the Foyle angler is considerably lower than that of his Canadian counterpart (Table 6).

Before leaving this topic it is worth considering the economics of a Scottish salmon fishery from the point of view of the fishing proprietor. Semple (1967) in discussing the 'mythical profits of the fishing proprietors' says:

> It is in assessing the precise value of these latter factors (i.e. salmon rod fishing) that difficulties arise. Returns of catches on individual rivers are confidential to the Secretary of State for Scotland and rod rents can vary tremendously. . . .
>
> Certainly high rents are charged in certain areas at peak periods of the year, and a legendary American tourist is said to have offered £700 for a week of high grade fishing. . . .
>
> This difficulty in obtaining precise information, the knowledge that high rents are sometimes charged, and the fact that demand has probably never been greater have all combined to perpetuate a myth that the landed gentry are making a great deal of money out of their fishing stretches. . . .
>
> Indications are, however, that this is far from the truth. . . .

TABLE 6

Estimated cost of salmon angling in the Foyle area and Nova Scotia

	Foyle Area Investigation	Canadian Sample Investigation	Canadian Full Investigation
	1966	1964	1964
Number of anglers	21	43	959
Total number of fish caught	145	92	3,462
Average catch per rod	6·9	2·1	3·6
Total number of rod days per salmon	2·6	10·9	5·6
Total expenditures	£891[1]	£2,190	£125,400
Average expenditure per angler	£47[1]	£51	£130
Average cost per salmon killed	£7[1]	£23	£36

[1] Only 19 anglers gave details of their angling expenses.

Not a penny is taken from the national purse to support this most prolific part of a national asset. The owners pick up the whole tab and, despite the myth, they are making little or no money from their sporting fisheries. . . .

Last year, a typical mid-river salmon rod fishery, representing a stretch of two and half miles on each side of the river (Tweed) drew £1866 in rents. As the table (Table 7) – an extract of audited accounts – shows, the profit was marginal. It was fortunate that no unusual expenditure was incurred, but the previous year, repairs to a cauld cost £300 and the fishery account showed a loss. . . .

1.6 Trends and fluctuations in the fisheries

There are a number of salmon fisheries in which the catches have shown downward trends and Netboy (1968a) has given dramatic accounts of these declines, particularly in the French and Spanish fisheries. Usually in any fishery after the 'period of abundance' there is a downward trend but this usually levels off with rational exploitation. However, in some fisheries where there has either been over-exploitation, or change in the river regime due to barriers or pollution, the trend has continued downwards to a point where the fishery is eliminated, as on the River Thames, or is virtually non-existent, as on the Tees.

In many cases the trend in the fisheries may be upward and many would consider this a good sign when in fact it might be the opposite. The actual amount of fish landed in a year is a poor guide to what is happening to any particular fishery. The real test is not the total intake of fish, which is called the 'total yield', but the average catch per unit of fishing effort, that is, per net, per trap or per rod, in a given time, say per

TABLE 7

Extracts from audited accounts of a typical mid-river salmon rod fishery on the River Tweed, showing a profit of £113.

Income		Expenditure	
Rents	£1866	Wages	£737
		Rates on houses	82
		Fishermen's perks	73
		Upkeep of boats	47
		Telephone	24
		Tweed assessment	172
		County rate	518
		Miscellaneous	100
	£1866		£1753

week, per day or per hour. This is called the 'density' of the catch, and the
first sign of a real decline in the supply of fish will be shown not by the total

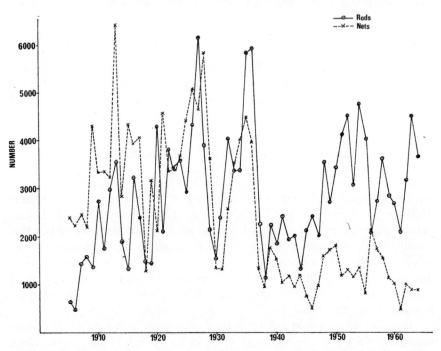

FIG. 5.   Annual salmon catches on the Wye, 1905–1964 (from Hellawell, 1966).

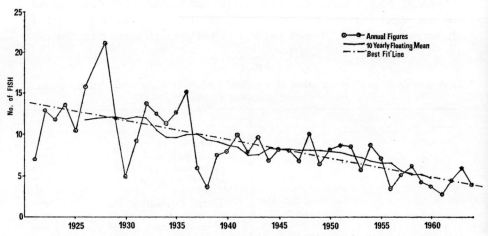

FIG. 6.   Annual salmon catches per unit fishing effort (rods only: 1921–
1964) (from Hellawell, 1966).

yield but in the density. The total yield could still go on rising while the density is declining. It has been shown by Hellawell (1966) from a study of the salmon fishery of the River Wye that, apart from low returns during the Second World War, the numbers of salmon handled have remained of the same order throughout, although they do fluctuate widely from year to year (Fig. 5). However, a study of the fishing effort showed that while the annual catch per unit effort does fluctuate considerably there has been a general decline over the years (Fig. 6). It is concluded that if the present downward trend continues at the same rate then the salmon population of the Wye will be almost completely depleted this century.

The reverse state of affairs was found in a study of the Norwegian statistics for the salmon and sea trout fishery between 1876 and 1965. Rosseland (1966) found (Fig. 7) that the catch per bag net is higher now when there are between 7,000 and 8,000 bag nets than it was in the 'seventies' and 'eighties' when the number of bag nets was from less than 2,000 up to slightly more than 4,000. His conclusion is that the salmon stock in Norway is at present at a rather high level. Apart from the probably good natural conditions prevailing, the reason for this may also be the better

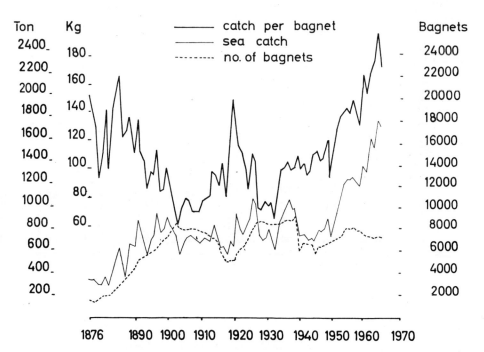

FIG. 7.　Yield of salmon fishery in the sea in Norway, 1876–1965 (from Rosseland, 1966).

control of illegal fishing, increased artificial propagation, the construction of a large number of fishways, especially in the northern part of Norway and better statistics.

A trend in the fishery may also be due to change in fishing methods or change in legislation. Ritchie (1920) shows the 'extraordinary decline' of the salmon and trout catches at the mouth of the Tweed by the Berwick Salmon Fisheries Company (Fig. 8). He accepts that part of this decline, from an average of 110,000 salmon and trout in the period 1842 to 1846 to less than 40,000 in the seventies is 'no doubt due to restrictive legislation controlling the size of mesh of salmon nets.' However, it is most unlikely that the slight change in mesh size could be responsible for such a large change in the average catch in this instance, and the decline could well have been due to pollution which was very bad in some parts of the Tweed watershed at that time. In recent years the salmon catches in the Tweed have shown the expected fluctuations between years and have now reached the levels of the 1840s, probably due to pollution control and the removal of the numerous caulds (weirs).

In the Greenland salmon fishery there is an upward trend in the annual catches possibly due to the fishery being of recent origin and its being in

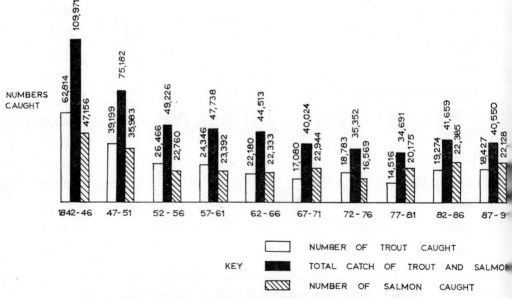

Fig. 8.   The decline of Tweed fisheries, as shown by the statistics of trout and salmon caught during fifty years. Each column indicates the average annual catch in a period of five years (from Ritchie, 1920).

the period of abundance. There appears to be no readily available data on fishing effort. It is hoped that there may be rational exploitation of this fishery as too great an increase in fishing effort may result in a downward trend and, as salmon in this fishery originate from many countries, this could have serious consequences.

In addition to definite trends there are also fluctuations which may be long or short term or, as Lindroth (1965a) calls them, primary and second-ary fluctuations. The short-term fluctuations are the expected variations in the size of the catches from year to year and some of these fluctuations of course result from differences in the numbers of nets or traps used. In a study of the salmon catches in the rivers of northern Sweden for the period 1860 to 1950 Lindroth (1950 and 1965a) found that fluctuations were remarkably synchronised not only for these rivers but for the Baltic countries as a whole, although they were not matched elsewhere. The trend of the catches in most of them was found to be similar, irrespective of whether the rivers were polluted or unpolluted, with or without power dams or with or without accessory artificial propagation. As the 'curves of capture' for almost every river running to the Baltic show a rather uniform appear-ance Lindroth speaks of a general 'salmon curve' (Fig. 9). The biological explanation of the long-term swings in catches is still obscure and Lindroth concludes that 'the main factors must be sought in changes in the biological balance induced by climatic factors.' Fig. 10 shows a hypothetical diagram illustrating Lindroth's views on the component fluctuations and their share in the total fluctuation. Much of this diagram will be more readily understood after reading the later chapters.

Another example of a long-term fluctuation is seen in the records of the catches at the Ballisodare Fishery in Ireland from 1880 to 1945 (Fig. 11). A periodic scarcity of salmon in the Maritime Provinces of Canada occur-ring on the average every 9·6 years was due to climatic factors (varying rainfall over a period of years) acting upon young salmon in the river (Huntsman, 1937).

A clear periodicity of 8–11 years was also shown to occur in salmon in the north of Russia, Norway and Canada by Berg (1935). Nikolsky (1969, p. 219) points out that the periodicity coincides with that of the aurora, from which Berg concluded that the factors governing the size of the year classes act during the river period of life.

Menzies (1949) discusses at length some possible causes for the annual or short-term fluctuations in the stock of Scottish salmon. He suggests that the reasons for the fluctuations in the stock may be spread over the whole field of the life history of the fish in both fresh and salt water. They may be linked with weather conditions on land or with usual or unusual movements of great bodies of water and seasonal or exceptional changes in the tempera-

c

ture and currents in the ocean. Fig. 12 shows that extreme variations occur and that little or no indication of regular cycles of good and bad years is apparent. The catch of salmon in a particular year is not necessarily a perfect index of the total run of fish. The effectiveness of nets is considerably influenced by the weather during both the working hours and the weekly close time. In a very dry year the effectiveness may be high and the size of the total run may be over-emphasised as a consequence. Angling conditions, too, may govern rod catches and these may bear no relation to the size of the total run.

Over the period 1914 to 1946 the first ten years produced relatively moderate annual fluctuations; the second ten years produced more extreme fluctuations and the third ten years showed a decline accentuated in the final three years 1944 to 1946 to a level of catch below that obtaining at any time since statistics of catch were first obtained in the eighties of last century. Probably some of this could be accounted for by a decline in fishing effort during the final years of the Second World War. A similar decline is seen in the Ballisodare fishery, but over the same period (i.e. 1943 to 1946) the salmon catches in the Baltic reached a peak above that obtaining at any time since 1890. In more recent years the Scottish catch has once more increased and has remained relatively stable for a number

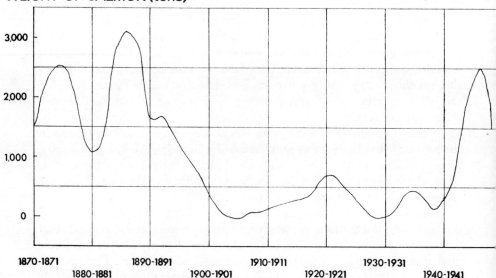

FIG. 9.   The 'salmon curve' (from Lindroth, 1950).

of years (Table 33). Hutton (1947) published a series of graphs showing salmon statistics for different parts of the British Isles from 1906 to 1945. The commercial landings for Ireland, Scotland, England and Wales handled at Billingsgate market, the Billingsgate total and the total catch by rods

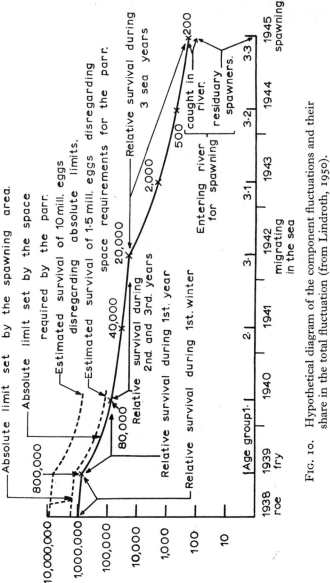

FIG. 10. Hypothetical diagram of the component fluctuations and their share in the total fluctuation (from Lindroth, 1950).

and nets on the River Wye for the thirty-year period 1911–1940 had been averaged separately. Then the annual figures from each of the five sources for the forty-year period were plotted as percentages above and below these averages. This gave five graphs, all to the same scale, which permitted comparison of the relative times of abundance and scarcity in each area. Kerswill (1955a) calculated the total Canadian commercial landings in the Maritime Provinces for the same period in the same way. He noticed a

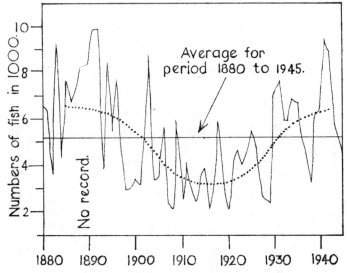

FIG. 11.   Fluctuations in the catches of salmon in the Ballisodare fishery (from Went, 1955).

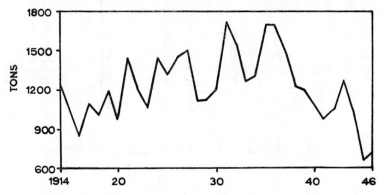

FIG. 12.   Weight of salmon caught in Scotland, 1914–1946 (from Menzies, 1949).

striking similarity between the fluctuations in the Canadian commercial
production and the British Isles. He concluded that these graphs indicate
that the availability of salmon on both sides of the North Atlantic has
been affected by common environmental conditions (Fig. 13).

The existence and varied explanations for fluctuations make obvious

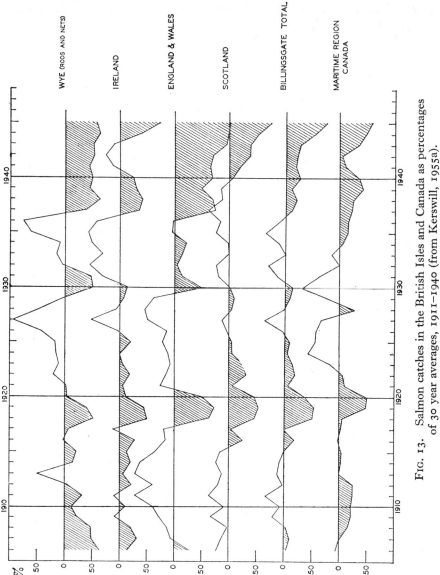

FIG. 13. Salmon catches in the British Isles and Canada as percentages
of 30 year averages, 1911–1940 (from Kerswill, 1955a).

difficulties for those in authority who may be required to assess the state of salmon stocks with a view to altering or reviewing the appropriate legislation. It also makes it very difficult to decide when to take appropriate action. For example, the netsmen and anglers may suggest various causes for a decline in their catches over a period of two or three years and request that the Government take steps to counteract these causes. It may be hard to convince the industry that their smaller catches may be only due to 'natural fluctuations'.

Chapter 2

THE TROUT AND OTHER MEMBERS
OF THE SALMON FAMILY

2.1 The fisheries for trout and other salmonids. 2.2 The sea trout fishery. 2.3 The brown trout sport fishery. 2.4 Rainbow trout farming. 2.5 Char. 2.6 Grayling. 2.7 Whitefish – powan and vendace. 2.8 Lake trout. 2.9 Danube salmon. 2.10 Introduction of Pacific salmon to Atlantic waters.

2.1 The fisheries for trout and other salmonids

While other members of the salmon family are not individually as important as the Atlantic salmon they are still a very valuable resource. Some, such as the brown trout, char and grayling are chiefly of value to the sport fisherman and tourist industry. Other salmonids support large commercial fisheries, particularly the sea trout and whitefish, the former is also a very popular quarry for the angler as well. The rainbow trout besides being a popular sport fish is also reared extensively in fish farms for the table.

2.2 Sea trout fishery

The sea trout, while not as valuable as the salmon, is a much-sought-after fish and many people hold it in higher esteem than the salmon. It supports a commercial fishery in a number of countries and as a sporting fish is usually more accessible to the average angler than the salmon. There are large commercial fisheries for sea trout in Denmark, England, Iceland, Ireland, Norway, Poland, Scotland and Sweden. The annual landings for Scotland from 1954 to 1968 are given in Table 8.

The methods employed in catching sea trout are the same as those used in catching salmon and usually sea trout are caught incidentally in the salmon fisheries. In some countries there are few fisheries specifically for sea trout, for example in England, Scotland and Wales most of the sea trout are caught at the salmon netting stations particularly in the tidal reaches of the rivers where sweep nets are employed.

Most sea trout rivers have a well-developed sport fishery and on some rivers sea trout provide more sport for anglers than the salmon. One exception to this is the Tweed, where large numbers of sea trout are caught by the nets but, although there is a large 'run' of fish up the river and its tributaries, very few are caught on rod and line except on the River Till.

In some countries sea trout are also caught on rod and line in the sea. In the Shetland and Faroe Islands the sea trout are caught in many of the voes. There is also good sea trout angling in the inner parts of the fjords of Norway and Sweden, and around the coast of Denmark.

The sea trout, being a migratory fish, is covered in many countries by the same laws that cover the salmon.

2.3 Brown trout sport fishery

Although there are practically no commercial fisheries for brown trout, this non-migratory form of the sea trout provides a valuable sport fishery in many European countries, where it is an indigenous species, and in many other countries around the world where it has been successfully introduced.

In Scotland, for example, brown trout fishing is the mainstay of the

TABLE 8

The annual Scottish catch of sea trout from 1954 to 1968. (Sources: *Scottish Salmon and Trout Fisheries*, Cmd. 2691 and *Fisheries of Scotland* (Annual Reports)

	Number	Weight (lb)
1954	179,375	388,253
1955	185,633	429,853
1956	184,097	402,085
1957	216,792	471,004
1958	207,802	469,128
1959	238,213	537,894
1960	219,655	504,048
1961	205,214	484,723
1962	278,421	644,161
1963	229,086	511,450
1964	263,524	642,880
1965	286,699	683,200
1966	244,778	556,228
1967	312,226	760,305
1968	209,491	526,486

angler of moderate means. In the Second Report on the Scottish Salmon and Trout Fisheries (H.M.S.O., Cmnd. 2691) the Hunter Committee consider that brown trout angling has a fairly important economic aspect in that many angling visitors and tourists are looking for trout fishing, sometimes in the form of angling holidays and sometimes for an odd day's sport in the course of a family holiday in Scotland. The Committee consider that the actual and potential demand for brown trout fishing is very large. In Scotland brown trout fishing has not been fully developed, which is not surprising when one learns that there are nearly 10,000 lochs, lochans and tarns containing trout in the north of Scotland and the Western Isles. In these remoter areas much of the fishing is owned or leased by hotels, which cater mainly for sport fishermen, and angling clubs are few in number. Much of the trout fishing can be had at little or no charge and on some rivers trout are held in disrepute because they eat young salmon.

There are not many reliable statistics for brown trout catches in Scotland but the catches at the greatest trout fishery in Scotland, namely at Loch Leven, Kinross-shire, are carefully recorded and details of these catches from 1955 to 1968 are given in Table 9. The annual yield from this loch is in the region of 7–10 lb/acre. The stock in this loch is maintained by spawning trout in the feeder streams. Detailed records are also kept by the Edinburgh Corporation for their reservoirs and details of catches and fishing effort on Gladhouse, a moorland reservoir are given in Table 10. The annual yield of this water is in the region of 2–3½ lb/acre. Frost and Brown (1967) give figures (lb/acre) for the crop taken by anglers off some man-made lakes in the British Isles and they are as follows: Sutton

TABLE 9

Details of brown trout taken on rod and line at Loch Leven, Kinross-shire, Scotland, from 1956 to 1968

	Number of fish	Weight (metric tons)	Average weight (oz)	(gm)
1956	55726	23·5	14·9	425
1957	56609	26·1	16·3	470
1958	51512	23·0	15·8	455
1959	48007	21·8	16·0	455
1960	85883	40·7	16·7	485
1961	50927	23·5	16·3	470
1962	45320	20·0	15·6	440
1963	51520	20·7	14·2	400
1964	26086	11·7	15·9	455
1965	33059	13·9	14·9	425
1966	49145	18·2	13·1	370
1967	31500	11·3	12·7	370
1968	37796	13·1	12·0	340

Bingham, 55; Weir Wood, 19; Chew, 11½; Blagdon, 5 to 6; Eye Brook, 5¼; Ladybower, 2½ to 5¼ and Lake Vyrnwy, 1.

There is a misguided belief that the right of fishing for brown trout in Scottish waters is public. This is not so; the right to fish for brown trout in any particular water belongs to those who own the land adjacent to the water. Under a separate Act of 1633 Loch Leven, Kinross-shire, is an exception, the fishing being reserved to a single proprietor. The only place which the public have a right to fish for brown trout is in tidal reaches of a river or sea loch that is also navigable. Even here care must be exercised in the Solway where the Esk is under English Law. At present no licence is required to fish for trout in Scotland. In England and Wales a licence is required and trout fishing is very much more expensive, and the mainstay of fishing for the angler of moderate means are the coarse fish such as roach and pike. A licence is also required to fish for trout in most other countries and Scotland is therefore unique in not making trout fishing permissible under licence only.

In Norway the fishing rights belong to the owner of the land. A Goverment licence is required to fish for salmon, trout, char and other freshwater fish, and the licence is valid for the whole country. This is a much better system than that existing in England where a licence is issued by each River Authority and is only valid in the area administered by that particular River Authority.

Brown trout have been introduced into several countries and successful sport fisheries have developed from these introductions in Argentina,

TABLE 10

Details of numbers, weight and yield of brown trout caught annually by rod fishermen on Gladhouse Reservoir, Midlothian [1]

	No. of Fish	Total Weight		Average Weight		Yield (lb/acre)	Fishing Effort (rod/days)
		lb	kg	oz	gm		
1957	2270	1368	622	9·6	270	3·4 (3·8)	836
1958	1734	1105	502	10·2	285	2·7 (3·0)	798
1959		No records					
1960	1650	1232	560	12·0	340	3·1 (3·4)	814
1961		No records					
1962		No records					
1963	1786	1233	502	11·1	315	3·1 (3·4)	789
1964	941	748	340	12·7	370	1·8 (2·0)	821
1965	1168	967	440	13·2	370	2·4 (2·6)	830
1966	1233	926	421	12·0	340	2·3 (2·5)	826

Figures in brackets denote kg./Ha.

[1] These details are for anglers fishing by licence only and do not include catches by anglers from one estate boat.

Australia, Ceylon, Chile, Falkland Islands, Kenya, Malawi, New Zealand, Peru, Tasmania and South Africa. The brown trout has also been introduced into waters on both sides of the North American continent.

2.4 Rainbow trout farming

The rainbow trout (*Salmo gairdnerii*) is a native of western North America and is very popular with sport fishermen. Besides being a good sport fish the rainbow trout is a very good fish for rearing in ponds with the result that rainbow trout farms have been established in a number of countries. Denmark has developed trout farming more than any other country in Europe. Rainbow trout culture started in Denmark about 1890 and by 1914 there were over 300 trout farms in Denmark. The fish were mainly sold fresh in Germany and when export to Germany was stopped, shortly after the start of the First World War, the market for Danish trout virtually ceased to exist and by 1919 there were only 10 trout farms still operating in Denmark. Between the First and Second World Wars the Danes ceased to be dependent on the German market for selling their rainbow trout and were eventually supplying countries all over Europe. Since the Second World War, the advance in deep freezing techniques has greatly increased their potential markets, both through pre-packaging for the consumer trade and in sale to more distant countries, notably North America.

At present there are between 700 and 800 rainbow trout farms in Denmark, nearly all of which are in Jutland, employing between 3,000 and 4,000 men (the Scottish commercial salmon fishery only employs 1,650 men and, because of the close season, these men are only seasonally employed). Some of the farms specialise in producing fingerlings or trout eggs for re-stocking lakes, rivers or trout farms in other countries. In addition there is a very small number of 'salt water' trout farms. Rainbow trout production in 1964 was in the region of 9,000 metric tons. Home consumption accounts for less than 1% of this total production and the remainder is exported, either alive, fresh in ice, deep frozen round, or deep frozen gutted in consumer packs. A quantity is smoked or processed in other special ways for particular markets. Table 11 gives the total amount by weight and value of Danish rainbow trout exports for the table market and Table 12 gives the details of the Danish rainbow trout exports by weight to different countries in 1962.

Rainbow trout farming is also carried on in Norway and in 1963 the total production of a small number of freshwater rainbow trout farms and about 30 salt water rainbow trout farms was in the region of about 400 tons. There is already a market for the large size red-fleshed rainbow trout produced by the salt water farms, and the small quantities of fish produced have a ready sale in Sweden and other countries.

More recently Unilever has started rainbow trout farming on the west coast of Scotland at Lochailort, Inverness-shire. The rainbow trout fry are put in freshwater tanks and the salinity of the water is gradually increased. They are then transferred to outdoor tanks and eventually to sea cages moored in the sea loch. Scottish rainbow trout production amounted to 20 tons (worth £10,000 in 1967, 47 tons in 1968 and 85 tons in 1969).

TABLE 11

Total amount by weight and value of Danish rainbow trout exports for the table market, 1955–1962, in thousand metric tons and thousands of pounds sterling

	Weight	*Value (£)*
1955	3·6	1,119
1956	3·9	1,287
1957	4·3	1,472
1958	5·2	1,733
1959	6·0	1,965
1960	6·9	2,018
1961	7·4	2,620
1962	7·6	2,804

Note. In the period 1950–1962 the weight of live rainbow trout exported from Denmark for stocking ponds or rivers in other countries, as opposed to direct table use, rose from 5·9 metric tons worth £16,786, to 28·1 metric tons, worth £93,929 in 1962. A greater weight of live fish was exported in 1960 and 1961, 49·9 and 50·8 metric tons respectively, but the value was less than that realised for 1962.

TABLE 12

Danish rainbow trout exported by weight, 1962, in thousand metric tons

Italy	1·8	France	0·1
U.K.	1·0	Holland	0·08
U.S.A.	1·0	Norway	0·08
Belgium	1·0	American Forces in Europe	0·07
Sweden	0·9	Finland	0·07
Western Germany	0·8	Austria	0·04
Switzerland	0·5	Other countries	0·07
Canada	0·1		

Note. France, Austria and Western Germany have considerable home production of rainbow trout. A number of the French trout farms are Danish owned. Switzerland imports large quantities of live trout. Norway imports live Danish trout in smaller sizes in order to stock her own trout farms, but little, if any, trout for direct table use.

2.5 Char

The Arctic char (*Salvelinus alpinus*) has a number of forms and vernacular names. In Great Britain it lives mostly in deep lakes but in other parts of the northern hemisphere the char frequents Arctic rivers as well. There are two principal forms of the char – the anadromous form which migrates to sea in the summer but returns to freshwater to spawn, and the land-locked form which remains in freshwater throughout its entire life.

In Iceland the Arctic char is a very important sport fish but the import- ance of the species in North America, has been confined, in the past, to its use as food for local use. For example in Canada it was of use to Eskimos and their dogs. However, in North America in the last ten years it has achieved status on the market as a luxury food item and renown as an excellent sport fish. Commercial exploitation mostly of sea-run fish, began on the Labrador coast in the early 1940s and has reached a peak annual production of 200,000 lb. According to Leim and Scott (1966), the average production in the area between 1944 and 1954 was 126,000 lb valued at $17,000. Smaller commercial catches, totalling approximately 100,000 lb annually, now come from Ungava, Frobisher and Cambridge Bays and the rivers to the west of the Mackenzie. Although no recent figures are available they are likely to have risen considerably. Char are now processed locally as char fillets, smoked char and char chowder and shipped south. The industry, run by the Eskimos, is under the direction of the Department of Indian Affairs. The fish are caught by means of gill nets, traps and spears. Land-locked char are of minor importance in North America. The sport fishery for Arctic char in rivers has also been expanding rapidly and at present total catches are estimated at more than 50,000 lb annually.

At one time there was a net fishery for char in Windermere, and Max- well (1904) also describes the taking of char with rod and line in this English lake:

> A couple of ash saplings about 12 feet long are placed in the stern of a boat. To each line is attached a plumb of lead weighing $1\frac{1}{2}$ lb or 2 lb, above which are attached four to six tail-lines carrying metal spinning baits. No reel is used; the line, about 26 yards long, trails behind the boat as it is rowed over the deep water, and a bell on each rod gives warning when a fish has struck.

The annual charge for a licence for plumb fishing was 5s. The licence for a char-net in Windermere cost £1 13s 4d. The char fishery was a fairly profitable industry owing to potted char being considered a great delicacy. The usual market price of char at the end of the last century was 1s 6d a lb. The average catch during the six years 1893–1898 was about 4,000 lb with a gross annual value of £250.

Ritchie (1920) refers to the enormous number of char in Loch Insh, Inverness-shire, which were caught as they moved into the River Spey to spawn. The fish were either netted or snared with a simple ring of brass at the end of a long stick. The fish were pickled with salt and preserved for winter use. Char are not so plentiful in Loch Insh nowadays. However, there are many lochs in the Highlands of Scotland, and in Ireland, where char fisheries could be developed.

Before leaving this section mention should be made of one other species of char which goes under the name of the North American Brook Trout or Speckled Trout (*Salvelinus fontinalis*) which, because it is so widespread, is probably the most sought after game fish in eastern North America. Its sale is prohibited in the Maritime Provinces of Canada except under permit and no estimate of the total catch is available. In the Province of Quebec some sale of trout is permitted; 25,000 lb were reported sold in 1953 but Leim and Scott (1966) feel this must be a small part of the total catch. Power (1966) refers to the unexploited populations of this fish in Ungava. He shows concern for these stocks becoming depleted by angling, when the region becomes more accessible, owing to the fish congregating in fast water for feeding during the summer.

This species was introduced to a number of Scottish lochs and rivers earlier this century but now there are only isolated records. These include a breeding population in a loch over 2,000 feet above sea-level in Wester Ross and a few recent introductions into lochs, and a stream in central Scotland. It has also been introduced into European and South African waters. In South Africa it was found to have very poor fighting qualities and is not very popular. However, this fish could fill a niche in Scottish Highland waters because it feeds at low water temperatures and can spawn in still water.

2.6 Grayling

Another sport fish which is highly prized in some countries (Austria, Canada, Finland, France, Yugoslavia and Sweden) and considered as 'vermin' in others (Scotland and parts of England) is the grayling (*Thymallus thymallus*). No large commercial fisheries exist for grayling and it is mainly a sport fish and has received high praise from many anglers. During the Second World War grayling appeared in some numbers on fishmongers' stalls in central England and sold successfully for about 3s 6d a lb. According to Peterson (1968), the grayling in Sweden has rarely been caught for sale commercially, but it is a popular fish with the housewife. On the very few occasions when grayling have been marketed it has usually been offered together with whitefish. In Sweden the grayling used to be fished intensively, probably by farmers, with nets and 'otters' and also from boats with a long line to which many flies were attached.

The grayling is in good condition during the autumn and winter months when the trout are out of season, and therefore the presence of grayling in trout streams extends the anglers' season. Unfortunately it is not much sought after in Scotland and the majority of anglers who do avail themselves of this sporting and edible fish are visiting anglers from northern England.

2.7 Whitefish

The Coregonids or whitefish are herring-like fish and include the powan (*Coregonus clupeoides*), the pollan (*C. albula*), the schelly (*C. lavaretus*) and a number of continental species which appear to be grouped under the common name of vendace and which include *C. peled*, *C. lavaretus* and *C. nasus*. Details of landings of whitefish in the countries in which they are fished for commercially are given in Table 13.

In Ireland the Lough Erne and Lough Neagh pollan used to be caught with nets and exported to the English markets. In northern Sweden there are important fisheries for whitefish in the rivers and coastal areas. In the rivers they are taken in seines during late summer and autumn when the fish migrate from sea to spawning grounds in the river. On the coast they are caught from May to November in bag nets of various designs, called 'storryssjor' or 'Kittor', and gill nets.

Whitefish are not sought after very much by anglers although angling clubs were formed many years ago for vendace fishing in the Lochmaben lakes (Castle Loch and Mill Loch) in Dumfriesshire, as the vendace was considered a great delicacy. There were two clubs, one was for the 'gentry' and the other for the working folk. The latter club consisted at times of as many as 2,000 people. Vendace were also fished for in these two lakes with

TABLE 13

Landings of whitefish (*Coregonus* spp.) in thousand metric tons.
(Source: *FAO Yearbook of Fishery Statistics*)

	1963	1964	1965	1966	1967	1968
Canada (Inland)	16·3	17·6	15·6	14·8	13·4	—
United States (Great Lakes)	9·2	6·8	8·0	7·5	7·6	6·7
Finland	6·2	5·6	5·8	6·9	6·3	8·1
Germany (East)	0·1	0·1	0·1	0·1	—	—
Poland	0·6	0·4	0·3	0·4	0·5	0·4
Sweden	0·8	0·7	0·6	0·8	0·7	—
U.S.S.R. (Inland)	20·2	16·3	16·6	14·9	14·7	14·1

small-meshed seines, the best days for fishing being when the weather was dull and windy, when the fish move out of the deep water and swim near the shore. It is thought that the vendace is probably now extinct in the Castle Loch.

This section would not be complete without mention of the fishery for the whitefish *Coregonus clupeaformis* in Great Slave Lake which lies in the Northwest Territories of northern Canada. While it is not the largest fishery of its kind (the amount of fishing done is only about 1/200th as much as that done in Lake Erie at one time) it has been studied in detail since the water was opened to commercial fishing in 1945. The results of the first ten years of commercial fishing are given in detail by Kennedy (1956). Fishing on this lake is done exclusively with bottom set gill nets of $5\frac{1}{2}$-inch stretched mesh, set both during the summer, and during the winter under the ice.

2.8 Lake trout

The lake trout (*Cristivomer namaycush*) is a resident of deep lakes in North America. It is a valuable fish for commercial and sport fishermen. Large commercial fisheries for this species occur on Great Slave Lake and elsewhere. At one time there was a large fishery in the Great Lakes but this disappeared due to the virtual elimination of this species by the sea lamprey (Plate 4). An abbreviated account of the relationships existing between the sea lamprey, the lake trout and the whitefish in the Great Lakes is given by Watt (1969). There is evidence to suggest that the stocks of lake trout are now beginning to recover. This is partly due to the planting, since 1958, of more than 19 million lake trout.

Lake trout were introduced into Swiss high alpine lakes in the later part of the nineteenth century but there is no evidence of any reproduction. Lake trout have also been introduced into Finland and Sweden. According to Nilsson (1967) 25 Finnish lakes have been stocked since 1957 and 55 Swedish lakes since 1960. So far no reproduction or interaction with native species, except predation on whitefish, has been recorded.

2.9 Danube salmon

The Danube salmon (*Hucho hucho*) is only found in the Danube river basin. It occurs singly and is regarded chiefly as a sport fish. It is also caught by the Danube fishermen in nets, and in mountain streams, by poachers with spears and forks by torchlight. In Poland a special fee must be added to fishing licences for trout waters if anglers want to catch this fish. It is protected from 1 December to 15 May and the minimum legal length at which fish may be taken varies between 50 and 80 cm; in Poland it is 60 cm total length. There is no other salmonid which has such a large minimum legal size limit.

Attempts have been made to introduce this species to rivers in Switzerland, Morocco, France, Belgium and England (the Thames) but only the Moroccan rivers gave positive results.

2.10 Introduction of Pacific salmon to Atlantic waters

While Pacific salmon are a little beyond the scope of this book, five of the six species should be mentioned in so far as they have been introduced into river systems draining into Atlantic waters. There are five species of Pacific salmon occurring in North America – the sockeye, blueback or red salmon *Oncorhynchus nerka*; the pink or humpback salmon (*O. gorbuscha*); the chum or dog salmon (*O. keta*); the coho or silver salmon (*O. kisutch*), and the spring, chinook or Quinnat (*O. tschawytscha*). The sixth species, the masu (*O. masou*) occurs in Japan. Foerster (1968) mentions a seventh species *O. rhodurus* or Biwa, also from Japan. Haig-Brown (1952) gives a description of the life histories of the Pacific salmon of North America.

It is the pink and chum salmon which have been introduced into the coastal Atlantic region. Some time ago (1900) the Quinnat was introduced successfully to the rivers of New Zealand's South Island and attempts were made in 1902 to introduce the sockeye salmon. Ricker (1954) discusses the earlier attempts at introducing the Pacific salmon species into rivers on the eastern seaboard of North America and gives reasons for justifying their introduction into waters outside their normal distribution. He states that the commercial salmon fishery of the west Atlantic takes about 5 million lb a year, as compared with about 150 million lb in British Columbia and about 1,000 million lb on the Asiatic side of the Pacific. The difference probably stems mainly from the fact that the two most numerous Pacific salmon live in rivers only during the spawning and incubation periods, and do not require the freshwater food or living space which appears to limit the supply of Atlantic salmon. Up to that time (i.e. 1954) attempts at transplantation of Pacific salmon to other waters had only been permanently successful in New Zealand. During the period 1933 to 1939 the Russians transferred approximately 9 million chum salmon eggs from the Far East to rivers in the Murmansk region without any practical success. The experiment was resumed in 1956, and between 1956 and 1959 the Russians transferred by air 48 million fertilised pink salmon eggs and 13 million chum salmon eggs from Sakhalin Island, north of Japan, to the rivers of the Kola Peninsula (Fig. 14). Up to 12 August, 1960, more than 40,000 sexually mature pink salmon had been caught off the coasts of the Kola Peninsula and the Tersk coast of the White Sea. Several thousand 'pinks' were also caught in the Norwegian fjords and rivers and smaller numbers in Icelandic rivers. One had also been caught off the Scottish east coast and one in a river in north-west England. From 1961 to 1964 only a few fish were recorded. However, in 1965 there was a good stock of pink salmon both in the sea and in many rivers and the catch amounted to several

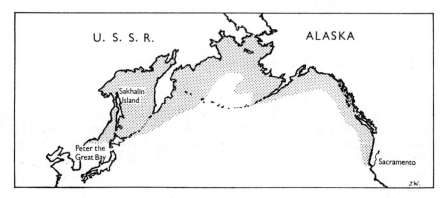

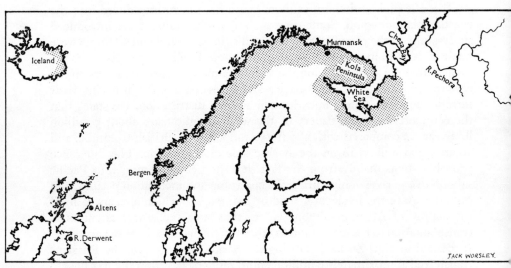

FIG. 14.   Distribution of the pink salmon. Shaded areas show (*above*) natural distribution. (*Below*) Areas and places where pink salmon from Russian experiments have been caught. Recaptures in Iceland have been in the rivers, while in Norway and Russia they have been in rivers and on the coast (from Shearer, 1961).

tons and in this year (as well as in 1961) a few fish were caught in Spits-bergen (Berg, personal communication). Again in 1966 and 1967 only a few fish were caught, one was taken off the Shetland Isles and another off the Scottish north-east coast.

In a personal communication Dr Berg said that there was little known about the occurrence of the chum salmon as the fishermen cannot distin-guish them from the Atlantic salmon. The first chum salmon to be caught was taken at Sørøya, Finnmark in 1963, and in 1965 eight chums were caught in the lower part of the River Tana, Finnmark and one was caught in the Mandalselve, Troms. The pink, chum and Atlantic salmon are depicted in Fig. 15.

Both Berg (1961) and Shearer (1961a) discuss briefly the biological impli-cations of the introduction of pink salmon and what effect it might have on the existing production of Atlantic salmon. The pink salmon, after spending two years in the sea, return to the lower reaches of the river to spawn. Their progeny migrate to sea almost straight after hatching and will therefore not compete with young Atlantic salmon.

A further experiment on pink salmon introduction has been carried out in Newfoundland by the Fisheries Research Board of Canada and the

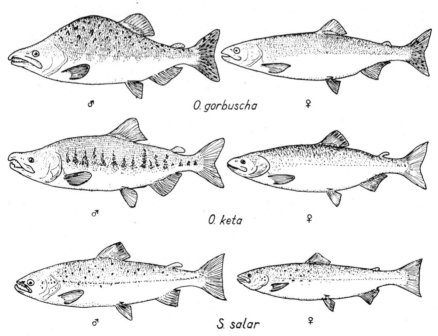

FIG. 15.   Pink, Chum and Atlantic salmon (from Berg, 1961).

Department of Fisheries. Pink salmon eggs were laid down in a specially prepared spawning channel of North Harbour River. The size of the transplants and the known adult returns are shown in Table 14. A full account of the Newfoundland experiments are given by Blair (1968).

In addition to the recent introduction of pink and chum salmon to European waters land-locked sockeye salmon, kokanee, have also been introduced to Swedish lakes but without any signs of successful reproduction.

More recently a large sport fishery has been created in the Great Lakes due to the planting of young coho salmon into some of the streams running into Lake Superior and Lake Michigan. The lake trout fishery in the Great Lakes, which yielded an annual commercial catch of 15,000,000 lb, was eliminated by 1962 by the invasion of sea lampreys through the $27\frac{1}{2}$-mile reconstructed Welland Canal which connects Lake Erie and Lake Ontario (Plate 4). With the absence of the predatory lake trout, alewives, which migrate to the Lakes from the sea, increased rapidly. It was then decided to introduce predators to control the number of alewives and those chosen were the coho and chinook salmon. In 1966 850,000 coho smolts from Oregon and Washington were introduced and in 1967 1,000,000 young chinooks along with more coho, were introduced. By the end of the 1967 season an estimated 25,000 adult coho salmon were caught in Lake Michigan and 15,000 in Lake Superior. Most of them weighed 11 lb or more. In addition some 80,000 were sold commercially by the state fishery agency. At the moment there are plans to increase the size of the liberations of cohos and chinooks and it is interesting to speculate whether this level of harvesting can be continued. Although there is no danger to the salmon from the lampreys, which are now controlled by spraying a lampricide, TFM with granular Bayer 73 as an additive, and by electrical barriers across their spawning streams, the stock of alewives may be rapidly reduced with a resulting decline in their predators. In addition the stocking programme should be viewed with some caution as the Great Lake Fishery Commission is concerned about the potential threat to its splake programme. Splake, a cross between the brook trout and the lake trout, were introduced

TABLE 14

Details and results of pink salmon introduction to Newfoundland

Year of transplant	No. of eggs (millions)	Year of adult return	No. of known adults returning
1959	0·25	1961	1
1962	2·50	1964	49
1964	3·40	1966	638
1965	3·30	1967	8440

into Lake Huron five years ago and major plantings are planned for 1969–1970. Canadian authorities fear that large numbers of adult coho would feed on the young splake thereby negating the money and effort involved in establishing this species. However, the Ontario Department of Lands and Forests planted 150,000 coho smolts in tributary waters of Lake Superior and Lake Ontario in the spring of 1969 in a further effort to improve the Great Lakes sports fishery.

There are potential dangers in introducing any of these species of Pacific salmon to waters draining into the Atlantic as there could well be an unforeseen change in their behaviour which might seriously affect native fish species. For example; there is already evidence that the behaviour of introduced pink salmon is changing. On some rivers they have been recorded moving much further upstream than they do in their native waters, and so they could conceivably compete with Atlantic salmon on the spawning grounds.

PART II

THE BIOLOGY OF THE RESOURCE

Chapter 3

THE ATLANTIC SALMON

3.1 General life history. 3.2 Return to the river: homing instinct;
age of fish at return; time of entry; factors affecting upstream
migration. 3.3 Spawning: change in appearance; fecundity; do
like breed like?; geographic variations. 3.4 Return to the sea: the
kelt and its value. 3.5 The early stages: fry and parr – their
growth and food; the smolt, factors causing its migration to sea.
3.6 Life in the sea: recaptures at sea; food and migrations.
3.7 Predation. 3.8 Parasites. 3.9 Disease.

3.1 General life history

With rare exceptions, the salmon depends on two distinct environments
for the successful fulfilment of its life history. (i) A freshwater environment
in which the reproductive and nursery phase of its life cycle occur and
(ii) a marine environment for its main feeding phase, during which rapid
growth is achieved.

The salmon enters the rivers at all times of the year; if it has spent
two, three or four years at sea before returning to freshwater it is known as
a 'salmon' and, depending on the time of year at which it returns, is called
either a spring, summer or autumn fish. If the salmon has spent only a
little over a year at sea before returning it is termed a 'grilse'. Quite often
there is little difference in the size of these fish, but their age can be determined by examining their scales, which lay down rings in a seasonal pattern.
On approaching freshwater the salmon stops feeding and will not feed again
until it returns to salt water as a spent fish or kelt, which may be six months
to a year or more later. Fortunately, this phenomenon makes little difference to the angler as salmon, for some inexplicable reason, take anglers'
lures into their mouths although not feeding. Once in freshwater the salmon

will migrate upstream at varying speeds depending on the time of year, water temperature and stream flow.

Spawning, or egg laying, starts in the late autumn. Some fish will lay their eggs in November, but those which have entered the river late in the season may not deposit theirs until January or February. By the time spawning commences salmon will have occupied suitable spawning grounds, which consists of silt-free gravel in areas extending from the upper reaches of the watershed down to tidal level. The salmon does not lay many eggs, relatively speaking; how many depends on its size. The number ranges between 2,000 and 15,000. A high fecundity is not essential because the eggs are well-protected in nests or redds under several inches of gravel. After spawning, most of the males die but a relatively small proportion of the females return to spawn a second time.

The eggs hatch in late March or early April and the alevins make their way up through the gravel to emerge as fry four or five weeks later when the yolk sac has been absorbed. At the end of their first year of life the fry are known as parr and they remain in this stage until the spring of their second, third or even fourth year or more, depending on stream conditions, when they turn silver and become smolts. At this stage they migrate to sea, the migration being triggered off by one or more environmental factors. The progeny of one fish do not necessarily all go to sea in the same year or return at the same time and this phenomenon gives obvious survival advantages to the species. The general life cycle of the salmon is summarised in Fig. 16.

While most salmon spend part of their lives in the sea there are some which are non-migratory. In several lakes in eastern North America there is a form known as a land-locked salmon, *Salmo salar sebago* (Girard), though their access to the sea is not barred. The fish is popularly called Ouananiche (Lake St John) or Sebago salmon (Nova Scotia, New Brunswick and the New England states). This lake salmon was distinguished from the Atlantic salmon on the basis of general shape, head size and spotting. Wilder (1947), in a comparative study of these two forms, made twenty-six body measurements and counts on the majority of 381 specimens of lake and Atlantic salmon. Adult lake and Atlantic salmon were found to differ generally in coloration, spotting and flesh colour, but he presented evidence that indicates that these are not inherent but result from differences in the environment and the diet.

In Lake Vänern in Sweden there is a non-migratory form of Atlantic salmon called 'blanklax'. This salmon enters the rivers, running into the lake, for breeding, and the smolts migrate to the lake, where they live pelagically, until they return to the rivers to spawn.

Land-locked salmon also occur in Russia in Lake Ladoga and in Norway

Salmon travel long distances in the sea and feed on a number of marine organism such as sand eels, herring and plankton

On approaching freshwater the salmon stops feeding

EGGS are laid in gravel in late autumn

SEA

RIVER

Parr become SMOLTS in the spring of their second, third, or fourth year of life and migrate to the sea in April, May and June.

After spawning the fish are known as KELTS and many die at this stage.

PARR remain in freshwater for two to three years, feeding on aquatic insects

FRY

ALEVINS hatch in early spring and emerge from gravel after 3–4 weeks ready to feed as fry

Fig. 16.   Life cycle of the salmon.

in Lake Byglandsfjord. There are also land-locked Atlantic salmon in South Island, New Zealand. The majority of the salmon originally planted in the New Zealand rivers running into Lake Te Anau descend only to the lake and, after feeding there, return to the head rivers to spawn. Their passage to the sea is not barred as the River Waiau flows out of this lake.

In Dalmatia a fish bearing a strong resemblance to a salmon parr lives in the rivers and is called *Salmo obtusirostris*. It has a smaller mouth than a salmon parr and more numerous gill rakers. *Salmo obtusirostris* may be derived from a colony of salmon parr found in glacial times when salmon might have entered the Mediterranean.

Berg (1943) gives an interesting account of a relict salmon called småblank from the River Namsen in Norway. These look very like salmon parr. This land-locked form remains in the rivers and does not migrate to a lake. According to Berg, "It is very abundant in the river higher up than the fall Fiskemoss where the salmon from the sea stop."

No land-locked races of salmon have been found in Scotland, although an occasional very large smolt has been caught in the hydro-electric reservoirs and there is at least one record of a female smolt with ripening ovaries.

3.2 Return to the river

Homing instinct. Probably one of the most intriguing aspects of the salmon's life history is its homing instinct. According to Izaak Walton, the return of the salmon to its parent river had already been established by 1653 by "tying a riband or some known tape or thread in the tail of smolts and catching them again when they came back to the same place usually six months after". Russel (1864, p. 54) refers to smolt marking experiments on the Tay in 1854, 1855 and 1856. The marking was by fin-mutilation, and while a small number of adult salmon were subsequently recaptured bearing marks on the fins that could have been due to this earlier fin-clipping, the results were considered inconclusive. The tagging experiments carried out on the River Tay in 1905 and 1906 by the late P. D. H. Malloch of Perth were among the first serious marking investigations carried out anywhere in the world. About 1·7% of the marked smolts were recaptured in the Tay as adult fish, thus demonstrating their return to their parent river. Some marked fish were, however, caught in other rivers which shows that the homing instinct is not always 100%. Since these early experiments many smolt-marking investigations have been carried out in Scotland, England, Canada, Ireland, Norway and Sweden, and all have demonstrated this homing instinct.

Many theories have been put forward to explain the way in which salmon find their way back to their parent river. Calderwood (1903a and

1903b) believed temperature was an important factor determining the choice of tributary or main stream. Others considered that current, temperature, quality of water and the amount and direction of light were all important factors influencing migration. Some workers suggested that the salmon on its return is responding to the carbon dioxide gradient of a fresh–salt water gradient while others believe that migratory fish follow a salinity gradient as they move upstream and that spawning takes place near the point where the salt content of the water is at a minimum. Probably the theory which has most acceptance is one derived from the work of Hasler and Wisby (1951 and 1954) which demonstrates the importance of stream odours in the orientation of fish. However, this theory is not new and almost a hundred years ago Buckland in 1880 suggested that salmon were assisted by their power of smell to find their way in the ocean, and also to find their parent river.

Huntsman (1952) considers that salmon return to their breeding grounds by a wandering mechanism rather than a homing mechanism. Huntsman tagged migrating smolts from two branches of the Moser River in Nova Scotia. On return as adults, the marked fish of both kinds ascended both branches but on the average 80% of the fish did ascend the home rather than the foreign branch. In the sea, the marked Moser salmon were taken mostly in the Moser outflow; but they were also taken in the outflows of certain neighbouring rivers in both directions along the Nova Scotia coast, which they would readily reach in wandering. However, they were not taken in one neighbouring river, the St Mary River, which drains country very different geologically and agriculturally from that drained by the Moser River and other neighbouring rivers. Huntsman considers that these facts indicate that in the sea Moser salmon avoid very foreign water, but not water sufficiently similar to the home water. He also found that the smolt tagging showed that many foreign fish, presumably from neighbouring rivers, also ascended the Moser River above the head of tide, sometimes exceeding the native fish in numbers. Otterström (1938) found that the salmon in the West Jutland rivers were partly of local and partly of foreign origin. Huntsman considered that home water does not direct the fish home but may stop the wandering and that very foreign water may actually be avoided by the fish. Other evidence of straying has been produced by Pyefinch and Mills (1963), Mills (1966 and 1968) and Carlin (1969a).

Another interesting aspect of homing instinct is that in which fish reared in one river, or in a hatchery fed by one river, and then released in another river, sometimes very far away and often under such conditions that they will leave this second river almost immediately, have returned to the river in which they were released. This indicates that, the memory of the smell of the home water is not imprinted during their early river life,

but during a few days before entering the sea or on their downstream migration. This phenomenon has been observed from the release of Scottish
hatchery-reared fish and by Carlin (1969a).

Carlin points out that the effect of this imprinting at the moment of
leaving the river is, however, not confined to the last stage of the return
migration, which is the wandering at the coast trying to locate the mouth of
the native river. But also the migration in the sea seems to be determined by
events in connection with the smolts leaving the river. Carlin illustrates this
well from the following example: Salmon eggs were taken from the Anger-
manälven and the young salmon were reared for two years in a hatchery in
southern Sweden. The smolts were transported to a hatchery at the river
Ume älv and kept there for a month. After that they were transported to
the river Lule älv and kept there for a week, during which time they were
tagged. Half the number of the fish were then released in the Lule älv,
and the other half in the Kalix älv, 40 miles to the north-east. Of those
released in the Kalix älv 3 were taken in the Torne älv 30 miles east of the
Kalix älv, 74 in the Kalix älv and 3 in the Lule älv. Of the fish released in
the Lule älv, 1 went to the Kalix älv, 150 to the Lule älv and 6 to the Ume
älv. In this case, in spite of the very complicated origin, the fish returned
mainly to the rivers of release. They are not very far apart, so this could
have been explained by the fact that all the fish had returned to the same
coastal area, and then sorted out the rivers according to the smell. *But*
this was not the case, as can be seen from Fig. 17. The two batches of fish
were quite well separated already when approaching the coast.

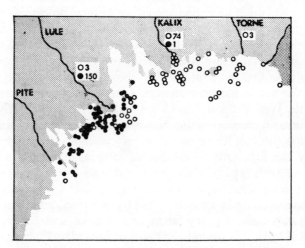

FIG. 17.   Recaptures of salmon tagged as smolts in the R. Lule (*black
dots*) and R. Kalix (*open rings*) (from Carlin, 1969a).

In 1960 some salmon ova from the River Indalsälven were sent to Poland and the resulting smolts were released in the River Vistula. A few fish went as far north as the Gulf of Bothnia, but none were taken near the Indalsälven. On the other hand 15 were taken in the Vistula or its estuary. They had therefore migrated south instead of going north, which they should have done if their migration had been guided only by an inherited kind of reaction to whatever stimulus is guiding their sea migrations.

Carlin concludes that the migration in the sea must also in some way be determined by the circumstances at the release, but, as he says "it is still quite impossible to imagine how fish distributed over a vast area of open sea and moving about in it for a couple of years, still can converge towards the place where they first entered sea water".

Age of fish at return. Salmon enter the rivers at all times of the year. Those fish entering the rivers between January and early May are called spring fish, while those entering the rivers during the summer are classified as summer fish if they have spent more than two years in the sea, but are called grilse if they have spent just over a year in the sea. Very rarely a fish may only spend a few months in the sea and return as 'pre-grilse'. Shearer (1963) records the capture of one in the River North Esk and Menzies (1914) records the capture of three, from the Helmsdale, North Esk and Forth respectively. Fish coming into the rivers during the autumn and winter are called autumn and winter fish, provided they are not late-running grilse.

The time of entry. The time of entry of the main runs of fish varies from river to river. Some rivers such as the Tweed, Tay, Findhorn, Spey, Inverness-shire Garry and Ness have early runs of spring fish while others, such as those on the west coast of Scotland, may have very few spring fish and the first large runs of fish only start to enter the rivers in June and July as grilse and summer fish. Again there are rivers such as the Tweed which have a large run of autumn fish which continues well into December. On the rivers Taw and Torridge in Devonshire there is a run of winter fish known as 'greenbacks' and a fishery for these has been established in the tidal reaches in December. Huntsman (1933) describes the very early run of salmon into the St John River, New Brunswick, which occurs almost a full year before spawning. Pyefinch (1955) discusses this classification of fish according to the time of year in which they enter freshwater and, using Went's account (1949) of types of winter fish, mentions the difficulties produced by this nomenclature. Pyefinch illustrates these difficulties admirably by quoting the following passage from Jones (1950a):

> ... the few 'spring fish' with little or no erosion of the scale edge were probably 'winter fish', i.e. fish which had that year's winter rings on the edge of their scales and had moved rapidly upstream from their

feeding grounds. Went (1949) suggested that this type of fish, if sexually mature, should be regarded as a 'late-running summer fish' despite the close band of rings on the edge of their scales. It is quite possible that these fish are the same type as the summer fish, but, if one regards the scale reading definitions at present in use, one could equally well call the late spring fish which are taken at the same time as the summer fish in April, May and June as 'early summer fish'!

However, this only illustrates the difficulties surrounding the scale interpretations of the few doubtful cases, and information on the age and composition of runs of fish is of great importance in any management plans, which is evident from the vast amount of literature on this subject which has been reviewed by Pyefinch (1955) and, for Irish rivers, by Went (1964b).

The salmon scale, like the scales of many other fish, appear under a microscope to consist of a number of ridges or rings formed successively around a small unringed centre or nucleus. The actual histology of the scale is very elaborate and reference should be made to the work of Wallin (1957) who has described in detail the growth structure and developmental physiology of the scale. Here it is sufficient to say that the scale is a growing part of the body and the spacing of the ridges or rings on it is an indicator of the rate of its former growth in the period when the rings were being formed. The growth rings seen on the salmon (and trout) scale are of two types (a) widely spaced rings characteristic of fast growth (summer growth) and (b) less widely spaced and less numerous rings indicative of slow or winter growth. From an examination of the scale, therefore, it is possible to tell how old the fish is (by counting the bands of winter rings), how much time it has spent in freshwater and, if an adult, how much of its time in the sea. If the length of the fish at capture is known it is possible to calculate its length at the end of each of its previous years of life (see page 281). It is also possible to tell whether it had spawned before, due to the presence of a spawning mark brought about by scale erosion, and how long ago, and how old and how large it was when it left the river as a smolt. However, recently White and Medcof (1968) have shown that scale readings alone do not give a dependable estimate of the number of times a salmon has spawned if it has spawned two or more times.

Because of the ease of obtaining scales without interfering with the market value of the salmon, much of the earlier research on salmon was centred around studies which could be made from scales. The volume of literature resulting from such studies is immense and has been listed in some detail by Pyefinch (1955), and Bergeron (1962).

Factors affecting upstream migration. A host of factors are said to be responsible for the entry of salmon into rivers and their subsequent upstream migration. Hayes (1953) found that fish move out of tidal waters into fresh

PLATE 5

A salmon on its way upstream leaps 12 ft to clear the Orrin Falls situated
a few miles downstream of the Orrin Dam in Ross-shire.

PLATE 6. The tail end of a 2 lb sea trout showing sea lice, some of which have the long 'tails' or egg sacs still attached to them.

PLATE 7. Salmon gill maggots on the outer fringes of the gills. Some have been taken off to show how they have eroded the gill.

water at dusk and light change may be the operating factor. He also had evidence that fairly strong onshore winds approaching 20 m.p.h. induce salmon to concentrate in the river estuary and eventually ascend. Peaks in the tidal cycles representing daily increasing differences between high and low tides seem to be effective in concentrating salmon on the coast and initiating a run into freshwater. Hayes showed that large natural freshets can initiate a major run of fish into the river provided the winds and tides are favourable. In cases where these two other factors were not favourable no run occurred.

Menzies (1931) describes how in dry weather, grilse which were held up in tidal waters, moved up the estuary just ahead of the tide, and fell back with the tide as it ebbed; but during a spate, tidal movements were ignored, and the fish entered the estuary and moved directly and rapidly upstream. Although Hayes found that temperature had little effect in initiating runs of fish, Menzies (1931) has shown that water temperature is of great importance to fish movement in the spring, and until the water temperature reaches 42° F there is little upstream movement of fish over obstacles. Lindroth (1952) estimated that the average rate of travel upstream of adult fish ascending the Indalsälven in Sweden was 10–20 km a day. It seemed to him as if the salmon which enter the river last travel farthest upstream.

Upstream migration is undoubtedly associated with thyroid activity as the salmon becomes sexually mature and Fontaine (1951) has suggested that the alternating periods of activity and torpor which characterise the behaviour of ascending salmon may be due to variations in the activity of the thyroid gland. As the season advances and the thyroid activity increases one might expect to see an increase in the urgency of upstream movement. Mills (1968) found that adult fish released downstream from a trap they had just entered re-appeared in the trap several times and that there was an increase in the persistence of this upstream movement as the season progressed.

At present a great deal of research is being carried out by the English river authorities, particularly the Lancashire River Authority, on the factors influencing upstream migration. Some of the factors being monitored, at weirs or counting sites, in relation to fish movement are air and water temperature, barometric pressure, humidity, precipitation, conductivity and flow. The effects of artificial freshets on upstream migration are dealt with in a later chapter.

Before leaving the subject of upstream movement mention should be made of the behaviour of fish at natural obstacles. Stuart (1962) carried out a most interesting study of the leaping behaviour of salmon and trout at falls and obstructions. The stimulus to leap was found to be closely related to the presence of a standing wave, or hydraulic jump, and the location of

D

the standing wave distant to the obstacle influenced the success of the leap. Thus in shallow fall pools and pools below sloping weirs the standing wave becomes located too far downstream for the fish to strike the crest of the fall on the upward arc of its trajectory. If the fish strikes the falling water on the downward arc it is immediately swept downstream. Salmon have been observed leaping at and surmounting vertical falls of up to 12 feet in height, such as those on the River Orrin, Ross-shire (Plate 5).

3.3 Spawning

Change in appearance. The adult male and female change in appearance after entering freshwater and as spawning time approaches. Some of the bones of the salmon grow substantially and there appears a new set of breeding teeth. The bones that increase their size and acquire new material include the main bones of the jaws, this is particularly noticeable in the male which develops a hooked lower jaw or kype. The parts of the skull growing at the breeding period require a large amount of material, mostly calcium. As the salmon does not feed during the time it is in freshwater (as a result of which it may lose about 25% of its body weight) the only material available is from other parts of the body. Comparing the enormous growth of the jaw bones and of the teeth with the relatively small absorption of the bones of the gill covers there would appear to be insufficient calcium to supply all the growing elements with necessary material. However, there is considerable absorption of the scales and Crichton (1935) and van Someren (1937) suggest that the calcium from this source is also used by the growing bones and teeth. In the case of the scale there is considerable scale erosion and what remains of the scale becomes deeply embedded in the spongy dermis.

Most Atlantic salmon spawn in the late autumn or early winter, though the onset of spawning in any particular year may vary slightly, probably due to environmental conditions. Calderwood (1901b) has given details of the duration of the spawning season in a number of Scottish rivers for the period 1892 to 1900. Spawning usually takes place in the upper reaches of the river system, where gravel suitable for the construction of the redds exists. However, spawning sometimes occurs only a short distance above tidal limits and has been observed occurring on the lower reaches of some of the eastern Canadian and northern Scottish rivers.

The most detailed account of the spawning behaviour of salmon is that given by Jones and King (1949) and Jones (1959), and readers are recommended to refer to these works for a complete description of spawning.

Fecundity. In a study of the fecundity of salmon in Scottish rivers Pope, Mills and Shearer (1961) showed that there is a relationship between the length of the salmon and the number of eggs produced. Although the year-to-year variations in this relationship are not significant, there are significant variations in the relationship between fish from different rivers. The average egg counts corresponding to a fish length of 70 cm, this being the average length of all salmon handled in the study, on each of the six rivers studied are:

Lyon	Blackwater	Garry	Dee	Conon	Meig
4943	5117	5370	5495	5572	6067

As egg number does not increase linearly with length, the classification of different rivers by reference to the number of eggs per unit fish length is not possible. However, as the power of L in the following relationships is constant from river to river, the fish of the same length from different rivers may be correctly compared:

Lyon $\quad\quad \log_{10} N = 2\cdot3345 \log_{10} L - 0\cdot622$
Blackwater $\quad \log_{10} N = 2\cdot3345 \log_{10} L - 0\cdot607$
Garry $\quad\quad \log_{10} N = 2\cdot3345 \log_{10} L - 0\cdot586$
Dee $\quad\quad \log_{10} N = 2\cdot3345 \log_{10} L - 0\cdot576$
Conon $\quad\quad \log_{10} N = 2\cdot3345 \log_{10} L - 0\cdot570$
Meig $\quad\quad \log_{10} N = 2\cdot3345 \log_{10} L - 0\cdot533$

It should be pointed out that, of the six rivers studied, three, the Blackwater, Conon and Meig, are tributaries of the one river system, whereas the other three are separate river systems. It seems reasonable to suppose that there are more chances of mixing of stock between tributaries of one river system than there are between the stocks of different river systems, so that the existence of significant differences between tributaries suggests that the significant differences between river systems may have less meaning, biologically, than might be supposed.

To assess the order of magnitude of the potential egg deposition on any river, if great accuracy in the final figure is not essential, it may be sufficient to employ the average equation for the above six rivers, namely:

$$\log_{10} N = 2\cdot3345 \log_{10} L - 0\cdot582$$

where N = number of eggs and L = length in cm.

Do like breed like? As has been mentioned earlier, particular rivers, or even tributaries of a river, may be characterised by the time of year when salmon enter them and by the proportions among them of grilse and salmon. These facts have been commonly interpreted as meaning that there are more or less distinct races in the various rivers, characterised by such behaviour and also by certain body proportions and other details of structure. This conception has been generally accepted and in the past a great deal of work was done in describing the characteristics of salmon of individual rivers from the results of studies of their scales. As White and Huntsman (1938) state:

> Even for one river the salmon may come in from the sea at quite different seasons and these 'runs' may differ considerably in character, such as size and body proportions. The theory has been extended to fit these facts by the supposition that there are more or less distinct early-running and late-running races in the one river.

The early-running and large fish are of most value to the fishermen, and White and Huntsman go on to say:

> It has been natural, therefore, that the fishermen have wished to have the theory of races put to practical use in two ways: first, by having the early and large fish used in fish cultural practice so that their numbers might be maintained and increased, and, second, by having the young from rivers with early-running and large salmon planted in those rivers where the local fish are late-running and small. To secure the early and large fish and to hold them until spawning time, was therefore, undertaken by the Fish Culture Branch of the Department of Fisheries of Canada, and proved to be a difficult and costly business. This made it desirable to ascertain whether the practice had any real justification.

There were conflicting views over whether local behaviour was heritable. To start with, late-running fish in the Miramichi River, New Brunswick, were tagged and liberated after spawning. Of those recaptured in the river after one or two years, and presumably ready to spawn again, 6 out of 16 were taken early in the summer. This raised doubts as to the distinctness of the early-running and late-running habits in individual fish. Calderwood (1930), however, has argued that the seasonal habit persists in individual fish, making use of the fact that of all the grilse (which run in summer) marked in Scotland, not one when recaptured as a salmon was taken in the spring. He also argued that the heavy netting of the salmon in summer and autumn on many parts of the coast of Scotland has caused the late-running grilse to decline and the spring salmon to increase, and that large catches of salmon in the summer and autumn in the Tweed district resulted in the Tweed changing in twenty-five years from a late river into an early river. He states: "If we do not accept the premise (the existence of early and late runs as separate local races of salmon) I am unable to account for the spring run in the Tweed in any other way." At the present time the Tweed has again a late run of autumn fish and, in the opinion of some, the spring run is declining and it would have been interesting to know how Calderwood would have explained this situation as the autumn fish enter the river after the netting season has closed. Huntsman (1931) concludes for the Miramichi River "that man's experiment lasting for more than 80 years in restricting fishing to the early run and in encouraging reproduction of the late run has succeeded neither in materially reducing the early run nor in materially increasing the late run".

It was apparent to White that a test was necessary in order to determine whether or not such peculiarity in behaviour is inherited. To carry out this test fry hatched from eggs of salmon in Chaleur Bay, near the mouth of the Restigouche River, New Brunswick, where salmon enter early in the summer as two sea-year and three sea-year fish, were planted in 1932 in the East Branch (without salmon) of the Apple River at the head of the Bay of Fundy. In this region the local salmon enter only in the autumn and nearly all as grilse. The Restigouche fish, as parr, grew more rapidly than the local fish, corresponding with the less-crowded conditions in the East Branch. The smolts were marked by removal of the adipose fin when descending to sea in 1934. Traps were placed on both branches in 1935 and in the autumn 92 marked grilse entered the East Branch and 6 the south branch. In 1936 5 marked two sea-year salmon entered the East Branch in the autumn and 1 entered the South Branch. No difference in appearance or behaviour was observable between the fish in the East Branch (from Restigouche parents), and the local salmon of the South Branch.

In summing up the results of the Apple River experiment White (1936a) says:

> The outcome of this experiment is quite clear. The Restigouche fish remained only two years in the Apple River instead of the three years characteristic of their native stream. Also they returned from the sea predominantly (95%) as grilse instead of as two sea-year and three sea-year fish, the behaviour in their native region. Finally, while in the Restigouche River a large number of the fish return as early-run fish and ascend the river as such, those introduced into the Apple River did not, on return, ascend as early-run fish, but were found both early and late in the estuary in common with the native stock. Water conditions in the river were probably not suitable for an early ascent, but later in the summer when there was sufficient water they did not ascend. Except in rate of growth in the river, for which obvious reasons have been given (i.e. less crowded conditions), the Restigouche salmon introduced into Apple River could not be distinguished by their behaviour from the indigenous salmon, and hence failed to show any evidence of a 'Restigouche' inheritance. Although the failure is definite as to any racial distinction between Restigouche and Apple River

salmon, the possibility of there being such distinctions in other places is not excluded. The significant point is that, in this instance, there has been a demonstration that environmental conditions, acting on the individual from the fry stage on, make the full observed difference in behaviour between Restigouche and Apple River salmon almost as great a difference as is to be found in the salmon in Canadian waters.

More recently the Salmon Research Trust of Ireland has undertaken the rearing of fish of known ancestry and their subsequent tagging, release and recapture. In these experiments, which are still continuing, fish derived from spring fish parents have returned as spring fish and those derived from grilse parents have returned as grilse. However, it was found that spring fish do not invariably breed spring fish nor do grilse invariably breed grilse, although the majority of smolts derived from grilse have returned as grilse. It was also noticed that there is a tendency for smolts of spring fish to return as grilse, and a similar situation has also been observed in hatchery-reared smolts in Scotland and Sweden where many fish, but by no means all, tend to return as grilse irrespective of their parentage. Obviously more research requires to be carried out on this subject, the results of which can have important applications.

Geographic variations. Geographic variation is common among many animals and plants. The differences may be internal or external, conspicuous or microscopic. In some animals geographic divergences are often due to non-genetic (phenotypical) adaptability, i.e. affected by the environment. In such cases the value of meristic characters as taxonomic tools is uncertain since there must be incontrovertible evidence for the genetic basis of any given variation. Among fish this phenotypical plasticity is very pronounced and has severely affected many studies of speciation and genotypical intraspecific variation. In the genus Coregonus the significance of gill rakers has been proved to be of genetic origin. Among most other fish however, the significance of most biometric characters is diffuse. These problems have been changed with the development of techniques for studying proteins close to the molecular level where qualitative differences can be shown to have a genetic basis, since enzymes and other proteins are direct products of the genes and differences in these reflect genetic differences.

Recently studies have been started to investigate the existence of distinct salmon races by the analysis of the haemoglobins by means of a microelectrophoresis technique. Wilkins (1967), observed differences in the pattern of the haemoglobin electropherograms of Scottish and Swedish salmon. However, Koch, Wilkins, Bergström and Evans (1967) found that the haemoglobins of Atlantic salmon of Scottish and Swedish origin exhibited the same type of starch gel electrophoretic pattern when analysed with the same buffer and the same pH. They therefore considered that the differences found by Wilkins cannot be attributed to a difference in geographical origin or genetic variation.

So at present no geographic variation has been found using the above method. However, Koch, Bergström and Evans (1964) did find that with an increase in the size of the salmon a developmental pattern is observed in each group of haemoglobins and a final pattern is reached in the sexually mature fish. The absolute size of the individuals is not important for the development of the final pattern as it appears in sexually mature dwarf individuals of the 'Namsen Blanken' race of Namsen River in Norway. It does not occur in precocious male parr. Wilkins (1968) suggests that geographic races may yet be determined by the rate of development of this final pattern.

Similar work to that described above has been carried out by Nyman (1965, 1966, 1967). Nyman looked at other proteins as well as blood, particularly enzymes and he was able to demonstrate interpopulation variations in a number of protein systems.

3.4 Return to the sea

After spawning, both male and female fish are known as kelts. The death rate after spawning is high, especially among male fish. According to Taylor (1968, p. 97), the fish suddenly develops Cushing's disease caused by an increased output of the hormone ACTH. Apparently the salmon contains some internal 'clockwork' which turns up its pituitary controls at the time of migration, and the over-stimulated pituitary causes the excessive output of ACTH.

However, Belding (1934) considers that the cause of the high mortality in salmon after spawning is a severe reduction in body weight. Physiologists have found that death occurs in animals during starvation when the body weight is reduced approximately 40%. The loss of between 31 and 44% in weight, according to the length of stay in the rivers, brings the salmon close to the line of physiological death. As a result it is so weak on its return to the ocean that it is unable to undergo normal recuperation. Salmon that are spawning for a second time are recruited from the more vigorous individuals which manage to recover their strength before being subjected to a hostile environment.

Some information on the proportion of the upstream run of spawners returning downstream as kelts has been collected at two points on the Conon River system in Ross-shire. On the River Meig the proportion of fish returning downstream as kelts over four years from an average upstream run of 333 fish was 14·4%, ranging from 10·2 to 24·6%. Unfortunately this information is incomplete as the trap, at which the information was collected, was flooded at times during the winter months. However, at Torr Achilty dam on the River Conon, where little spilling occurs, the proportion was much higher and, with an average upstream run over six years of 2,300 fish, the proportion descending was on average 26%, ranging from 20 to 36%.

The proportion of previously spawned fish in the rivers of various countries is very similar on average and is in the region of 3 to 6%. However, there are some short course rivers, such as those in the west of Scotland and parts of eastern Canada where the proportion of previously spawned fish may be as high as 34%. Nall (1933) has recorded a salmon caught in Loch Maree on the west coast of Scotland which had spawned four times. It was 13 years old and is probably the oldest recorded Scottish salmon. Observations show that there are two main periods when the downstream movement of kelts occurs, one being in November and December and the other in April and May. However, these records of kelt descent have been made at, or a short distance below, hydro-electric installations where delay in descent is known to occur, and therefore the time of descent in an uncontrolled river may be different.

Although fish liberated as kelts may at times tend to stay in the estuary or in the sea within the influence of the river, kelts do undergo long-distance migrations. Menzies and Shearer (1957) give details of a kelt tagged at Loch na Croic on the River Blackwater, Ross-shire, which was recaptured 1,730 miles away on the west coast of Greenland. Went and Piggins (1965) also record kelts tagged in rivers in the west of Ireland being recaptured off the west coast of Greenland.

The absence periods or lengths of time salmon spend in the sea between spawnings have been classified by Jones (1959).

1. Short period. A few months duration, i.e. when a kelt goes down in spring and comes up the following autumn to spawn again.
2. Long period. About a year, i.e. a whole summer and winter spent in the sea.
3. Very long period. A stay in the sea of about 18 months.

Since the beginning of the century over 22,000 kelts have been marked in Eire and of these 490 have been recaptured in the river as clean fish and 486 or 99·2% of these recaptures were made in the river in which marking was done or in the estuary thereof. This indicates a marked homing instinct in the previously spawned fish.

The kelt and its value

There has been some controversy over the value of the kelt to the commercial and rod fisheries, and opinions differ from country to country.

In Canada, for example, there is a rod fishery in the spring for kelts or 'black salmon' on the Miramichi. Kerswill (1955b), in his conclusions on the assessment of the effects of black salmon angling on Miramichi salmon stocks, states:

> Although the Miramichi black salmon fishery takes some of the early-run stock of salmon, there is small chance that these would become available again to fishermen even though they were spared. Less than 10% of Miramichi salmon have come into freshwater previously for spawning. Recent tagging of incoming salmon throughout the season has shown that the proportion of the late-run fish taken by black salmon anglers in the following spring is greater than the proportion taken of the early-run fish. The black salmon fishery appears to be a worthwhile use for the late-run stock which is quite plentiful in the Miramichi area. In weighing the merits and disadvantages of black salmon angling these points must be considered carefully, as well as the financial benefits derived from this popular sport fishing. Wanton destruction of black salmon is to be avoided, of course, since some of the largest early-run salmon in future years will be the survivors of the earlier spawning.

Harriman (1960) describes the 'black salmon controversy' and quotes the opinions given him by a number of salmon experts from different countries. Two only will be quoted here, one from 'each side of the house' as it were. The first one is from Menzies' *Report on the present position of the Atlantic salmon fisheries of Canada* (Atlantic Salmon Association Document No. 17) 1951:

> Like drift netting in the sea, black salmon angling, in plain language, 'kelt fishing', has become an established practice on the Miramichi River, and is engaged in to a lesser extent on two or three other rivers. It is a queer form of sport but, apparently some people enjoy it, though one cannot imagine anyone enjoying the eating of a kelt; the justification appears to be that the anglers provide employment and bring money into the area which otherwise, at that time, would not have the benefit.
>
> Expediency, or financial gain, seem poor excuses for this departure from the law and from normal sporting standards, even if harm done to the stock is small. I recommend that the law should be strictly enforced in the other rivers, and serious and immediate consideration should be given to taking the same step on the Miramichi.

In a letter to the Narraguagus Salmon Association (31 October, 1959) Menzies says:

Scale reading shows that the previously spawned fish constitute in our (Scottish) rivers between 3 and 5% of the total stock. Consequently, in a normal river, if the entire kelt population were destroyed, the stock would be reduced by no more than 5%, although necessarily this would have a cumulative effect. This last point, the cumulative effect, is, I think, important, especially since nearly all the kelts which survive until the spring and are then caught are females.

In Scotland and throughout Great Britain, the taking and killing of kelts has been illegal for all time.

Carlin is of the opposite opinion and in his letter to the Narraguagus Salmon Association (23 January, 1960) says:

The regulation of kelt fishing is different in different parts of Sweden. In the rivers of the northern part of our east coast, the closed season is usually from September 1st to December 31st, although in some cases the salmon fishing is closed until May to protect the kelts. A very rough estimation, founded on tagging experiments, gave the results that, if the kelts are spared, about one third of them would be taken later as mended fish, and the individual fish would have increased about three times in value.

My personal opinion is that the salmon fishing could be free after the spawning season unless the salmon population is so low that the kelts are urgently needed to increase the salmon population.

Harriman (1960) in his conclusion says:

In light of overwhelming evidence and opinion as to the wisdom of legalising black-salmon angling, it is submitted that the Maine Sea-Run Salmon Commission should not only reverse its decision with respect to the Narraguagus but should outlaw black-salmon angling on all Maine streams until such time as it becomes evident that additions to the spawning stock are in excess of requirements.

Probably the best evidence put forward for conserving kelts, in Ireland at least, is that given by Went (1964b):

In Irish waters it has been obvious that the returned kelts may make fairly substantial contributions to the stocks of salmon. In the Shannon the proportion of previous spawners has varied considerably from year to year. In the year 1941, for example, by weight the previous spawners amounted to 7·3% of the total. From other investigations we know that of the previous spawners at least four out of five are females, so we can assume that female previous spawners in 1941 represented 5·8% of the total stock by weight. In the maiden fish, as far as we can ascertain in this river the sexes are more or less equally abundant.

Now the number of eggs spawned by a female is roughly proportional to her weight and if we take 500 eggs per lb of body weight as a round figure then 100 pounds of spawning fish in the Shannon might be expected to yield the following eggs:

Previous spawners – – – – – – –
Females 5·8 lb = 5·8 × 500 = 2900
Males   1·5 lb   Nil

Maiden or unspawned fish
Females 46·35 lb = 46·35 × 500 = 23175
Males   46·35 lb   Nil

Total   26075

On that basis in the Shannon the previous spawners would have accounted for 11·1% of all the eggs deposited or, say, 1 in 9, certainly a worthwhile contribution.

It is stated in the Report of the Committee on Salmon and Freshwater Fisheries (The Bledisloe Report) in 1961 (Cmnd. 1350) under Section 89:

> In England and Wales only about 5% of the salmon entering our rivers survive to spawn a second time, so if a fisherman takes a kelt there is a large chance that it would have died anyway and therefore that it would not have contributed to the future stock. If, indeed, a river is so short of fish that it depends on the maintenance of the population of fish which have spawned before, then clearly it is being overfished and the effective remedy is a reduction of fishing by means of an increased annual or weekly close time, reduction of netting, or even by restriction of angling.

Some adult fish, generally females, may not spawn due to either some physical abnormality or absence of one of the opposite sex. These fish are known as baggots or rawners and return to the sea with eggs or milt unshed.

There are a number of physical differences which are supposed to distinguish a previous spawner from a virgin fish. These are: (1) Previous spawners are not truly silvery, but have a golden sheen on their scales (but apparently some late-running virgin fish may also have this golden sheen!). (2) Previous spawners generally have many more spots, especially on the back and gill covers. (3) Previous spawners invariably have gill maggots (*Salmincola salmonea*) on their gills. (4) The scales of previous spawners show a spawning mark. I would be reluctant to use the first two characteristics and I would qualify the third by saying that fresh-run previous spawners will have gill maggots while fresh-run virgin fish will not; as after virgin fish have been in the river for some time they also will carry gill maggots. Kelts also have gill maggots and I have witnessed many arguments among anglers as to whether a certain fish which had been killed was a kelt or a previous spawner, and I have generally been brought in to decide with a scale examination. However, it is usually possible to recognise a fresh-run previous spawner from a kelt by its general appearance, but the reasons one gives would not necessarily stand up to expert cross-examination.

3.5 The early stages

Fry and parr – their growth and food. The eggs deposited in the redds may be under 6 to 12 inches of gravel and the time required for their hatching ranges from 70 to 160 days depending on water temperature. On hatching, the fish, which is about half an inch long, is called an alevin and possesses a large yolk sac attached to its under surface. The alevins move about in the gravel as a result of phototaxes and rheotaxes (Dill, 1969). At first they move obliquely downwards but, after a few days, the direction of this movement changes and they move obliquely upwards. The alevins then remain a few inches under the surface until the yolk sac is nearly absorbed, after which they emerge from the gravel. Only in the last few years have any serious studies of egg and alevin ecology been made (Brannon, 1965; Marr, 1966; Dill, 1967 and 1969, and Bams, 1969).

After emergence the young fish are known as fry and during the first few weeks there is a high mortality due to starvation, predation and competition for space. The fish remain in the fry stage for about a year, at the end of which time they are known as parr and can be recognised by the dark blotches or 'parr marks' along each side of the body which are usually more conspicuous than those on the trout. The characteristics by which the salmon parr can be distinguished from the trout are the relative length of the maxilla and the number of scales in an oblique series from the posterior edge of the adipose fin, downwards and forwards to the lateral line. In the salmon the distal point of the maxilla extends only fractionally behind the mid-point of the eye to give a mean ratio of $1·06:1·0$ and $1·09:1·0$ for the $5·0$ to $9·9$ cm and $10·0$ to $14·9$ cm length groups respectively. The mean ratios for trout of comparable sizes are $1·20:1·0$ and $1·27:1·0$. A scale count of 11 is the average value for salmon and 14 for trout (Rogers, Crichton and Piggins, 1965). Other characteristics which these authors investigated for their suitability as identification features were relative thickness of the caudal peduncle and degree of forking of the tail, but neither were suitable features upon which to base identification. The characteristics of the salmon parr, the trout and the brook trout are compared in Plate I (Frontispiece).

Most of the studies on fry and parr have been concerned with their food and growth. Allen (1940 and 1941a), in a study of the fry and parr in the River Eden, England, has shown that growth takes place from early April until late October but does not occur during the winter months. This growth can be divided into two parts, an early period of rapid growth lasting until mid-August in the first year and mid-July in the second year, and a later period of slow growth. This change during the summer from rapid to slow growth he felt may be caused by either the high water temperature or some other external cause; or possibly by changes within the fish. The former factor governs the availability of the food, the latter the degree of selection, which tends to increase as the stomach becomes fuller. In a study of the food, growth and population structure of young salmon and trout in two Scottish highland streams Egglishaw (1967) found that the variation in the kind and amount of food found in the stomachs of salmon and trout is very large. A great deal of this variation, and the apparent selection of food by some fish, can probably be attributed to the distribution or behaviour of certain benthic organisms and the type of habitat in which they are feeding. Salmon from pools in the River Almond for instance, contained significantly more emerging chironomidae and terrestrial organisms than salmon from the riffles. Both Egglishaw (1967) and Mills (1964a) found that trout tend to eat more terrestrial organisms than salmon parr.

Young salmon are territorial and this behaviour has been closely observed by both Kalleberg (1958) and Keenleyside and Yamomoto (1962). The young fish tend to remain in one place, their territory, in the stream for long periods. Tagged parr and fin-clipped fry were observed throughout the summer and early winter in a 1,000-foot study area of a small coastal stream by Saunders and Gee (1964). Tagged parr were usually found in or near places of original capture which the authors designated as homes. Parr whose homes were in pools, which appeared to be as suitable habitats as riffles, and those in adjacent riffles appeared to stay in their respective habitats. Some returned to their homes after having been moved as much as 700 feet upstream or downstream. The fry were most numerous in shallow riffles and appeared to remain within small areas of the stream during summer but moved into parr habitats, the pools and deep riffles, in autumn.

Menzies (1927) believes that the length of the parr at the end of its first year of life is an index of its growth throughout life. He considers that "a short parr makes a poor, or an old, smolt, and makes poor growth in the sea. A long parr makes a good smolt and grows well throughout its marine existence".

A varying proportion of male parr attain sexual maturity before leaving the river and Jones (1959) described their presence on the spawning grounds in large numbers in November and December. Jones made extensive observations on the spawning behaviour of adult salmon and ripe male parr and concluded that the presence of ripe male parr was to ensure fertilisation of the eggs in case of inadequate fertilisation, or lack of fertilisation, by the adult male.

It is little more than a hundred years ago that the salmon parr was still considered by some to be a distinct species, *Salmo salmulus* (Ray.). Some considered it to be the hybrid offspring of salmon and trout but Stoddart (1831) was quite certain that parr were the young of salmon. It was not until Shaw's experiments of 1836 and 1837 at Stormontfield Ponds that the eggs of salmon were artificially fertilised with adult salmon sperm and the young were reared. In 1840 Shaw first proved that the progeny of such a fertilisation were indistinguishable from parr in the rivers. However, the parr and salmon controversy still raged, particularly in the Courts of Law, so much so that Henry Flowerdew published a book in 1871 entitled *The Parr & Salmon Controversy, with authentic reports of the legal judgements and judges' notes in the various law suits on the parr question, and also a brief sketch of some incidents connected with the dissemination of the modern parr theory.*

Elson (1957a) presented evidence from both sides of the Atlantic to show that, as a general rule, parr which have reached a certain size (10 cm) towards the end of one growing season are likely to become smolts at the next season of smolt descent.

Parr have two main periods of movement; during the spring and during the autumn and early winter. The autumn movement frequently consists mainly of ripe males, while the spring movement consists of forerunners of the coming smolt migration and younger fish which have either been displaced by more aggressive individuals or are in search of larger territories. Calderwood (1906a) indicated that the number of parr caught in the Tay estuary increased in November and that some were becoming silvery which suggested that they were perhaps migrating to sea. However, more recently Europeitseva (1957) explained the presence of increasing numbers of parr in a creek in the autumn to smolts, which had not entered the sea earlier, reverting to parr. Shearer (personal communication) has found large numbers of parr in the estuary of the River North Esk, Angus, in the autumn and believes that they may be going to sea at this time.

The smolt, factors causing its migration to sea. The length of time the salmon parr spend in the river before going to sea as smolts varies with the geographical location of the river. In the Hampshire Avon, Jones (1950b) found that over 90% of the smolts were yearlings, while in northern Scandinavia parr stay in the rivers for seven or eight years. Smolts in the northern Scottish rivers are mostly two and three years old, and a very few four years old. Jones (1959) considers that this differential migration is related to temperature, day-length and feeding, and that it affects the subsequent growth rate of the fish.

In the spring during transformation of the parr to the smolt stage, or smoltification as the process is called, the length–weight relationship of the fish changes, a sub-cutaneous deposit of guanin is laid down, concealing the parr markings and the pectoral and caudal fins turn black. Allen (1944) determined the degree of smolt development on the Thurso River, Caithness, and found that the average rate of development was about 0·08 per day on a colour scale where 4·0 represents full development.

In addition to the associated changes in appearance, smolt development consists of the development of susceptibility to migration producing stimuli. A number of attempts have been made to correlate the onset of the main migrations with various environmental factors such as rainfall, radiation and water temperature.

It has been found that during the early (April and early May) part of the smolt migration smolt movement is during the hours of darkness but later on (late May and early June) movement occurs during the middle part of the day (Munro, 1965a). It is likely that smolts drop downstream tail first, although in a lake they almost certainly swim actively downstream. At natural falls, traps and screens the fish I have observed have always been heading upstream against the current. The speed at which they migrate downstream varies between 0·29 and 1·27 miles per day (Mills, 1964a), the speed varying with the nature of the river; migration through a lake is usually slower.

It seems likely that smolts need some time to become acclimatised to saline conditions. Calderwood (1906a) and others have noticed that smolts may remain in the estuary for a short time for this purpose before entering the sea. There are many rivers which have no estuary, such as those on the north-west coast of Scotland, and here the smolts must go straight from fresh to salt water, although as there must be some mixing of fresh and salt water at the river mouth the transition will not be abrupt. Huntsman and Hoar observed smolts at the mouth of the Magaree River, Cape Breton Island, lying completely inactive for a time after entering the sea.

3.6 Life in the sea

Recaptures at sea. Once the smolts have entered the sea little is known of their movements. Smolts from northern Swedish rivers have been caught in the Gulf of Bothnia and have been recorded taking insects blown off the land. Tagged smolts released in these northern Swedish rivers are later recaptured as adults in the southern Baltic (Fig. 18) by fishermen from a number of Baltic countries. Here the picture of the salmon's migrations is fairly complete, but for smolts entering the North Sea and Atlantic from the rivers of the British Isles, Canada and Norway the picture is far from complete. With the advent of the Greenland fishery much more is now known about the sea life of the Atlantic salmon than was previously known. However, the general picture of the salmon's sea life can only gradually be pieced together from isolated records. Balmain and Shearer (1956) summarised the records of salmon and sea trout caught at sea. Over the period 1888–1954 there are only 78 Scottish records of salmon taken at sea and these describe the capture of approximately 90 clean salmon, 10 salmon kelts, 5 grilse and 3 pre-grilse. It is perhaps the capture of pre-grilse which is the most interesting as it gives us a picture of their distribution during the

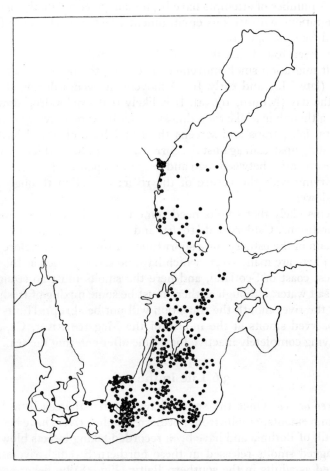

Fig. 18. Map showing recaptures (*black dots*) from a smolt-tagging experiment in the River Indalsälven (*black square*) in May, 1961 (from Carlin, 1969a).

first year of their life at sea. The salmon captured at sea have been taken in drift nets, trawls and nets set for the capture of garfish and prawns.

More recently records of captures at sea have increased rapidly and many of these have been published in the Scottish Fisheries Bulletin. One of the more interesting recaptures was of a pre-grilse off Greenland. Many of these records have been collected as a result of the examination of the stomachs of other fish. This is particularly useful as it gives us an idea of the sources of mortality at sea. Among the fish recorded eating salmon are the skate (*Raia batis*), halibut (*Hippoglossus vulgaris*), cod (*Gadus morrhua*) and porbeagle shark (*Lamna cornubica*). The salmon taken by the porbeagle shark were $5\frac{1}{2}$ lb and 8 lb in weight respectively, while those taken by cod ranged from 6 to 18 inches in length. The smallest of these fish were little more than smolts and Piggins (1959) has recorded another member of the cod family, the pollack or lythe (*G. pollachius*), taking smolts.

Perhaps some of the most interesting records of salmon caught at sea are of (1) a fish taken by the weather ship *Weather Surveyor* when on station 'India' (59°00′ N, 19°00′ W) in June. (2) Four salmon caught by the Danish research vessel *Dana* during drift netting experiments in the Irminger Sea at the end of June, 1966 (Jensen, 1967) along the 62°00′ N latitude and (3) two fish tagged as kelts in the River Polly on the west coast of Scotland and one fish tagged as a smolt in the River Meig, in the north-east of Scotland, caught by Faroese line vessels north of the Faroes (Munro, 1969).

Food and migrations. The sea food of salmon consists chiefly of fish such as herring, capelin and sand eels and large zooplankton organisms, particularly euphausiids and amphipods. Pyefinch (1952) records the following organisms from a pre-grilse caught off the Faroes: amphipods (*Themisto gracilipes*), euphausiids (*Thysanoessa longicaudata*) and sand eels (*Ammodytes lancea marinus*). The food of Scottish drift-net-caught salmon was similar and included polychaete worms (*Nereis* spp.), amphipods (*Parathemisto* spp.), euphausiids (*Meganyctiphanes norvegica*) and herring, sprats, whiting and sand eels. The salmon caught in the Irminger Sea had been feeding on amphipods (*Themisto gaudichaudi*) and squid (*Brachioteuthis riisei*), while Shearer and Balmain (1967) found that the salmon in the Greenland area had been feeding mainly (86%) on capelin (*Mallotus villosus*). Thurow (1968), in a study of the food, behaviour and population mechanism of Baltic salmon estimated that a 'clean' salmon more than 60 cm long consumes not less than 50 gm of food a day. He also estimated that more than 16,000 tons of sprats are eaten by the exploitable part of the Baltic salmon stock in a year. He considered that the growth rate of adult salmon is largely determined by the amount of food available during the first few months in the sea.

Since a salmon fishery was developed off the west coast of Greenland in 1957 our knowledge of the sea migrations of salmon has increased enormously due to the recapture in this area of tagged smolts and kelts from Canada, England, Ireland, Scotland, Sweden and the United States (Maine). The capture of salmon off the Greenland coast during the autumn months in recent years, together with the recapture of a large number of fish which had been tagged in rivers on both sides of the Atlantic, supports Menzies' hypothesis that the feeding ground of Scottish salmon lies in the vicinity of Greenland and that it is shared with salmon from elsewhere in northern Europe and from the Atlantic seaboard of North America. Until recently the recapture of tagged fish off Greenland only indicated where some of the salmon originated, but there was no evidence to show where the salmon in Greenland waters were destined to spawn. However, after extensive tagging of these fish and subsequent recaptures in Canadian, Irish and Scottish waters (Pyefinch, 1967 and 1968) we now know where some, at least, are destined to go. It only remains to demonstrate a two-way migration by capturing a fish off Greenland which had been tagged in home waters, releasing it and catching it once more in home waters.

Carlin (1969a) gives a very interesting account of the migration of Swedish salmon. He suggests that while the waters off west Greenland may be the main feeding grounds for all the European as well as for the American salmon, there are also some indications of feeding grounds for salmon in the eastern part of the Atlantic. Some Swedish fish have been recaptured off the coast of northern Norway far away from what could be expected to be the normal route from Greenland to Sweden. Furthermore, a very large number of salmon smolts have been tagged in Norwegian rivers, but none of them have ever been recovered in Greenland. The proportion of salmon caught at Greenland in relation to the catch in home waters Carlin thought also to be lower for fish tagged in Sweden than for fish tagged in Canada and the British Isles. On the other hand, Soviet scientists have reported catches of young feeding salmon in the open sea far off the Norwegian coast, among them also one salmon tagged in the river Lagan on the Swedish west coast. From this evidence Carlin suggests, quite rightly I think, that we can assume that the main feeding grounds for salmon from England, Scotland and Ireland and also to some extent from Sweden and possibly southern Norway are situated in the western part of the North Atlantic, but that some salmon from Sweden and perhaps the major part from Norway and the Soviet Union may grow up in the eastern part of the North Atlantic.

A wealth of literature exists on the coastal movements of adult salmon which have been caught and tagged offshore. The results of the Scottish tagging operations have been summarised by Calderwood (1940). Similar experiments have been carried out off the coasts of Norway and Canada and in the Baltic and the results of many of these experiments have been summarised by Menzies (1949) and Carlin (1969a).

Other tagging experiments have been carried out off the east coast of Scotland and the Irish coast. Most of the results of the Irish investigations have been reviewed by Went (1964b).

The value of these tagging operations has been to provide data on the coastal movements of adult salmon, the general direction of these movements and the rate of migration. Pyefinch and Woodward (1955) suggest that the proportion of fish recaptured in their experiment off the Scottish east coast give some indication of the proportion of catchable stock removed along a heavily-netted section of coast and that the rate of recapture gives some idea of the rate at which salmon penetrate the barrage of coastal and estuarine nets.

3.7 Predation

Some mention has already been made of predation in the sea. The most important known marine predator of Atlantic salmon is the grey seal (*Halichoerus grypus*). Rae (1960) gives a very full account of the distribution of both the grey seal and the common seal and their relation to the Scottish fisheries. It was found that there was considerable damage to fish, to nets and to fishing power and there was also probably a diversion of fish from the nets by the seals. Rae and Shearer (1965), on the basis of the number of seals seen by fishermen in the vicinity of the nets when they are being fished, estimated that 147,888 salmonids were killed by seals on the Scottish east coast from 1959 to 1963. The average annual monetary loss to the salmon industry on the Scottish east coast was estimated at about £67,000 if all these fish had been caught by fishermen. The grey seals are shot near salmon nets along the Scottish coast and an annual cull of pups is carried out on some of the seals' breeding grounds. However, now that the majority of the coastal nets are made of the stronger synthetic fibres, net damage has lessened considerably. This means that the seals cannot reach the trapped salmon easily and as they cannot 'hole' the nets there is not the reduction in fishing effort which used to result from damaged nets. As Lockie (1962) points out there are serious gaps in our knowledge of grey seals which should be filled if one is to assess the importance of the seal as a competitor with man for salmon. These include: (1) Annual mortality of the various age groups; (2) the exact age at which breeding commences in each sex; (3) the distribution of immature animals; (4) the age groups frequenting the salmon nets and, (5) a food study that takes into account the limitation of stomach analysis and the difficulties of sampling in the field.

The adult and juvenile stages of the salmon are particularly vulnerable in the relatively confined areas of rivers and streams and the predators of salmon can be listed as follows (a) *Fish*: pike, perch, chub, eels and trout. (b) *Birds*: cormorant, shag, black-headed gull, common gull, goosander, red-breasted merganser, belted kingfisher, heron and osprey. (c) *Mammals*: otter and mink. An account of predation on freshwater fish by animals other than fish has been given by Mills (1967a).

Both pike and trout can be serious predators of salmon fry, parr and smolts. For example it was estimated that 10% of the smolt run on the River Bran, Ross-shire, in 1959 and 1961 was eaten by pike.

There have been a number of studies made on bird predators and the results are often conflicting, as the extent to which predators ate young salmon varied from area to area. White (1937, 1939a) considered that the American merganser was a serious predator of young Atlantic salmon in eastern Canada, while Munro and Clemens (1937) found that in western Canada it did not affect the production of Pacific salmon (*Oncorhynchus* spp.). In Michigan it was felt that 'merganser control' was only necessary at certain times in the winter, but in Oklahoma it was found that these birds were beneficial as their diet was composed largely of coarse fish. Similarly in Europe the goosander was found to be a serious predator of young salmon in the Swedish River Indals and on some northern Scottish rivers. Madsen (1957), however, considered that it did little harm in Denmark as it ate mainly cyprinids, although to some extent it might be considered harmful because it ate eels and might affect the eel fishery, although Coldwell (1939) considered that the American merganser was benefiting the salmon fisheries because it ate eels.

Salyer and Lagler (1940) found the red-breasted merganser to be of little importance to fish management in Michigan, while White (1939b) concluded that, while feeding in freshwater areas, there is no difference in the food of the red-breasted merganser and the American merganser. In Scotland, Ireland and Norway the red-breasted merganser is only considered to be harmful to young salmon stocks on certain rivers.

The mean daily food intake is frequently used to calculate the total number of fish eaten in any particular area. White (1936b) estimated the numbers of fish consumed by kingfishers on 30 miles of stream on the Northeast Margaree River, Nova Scotia, to be 330,000 young salmon, 50,000 trout and 40,000 other fish. In the same way White (1957), basing his calculations on an average weight of salmon parr of 9 gm, estimated that it took 32 kg of fish to rear a single American merganser to full growth (of which 46% or 15 kg are young salmon; the 15 kg is equivalent to 1,584 salmon parr). He also estimated that 1,200 mergansers shot on the Miramichi River represent an annual consumption of over 1,900,000 salmon parr.

White (1939a) carried out an experiment to test the value of control of fish-eating birds on the numbers of young salmon on a tributary of the Northeast Margaree River, Nova Scotia. After years of unrestricted feeding by a number of fish-eating birds, 1,834 salmon smolts were taken in a trap when descending in the spring of 1937. After a year of predator control 4,065 salmon smolts were taken in the trap in the spring of 1938. The differences in these figures could be due to no more than year-to-year fluctuations in the smolt run, but White considered that the results indicated that these birds have a significant effect in reducing smolt numbers, although he admitted that this could not be proved and that further studies were needed.

A more detailed experiment was carried out some years later on the Pollett River, New Brunswick, by Elson (1962a). Hatchery-reared Atlantic salmon underyearlings were planted annually for nine years in a 16-km stretch of the river and the smolt production from each planting was measured by counting descending migrants at a trap at the lower end of the experimental area. The average annual smolt production from the first five annual plantings of between 16,000 and 250,000 underyearlings was 3,000. American mergansers and belted kingfishers were then controlled, and the average annual smolt production, from the final four plantings of 250,000 underyearlings annually, was nearly 20,000 (13,600 to 24,300). Control of these birds had thus made possible an increase in average smolt production of not less than five times. However, Lack (1966) felt that, while these birds ate many fish, their ultimate influence on the size of the fish population was not, in his view, established by Elson, since there was effectively only one year of comparable observations before the birds were controlled and the low densities of fish before bird control might have been due to some other factor. While it is true that only in one year prior to control were 250,000 underyearlings planted, while in the four years of control 250,000 were planted annually, Elson stated that the initial plantings (i.e. before bird control) used about 16,000 underyearlings in order to permit maximum survival rates without waste due to overstocking. Late, heavier plantings were used to measure the total capacity of the area to produce smolts. From this study Elson was able to produce a rule-of-thumb for successful merganser control. The average population density of American mergansers on these streams was about 10 birds per 24 km of stream of 9 m width (about 1 bird per 25 hectares) but the effect of control is slight until the population density is reduced to 3 birds/24 km/9 m width (about 1 bird per 8 hectares). Reduction of the merganser population below this level, however, has an increasingly advantageous effect on smolt production down to a population density of 1 bird/24 km/9m (about 1 bird per 22 hectares). Any further reduction had little effect.

3.8 Parasites

The parasites of salmon which are most well known are the ecto- or external parasites. There are those which attack the fish in the sea and those which attack the fish when it enters brackish or freshwater.

(a) *Invertebrates*. The marine invertebrate parasite most well known is *Lepeophtheirus salmonis* (Plate 6), or the sea louse as it is called by fishermen. It only lives for a short time in freshwater and its presence on salmon in freshwater is therefore a good indication that the salmon is only recently in from the sea. The female sea lice, which often have long egg sacs or 'streamers' are most conspicuous. Hutton (1923) has found sea lice on salmon in the River Wye 120 miles upstream and believes that they may survive in freshwater for over a week when the water temperature is low.

White (1940b) describes the damage caused by 'lice' and mentions the capture of a grilse so heavily infested that its body colours from above were obscured by the brown parasites.

White believed that the death of a number of salmon in the Moser River in August, 1939, was partly due to areas of abrasion caused by the lice. Practically all the salmon running during July and early August were very badly infested with the parasites and the later ones showed white patches over the frontal region, on the opercula, along the occipital region and extending posteriorly along the nape. White felt that these abrasions were not severe enough of themselves to cause death. However, some days later dead fish were found with the skin over part of the head sloughed away exposing the muscle beneath. White found that on many of the fish which were severely infested the skin was loose over the same areas. It was also noticed that when the 'lice' were scraped off the skin readily came away exposing the flesh beneath. Before the skin sloughs off there is a distinct white area over these infected regions and White believes that this condition is the same as that described by Calderwood (1906b) as 'white spot disease'. Calderwood also recorded it from salmon under the same conditions as those in which the infected salmon in the Moser River were existing, namely in very low water when the fish were prevented from ascending the streams and were congregated near the mouths. Calderwood attributed the injury to sunlight.

The life history of *Lepeophtheirus* was later described by White (1942b) and he records finding bits of fish skin with melanophores in the digestive tracts of the sea lice and he also observed them taking into their mouths minute pieces of chopped skin which had been fed to them.

The most well-known freshwater parasite of salmon is the gill maggot *Salmincola salmonea* (Plate 7). This organism, like *Lepeophtheirus*, is a parasitic copepod but is not free-living and bears little resemblance to

Lepeophtheirus. Its life history and ecology have been fully described by Friend (1941). Salmon are infected by this parasite in fresh water. The free-swimming larvae attach themselves to the gills of a salmon while it is in freshwater. On becoming attached to the gills it eventually moults twice and becomes either a mature male or a first-stage female, both of them can move about on the gills. After copulation the male dies, but the female develops an attachment organ and can no longer move about on the gills. About six months after copulation eggs are produced. A moult follows and the eggs are extruded; two further sets of eggs may be extruded by the female before the salmon returns to the sea. If the kelt returns to the sea before these later generations of eggs have been extruded reproduction is inhibited in the sea and will not be resumed until the fish returns to fresh-water. Then the parasite lays its eggs and drops off the gills; the fish is then liable to re-infection. The epizootic significance of the parasite is compara-tively slight, it causes some injury to the ends of the gill lamellae to which it is attached. The salmon shows definite seasonal variations in its suscepti-bility to infection. In the pre-spawning period infection intensity averages 11·2 copepods per fish; in November it increases to 20·8, and in December to February, up to 53·7 copepods per fish.

An attempt was made to establish the life span of the copepod. If the salmon remains in the sea for only one summer on its second visit to that environment and re-enters the river in the autumn to spawn a second time, the copepod probably lives about one year. The cycle in this case is – infection in the river in late autumn or winter, maturation in freshwater for six months, growth in the sea in the summer, reproduction in the river and death in the spring. However, in cases where the salmon spend a year or more in the sea before returning to spawn a second time, some of the cope-pods remain alive and continue to grow until they are two to three times larger than usual.

Another freshwater parasitic copepod is the freshwater louse *Argulus foliaceus* (Figure 19). The organism is disc-shaped and flat-bodied and attaches itself to its host by two suckers under the front end of its body. Between the suckers is a 'poison spine' and just behind the suckers a suctorial mouth or proboscis. *Argulus* lives on the gills or body surface of the fish and perforates the skin of its host with its proboscis to suck its blood. According to Ivanfi (1927), it feeds only on the plasma, since the proboscis is not wide enough for the passage of blood cells. Its 'poison spine' causes a small local infection, but the blood sucking causes a general weakening of the organism. According to a number of authors, *Argulus*, by glands connected via efferent ducts to the proboscis, also has a toxic action on fish. Only this can explain the rapid killing of young fish by one or two parasites.

The leech *Piscicola geometra* is parasitic on salmon, as well as other fish, and is adapted to life in cool, well-aerated water. It is found in fast-flowing streams and on the wave-washed shores of eutrophic lakes and occurs most frequently in hard waters.

In February, 1967, these leeches were found on salmon taken from the Tweed at Kelso, Roxburghshire. Most of the salmon were kelts and according to reports about 50% of the kelts seen were infected. Although the leeches were found on all parts of the fish they occurred mainly around the dorsal and pectoral fins, the flanks and caudal peduncle. The number of specimens per fish varied from one to fifteen.

This leech is a little over an inch long and is olive brown in colour. The body, which is cylindrical, is divided into numerous small annuli and along the lateral margins are pulsating vesicles. There are powerful suckers at the anterior and posterior end of the organism and the anterior one forms a conspicuous dilation on the head region.

A number of internal parasites occur in both the juvenile and adult stages of the salmon and include representatives of the trematodes (flukes), cestodes (tapeworms), acanthocephalans (spiny-headed worms) and nematodes (round worms). One of the largest of these is the tapeworm *Eubothrium crassum* which, in its adult stage, may measure between 12 and 60 cm in length and occurs in the pyloric caecae. The intermediate hosts of this parasite are copepods (e.g. *Cyclops strenuus*) and the perch (*Perca fluviatilis*). A list of the parasites infecting the Atlantic salmon is given by Hoffman (1967).

Ecological studies of the parasites of the salmon have been made by Heitz (1918) and Dogiel and Petrushevski (1935). Heitz, in a work devoted to the salmon of the Rhine, described the gradual reduction of the parasitic

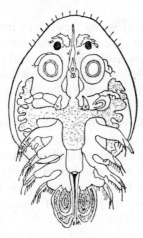

FIG. 19
The fish louse – *Argulus foliaceus* (from Dogiel, Petrushevski and Polyanski, 1961).

fauna with the progress of the fish upstream. Dogiel and Petrushevski succeeded in obtaining a full picture of the changes in the parasite fauna of the salmon throughout its entire life cycle, having collected data not only on the adult fish, but also on the young inhabiting the upper reaches of the rivers. Data were collected from the rivers Onega, Vyg and tributaries of the North Dvina. The freshwater parasite fauna of the young fish was found to be comprised of twelve species. The young fish acquires this fauna gradually with the progress of growth, this slow build-up lending support to the rule of the age dynamics of parasite fauna. It was found that a considerable proportion of the three to four months old fish were completely free of parasites. Almost all the fish of the 1 + group were infested, the four-year-old fish retained the same number of parasitic species as the 2 + and 3 + group fish, but their incidence and the intensity of infestation became higher.

The process of this gradual development of the parasite fauna in small salmon may be expressed by the mean number of parasitic species in infested fish of various ages. For the three to four months old fish this number is 1·0, for the 1 + group it is 1·3, for the 2 + and 3 + it is 2·3 and for the 4 + it is 2·7.

Once in the sea it was found that the salmon frees itself completely of its freshwater parasites and acquires parasites of marine origin. The parasite fauna of fifteen species, found in the salmon on its return to freshwater, included only three freshwater parasites. Even these few freshwater parasites, however, were not survivors of the salmon's original parasite fauna but were newly acquired by it during its ascent of the river. All the marine species accompany the salmon on entering freshwater. Once in freshwater the salmon begins to lose its marine parasite fauna. The first to go are the ectoparasites, subjected to the direct influence of freshwater. For example, all salmon caught in Belomorsk on the White Sea (mouth of the River Vyg) were infested with *Lepeophtheirus*. The salmon caught about 10 km up the river from that town were only 25% infested, while farther upstream they were completely free of *Lepeophtheirus*. The loss of ectoparasites is followed by the gradual loss of the marine intestinal parasites, the decrease in the number of species and the intensity of infestation being inversely proportional to the length of time spent by the host in freshwater.

The use of certain indicators enabled Dogiel and Petrushevski to distinguish the autumn fish from the spring and early summer fish by the presence of fewer marine parasites in the latter. A similar picture was obtained by Heitz, who compared salmon of the upper and lower reaches of the Rhine. The infestation with *Eubothrium crassum*, however, showed some differences. The number of scolices (heads) found in the gut of fish from both groups was approximately the same, but in that of the spring fish the strobilae (bodies) of the worms were generally shorter due to the breaking off and loss of almost all the proglottids (segments of the body containing the eggs). This resulted in the mean total weight of worms from the gut being considerably lower in the spring fish (2·8 gm) than in the autumn fish (24·3 gm).

The parasites of the body cavity, not exposed to the direct influences of the freshwater and unable to leave their habitat, are only little affected by the migration of the host. This is shown by the larvae of the nematode worm *Terranova decipiens*, which were equally abundant in both groups of salmon.

The small number of freshwater parasites acquired by the salmon in its ascent of rivers is due to the behaviour of the fish at this stage of its life history. The salmon does not feed during its upstream journey, so that one of the main paths of infection, the gut, remains closed.

Vertebrates. Without doubt the most important vertebrate parasite of salmon is the sea lamprey *Petromyzon marinus*. The damage of the sea lamprey inflicted on the fisheries of the Great Lakes has already been described and the lamprey has been the subject of much research in that area. Unfortunately there is little information on its effects on Atlantic salmon stocks. Malloch (1910) describes them being caught in the salmon fishers' nets on the Tay when they are ascending the rivers in May and June to spawn. They are present in a number of Scottish rivers and can be seen at spawning time carrying stones in their sucker-like mouths to build their 'nests' in which the eggs are deposited. In June and July recently formed depressions or 'clean' areas of gravel may be noticed in streams and these may be due to the spawning activities of lampreys.

Occasionally salmon are caught in the nets with lampreys attached to their flanks and at other times only the presence of large wounds inflicted by this parasite are evidence of attack. It is not known how many salmon die from lamprey attacks. Williams and Gilhousen (1968) showed that at times there may be a high incidence of lamprey parasitism on sockeye and pink salmon. One stock of Fraser River sockeye salmon bound for a tributary, the Adams River, were first examined while still in the lower reaches of the Fraser and it was found that 67% had been attacked by the lamprey *Entosphenus tridentatus* and 6% bore wounds classed as severe. Later, on the Adams River spawning grounds, many wounds showed signs of healing and comparable percentages of wounded fish were 57% overall and 5% severe. Mortality of the Adams River run during upstream migration was calculated at less than 2%. Other runs of sockeye entering the lower Fraser at the same time as the Adams fish showed a 65% overall incidence of lamprey wounds and a 3% incidence of severely wounded fish. Among pink salmon examined in the lower Fraser, the incidence of wounded fish was only 20%, and less than 2% carried moderate or severe wounds. Although mortality of sockeye and pink salmon was considered to be negligible during up-river migration, some evidence suggested a possibly greater mortality in Georgia Strait prior to entering the river.

The incidence of lamprey attack on land-locked Atlantic salmon has been studied by Davis (1967) in Love Lake, Maine. It was found that young sea lampreys (*Petromyzon marinus*), newly transformed from the larval stage, were attaching themselves and in many instances feeding upon the salmon. Examination of 660 salmon from 4·5 to 23·5 inches long revealed that 85% had been attacked.

3.9 Disease

The salmon is subject to a number of diseases, some of which can be responsible for very high mortalities. The diseases include furunculosis, Dee disease, kidney disease, salmon disease, ulcerative dermal necrosis, vibriosis and columnaris.

Furunculosis. This is a well-known disease of salmonids and is caused by the bacterium *Aeromonas salmonicida*. The bacterium is short, non-motile, Gram-negative and non-spore forming. Salmon which are suffering from furunculosis show a variety of external symptoms ranging from congestion of the fins, haemorrhage at the vent and furuncles. At times the only external symptoms may be congestion of the fins and at other times there may be no external symptoms.

The disease has been recognised for over fifty-five years as a cause of death during the summer, especially when the rivers are low and the water temperature rises to 55° F. Serious outbreaks have been recorded when there have been large concentrations of fish assembled below falls and in pools during low water conditions. However, Smith (1960, 1962) reported a high incidence of furunculosis in kelts in some Scottish rivers in the winter of 1958–1959 and 1960–1961 and a lower incidence in 1959–1960. A high incidence was also found in kelts in some English and Welsh rivers in 1958–1959, but a very low one in Irish rivers in 1960–1961 and 1961–1962.

An interesting feature of the disease in kelts is that many of the fish suffering from it are less likely to develop external symptoms than unspent fish. Smith (1962) showed that of 194 unspent fish with the disease, 142 (73·2%) showed some external sign while only 51 (33%) of 172 kelts with furunculosis showed external symptoms. Smith also showed that over the period October to December, i.e. the period when most of the dead kelts are found, only 43% of the unspent fish showed external symptoms, a proportion much closer to that found for kelts. Thus, as Smith states:

the possibility of an unspent fish developing external symptoms is much greater in the summer months, though any unspent fish is more likely to develop such symptoms than a kelt. This does not agree with the observations that at higher temperatures during the summer, fish are more likely to die from an acute infection of furunculosis (in which there are no external symptoms), than from a chronic infection (where furuncles are present). It might, however, explain why the incidence of furunculosis in kelts has hitherto gone unnoticed.

Smith noticed that male kelts seem to be more susceptible to furunculosis than unspent males. She rightly points out that as some or most of the kelts which die are suffering from furunculosis, their importance as sources of infection should be borne in mind. It was found that the bacteria are viable for as long as three to six months under certain conditions and as most of the kelts die soon after spawning there is the possibility of direct infection of unspent salmon entering the river during the winter. Some smolts were also recorded as dying from furunculosis and their infection was attributed to the presence of diseased kelts. Recent investigations have shown that the viability of *A. salmonicida* in sea water is not negligible, so that its survival in the tissues of a host adapted to sea water seems a distinct possibility. Therefore, *A. salmonicida* may not only pass from one adult host to another, it may also pass from an adult host to a juvenile host and survive a period in the sea, with the consequence that at least part of the returning migrants are infected before they reach freshwater.

There has been a certain amount of confusion over the classification of '*Bacterium salmonicida*'. As the systematic position of this organism was in doubt, forty-two strains of '*Bacterium salmonicida*', six of a non-pigmented fish pathogen and forty-two Aeromonas strains were compared morphologically, culturally, biochemically and metabolically by Smith (1963). The results, which were computed electronically, showed a distinct difference between '*B. salmonicida*' and the Aeromonas species. On the grounds of this variation in morphology, culture and biochemistry, Smith suggested that '*B. salmonicida*' be removed from the genus *Aeromonas* and given a generic place in the family Pseudomonadaceae. The name *Necromonas salmonicida* was suggested as an alternative to '*B. salmonicida*'. However, in a recent paper on the pathogenicity of '*Bacterium salmonicida*' in sea and brackish waters Scott (1968) uses the name *Aeromonas salmonicida* (Griffin) and this remains the accepted name (Smith, personal communication).

Dee disease. This disease is so called because it was first described in salmon from the Aberdeenshire Dee in 1930, and first recorded in the Second Interim Report of the Furunculosis Committee (1933). The fish were found to have small necrotic lesions on their spleens. From these lesions a small Gram positive bacillus could be demonstrated but could not be grown successfully on culture media.

Fish suffering from this disease may show congestion of the fins, haemorrhage at the vent and, in a very few cases, haemorrhagic spots on the muscle. As Smith (1964) points out, such symptoms are found in other fish diseases so they are of little value in the diagnosis of Dee disease. Internally the salmon shows very characteristic lesions, the most prevalent one being petechial haemorrhage of the muscle lining the peritoneum. The next organ most often affected is the kidney which, instead of its normal uniform reddish-brown colour, develops greyish-brown areas and, if the disease is more advanced, these areas develop an almost cyst-like appearance. The spleen is the next in order. On its surface a number of creamy-white lesions, which vary in size from pin-head to about 4 mm in diameter, develop. The number of such lesions varies from fish to fish, ranging from a very few to a large number, which gives the spleen a peppered appearance. The liver exhibits similar pathological changes but here the number of lesions is often smaller, and as a whole the liver is less often affected in this manner. Occasionally the swim bladder is covered with petechial haemorrhages. The above symptoms are those most often found in Dee disease, but early in the year the pathology of the disease is somewhat different. At this time the spleen, liver, gonads and even the swim bladder and peritoneal muscle are partially or completely covered with a white membrane. This membrane is not firmly attached to any of these organs but can be peeled off leaving the surface of the organ apparently unharmed. In this type of infection, the pericardial sac is occasionally filled with a milky fluid consisting of tissue cells and the Gram positive bacilli.

There is no sharp boundary between the two forms and so in some salmon both the necrotic lesions and the white membrane are manifested. The second clinical picture was thought to represent a chronic infection so the water temperature of the river was studied to see if there was any correlation of type of symptom with water temperature. It was found that salmon which had white membranes on their spleen or liver were nearly all found dead when the water temperature ranged from 35° to 49° F; those with both white membranes and necrotic lesions from 45° to 51° F, and necrotic lesions only from 44° to 63° F (Fig. 20).

Smith (*loc. cit.*) considered that the organism most probably belongs to the *Corynebacteria* spp. She also concluded that Dee disease is very similar to or identical with kidney disease which has been described in Pacific salmon by Earp, Ellis and Ordal (1953) and in *Salvelinus fontinalis, Salmo trutta* and *S. gairdnerii* by Snieszko and Griffin (1955). A summary of the pathological symptoms recorded by these workers together with those recorded for Atlantic salmon are given by Smith (1964).

Salmon Disease. Salmon disease was noticed originally in the spring and autumn of 1877 in the Border Esk and Nith. It soon spread to the Eden and neighbouring rivers and in the spring of 1879 it was observed in the Tweed. It had spread to other rivers in the south-west of Scotland in 1880 and by 1882 had spread to North Wales and to the Tay and North Esk in Scotland.

The first symptoms of this disease was the appearance of small greyish or ashy discolorations of the skin, usually upon those parts of the body which are devoid of scales, such as the top and sides of the head, the adipose fin and the soft skin at the bases of other fins. A detailed description of the symptoms of the disease appears in the *21st Annual Report (for the year 1881) of the Inspector of [Salmon] Fisheries (England and Wales)*:

> When a patch of diseased skin has once appeared it rapidly increases in size and runs into any other patches which may have appeared in its neighbourhood. The marginal zone, constantly extending into the healthy surrounding skin, retains its previous characters, while the ashy central part changes. It assumes the consistency of wet paper and can be detached in flakes, like a slough, from the skin which it covers. If the subjacent surface is now examined it will be found that the epidermis has disappeared and that the surface of the vascular and sensitive derma beneath is exposed. As the diseased area extends, the papyraceous coat more and more completely takes the place of the epidermis until, in extremely bad cases, it may invest the back and sides of a large salmon from snout to tail.
>
> The affection, however, is not confined to the epidermis. As the patch acquires larger and larger dimensions, the derma in its centre becomes subject to a process of ulceration, and thus a deep bleeding

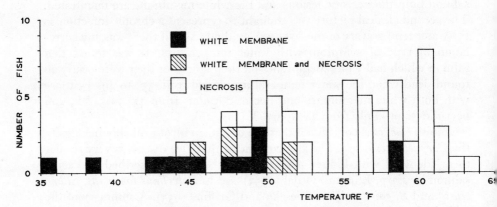

FIG. 20.   The relationship between water temperature and the symptoms developed by salmon suffering from Dee disease (from Smith, 1964).

sore is formed, which eats down to the bones of the head and sends off burrowing passages, or sinuses, from its margins.

Huxley (1882) believed that salmon disease was caused by the fungus *Saprolegnia ferax*. However, Patterson (1903) established the fact that *Saprolegnia ferax* did not constitute in itself the active agent in the disease. He considered that salmon disease was due "to the invasion of the tissues of the fish by a special bacillus *Bacillus salmonis pestis*". The bacillus was said to gain access through abrasions or ulceration of the skin, and the disease was apparently not contracted when the skin of the fish was in a healthy state. Patterson (*loc. cit.*) also found that (i) *B. salmonis pestis* can be transmitted from dead diseased fish to other dead fish in the water, (ii) the disease can be transmitted from dead fish to living fish in the same water, (iii) the fact that the bacillus grows profusely when placed in a freezing mixture of ice and salt, while a temperature of 37° C soon destroys it, shows that the cold season is more favourable to its growth.

In the *22nd Annual Report (for the year 1882) of the Inspector of [Salmon] Fisheries (England and Wales)* it was said:

What is known of the history of the 'salmon disease' brings out the curious fact that the epidemic, starting apparently from a centre near the Solway, and extending thence to the Scottish rivers both east and west of this point, has spread to nearly all the English and Welsh rivers on the west coast in pretty regular rotation, from Cumberland to Herefordshire; while, on the east, it has spread only very slightly, if at all, south of the Tweed, notwithstanding the fact that larger numbers of diseased fish have been found in the Tweed than in the Eden, the first and worst affected of all English rivers.

Over 6,000 diseased salmon were taken out of the Eden between 1878 and 1883 (up to 31 May).

The report also commented on the fact that, in the rivers in which the disease had been most virulent, the salmon harvest had increased rather than diminished.

Ulcerative dermal necrosis. There are many reasons for believing that ulcerative dermal necrosis, or U.D.N. as it is popularly called, is the same disease as the 'salmon disease' which occurred at the end of last century. The pattern of the spread of the disease is similar, the symptoms are remarkably alike, even to some authorities (Stuart and Fuller, 1968) believing that *Saprolegnia* spp. may be the causative organism, and the presence of a direct relationship between the prevalence of the disease and low water temperature (Elson, 1968a) (Fig. 21).

U.D.N. was first observed in epidemic proportions in a number of rivers in south-west Ireland during 1964–1965 and full details of this are given in reports prepared by the Fisheries Division of the Department of Agriculture and Fisheries of Ireland in August, 1966, and April and May, 1967 and which were also published in *Salmon Net* (1967). During 1966 the disease spread to the Lancashire, Cumberland and Solway river systems. By the end of 1967 the disease had spread to all east coast rivers from the Tweed to the Nairn with the exception of the Forth and Tay and, on the west coast, from the Solway Firth to the River Ayr. In 1968 cases appeared in the Forth, Tay, Ness and Conon river systems. The progress of the disease up the east coast of Scotland resembled that in Ireland, in that, for no apparent reason, one river might remain clear of the disease while its immediate neighbours were seriously affected. Elson (1968a) suggests that it is possible that sea trout may have contributed to the spread of the disease

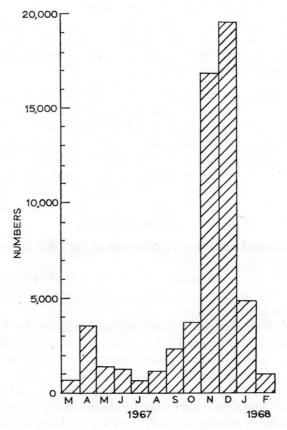

FIG. 21. Monthly numbers of diseased salmonid fish from Scottish rivers where U.D.N. is suspected of being the major contributory cause to disease (from Elson, 1968).

PLATES 8–10

Salmon (top) and sea trout (below) showing the differences in the shape
of the head and the tail.

PLATE 11. A salmon infected initially with ulcerative dermal necrosis and later, as a result of this infection, with fungus.

PLATE 12

Whirling disease – rainbow trout showing spinal curvature.

PLATE 13
Whirling disease – rainbow trout with blackened tail owing to loss of pigment cell control.

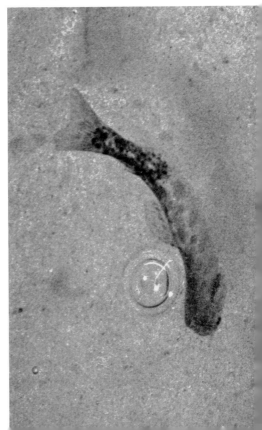

as these fish may move from estuary to estuary. In the rivers Deveron and Spey sea trout were seriously affected for almost two weeks before any diseased salmon were observed.

Pyefinch and Elson (1967) describe the symptoms of the disease in some detail:

> The first signs of this disease are the appearance of small bleached areas of the skin, on the head, back and near the dorsal fin and on the tail (Plate 11). As the disease progresses areas of a bluish-grey, slimy growth develop over these bleached areas, making the fish very conspicuous in the water. The appearance of the fish at this stage has been likened to that of a fish heavily infected with fungus but, if the fish is taken out of the water, the affected patches show none of the woolly or fuzzy appearance which characterises a fungal infection; instead they resemble masses of sodden blue-grey blotting paper. Further these slimy masses can readily be pulled away, exposing inflammation or shallow ulceration of the underlying skin.
>
> As the disease progresses, more patches appear and the others spread, so that considerable areas over the head, back and the 'wrist' of the tail are affected and, at this stage, the head may be so badly affected that it seems largely covered by raw, reddish areas. As often happens when the skin of a fish is damaged, fungus may infect these exposed areas but it is important to recognise that this fungal growth is a secondary effect, consequent upon primary infection, and not a primary symptom. Once established, however, the fungus spreads and, in the most advanced stages of the disease, the head and tail regions of the fish may be largely covered with fungus.

Elson (1968a) also mentions that the gall bladder is commonly affected. In fish showing the early stages of the disease the gall bladder is enlarged but in the more seriously affected fish it is often found to be empty. Certain actions such as aquaplaning and jumping with an agitated flapping movement have been described as characteristic of infected fish. Recently (July, 1968), it has been found that there is a marked depletion of serum protein in diseased fish. Adult salmon appear to be much more susceptible to the disease than juveniles and relatively few infected parr and smolts have been recorded.

In the report prepared by the Fisheries Division of the Department of Agriculture and Fisheries of Ireland in August, 1966, it mentioned that Dr Jensen suggested that the disease was 'Columnaris', but was insistent that this diagnosis would have to be proved by the isolation and culture of *Chondrococcus* (*Cytophaga*) *columnaris* and the subsequent reproduction of the disease in healthy salmon by infection with bacteria thus cultured.

E

Dr Snieszko examined further diseased salmon and isolated *Aeromonas liquefaciens* and a *Pseudomonas* species. While these are well-known fish pathogens in Europe Dr Snieszko was not convinced of their significance in this disease.

Further examination of diseased salmon showed the presence of 'columnaris' organisms and fungi of the *Saprolegnia* type and attempts were made to conduct small-scale infectivity experiments. A number of these experiments were conducted with all of the above bacteria using both injection and water infectivity processes. While it was repeatedly possible to kill fish and isolate the specific organisms used from the infected tissues thereby demonstrating their pathogenicity, the true lesions of U.D.N. were not reproduced.

The lack of knowledge of the surface bacterial populations of healthy salmon made it necessary for a study to be made of the normal skin flora of salmon in marine, estuarine and river environments in which no disease had been encountered. One of the things that emerged from the survey was that 'columnaris' type bacteria could be isolated from the skin of 36·5% of all fish examined from non-affected areas.

Elson (1968a) describes examining fresh-run infected salmon within five minutes of their capture in nets in the tidal reaches of the Tweed. These fish exhibited the typical ulcerated areas on the head but no fungus. Salmon, heavily infested with sea lice but showing shallow ulcerations of the head have also been taken in coastal nets off the north-east of Scotland (Elson, 1968b) which suggests that some fish are infected with U.D.N. before they reach freshwater. From an examination of the salmon from the tidal reaches of the Tweed Elson found that bacteria were neither culturable nor demonstrable but microscopical preparations of liver and kidney impression smears revealed the presence of inclusions within the cells which indicated a possible virus infection. Carberry and Strickland (1968) in Ireland claim to have produced the disease in apparently healthy fish with the use of bacteria and fungus-free filtrates of infected fish tissues and this could indicate a virus involvement. It was also found that the aetiological agent of U.D.N. was resistant to antibiotics and was smaller than 200 mμ in size. Roberts (1969) considered that the microscopical appearance of the early lesions suggest that a virus is responsible but that it is only the harbinger of the initial skin damage which allows both loss of body proteins and attack of unprotected tissue by fungi. No abnormalities were detected in any organs other than the skin. Roberts, Shearer and Elson (1969) found no definite evidence to suggest a primary virus aetiology, but the lesions resembled those produced in the virus disease of cattle known as mucosal disease, where secondary infection is again a common occurrence.

While the work to isolate the causative organism of U.D.N. went on, the numbers of infected salmon in Scottish rivers rose and from March, 1967 to 25 February, 1968, a total of 41,234 infected salmon and grilse were removed from Scottish rivers. This total is 12·6% of the provisional Scottish catch of salmon and grilse for 1967 by all methods of fishing.

However, a note of hope is sounded by Elson (1968a):

> During the last decades of the nineteenth century, a disease character-ised by clinical symptoms similar to those of U.D.N. occurred in many Scottish rivers. This took some time to die out, e.g. the River Tweed was seriously affected over the fifteen-year period from 1879 to 1893, and though there are now methods for treating bacterial fish disease which were not available seventy or eighty years ago, these are econ-omically impracticable in an open river system and recovery must still, presumably, depend upon a balance taking place between the host and the pathogen by the process of natural selection. In this context, a certain number of kelts have been observed to show repair tissue, and experiments carried out in Ireland have indicated that the progeny of diseased salmon were apparently healthy and showed no evidence of U.D.N.

Munro (1970) points out that many high annual catches were made over the period of the outbreak in the late nineteenth century, indicating that the species was never in danger of extinction; indeed the disease may have occurred as a result of an exceedingly large population. Munro considers that similar factors may have operated to start the present outbreak, though available information is too meagre to draw such a conclusion.

Vibriosis. The causative organism of this disease is the common marine bacterium *Vibrio anguillarum* which is a Gram negative, motile, curved rod. This organism is also pathogenic to sea trout, eels, perch, plaice and saithe.

The symptoms of the disease are haemorrhagic spots on the body, particularly on the belly. Internal organs often show signs of degeneration. Because it is a marine bacterium salmon in salt and brackish water are often affected, but it also occurs on salmon in most rivers. Frequently infected fish showing signs of vibriosis are believed to be suffering from furuncu-losis which has similar symptoms. For this reason a bacteriological exam-ination is necessary before the disease can be diagnosed.

Chapter 4

THE SEA TROUT

4.1 Sea trout and brown trout – a confused taxonomy. 4.2 Life in freshwater. 4.3 Life in the sea. 4.4 Return to the river. 4.5 Parasites and disease. 4.6 Salmon × sea trout hybrids.

4.1 Sea trout and brown trout – a confused taxonomy

The sea trout and brown trout are now considered to be the migratory and non-migratory forms of the same species, *Salmo trutta*. The sea trout migrates to and from the sea, while the brown trout spends its whole life in freshwater. Some trout adopt the intermediate habit of frequenting the brackish waters of estuaries and are often called slob trout.

Frost and Brown (1967) give a very good review of the taxonomy of the trout and say that:

> it has been shown experimentally that sea trout which are prevented from migrating to the sea can grow and spawn in freshwater like typical brown trout, but as they grow older they become silvery in colour as do the older brown trout in lakes such as Windermere. There are therefore no real grounds for considering 'sea trout' as anything more than brown trout in which the migratory habit is very well developed. Indeed, typical brown trout transplanted to some parts of New Zealand and to the Falkland Islands found their way to the sea and became anadromous.

There were at one time believed to be ten species of trout in the British Isles: the sea or salmon trout (*Salmo trutta*), the sewin or western sea trout (*S. cambricus*), the finnock or eastern sea trout (*S. brachypoma*), the Galway sea trout (*S. gallivensis*), the Orkney sea trout (*S. Orcadensis*), the river trout (*S. fario*), the great lake trout (*S. ferox*), the gillaroo (*S. stomachicus*), the Welsh black-finned trout (*S. nigripinnus*) and the Loch Leven trout

(*S. levensis*). Tate Regan grouped all these and the continental varieties together and called them *Salmo trutta*. Trevawas (1953) reviewed this problem of classification and concluded that Tate Regan was justified in grouping together all the so-called varieties.

In their account of the distribution of the trout *Salmo trutta* Linn. Frost and Brown (1967) mention that:

> it is indigenous to Europe, North Africa and north-western Asia. Sea trout are found from Iceland to Scandinavia, the White Sea and Cheshkaya Gulf in the north, in the Baltic, North Sea, English Channel and Atlantic Ocean as far south as the Bay of Biscay. Brown trout live in rivers emptying into all these and also in rivers entering the western Mediterranean and the northern part of the eastern Mediterranean, but there are no sea trout in that sea. Brown trout also live in Corsica and Sardinia. There are trout in the Black and Caspian Seas and in their tributary rivers and in the Aral Sea and the River Oxus.

It also extends eastwards through Persia to the northern slopes of the Himalayas. McCrimmon and Marshall (1968) give a very detailed account of the world distribution of brown trout. They conclude that any future expansion in the world distribution of the brown trout, with the possible exception of Asia, is unlikely.

> Berg (1932) listed six subspecies of *Salmo trutta* as follows:
> *Salmo trutta trutta* in northern and western Europe.
> *S. t. labrax* in the Black Sea and its tributaries.
> *S. t. caspius* in the Caspian Sea and its tributaries.
> *S. t. aralensis* in the Sea of Aral and the River Oxus.
> *S. t. macrostigma* in the Mediterranean region.
> *S. t. carpione* the large trout of Lake Garda in Italy.

4.2 Life in freshwater

The sea trout has a similar life history to that of the salmon. It spawns in freshwater and returns to the sea. The young pass through a fry and parr stage before they migrate to sea as smolts. It is thought that the sea trout is less marine in its habits than the salmon and remains within the vicinity of the coast. The sea trout does not remain long in the rivers after spawning and will return to freshwater several times and there are records of fish which have spawned up to twelve times. Thus once a sea trout has reached maturity it can contribute to future stocks over several years. The adult sea trout also differs from the adult salmon in that it feeds in freshwater. The sea trout may spawn on finer gravel than salmon and often the spawning grounds of the two species differ. Fig. 22 outlines the general life history of the sea trout. Plates 8–10 depict the differences in shape of an adult salmon and a large adult sea trout.

The rate at which young sea trout grow and the age at which they enter the sea as smolts varies widely over their geographical range. A great deal of information on the river life of sea trout, particularly in Scotland and Ireland, has been published. Nall has studied the sea trout of more than sixteen Scottish rivers and eleven Irish rivers and his results, besides being published in a series of reports including those of the Fishery Board of Scotland (Salmon Fisheries Series), also appear in his book *The Life of the Sea Trout* (1930). In his book he also describes the age and growth characteristics of

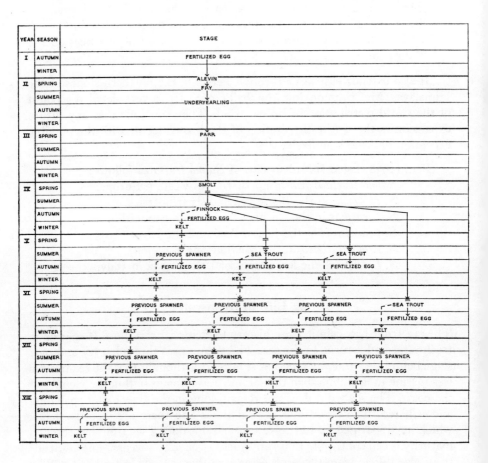

Fig. 22.   Life history of the sea trout (from Her Majesty's Stationery Office. Cmd. 2691).

sea trout of English, Welsh, Irish, Norwegian and Baltic rivers. Later information on Irish rivers has been reviewed by Went (1962). A number of studies of sea trout of the Vistula River, Poland, have been made by Zarnecki (1956).

Most of the information collected on sea trout from so many rivers in these countries, chiefly from examination of their scales, has been of great value in building up our knowledge of their characteristics. Most of this information is factual, however, and little research has been carried out on the ecology of this species. Went (1962) says in his opening remarks to his review of investigations on Irish sea trout "Sea trout have received less attention in Ireland than salmon and the reason for this is obvious. They are very important from the angling point of view in many parts of Ireland but, taking the country as a whole, both from the sporting and commercial points of view they are less valuable than the salmon."

Little is known of the ecology of young sea trout in streams or of their inter-relationships with young salmon. Nilsson (1967) describes the inter-action between these two species and states that when living separately the species have similar food habits, but when living sympatrically they are segregated into separate food niches. He refers to Lindroth (1955b) who demonstrated that juvenile Atlantic salmon and sea trout were segregated into separate food niches when living together in a Baltic river, but that the salmon on the Atlantic coast of Sweden, in the absence of trout, pre-ferred a habitat corresponding to the trout habitat in the Baltic river. In this connection it would be interesting to know something of the sequence of spawning in a stream used by both salmon and trout and how far the distribution of spawning fish was related to time of arrival in the stream.

4.3 Life in the sea

It is believed that sea trout, on entering the sea as smolts, do not move far away from the coast, although they may move some distance along it. For example, Nall (1955) gives records of sea trout kelts tagged in the Tweed and recaptured outside this river. In a northerly direction, two had travelled to the Forth and four to the Tay. In a southerly direction, one had made its way to the mouth of the Coquet, one to Blyth near North Shields, one to the Yorkshire coast, one to the Norfolk coast and one to the Dutch coast. These results tie in well with the work of Swain and Hartley (1959). In 1950 and 1955 Hartley and Swain tagged sea trout off East Anglia where, during the summer months, large numbers of sea trout are caught by seine netsmen, although the rivers in that area do not contain sea trout. A few fish were recaptured later off the Northumberland and Yorkshire coasts and in the Northumbrian rivers. More recently sea trout kelts were tagged in the Tweed and Coquet and in the few months following tagging most of the recaptures were made off the Norfolk and Suffolk coasts and a few were reported from the coasts of Belgium, Holland, Denmark and Norway. Nearly all the recaptures of fish which had spent over a year at sea were made off the Northumberland coast or in the parent rivers.

Went (1962) reviews the information available on the movements of Irish sea trout. Most of the recaptures of tagged sea trout were within the area of the river system in which they were tagged.

Balmain and Shearer (1956) summarise the records of sea trout caught at sea off the British Isles over the period 1927–1954, and Shearer (1957) gives further records for 1956. The majority of the fish were captured in drift nets, presumably set for herring. Most of these sea captures were made in four areas – off the Buchan (north-east Scotland) coast, off the East Anglian coast, off the Danish and Dutch coasts and off the coast of Argyll. The fish caught off the Buchan and East Anglian coasts are largely those which have migrated to sea in the spring of the year in which they were caught. The catches off the Danish and Dutch coasts also contain fish in their first year of sea life, though some older fish are also present. Little is known about the sea trout off the Argyll coast. The stomach contents of many of the sea trout caught at sea have been sand eels (*Ammodytes* spp.). Other fish recorded in sea trout caught at sea have been sprats (*Clupea sprattus*), gadoids and salmon smolts.

4.4 Return to the river

Some of the sea trout smolts do not go far out to sea, but enter the rivers again in the late summer and autumn after being only a few months in the sea. At this stage they are called by a variety of names depending on the district, the names most frequently used are whitling, herling and finnock. Although some of these visit freshwater in the autumn of the year in which they migrated as smolts only a small proportion of them spawn. The majority of them, even if they penetrate far upstream, do not spawn. Some of these young sea trout enter the rivers in the following spring while others, which came in the previous autumn, return to the sea. Not all sea trout return to the river within a year of entering the sea as smolts and those which don't will return as adults from the second spring or summer after migration.

Concerning young sea trout, i.e. whitling or finnock, the question often asked is whether their return to the water after being caught is justified. Went (1962) says:

Some owners of sea trout fisheries return all sea trout below a certain size to the water in the belief that they will produce larger fish in the years to come. A return of small fish, say below 12 inches, is likely to increase the number of larger fish in future years, although to what extent fish returned to the water survive we do not yet know. Nor do we know whether the age group in which a sea trout returns to the river is based on genetical considerations.

In referring to the small size of sea trout along the western seaboard of Ireland, which Piggins (1967) attributes to the relatively poor sea feeding along the narrow Continental Shelf off the western Irish coast;[1] Piggins raises the same question. He feels that in returning rod-caught finnock the fishery is being utilised inefficiently in terms of its function as a primary producer of fish-flesh. However, as he says:

> In terms of the intangible value of sporting fishing it might be thought worthwhile to return 100 small fish in the hope that one-quarter of them will survive to the following year at one-third of their original weight. These estimates are the most optimistic possible since survival from a summer rod-caught finnock is almost certainly less than that of a finnock kelt in the following spring.

Piggins also points out that it is not known whether finnock make a significant contribution to the breeding potential of sea trout stocks, in terms of either fecundity or viability of their genital products, out of 700 tagged finnock only 1 survived for five years, by which time it weighed only $2\frac{1}{4}$ lb.

Sea trout, like salmon, home to their parent river. A study of the homing behaviour of sea trout in the Aberdeenshire Dee has been carried out by Shearer (1959a). Sea trout caught in a trap on one of the tributary streams were tagged and transferred to various points on other tributary streams entering the Dee, upstream and downstream of the parent stream, and to points on the main river ranging from just above tidal limits to about 70 miles from the sea. The results obtained showed that the numbers of sea trout returning from each transfer site were, roughly, inversely proportional to the distance of the site from the trap on the parent stream. It was particularly interesting to find that sea trout returned from positions upstream as well as downstream from the trap. Some fish moved nearly 50 miles downstream to re-enter the parent stream. The results also suggested that the ability to return to the parent stream did depend, to some extent, upon whether the fish were transferred well in advance of or near to the time when they were likely to spawn; greater numbers of those transferred well in advance returned to the parent stream. It was also found that plugging the nostrils of the fish also reduced the ability to return.

---

[1] Fish from stock of large Swedish sea trout were reared by Piggins and released as smolts in 1964, but returning adults were the same size as native Irish stocks.

From tagging experiments in Poland, Zarnecki (1956) showed that sea trout originating from the Vistula basin and released in the Vistula tributaries all returned to the river. Similarly, sea trout originating from Pomeranian rivers and released into these rivers were recaptured in Pomeranian rivers and did not enter the River Vistula which was very close. Some of Zarnecki's experiments confirmed the hypothesis of imprinting, as sea trout originating from Pomeranian rivers and released into the tributaries of the Vistula returned to the release sites and not to their native rivers.

Generally speaking, in the British Isles it is found that the homing instinct of sea trout is not as strong as in salmon, and often sea trout return to other local rivers and not the river they left to go to sea as smolts.

Unlike salmon, sea trout, on returning to the river, do feed in freshwater. Piggins (1967) found that sea trout caught during the day in freshwater rarely contain food in their stomachs, but a number of those caught at night have been found to have been feeding. It is well known among anglers that the best time to catch sea trout is at night. From the evidence presented by Piggins for the sea trout he examined, approximately 20% of the adult fish continue to grow in freshwater.

4.5 Parasites and disease

The sea louse *Lepeophtheirus salmonis* is a common external parasite on sea trout. They are most common on fish during the summer and autumn. Nall (1937) found few lice on sea trout in March, but in August recorded them on 63% of the whitling and 75% of the adult sea trout netted in tidal water; and on 27% of the whitling and 50% of the sea trout netted in estuarial water.

A gill parasite sometimes found on sea trout is the trematode *Discocotyle sagittata*. If this parasite occurs in large numbers the gills may be covered with copious amounts of mucus and become pale through lack of blood and death may result. A trematode frequently occurring in sea trout is *Crepidostomum farionis* which inhabits the intestine, pyloric caecae and gall bladder.

Many other internal parasites which infect salmon also occur in sea trout and an account of some of these is given in *The Trematoda of British Fishes* by Dawes (1947).

There is little information on the parasitism of sea trout by lampreys but damage on sea trout which could be attributed to lamprey attacks is given by Smith (1957). The proportion of sea trout showing this damage in Montrose Bay and the mouth of the Aberdeenshire Dee on the east coast of Scotland was as high as 30% but only 3% at the mouth of the Tweed.

The sea trout suffers from the same diseases as salmon, although the degree of susceptibility may vary between the two species. For example Elson (1968a and b) noticed that sea trout in the rivers Deveron and Spey did not exhibit any of the distinct ulcerations characteristic of ulcerative dermal necrosis but had a piebald appearance due to an extensive covering of fungus.

4.6 Salmon × sea trout hybrids

Early work on salmon hybrids has been described by Alm (1955). More recently salmon and sea trout hybrids have been produced in Ireland (Piggins, 1965). The hybrids described by Piggins were the result of a single experimental cross between a small female grilse ($3\frac{1}{2}$ lb) and a male sea trout (3 lb). The resulting progeny from the cross were found to have a much better growth rate than either salmon or sea trout maintained under the same hatchery conditions. At the end of two years these hybrids averaged about 12 inches in length. In the autumn of their second year the growth rate began to decline when both sexes became sexually mature, but they continued to grow at a reduced rate and at four and a half years of age their average size was $17\frac{1}{2}$ inches and 3 lb. Some of the F_1 hybrids were released into a lake and one was caught at $7+$ years old and weighed almost 7 lb. The hybrids were found to be hardy and disease resistant.

Piggins found it was possible to breed from the F_1 generation. He also successfully back-crossed male and female hybrids with the opposite sex of both salmon and sea trout and the resulting offspring have been reared. The progeny of hybrids back-crossed to salmon show a strengthening of salmon-like characters while the back-crosses to sea trout resemble the trout more closely. It would seem, therefore, that this hybrid strain possesses considerable plasticity in its ability to breed both *inter se* and with either parent stock. The F_2 generation hybrids have been reared for two years in a hatchery and released in a landlocked lake and their subsequent growth rate has been much above normal for trout in the area.

Chapter 5

THE BROWN TROUT

5.1 General life history. 5.2 Migration and spawning. 5.3 Survival, behaviour and movements of immature fish. 5.4 Growth. 5.5 Feeding habits. 5.6 Predation. 5.7 Parasites and disease. 5.8 Ferox trout.

5.1 General life history

The brown trout is indigenous to Europe, North Africa and west Asia and has been introduced into nearly all parts of the world where conditions are suitable for its survival (Fig. 23).

There is a great variation in form and colour among individual brown trout not only from different localities but also from the same water. The colour of the back varies from bluish-grey or olive through yellows and browns to nearly black, while the belly may be white, silvery or golden-yellow and the sides have silver or golden reflections; the spots may be red or brown, oval stellate or haloed and they may vary considerably in size, number and distribution. The dark pigment cells (chromatophores) in the trout skin are under the control of the eye so that the trout are able to change colour to some extent to match their background.

It is said that pink flesh and many red spots are characteristic of trout which eat a high proportion of crustaceans and molluscs. For example a variety of brown trout known as the gillaroo which occurs in some Scottish and Irish lakes is yellow and gold with large brown and numerous red spots. These fish are said to live only on snails and have hard, thick-walled stomachs. It has also been noticed that trout in some lakes lose the pink colour in their flesh after spawning, so that some of the trout in the lake may have red flesh while others have white flesh. Vladykov (1956) found that in brook trout (*Salvelinus fontinalis*) fish approaching spawning have flesh of a much brighter hue and are better tasting than young or spent individuals.

In temperate regions in the northern hemisphere the brown trout become ripe and spawn between October and February, the normal time being between October and December; they are never found in breeding condition outside this period.

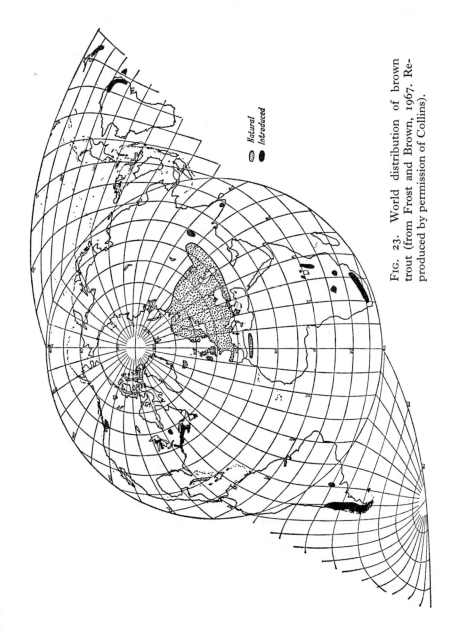

FIG. 23. World distribution of brown trout (from Frost and Brown, 1967. Reproduced by permission of Collins).

Spawning usually takes place in running water, although on occasions they may spawn in lakes especially when the inflowing or outflowing streams are unsuitable for spawning. Trout living in lakes migrate into the feeder stream, while trout living in rivers may, or may not, move up the main river and into the tributaries to spawn. The spawning areas are usually in fast flowing water where there is suitable gravel in which to deposit the eggs, but not in turbulent riffles.

The time the eggs take to hatch depends on water temperature. The alevin becomes a fry when the yolk sac has been absorbed and the small fish begins to feed. The 'parr' marks are visible even in young fry and become more obvious when the fish grow older. The red edge of the adipose fin, which is characteristic of the trout, appears early in the fry stage. There is considerable mortality during the fry stage. As trout are strongly territorial and aggressive the young fish which cannot find a 'territory' move down-stream, or upstream, in search of a vacant niche. The young fish live in the nursery stream for one to four years before moving into the main river or lake. On reaching maturity the fish home to their parent stream to spawn. In many trout populations each surviving trout spawns every year after it has first spawned, but some fish, living in large lakes such as Winder-mere, may spawn only every second year. The life span of the trout varies from water to water.

5.2 Migration and spawning

Trout may start their spawning migration several weeks or only a few days before spawning. Although trout living in lakes may start to congregate around the mouths of the spawning streams from the end of August, as was noticed in Loch Leven, Kinross-shire, by Munro and Balmain (1956), they may not ascend the streams until October or November. This spawning migration is usually associated with a rise in water level and Munro and Balmain observed that on every occasion the commencement of a run was associated with an increase in water level, and they concluded that an increase in water level or some change in the nature of the water associated with such a rise is the most important stimulus inducing the upstream migration of trout to the spawning grounds.

Stuart (1953a) considered that, although spates may be one of the factors inducing runs and facilitating the passage of fish, stream temperatures were more important than spates. He recorded that the main spawning runs into the tributary streams of Dunalastair Reservoir occurred only after the temperature had fallen to 6–7° C and considered that the spawning runs are inhibited when the temperature of the stream is higher than that of the loch. Munro and Balmain found that in one of the spawning tributaries of Loch Leven water temperature conditions within the limits recorded (5–9° C) are not of importance in governing the migrations of spawning trout. However, the greatest difference between the temperatures of the loch and the stream recorded by Munro and Balmain during the period of their observations was only 2·6° C. Other factors which may inhibit migration are turbidity and acidity.

Stuart (1957) carried out a number of experiments to demonstrate homing behaviour in trout. He was able to demonstrate this homing instinct by (i) marking juvenile trout in streams running into Dunalastair Reservoir, Perthshire, and recapturing them as mature fish ready to spawn in their stream of origin and in *none* of the other streams. (ii) By removing ripe trout already present in their home streams and transporting them to a stream on the opposite side of the lake. These transfer experiments were carried out a number of times in different years, and up to 100% of the transported fish were recaptured in their original streams. More than 3,000 trout were marked in these experiments and yet only one of them could definitely be classed as having strayed. Although these observations in Dunalastair Reservoir are a convincing demonstration of homing in brown trout, as Pyefinch (1960) points out, they should not be held to imply that homing behaviour is as exact in salmon and sea trout. The total area of Dunalastair is small, so the trout probably could not migrate far from their parent stream and, on return, the choice of spawning streams would be limited.

Potential spawning sites are characterised by the presence of water currents flowing downwards into the gravel and the female trout become aware of these currents during their movement upstream and select these areas for spawning. The location of these sites is towards the tail of the pool where the gravel slopes gently upwards (Fig. 24).

The spawning act is very like that of the salmon. Curtis (1949) has produced a summary of many observations on spawning trout and a description of this is given by Jones and Ball (1954) and Pyefinch (1960).

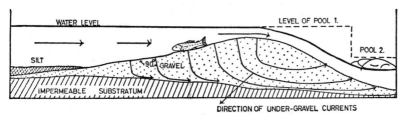

FIG. 24. Section through the substratum of a typical stream pool showing its relation to the principal water currents and the position of the female trout on the gravel before excavation of the redd. (By Stuart, reproduced by permission of Collins.)

If an ideal spawning site is not available trout will either not spawn or else deposit their eggs in an unsuitable site. For example, Stuart (1953a) found in Loch Moraig, Perthshire, that trout confronted with a relatively high temperature barrier refused to enter an easily accessible stream, but spawned instead on a gravel patch in the loch itself. In cases where the eggs and milt are not shed they are absorbed eventually by the tissues. In the case of the female the contents of the eggs are absorbed but the chorion or shell remains and Stuart found in a number of female trout a hard, compact wad of chorion membranes lodged in the anterior end of the body cavity. He believed that this was responsible for the death of a number of female trout each year. So where natural spawning facilities are lacking the larger female trout population may gradually die off.

Once the eggs are fertilised and in the gravel their rate of development will depend on water temperature. The average time between fertilisation and hatching at different water temperatures is given in Table 15.

5.3 Survival, behaviour and movements of immature fish

For several days after the trout alevins (Fig. 25) emerge from the gravel as fry they will move down into the gravel if disturbed. However, after some days of active feeding the fry gradually begin to disperse from the redds and start to station themselves some distance away from each other, thus exhibiting the first signs of territoriality so characteristic of older trout. Those fish unable to find a territory tend to move downstream until an unoccupied territory is found. The larger fry are more dominant and presumably hold the most favourable territories for food and shelter. As a result of this it is

TABLE 15

The average time between fertilisation and hatching for brown trout eggs at different temperatures. (From Frost and Brown, 1967)

Water temperature		Incubation time
°C	°F	Days
2·0	35·5	148
3·6	38·5	118
4·7	40·5	97
6·0	43·0	77
7·8	46·0	60
10·0	50·0	41
11·0	52·0	35
12·0	53·5	27

usually the smaller, subordinate fry which disperse downstream, particularly during times of drought and flood. Elliott (1966) recorded a downstream
movement of fry (about 2·5 cm long) while sampling drifting invertebrates
in a Dartmoor stream. The catches in both March and April indicated that
downstream movement occurred chiefly at night, being at a maximum
in the early hours of the night. Those fish that cannot find a territory die of
starvation. Under normal conditions there are usually too many fry and the
excess die. The mortality during the fry period of life is usually very high.

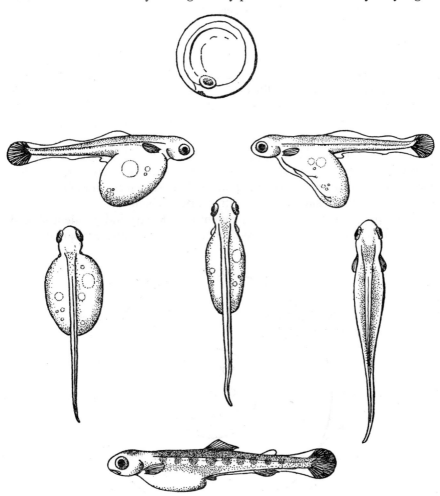

FIG. 25.   Stages in the development of the alevin from the time of
hatching until a few days before emergence from the gravel (from Stuart,
1953).

Le Cren (1961) (Fig. 26) showed a 94% survival from the egg to the fry stage, but only a 2·7% survival during the fry stage. Le Cren assumes an annual survival of 50% after the yearling stage. Frost and Brown (1967) give survival rates of brown trout of different ages in Three Dubs Tarn in the Lake District (Fig. 27). These show the expected low survival in early life. This is then followed by a 53% survival in the third year, but only a 35% survival for the fourth to eighth years; these fish mature at four years old. However, as Frost and Brown point out, the actual survival may vary greatly from average figures according to climatic and other environmental changes and the earliest stages are generally the most vulnerable to adverse conditions.

McFadden (1969) has produced a diagram (Fig. 28) showing the network of processes operating over successive short intervals of time during a single growing season in the life of a salmonid fish. The relative importance of the various density-dependent and density-independent factors will change with time. For example, under the conditions prevailing during one interval, emigration rate might be high and reduce the initial density of the fry so effectively that the death rate remains low. During a subsequent interval, changes in the size of fry, their territorial behaviour, or other factors may throw greater weight upon death rate as a mediator of numerical change, with the result that emigration rate is changed.

Perhaps the terms density-dependent and density-independent should be clarified. Processes which are *density-dependent* cause a population to

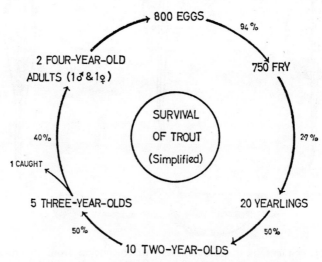

FIG. 26.   Diagram of the survival of a typical trout brood (from Le Cren, 1961. Reproduced by permission of Collins.)

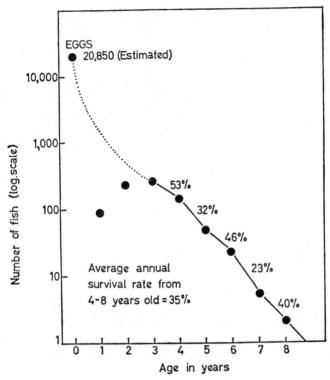

FIG. 27.   Survival rates of brown trout of different ages in Three Dubs Tarn (from Frost and Smyly, 1952; and Le Cren, 1961. Reproduced by permission of Collins).

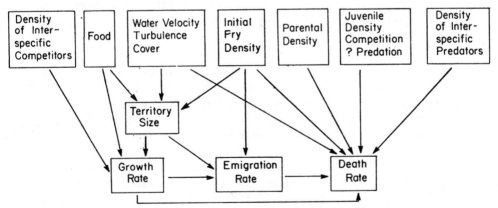

FIG. 28.   Summary of factors which effect changes in numbers of stream-dwelling salmonids during the fry and parr stages (from McFadden, 1969).

increase when density is low and to decrease when density is high; for example, high death rates or low growth rates at high levels of population density and the opposite at low densities. *Population regulation* refers to the operation of density-dependent factors. Distinguished from population regulation is *population limitation*, which refers to reduction or restriction of population below the level of abundance it would otherwise have attained, with the intensity of reduction or limitation not being a function of population density. For example, predation may remove a fixed fraction of a stock, independent of its density, with the result that the population persists at a lower level of abundance than in the absence of predation. Populations are *limited*, in the sense used here, by the operation of *density-independent* factors. Population limitation does not regulate population size.

Besides there being a movement of trout fry there is also, at certain times of the year, a movement of older trout. Movements of older trout vary from locality to locality, for example Mills (1964b and 1969a and b) has shown that there can be a considerable downstream movement of trout which seems to occur throughout the whole year, while Stuart (1957) has found that young trout, living in streams feeding a loch, move into the loch in the autumn and return to the streams in the spring. There is probably considerable to-ing and fro-ing of fish in streams throughout the year, although this may not always be the case as Allen (1951) found that trout in the Horokiwi stream moved very little during their lives.

5.4 Growth

A regular annual growth-rate cycle in wild and hatchery yearling brown trout has been demonstrated by Swift (1961); the fish have a high growth rate in the spring and autumn and a low growth rate during the summer and winter of each year.

The growth rate of trout is influenced by a number of physical, chemical and biological factors. In addition, Southern (1932) mentioned that some authorities considered that it could also be affected by hereditary characters of the stock of trout, the size of the egg from which it develops and the amount and kind of food available. With regard to hereditary characters, some people are inclined to believe that the size attained by trout is governed by their hereditary constitution. This belief is said to account for the popularity of certain 'breeds' of trout for restocking, such as Loch Leven trout. It is also believed that trout suffer in size from inbreeding. There is no evidence to support these beliefs. There are, however, many cases where small trout have increased in size after being transferred from a water producing only small trout to a water where conditions were more favourable for growth. Dahl (1919) summarised the results of his investigations on the growth of trout saying "no trout may apparently be considered as possessing definite and hereditary capacities for a definite kind of growth. Growth appears always to be a product of exterior influences."

Southern concluded that brown trout grew more rapidly in alkaline than acid waters. However, Pentelow (1944) believed that growth rate depended more on the relation between the trout population and the food supply than on the chemical composition of the water. Trout can grow to a large size in acid and alkaline waters and Pentelow pointed out that the survival rate of trout in acid waters is much higher in the early stages due to the physical suitability of the spawning grounds and in their later stages due to the lack of predation by coarse fish. The second reason is a little less easy to understand as the only coarse fish which can feed on larger trout are pike and these occur in acid as well as alkaline waters. Certainly competition from coarse fish might be considered a more justifiable reason than predation. The high survival rates, and consequently high population densities thus leads to a slower growth rate in acid waters. In a comparison of the bionomics of trout in three Devonshire streams Horton, Bailey and Wildson (1968) found that the faster growth rate in one stream is correlated with low fish densities due to unfavourable spawning and to high bottom fauna production. Poor growth rate in the other two streams, it was suggested, may be due to lack of bottom fauna, correlated with favourable spawning grounds and very large fish densities.

Frost and Smyly (1952) found that the rate of growth in Three Dubs Tarn in the Lake District probably varied inversely with the population density. Campbell (1961) describes the growth of brown trout in acid and alkaline lochs in Scotland and points out that the density of trout populations, and consequently the relative amount of food available, is nearly always ignored in considering the reasons for slow and fast growth in trout. Campbell was able to show that the growth of trout in some Scottish lochs with little or no spawning facilities was much better, regardless of the pH and alkalinity, than in lochs where spawning facilities were good (Table 16).

While the presence or absence of spawning facilities may influence the growth rate of trout in lochs, physical factors existing in fast-running streams may influence trout growth more than population density. For example, in a forest stream (Mills, 1967c, 1969a) found that the population density of trout was higher in that part of the stream which flowed through a recently-planted section of forest, where there was abundant vegetation and cover, than in a section of stream immediately downstream which flowed through old forest with no undergrowth and little cover. Although there is abundant food readily available in the form of *Gammarus pulex* it is not utilised as much as one might expect and terrestrial insects form a large part of the trout's diet at the time of the year when growth rate is greatest.

Although there are these differences in the two sections of a stream the growth rate of trout is the same in both sections and it is considered that the low temperatures, which rarely rise much above 10° C, are responsible for the slow rate of growth. Swift (1961) showed in experimental work with constant-environment aquaria, together with the results of field work, that water temperature is the main external environmental factor influencing growth rate, maximum growth rate being achieved at 12° C.

5.5 Feeding habits

The feeding habits of brown trout have been studied in considerable detail and the diets of trout from different waters have been listed by many authors. Trout are very catholic feeders and crop the bottom fauna, the fauna being carried downstream in mid-water (the drift) and also organisms which fall on to the surface of the water. At certain times of the year trout take a large part of their food from the water surface.

Egglishaw (1967) made a study of trout and salmon in two streams in the Scottish Highlands and, among other things, studied the seasonal changes in the food consumed (Figs. 29 and 30). It was found that there was less food in the stomachs of both trout and salmon during the colder months of the year, November to February, than during the warmer months. However, as Egglishaw points out, stomach contents give little indication of the rate of feeding because the rate of digestion is related to temperature. At low temperatures the rate of digestion is extremely slow and food may remain in the stomach for several days. The amounts con-

TABLE 16

The growth of brown trout in Highland lochs with a range of alkalinities

Loch	pH	Total Alkalinity[1]	Length (in cm) at end of Winters			
			1	2	3	4
Loch Lanish[2]	8·7	77·6	8·7(11)	21·2(11)	36·1(7)	43·1(6)
Loch Borralie[2]	8·4	109·0	9·1(15)	23·1(15)	32·1(10)	40·3(4)
Unnamed Loch[2]	5·7	<1	8·6(3)	20·2(3)	30·6(3)	39·5(3)
Loch nan Ealachan[2]	7·6	27·2	7·6(19)	21·7(19)	32·5(12)	38·9(11)
Loch Croispol	8·6	97·7	5·8(21)	17·1(21)	29·4(21)	35·8(18)
Glutt Loch[2]	4·9	<1	6·3(9)	13·7(9)	20·8(9)	33·6(9)
Fincastle Loch	8·6	60·5	6·5(168)	15·6(168)	22·2(168)	24·4(80)
Loch an Daim	7·7	44·4	4·2(100)	11·7(100)	18·9(98)	23·6(23)
Strathkyle Loch	6·5	4·2	6·5(163)	15·5(163)	20·4(163)	23·5(33)

All lengths calculated from scales. The figures in brackets indicate number of trout in age group.
[1] Parts per million of calcium carbonate.
[2] Indicates spawning poor or non-existent.
(From: Campbell, R. N. 1961, *Salmon and Trout Magazine*, No. 161, pp. 47–52.)

sumed in the summer months compared with the amounts consumed in the colder months would probably be several times larger than the relative amounts of food in the stomachs at these times.

A study of the feeding habits of trout in a Dartmoor stream was made by Elliott (1967) to assess the importance of invertebrate drift. He found that nearly all the common members of the benthos and drift occurred in the trout stomachs, but only the older trout contained the larger members of the benthos and drift. Most of the animals taken exclusively from the drift were only important as constituents of the diet in the summer, while those taken chiefly from the benthos were important in both winter and summer. Elliott also examined the stomachs of trout taken at night and found that they were feeding in the early hours of the night during the summer months. He concluded that the availability of many benthic

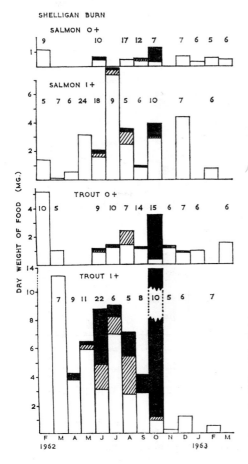

FIG. 29

The amount of invertebrate food present in salmon and trout from the Shelligan Burn. The number of fish on which the measurements are based are given for each column (from Egglishaw, 1967).

animals increased at night and that the trout were utilising this readily available food either as drift or from the tops of stones. As well as eating invertebrates, trout eat other fish species and at times they may be serious predators of young salmon.

5.6 Predation

A formidable list of animals that eat trout could be compiled and an equally long list of authors who have recorded predation on trout could also be drawn up. Probably the most common predators are the otter (*Lutra*

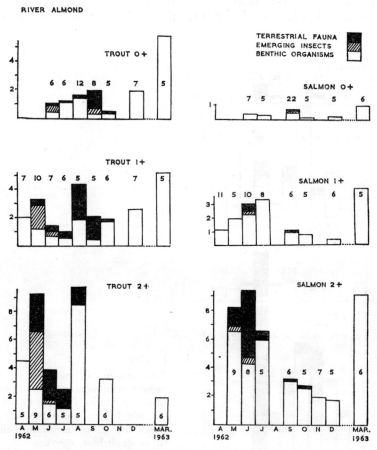

FIG. 30. The amount of invertebrate food present in salmon and trout from the River Almond. The number of fish on which the measurements are based are given for each column (from Egglishaw, 1967).

lutra), the cormorant (*Phalacrocorax carbo*) and the pike (*Esox lucius*). A bird which has recently reappeared on the Scottish scene as a trout predator is the osprey.

Stephens (1957) has made a thorough study of the otter and its feeding habits. She considered that, although the otter ate trout, it did little harm to trout populations in their natural environment but it might cause considerable damage at trout hatcheries.

Mills (1965a) examined 129 cormorant stomachs from Scottish inland waters and found that the average size of brown trout taken was 10 inches, while fish of up to 18 inches (2½ lb) were eaten on occasions. Because cormorants feed on trout of a size that are of immediate value to the angler their control may be beneficial where their numbers on trout lochs are high. But where trout may be small and numerous, as in acid hill lochs, the presence of cormorants might result in an improvement in the size and quality of the trout by reducing the population.

Pike can be very serious predators on trout and in many trout waters their numbers are often controlled by netting. In a study of pike predation in three Irish lakes Toner (1960) found that in Lough Mask 67·2% of the pike were feeding exclusively on salmonids, while in Lough Conn and Lough Corrib the figures were 58·3% and 54·2% respectively. In Denmark Larsen (1965) found that the food of pike was almost the same as that preferred by trout and that a definite food-competition exists between these two species, especially between the smaller pike, of up to 40·0 cm in length, and the young trout. In addition to demonstrating competition between these two species Larsen also found that predation by pike in these streams can be serious and he estimated that the presence of 100 pike in a trout stream will entail an annual loss of about 2,500 trout.

5.7 Parasites

Many of the external and internal parasites of salmon and sea trout are also found infecting brown trout. There are the external parasites *Argulus* and *Piscicola*, the gill parasites *Discocotyle* and *Gyrodactylus* and the tapeworm *Eubothrium* to name only a few. The well-known gill maggot *Salmincola salmonea* of the salmon, however, is rarely found on brown trout.

Thomas (1964) made a study of the populations of the helminth parasites in brown trout on the River Teifi in Wales. He found that only six species of helminth occurred commonly in 905 fish he examined. Each of these had a preference for certain microhabitats in the host; *Discocotyle sagittata* and *Phyllodistomum simile* are restricted to the gills and the urinary bladder respectively; *Dacnitis truttae* and *Crepidostomum metoecus* occur chiefly in the region of the pyloric caecae and *C. farionis* and *Neoechino-*

rhynchus rutili mainly in the alimentary canal behind the caecae. There was no significant increase in infestation with increase in age of the trout.

Those parasites more commonly found in the trout than in the salmon are the larval stages of the fluke *Diplostomum*. This parasite, in one of its larval stages, encysts in the eye of the fish causing opacity of the lens and 'pop eye'. The parasitised fish is eaten by a fish-eating bird where the larval parasite changes into its adult form (Fig. 31). The tapeworm *Diphyllobothrium* also spends one of its larval stages in the trout, the adult stage living in the guts of birds and mammals.

Infection of trout with the plerocercoid (larval) stage of species of *Diphyllobothrium* is widespread. Epidemics caused by the larvae of *Diphyllobothrium* in trout have been recorded from the British Isles, Canada and the United States. The species of *Diphyllobothrium* infecting trout is not

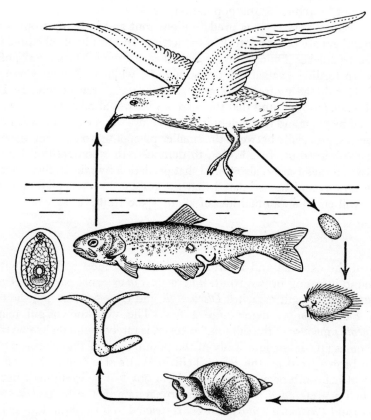

Fig. 31.   Life cycle of *Diplostomum spathaceum*. (After Schäperclaus, from Dogiel, Petrushevski and Polyanski, 1961.)

known in many cases, but at least two species are involved, *D. dendriticum* and *D. ditremum*. The definitive (final) hosts of both species are fish-eating birds.

As with many other parasites, the degree of infestation by *Diphyllobothrium* in the trout increases with size and age. Fraser (1960) studied an outbreak of Diphyllobothriosis in a reservoir in the west of England and found the heaviest mortality occurred in three-year old trout. During the height of the epidemic the trout died in greater numbers in the summer months, particularly July and August, than during the winter. The external features often give no indication of infestation and the brown trout appear healthy and normal in colour. However, heavily-infested trout, which are in a dying condition, are emaciated, sluggish and disinclined to move unless disturbed. Often the mass of encysted larvae in the body cavity can be felt when holding the trout and bleeding from the abdominal pore in the female is common.

The cysts are smooth, round, cream in colour and not calcified, their size varies with the size of the encysted plerocercoids, reaching a maximum diameter of 1·0 cm. The larvae are most frequently found encysted among the pyloric caeca and on the outside of the stomach. Cysts are rarely found on the intestine. In heavy infestations cysts frequently obscure the entire stomach, and other organs are also affected, namely the liver, gonad, spleen, surface of the swim bladder and occasionally the abdominal musculature.

The larvae of nematodes or round worms of such species as *Eustrongylides* also form cysts which are round and somewhat flattened. They can usually be distinguished from the spherical cysts of *Diphyllobothrium* and of course contain a small round worm which, in the case of *Eustrongylides*, is usually red in colour.

Other parasites also have a number of deleterious effects on their hosts. The leech *Acanthobdella peledina* can damage the skin of salmonids, causing the appearance of small round wounds and when present in large numbers can cause complete destruction of the fins. Leeches, such as *Piscicola*, can also cause serious mechanical injuries to the gills. The parasites of the alimentary canal, such as the tapeworm *Eubothrium crassum*, can cause partial obstruction of the gut, as can the spiny-headed worm *Echinorhynchus truttae*. Many other organs can also be affected, for example the encysted larval stages of the tapeworm *Triaenophorus nodulosus*, parasitic in its adult stage in the gut of the pike, can cause diseases of the liver (Fig. 32). The myxosporidian (a protozoan) *Myxosoma cerebralis*, which is parasitic in the cartilage of the trout, causes destruction of the balancing organs and consequently affects the co-ordination of movements resulting in what is known as the 'whirling disease'. A characteristic blackening of

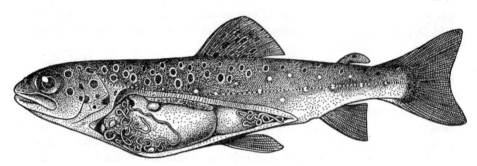

FIG. 32.   Trout infested with *Triaenophorus* (from Dogiel, Petrushevski
and Polyanski, 1961).

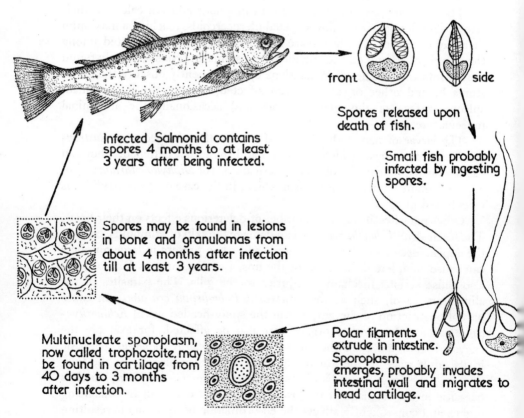

front   side

Spores released upon
death of fish.

Small fish probably
infected by ingesting
spores.

Infected Salmonid contains
spores 4 months to at least
3 years after being infected.

Spores may be found in lesions
in bone and granulomas from
about 4 months after infection
till at least 3 years.

Polar filaments
extrude in intestine.
Sporoplasm
emerges, probably invades
intestinal wall and migrates to
head cartilage.

Multinucleate sporoplasm,
now called trophozoite, may
be found in cartilage from
40 days to 3 months
after infection.

FIG. 33.   Life cycle of *Myxosoma cerebralis* (after Hoffman, from Elson, 1969).

the tail region of the trout, spinal curvature and exhaustive tail chasing movements are symptoms associated with this disease. It is common in hatchery-reared salmonids, but until recently (Elson, 1969) was not found in Scotland. The life cycle of this parasite is depicted in Fig. 33 and trout infected with the disease are shown in Plates 12 and 13.

All these effects of parasitic infestation are likely to have an effect on the condition and growth rate of trout and it is interesting to note that Frost and Brown (1967) suggest that as trout eggs are free of parasites, the extra-ordinarily good growth of trout when first introduced into countries such as New Zealand and Kenya may be due partly to this complete freedom from internal parasites. While this is an interesting suggestion, there are so many other factors which might govern the growth rate of trout introduced to a new environment it would be difficult to demonstrate. However, their suggestion is borne out to some extent by Dix (1968) in a study of hel-minth parasites of brown trout in Canterbury, New Zealand, who found that there was a reduction in the parasitic fauna when compared with that of trout in their native habitat. There is a general occurrence, however, of parasitic groups of low host specificity.

5.8 Ferox trout

Ferox trout were at one time considered to be a separate species *Salmo ferox*. They are in fact large predatory brown trout inhabiting deep lakes. Some people believe that the presence of char in a lake is an indication that ferox trout are also present. Certainly large, deep Scottish lochs containing char also hold large trout and Hardie (1940) devotes a considerable part of his book *Ferox and Char in the Lochs of Scotland* to this association.

Chapter 6

OTHER MEMBERS OF
THE SALMON FAMILY

6.1 Rainbow trout. 6.2 Brook trout. 6.3 Arctic char. 6.4 Grayling.
6.5 Whitefish. 6.6 Danube salmon.

6.1 Rainbow trout

The Pacific rainbow trout (*Salmo gairdnerii*) comprise a very variable and complex group of related forms. The three main forms are the steelhead trout (*Salmo gairdnerii gairdnerii*) which has an 'inbuilt' sea-going rhythm like the European sea trout (*Salmo trutta*), the rainbow trout of coastal rivers (*Salmo gairdnerii irideus*) with an occasional sea-going habit, and that of inland waters such as the Kamloops trout (*Salmo gairdnerii kamloops*).

Leim and Scott (1966) in referring to the biology of the rainbow trout introduced to eastern Canada say that it behaves in the same way as in its native waters of the Pacific coast, that is, the species may go to sea but usually remains in freshwater. One assumes that they are referring to the coastal river form (*S. g. irideus*). Landlocked populations occur in lakes without access to the sea, but even when ready access is available, fish may or may not migrate.

The coastal river form spawns in the spring while that of inland waters, some of which are known as 'Shasta' rainbows, breed in the autumn or early winter. The migratory form, the steelhead, enters the rivers throughout all months of the year, particularly in the early spring.

According to Worthington (1940 and 1941) the importations of rainbow trout into Britain prior to 1890 were of the pure 'Shasta' race, but subsequently the crossing with other races, such as the steelhead, in American and European hatcheries led to mixed strains which became further confused in Britain and were generally referred to as *S. irideus*. The original hatchery rainbow trout were taken from the McCloud River, California and Needham and Behuke (1962) produce evidence to show that the original 'Shasta' rainbow trout used for hatchery work was actually the result of mixing two types of rainbow trout: a resident, fine-scaled form and the anadromous steelhead.

Rainbow trout can tolerate higher water temperatures and lower oxygen concentrations than brown trout. They also tend to grow faster than brown trout under similar conditions, and under very favourable conditions they have a very good growth rate. Shallow limestone lakes with a high pH appear to be most favourable. In Lough Caragh in Ireland introduced rainbows reached seven lb weight in three years, while in New Zealand and Chile they have grown even faster. In a study of five lakes near Rotorua, North Island, New Zealand, Fish (1968) found that rainbow trout production was correlated with the trophic status of the lakes as indicated by their temperature and oxygen content. There was no clear relationship between lake size and trout production, but trout production decreased as the environment became more eutrophic.

Although rainbow trout will reach maturity in natural waters in Scotland they do not generally breed. It is therefore necessary to restock these waters with hatchery-reared fish. Some English reservoirs, such as Blagdon and Chew, contain stocks of large rainbow trout and a breeding population has been established in a few English waters, the northernmost being in the River Dove in Derbyshire. In Scotland a breeding population exists in the Lake of Menteith.

Rainbow trout have been successfully introduced into a number of other countries around the world including Australia, India, Kenya, Malawi and South Africa and in most of these countries breeding populations exist.

A number of hybrid experiments have been conducted by hatchery personnel involving the crossing of rainbow trout and brown trout. One experiment, which involved fertilising rainbow trout ova with brown trout milt, resulted in a trout known as a 'brownbow'. The 'brownbow' is similar in appearance to the rainbow but rather darker and less attractive. However, 'brownbow' ova fertilised with the milt of brown trout produced very attractive 'sunbeam' trout. There is usually a very high mortality due to different chromosome numbers in the two species.

6.2 Brook trout

The brook trout (*Salvelinus fontinalis*) is native only to eastern North America, attaining its greatest abundance in the maritime areas such as the Hudson Bay watersheds of Manitoba, Ontario and Quebec, Newfoundland, Prince Edward Island, Nova Scotia, New Brunswick and northern New

England. It has been introduced to a number of other countries around the world with varying success. An account of the world distribution of this species has been produced by McCrimmon and Campbell (1969).

The brook trout is sometimes called the speckled trout and also the sea trout due to its occasional sea-going habit. It is not known whether it develops this habit in countries to which it has been introduced and accordingly it may help to have a description of its sea coloration should it appear in introduced waters. The colours of the sea-going form and the freshwater form are quite different, except that in some waters sea-run fish go through a transition before leaving and after returning to freshwater. The trout living in salt water are steel-blue or green on the back, with cheeks and sides silvery, belly white; pectoral, pelvic and anal fins usually white or grey tinged with pink, dorsal fin greyish-green, mottled with grey; the flanks have 8 or 9 very pale orange spots. When the sea trout enter freshwater they gradually lose the guanin and tend to assume the colours of the freshwater form. There is considerable colour variation in the freshwater form depending on the habitat. Young brook trout exhibit 8 or 10 parr marks on the sides.

Wilder (1952) made a comparative study of anadromous and freshwater populations of brook trout in the Moser River system, Nova Scotia. He found that Moser River fresh-run sea trout generally differed from Moser River freshwater trout in having smaller head parts, shorter fins and more terete bodies. These differences were evident in both sexes but more striking in male trout. However, the sea trout and freshwater trout did not differ significantly in any of the meristic structures counted, and Wilder concluded that, on the Moser River system, they constitute one taxonomic unit.

The brook trout, which is a char, may be distinguished from the arctic char (Salvelinus alpinus) by its almost square tail, that of the arctic char being forked; and by the presence of pigmented patterns on the dorsal and caudal fins, while those of the arctic char are without any pattern. It differs from the Atlantic salmon in having a larger mouth, smaller scales and lacking black spots and teeth on the shaft of the vomer.

Anadromous brook trout in New England and eastern Canada have a definite migratory pattern. In Massachusetts, they migrate to sea after spawning in late October to early December and return in late May, June and September (Mullan, 1958). Seaward migration of smolts, kelts and large immature fish occurs in April, May and early June in the Moser River, Nova Scotia. Fish return to freshwater in June, July and August. When in the sea brook trout tend to remain within the general influence of the parent river.

Freshwater populations of brook trout do not migrate extensively. An

PLATE 14

A whitefish (*Coregonus lavaretus*) from northern Sweden.

PLATE 15

This severe mortality of brown trout was attributed to pollution from a tannery.

overall short upstream movement may take place during the spawning season and the reverse may occur during the colder months. Spawning takes place between September and November and the females produce about 1300 eggs per pound weight of fish. Incubation time depends on water temperature and is 85 days at 40° F and about 210 days at 33° F.

Disease, predation or starvation during the first year of life determine the population size in brook trout populations. According to Latta (1969), it has not been shown that predation either by other brook trout or by other vertebrates accounts for the loss of fry. Although it has been demonstrated that brook trout are relatively long-lived in the face of starvation, the possibility exists that a rather short period of starvation may deter them from feeding effectively or assimilating the food they do obtain. Starvation undoubtedly lowers their resistance to biological and physical stresses of the environment such as predation or increases in stream flow.

An interesting example of population regulation was observed in a long-term study of a brook trout population by McFadden, Alexander and Shetter (1967). It was found that the survival of adult fish tended to increase, leading to larger numbers of spawners. The larger egg complements which resulted tended to experience lower survival, thus largely preventing substantial increases in population size.

Brook trout have been hybridised with brown trout to give an infertile 'tiger' or 'zebra' trout, the eggs of brown trout being fertilised with sperm from male brook trout. Harrison (1963) considered that they were a very useful fish in the climate of Cape Province, South Africa and were a very game fish. Another hybrid called a 'splake' has resulted from crossing a male brook trout with a female lake trout (*Cristivomer namaycush*). This fish has been introduced into some of the Great Lakes.

6.3 Arctic char

The arctic char (*Salvelinus alpinus*) has a circumpolar distribution in the northern hemisphere. In the more northerly part of its range it is frequently migratory, spending part of its life in the sea and hence its popular names sea trout and Hudson Bay salmon in parts of northern Canada. It occurs more frequently as a land-locked form in the southerly part of its range, where it lives in deep lakes and is called the Alpine char (*Salvelinus salvelinus*). Holčík and Mihálik (1968) describe four main forms:
(1) the normal medium-sized form feeding on plankton and benthos; (2) the predatory form ('Wildfangsaibling') feeding on fish and attaining a weight of 8–10 lb; (3) the 'Schwarzreuter' form characteristic of the Alpine lakes with very little food to be found, a pigmy form barely attaining a length of 4–6 inches and a weight of 3 ounces, feeding on plankton; (4) the deep-

F

water form ('Tiefseesaibling') living at a depth of 100–350 feet, feeding on plankton and bottom fauna and growing to a length of 4–8 inches.

There are a variety of forms or sub-species of this fish and there still exists a great deal of confusion over the taxonomy of 'char' or, as they are sometimes called, 'charr'. In Canada Leim and Scott (1966) refer to S. *aureolus*, S. *marstoni* and S. *oquassa* as being S. *alpinus* derivatives. Certainly since the time when char became isolated in mountain lakes they have developed along certain lines, so that each isolated group has some different meristic characters, such as variations in numbers of gill-rakers, fin rays and scale counts, which make them recognisable as different species. Tate Regan has listed a large number of species which all exhibit quite marked differences. However, some authorities consider that they are only sub-species or varieties of the arctic char S. *alpinus*. J. Travis Jenkins (1925) gives a very full account of the various 'species' of char and describes their distribution. Char display a variety of rich colours, particularly during the breeding season when they may have brilliant red bellies and hence their name, in some areas, red trout.

In recent years Went and Twomey have made a systematic study of char in Irish loughs and consider Cole's char (S. *colii*) to be the most widely distributed species in Irish waters.

Arctic char in Canadian waters go to sea after spending a number of years in freshwater. They leave the rivers in spring when the ice breaks up and remain relatively close to the shore. They return to freshwater in July and August and there is no evidence that any remain in the sea during the winter. Spawning takes place in September and October on gravel in lakes and deep holes in the rivers. Similar behaviour occurs in Scandinavian waters. For example in the Vardnes River in northern Norway char migrate to sea in spring where they remain to feed during the summer. They return to the river in early autumn to spawn and winter in a small lake (Mathisen and Berg, 1968).

Frost (1963 and 1965) describes an interesting situation in Windermere char, *Salvelinus willughbii*. These fish are either autumn spawners or spring spawners. The autumn spawners have their main breeding period in November, most of them spawning on the lake shore in shallow water and some in the main inflowing stream. The spring spawners spawn in February and March in the lake only and in deep water. It seems highly probable, from the scale pattern and gill-raker number, as well as from the time and place of spawning, that there are two distinct self-perpetuating populations. From rearing experiments in ponds Frost found no evidence that breeding time is inherited and cross-fertilisation experiments reveal no genetical barrier. As Frost says: "although the possibility of some genetical difference cannot be ruled out, the evidence so far suggests that imposition and imprinting are sufficient to explain the division of Windermere charr into autumn and spring breeding populations".

6.4 Grayling

According to the Synopsis of Biological Data on European grayling *Thymallus thymallus* (L) by Jankovic there are four independent species of grayling in Eurasia: these are *Thymallus thymallus*, *T. brevirostris*, *T. nigrescens* and *T. arcticus*. Jankovic deals at some length with the taxonomy of this genus; he also gives the standard and common vernacular names of the grayling used in twenty-one countries and the ranges of systematic characters of grayling populations.

The European grayling is found from 42° 35′ N to almost 70° N and from 65° E to 5° W. Grayling live mostly in the middle course of cool, not very swift rivers with gravel and sandy bottoms. In northern Europe they depend less on rivers and streams and occur abundantly in lakes and also in the coastal waters of northern Sweden and Finland.

The areas occupied by the adult grayling are mainly the typical grayling zones of rivers as described by Huet (1959):

> The grayling zone is characteristic of rivers and larger rapidly-flowing streams. The gradient is generally less than in trout waters and the riffles and rapids are usually separated by pools. The more rapid stretches are inhabited by trout and grayling and the calmer waters in between by the running-water cyprinids. . . . The stream bed is usually of finer material than is common in the trout zone and often is largely of gravel spread out and washed clean by the current.

In northern Europe the 'grayling zone' is less well-defined as grayling may occur from the mountain areas to sea-level.

Grayling spawn in the spring, when the water temperature is above 4° C, between March and the end of May, although in northern Swedish rivers spawning may not finish until mid-June.

Fabricius and Gustafson (1955) found a clear-cut activity rhythm in spawning areas. The males occupy their special enclosed territories in the spawning area in the late morning or early afternoon and leave them at midnight. Maximum spawning occurs between noon and 1900 hours when the water temperature is at its highest. If the water temperature drops during the spawning period spawning may stop for a few days.

Grayling spawn near their normal dwelling place if the water depth, substrate and other conditions are favourable. However, if the area in which the grayling usually live contains no favourable spawning gravel, or if the water temperature in the river or lake is very low at spawning time, the grayling migrate to warmer neighbouring tributaries to spawn. In Sweden the grayling along the coast move into the rivers to spawn, although they are known to spawn along the coast in the northern part of the Gulf of Bothnia.

The eggs are laid about 10 cm deep in the gravel to which the eggs adhere. Grayling eggs in the Indalsalven, Sweden, take about three weeks to hatch while the water temperature rises from 5 to 12° C. The fry remain near the redds some months on occasion, living in the shallow gravelly areas of the streams near the banks. According to Gustafson fry hatched in small tributaries of lakes seem to move downstream into the lakes soon after hatching, and Peterson (1968) refers to the fry going down the rivers to coastal waters.

Most of the fish living in the grayling waters feed on the eggs of grayling, including the grayling themselves. When young, grayling are found on the same sort of river bed as salmon and trout of the same age, i.e. on beds of coarse gravel over which a fairly rapid current is passing. During their first year of life they behave like young salmon and trout in that when disturbed they will take cover under stones.

Young grayling feed on plankton and smaller larval and nymphal stages of the chironomidae, trichoptera, plecoptera and ephemeroptera. Larger grayling feed on the larger larval and nymphal stages of these groups and also molluscs, particularly the river limpet *Ancylus fluviatilis*, which are crushed in the grayling's muscular stomach. It has been found in Sweden that grayling take large numbers of salmon and trout eggs. Large grayling have also been recorded taking other fish species, including roach, perch, whitefish and sticklebacks.

Many anglers believe grayling have an adverse effect on trout and young salmon as they consider they compete with them for the same limited food supply. In a study of the feeding habits of trout and grayling in northern Swedish rivers Muller (1954) found that both occupy different niches, and that there is no similarity between them regarding the selection of bottom fauna as food. This is not surprising if one compares the structure of their mouths. Trout have big mouths, terminally placed and large sharp teeth, while grayling have very small mouths which are ventrally placed and no teeth. However, Jankovic (1964) states: "Grayling and trout are mutual competitors. In smaller streams this often results in trout dominating the colder and swifter parts of the system, while the grayling dominates the lower parts of the river."

When grayling were introduced into a small brook inhabited by sea trout in Jutland, Denmark, the quantity of trout was severely reduced, and in Lake Anjan in central Sweden the trout and char were heavily reduced after the introduction of grayling which multiplied rapidly. In some parts of Scandinavia where lakes are dammed and converted into reservoirs, and where the bottom fauna decreases to some 20% of the pre-damming level, trout numbers decline while the numbers of char and grayling remain relatively unchanged or even increase. In many water systems of the higher parts of western Sweden, trout are reported by many anglers to be decreasing, while the grayling is increasing and this is believed to be due to the amelioration of the climate. So, both a change in the environment and the climate might be reasons for an increase in grayling in certain waters.

Like other members of the salmon family, the grayling is parasitised by the tapeworm *Eubothrium crassum* and the larval stage of the tapeworm *Triaenophorus nodulosus*. The fluke *Crepidostomum farionis* may cause emaciation and intestinal catarrh. The grayling is also attacked by *Argulus*.

The bacterial disease furunculosis may infect grayling where the disease is rife. There is also a very infectious bacterial disease known as grayling pox which has been scarcely studied and is most common in Slovakian and Carpathian waters. At high water temperatures in the summer the grayling also suffer from 'spot disease' which causes a necrosis of the skin and muscles with the appearance of black spots.

6.5 Whitefish

There are a number of species of whitefish or coregonids, and the species in this genus, *Coregonus*, resemble one another very closely (Plate 14). A great deal of work has been done in Sweden on the speciation problem of this genus and it has been found that the number of gill-rakers can be used as a taxonomic characteristic. The coregonids occurring in the British Isles, using the nomenclature given by Wheeler (1969), are:

Scotland (1) The Lochmaben Vendace – *Coregonus albula*, now only occurring in the Mill Loch near Lochmaben, Dumfriesshire.

(2) The Powan – *C. clupeoides*, occurring in Loch Lomond and Loch Eck.

England (3) The Cumberland Vendace – *C. albula*, found in lakes Derwentwater and Bassenthwaite.

(4) The Schelly – *C. lavaretus* in Haweswater, Ullswater and Red Tarn.

(5) The Houting – *C. oxyrhinchus*. This is a migratory species living in the south-eastern part of the North Sea and breeding in some continental rivers and occurring only occasionally in some English rivers in the south-east.

Ireland (6) The Lough Neagh Pollan – *C. albula*.
   (7) The Lough Erne Pollan – *C. albula*.
   (8) The Shannon Pollan – *C. albula*.

Wales (9) The Gwyniad – *C. lavaretus*, present in Lake Bala.
There is still much taxonomic work to be done on this genus.

Slack, Gervers and Hamilton (1957) made a detailed study of the powan in Loch Lomond. The powan was found to spawn in early January on the lake bed where stones and gravel were situated off headlands and on submerged offshore banks. Unlike most other salmonids, the eggs are scattered at random and are only adhesive a short time after fertilisation. An interesting aspect of this study was the estimation of predation on the powan eggs. The predation is particularly heavy in the first few weeks of their embryonic life from adult powan, which stay on the spawning grounds for about two months, and the larvae of a caddis fly, *Phryganea* (Fig.34). During one season 65% of the stock of eggs was killed by *Phryganea*, a further 30% were either infertile or had died from other causes, such as fungal attack. A 95% mortality at the egg stage is extremely high and much

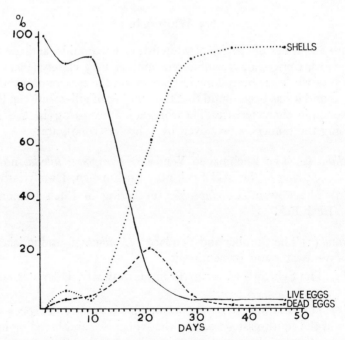

Fig. 34. The predation of *Phryganea* larvae on eggs of powan (from Slack, 1955).

higher than that occurring in other salmonids where the mortality at the egg stage is often as little as 5%.

Slack (1955) found that some of the factors controlling the numbers of mature fish were predation by pike and lampreys (17% of about one thousand powan examined showed fresh or, more often, healed wounds made by *Petromyzon*).

In a study of the diet of the adult powan Slack, Gervers and Hamilton found that the majority of their food consists of planktonic organisms and from June to November it constitutes 85% of their diet.

One of the most important species of whitefish occurring in North America is *Coregonus clupeaformis*. This species, which spawns in lakes in late October or November, is mainly a bottom feeder.

A lake dwelling form in the deep lakes of north Germany, particularly in Pomerania, is the lavaret (*C. lavaretus maraena*). It is often kept in fishponds (e.g. Czechoslovakia) and recently in artificial reservoirs.

An example of the care and work that is involved in separating the coregonid species is seen in a study of the *Coregonus* populations of the Sundsvall Bay district in Sweden. By means of gillraker counts on more than 1300 specimens Lindroth (1957) was able to divide the populations into two groups. In a rearing experiment it was proved that the number of gillrakers is genetically fixed and that the two groups are therefore genetically different and can be ranked as species. These two species are *C. lavaretus* which spawns in the large rivers and *C. nasus* which spawns by the coast. The offspring of *C. lavaretus* leave the rivers passively as eggs and fry.

Some work on the hybridisation of coregonid species has been done by Svärdson (1949, 1950 and 1952) and Maitland (1967). Experiments such as these will be of considerable value in that they will produce some evidence on modifications caused by the environment.

6.6 Danube salmon

The Danube salmon or Huchen, *Hucho hucho* (L.), occurs in the Danube river basin, preferring the upper reaches of the tributaries of this large river in the following countries: German Federal Republic, Austria, Czechoslovakia, Poland, Hungary, Romanian People's Republic, Bulgaria, Yugoslavia and Russia. The rivers in which it occurs in these countries are listed by Prawochensky and Kolder (1968) in their Synopsis of Biological Data on *Hucho hucho* published by F.A.O.

The Danube salmon is a spring spawner, spawning in March and April in the upper courses of highland rivers. During this time the fish are red in colour and are called 'Rotfish' or 'Rothuchen' in Austria and Germany. After spawning, the adults go downstream and keep close to deep places and rocks where the Näsling or Broad-snout *Chondrostoma nasus*, their principal food, occurs.

The habitat requirements of this large fish, which can grow up to 2 metres in length, are: well-oxygenated water; water with a maximum temperature of $+15°$ C; river bed of coarse sand and gravel; waters with a fast, strong current and deep holes, and plenty of food.

The young fish are fierce predators and remain about a year in the spawning areas before dropping downstream in search of deeper water. The fish grow rapidly and may live up to 20 years. The food of the Danube salmon is mainly fish. It feeds on all available species. In spring it feeds on cyprinidae which gather in the spawning areas. In summer it preys mainly on the näsling or broad-snout, which live in shoals, and, in autumn and winter, seeks the deeper water where other fish spend the cold season in large numbers. Because this species is such a predator it is not popular with some fishermen who believe that it destroys the trout and grayling populations.

PART III

THE ENVIRONMENT,
THE RESOURCE AND MAN

Chapter 7

THE AQUATIC ENVIRONMENT

7.1 Biochemical cycle. 7.2 A lake environment. 7.3 Running
waters. 7.4 Habitat needs of salmonid fish. 7.5 Inter-relationships. 7.6 Ecological succession. 7.7 Production.

7.1 Biochemical cycle

In order to achieve successful conservation and efficient management, and
plan other development schemes, it is essential to know something of the
environment in which the animal lives and the habitat requirements of that
animal. This knowledge is also essential for those responsible for land and
water development schemes so that they may know how they are going to
affect the environment and what changes in the environment are likely to
occur. Unless one is familiar with the basic principles, such as the biochemical cycle, one cannot appreciate, for example, differences in the
various types of lake, nor the existing inter-relationships.

Due to the energy from the sun in the form of light and heat the mineral
substances or nutrients, including carbonic acid which is present in the
water, are converted or transformed by the green plants (the producers)
into organic substances. The nutrients in solution originate from (1) the
ground with which the water is in contact – the geology of the area is therefore important; (2) atmospheric precipitation; (3) mineralisation of detritus,
accumulated in the water, by bacteria and fungi, and from products in the
detritus or from outside; (4) outside sources such as industry and agriculture.

The aquatic vegetation includes the lower plants in suspension in the
water, the phytoplankton (diatoms and desmids), those covering the surfaces of the stones, etc., the filamentous algae and the higher plants –
submerged, floating or paludal (marsh). Some of this vegetation is consumed either living or dead by the herbivorous invertebrates and fish

(primary consumers), while some is reintroduced into the biochemical cycle in the form of detritus by fungi and bacteria (decomposers). Some of the herbivores are consumed by the carnivores (secondary consumers), while others escape the carnivores and are reintroduced into the cycle after death due to bacterial activity.

Within the carnivorous fauna the weaker or smaller organisms form, living or dead, part of the food for other carnivorous elements. An essential metabolic phase of the biochemical cycle in the water is the mineralisation effected by bacteria. The detritus accumulated from the death of the flora and fauna, as well as the detritus coming from outside, are broken down by invertebrates and bacteria and reintroduced into the biochemical cycle as simple elements which can be used by green plants in assimilation. In addition to this source of elements there is that which comes from the faeces of the whole aquatic fauna.

7.2 A lake environment

There are three major zones in a lake – the littoral, the limnetic or offshore zone and the profundal zone which occurs below the light compensation level. The littoral or shallow zone may be large in relation to the area of the lake or small, depending on the formation of the lake basin. The littoral area is that in which the rooted aquatic vegetation will occur depending on the nature of the bottom. A large littoral zone is usually indicative of relatively high organic production. The limnetic or offshore zone extends down as far as the light compensation level. The flora in this zone consists chiefly of phytoplankton.

During the summer months a typical lake may be divided into an upper warm epilimnion and a lower cold hypolimnion, which are to all intents and purposes completely separate. All plant growth takes place in the epilimnion. This division or stratification of a lake into two parts is of great importance. The division into two layers starts to occur after winter when the lake has a uniform temperature from top to bottom of about 4° C. As the sun increases in strength with the lengthening days the upper layers of the lake will be warmed. It is only the upper layers that are warmed because the heating part of the sun's rays is soon absorbed in water. Water has the greatest specific heat and, as it is so great, a lake must absorb vast quantities of heat to increase its temperature by 1° C. Warm water is lighter than cold water and consequently floats on top of it. By early summer the two layers are established with such a big temperature difference between them that they remain separate for the rest of the summer, although in shallow lakes there may never be this division owing to constant mixing due to wind and currents and this is the position in most Scottish lakes. The area between the epilimnion and hypolimnion, where the temperature changes rapidly, is known as the thermocline (Fig. 35). Once there is this firm demarcation, the warm upper layer of water increases in temperature relatively rapidly, and it also increases in depth because when disturbed by the wind it mixes with eddies of cold water from below. The rivers and streams flowing into a lake are usually at a temperature well above that of the hypolimnion and will therefore mix only with the epilimnion.

With the shortening of the days in the autumn, and lower air temperatures, temperature is lost by radiation. The epilimnion begins to cool down and is eventually eliminated by severe wind action causing an 'overturn' so that the whole lake assumes the same temperature.

Since light does not penetrate far into water, plant growth is only possible in the upper layers, and is nearly always confined to the epilimnion. Algae are present in the water all through the winter. Early in the year these algae begin to multiply and become very abundant producing concentrations known as 'blooms' (Fig. 36). Shortly after the main production of algae comes the period when the minute floating animals or zooplankton appear in large numbers.

These various plants and animals die and decompose. Some of the decaying fragments sink into the hypolimnion and decay at a slower rate on account of the low temperature. Oxygen is used up during the decomposition process and there is no source from which the oxygen may be replenished. Consequently the concentration falls steadily through the summer. The extent of depletion of the oxygen in the hypolimnion depends on the amount of decaying matter and on the depth of the thermocline. Productively

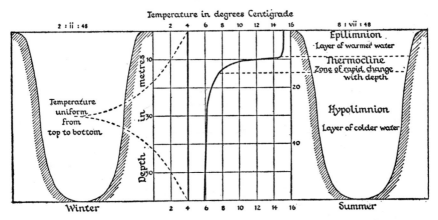

FIG. 35. Temperature of Lake Windermere at different depths on 2 February 1948 and 8 July 1948 (from Macan and Worthington, 1951. Reproduced by permission of Collins).

'rich' lakes generally are subject to greater oxygen depletion during the summer than 'poor' lakes, because the 'rain' of organic matter from the limnetic or littoral zones into the profundal zone is greater in the former.

The type of lake that concerns us in relation to salmon and trout are divided into two categories, those that have a low primary productivity and those that have a high primary productivity. Those with a low primary productivity are known as oligotrophic (few foods) lakes which either lie in a glacial rock basin or are made artificially in mountain regions. These lakes are deep with the hypolimnion larger than the epilimnion. There is a very small littoral area and plants are scarce and plankton density is low. Plankton blooms are rare since nutrients rarely accumulate in sufficient amounts to produce an outburst of phytoplankton. Because of low productivity of these lakes, the hypolimnion is not subject to severe oxygen depletion, therefore cold-water fish such as lake trout, char and whitefish are characteristic of, and often restricted to, the hypolimnion of oligotrophic lakes. Oligotrophic lakes are still 'geologically young' and have changed but little since the time of formation.

Eutrophic (good foods) lakes are shallower, have a small hypolimnion and a greater primary productivity and are usually situated on plains. Littoral vegetation is more abundant, plankton populations are denser and 'blooms' are characteristic.

While lakes can generally be divided into oligo- and eutrophic types there are some which have the appearance of, say, oligotrophic lakes but are rich in nutrients, and vice versa.

There are also some lakes classified as being dystrophic. These are rich in organic matter, which consist of undecomposed plant fragments such as peat. There is little decomposition because of a deficiency of calcium. The result is a considerable accumulation on the bottom of a characteristic deposit, but a scarcity in solution of nutrient salts on which plant life might be supported. These waters are often stained brown.

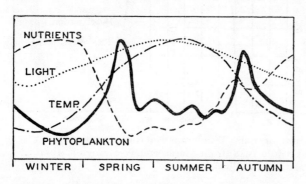

FIG. 36

The probable mechanism for phytoplankton 'blooms' (from Odum, 1951).

7.3 Running waters

Running waters differ from lakes in a number of respects: usually the depth of all running water units is small compared to lakes; with the exception of those channel expansions sometimes known as river lakes, the water is confined to a relatively narrow channel; the whole volume of water flows in one direction; physical, chemical and biological conditions gradually change with distance along the main channel and in a definite direction. Stream systems increase their length, width and depth (to base level) with increasing age, this is in distinct contrast to the reduction process characteristic of all standing water units. There is a permanent removal of eroded and transported materials in running waters. At any position along the course of a running water unit, materials eroded at that point and all materials momentarily suspended or dissolved at that level are transported downstream with no opportunity of return. In lakes, such materials commonly remain within the basin. Physical factors of a running water environment are often relatively more important than they are in lentic situations. Most streams produce within themselves little basic food materials but depend much more upon the contribution from the surrounding land than do most lakes.

The course of a river may be divided into a number of zones (Table 17). A river usually originates in a hilly or mountainous region, where the gradient is steep, and it flows to the sea passing through land where the gradient becomes less and less steep and the flow of the river consequently becomes slower. One therefore starts with a torrential zone (sometimes classified as a Highland Brook) where the flow is fast and where no animals can maintain themselves because of the water velocity and where only boulders or bedrock make up the bed of the stream. The torrential zone in its lower section becomes the trout zone or troutbeck, the flow is still fast but gravel and stones are able to withstand normal flows although less stable gravel may be set in motion during floods. Here a bottom community of animals specially adapted to withstand the velocity of the water has become established. As the gradient becomes less steep the river passes into the grayling zone or minnow reach. Here some silt has been deposited in the quieter areas such as the eddies and pools, and aquatic plants become established. More animals are able to find shelter and food in this habitat and there is consequently a higher species diversity. In the lower reaches of the river the gradient is shallow and this section of the river (known as the coarse fish reach or an upper barbel zone and a lower bream zone) is the area in which there is less transportation of stones and silt, and more deposition. In this zone the habitat requirements, such as silt-free gravel for spawning, high dissolved oxygen concentrations and suitable water temperatures, for salmonids are no longer present. These fish are now succeeded by the cyprinids which have different reproductive requirements and which are able to tolerate the lower dissolved oxygen concentrations, warmer water temperatures and greater turbidity which are characteristics of this part of the river.

Not all rivers have these courses. The first obviously depends on the existence of hills which are fairly high and not permeable to water as, for example, chalk hills are. Or the later ones may be missing, and a torrential zone may run into the sea with no slackening of the current. Rivers change during the passage of time and the changes are in the direction of shorter and less torrential mountain courses and longer and more meandering lowland courses. Macan and Worthington (1951) say that it is convenient to speak of a young or primitive and an old or evolved river, applying these terms not as an indication of the tale of years but as an indication of the stage of development which has been reached. For this reason salmonids thrive best in what are actually temporary communities.

TABLE 17

Huet's classification of European river zones (Huet, 1949, 1954)

	Trout zone	Grayling[1] (Minnow) zone	Barbel[1] (Chub) zone	Bream zone
Gradient	very steep	steep	gentle	very gentle
Current	very rapid	rapid	moderate	slow
Type of fish fauna	salmonid	mixed, with salmonids predominating	mixed, with cyprinids predominating	cyprinid, with predators

Fishes usually present (those underlined are most common; those in square brackets are uncommon)

	trout, salmon parr, minnow, bullhead, stoneloach	fish of trout zone grayling[1] cyprinids of running water [complementary cyprinids] [complementary predators]	[fish of trout zone] [grayling] cyprinids of running water complementary cyprinids complementary predators [cyprinids of still water]	[cyprinids of running water] complementary cyprinids complementary predators cyprinids of still water

Cyprinids of running water include: barbel[1], chub, dace, gudgeon, bleak.
Complementary cyprinids include: rudd, roach.
Complementary predators include: perch, pike, eel.
Cyprinids of still water include: tench, bream, white bream, carp.
[1] The grayling and barbel have limited distributions in British waters but are much more common in continental rivers.

7.4 Habitat needs of salmonid fish

In order that a given population of fish can exist it is necessary that the fish are able to live and develop normally. This means that the ecological conditions must be satisfactory. If any one of the required conditions for a particular species is altered, even though all the others are acceptable, the habitat will no longer be suitable for the successful life cycle of that species. It is therefore important that when a habitat is managed all conditions necessary for the successful existence of the species under consideration are available. If we have a look at some of the requirements the effects of altering the habitat will be appreciated.

Respiratory needs. The needs are very different from one species to another. Salmonids require a high dissolved oxygen concentration. The importance of dissolved oxygen, essential for the respiration of the fish, is very marked. Fish are very sensitive to any decrease in the volume of oxygen and die of asphyxia very quickly. It is important, therefore, that fish never have to withstand a lethal dose even for a short period.

The amount of dissolved oxygen in the water depends mainly on the water temperature, the amount of organic matter, and underwater vegetation. In natural waters the most important factor influencing the amount of dissolved oxygen is temperature, and the higher the water temperature the lower the dissolved oxygen concentration. Oxygen consumption, especially through the oxidation of organic matter, is also increased with increase in water temperature.

The amount of dissolved oxygen also depends on the quality of organic substances found in the water. If this quality is high, the oxidation of these substances uses up a considerable amount of the dissolved oxygen in the water, and the concentration can decrease below the necessary minimum. This can happen from natural causes. It happens during the stagnation period in the hypolimnion of eutrophic lakes; it also happens in winter under the ice in stagnant water that has a weak current; it often happens in water polluted by organic matter from domestic sewage and some types of industry.

The amount of dissolved oxygen normally required by fish, and the minimum concentration they can tolerate, differ drastically from one type to another. The minimum dose permissible for trout is from 5·0 to 5·5 mg per litre. Quantities that are markedly lower can be tolerated, but only for a short time. There are no absolute minimum amounts supported by fish, they depend on many ambient factors such as temperature, and those properties of the fish itself such as species, age, size and activity. Young fish or breeding fish have greater needs, for example salmonid eggs lying in the gravel need water rich in oxygen.

In practice natural salmonid waters should have a dissolved oxygen concentration of at least 80% of saturation, locally and temporarily this amount can be reduced to not less than 5 mg per litre.

Reproductive requirements. The most important reproductive requirements are temperature and a suitable substrate. As temperature is an important factor affecting so many physiological conditions I shall deal with it separately later.

The nature of the stream and lake bed is most important for the spawning of salmonids. Trout kept in ponds, or even in streams with a sandy bottom, do not reproduce. Trout, like salmon, require fast-flowing streams with a stony or gravelly bottom. In these conditions they can lay their eggs and the stream flow provides a constant supply of oxygen-rich water. Equally important is the free access to these spawning places. Access can be inhibited or made impossible by dams and pollution. Damming often results in a change in the water temperature. This in turn can cause a modification in the composition of the fish population. Alteration of ecological conditions in reservoirs with fluctuating water levels reacts in different ways upon the species of fish which spawn in lakes. In several species the presence of the correct spawning substrate is of greater importance than depth and such species are able to increase the vertical extent of their spawning ranges to take advantage of suitable gravel uncovered by erosion when the water levels are lowered. Thus char in Sweden and lake trout in Canada were not eliminated due to eggs being stranded by falling lake levels, but extended their spawning into deeper water. In Sweden, grayling also extended their spawning sites from riverine gravels to eroded lake shores.

Conditions of habitat. Certain species of fish live in open water, either in the median zone of streams or in the pelagic region of lakes and ponds. Other types of fish living in the marginal or littoral zones of streams need aquatic vegetation and the protection of the cover provided by riverside vegetation, which also provides food in the form of terrestrial insects for the fish and also invertebrate fauna. Trout in streams need sheltered areas and hiding places in the form of stones and boulders. If any of this protection is missing as a result of damming, dredging or tree felling the fish may leave that habitat.

Temperature. Water temperature is a critical factor in the life of fish and other water organisms. It affects to a considerable degree respiration, growth and reproduction of fish. Each species of fish has a thermal tolerance zone in which it behaves in a normal manner; also there is a zone of higher temperature and one of a lower temperature in which the species can survive for a certain length of time above and below which the temperatures are lethal. A gradual and regular acclimatisation allows certain species of fish to survive in temperatures that would be fatal if they occurred suddenly. Fish adapt themselves quickly to a rise in temperature, but less easily to a drop in temperature. Varley (1967) distinguished three groups of fish according to upper lethal temperatures:

(a) Fish with upper lethal limits below 28° C and having optimum temperatures for growth between 7 and 17° C, e.g. salmonids, these are stenotherms.

(b) Fish with upper lethal temperatures between 28° C and 34° C and spawn only at temperatures of 10° C or more, e.g. pike, perch and roach.

(c) Fish with upper lethal limits above 34° C and spawn only when the water temperature is 15° C or higher, e.g. carp, tench and probably rudd and bream; these are eurytherms.

Water temperature influences the growth of fish considerably, the optimum temperature varying according to species. The variation in rate of growth in relation to water temperature has already been mentioned.

Temperature is also an important factor in fish reproduction. Fish only spawn when the water reaches a suitable temperature, for example some salmonids (salmon, trout, char and whitefish) spawn in winter at low temperatures while others, such as grayling, the Danube salmon, and rainbow trout spawn in spring when the water temperature is rising.

It has also been shown with regard to both the migration of adult salmon and the downstream migration of smolts that temperature is an important factor.

Acidity. There are a number of other water properties needed by fish which, if altered, may affect their habitat and numbers. One of these is the pH or acidity. The best water for fish is that which possesses a slightly alkaline reaction, in other words a pH of between 7·0 and 8·0. Fish can tolerate acid or alkaline pH levels but the limits should be between 5·0 and 9·5.

Miscellaneous. The presence of suspended and dissolved matter in the water is of great importance to fish. If the water is too turbid its productivity may be affected. The shortage of light prevents or interferes with plankton and aquatic plant production. Tarzwell (1957), for instance, mentioned finding seven times fewer organisms in a river downstream from a mine than upstream. However, Hamilton (1961) concluded that high turbidity produced by finely divided organic matter does not, by itself, affect adversely the bottom fauna in a shallow lotic environment. It is only when a thick layer of such material covers the bottom that the normal fauna cannot be found. While turbidity can be due to natural causes, such as milky and cold water following melting glaciers or snow, it can also be the result of pollution caused by quarries and gravel pits. Turbidity can be caused by solid particles that settle quickly or by colloidal matter that remains in suspension for a long time. Erosion from various causes, especially deforestation, can have serious and damaging consequences.

In general, turbidity is more harmful to the nutritive richness of the water than directly to the fish. Disturbed water and the resultant deposits can also interfere with or completely prevent the reproduction of fish by destroying the eggs or spawning beds (Hamilton, 1961). There are also some dissolved substances present in natural waters which are harmful to fish such as excess iron and sulphur.

7.5 Inter-relationships

As Nikolsky (1963) states:

> The inter-relationships between the fish and the elements of its environment are not isolated, they are interdependent, and any changes in one system of relationships inevitably produce changes in the other; all the inter-relationships of the organism with its environment are interconnected. The character of the interaction of the fish with any particular elements of its environment depends to a significant extent upon the condition of the fish itself; its state of nourishment, fat content, state of maturity, etc. A fish can react differently to the same stimulus according to its biological condition. All these factors must be taken into account in studying the interactions of the fish with any particular element of its abiotic or biotic environment.

A number of terms have been applied to these relationships. Macan (1963) uses 'predation' when one species reduces the numbers of another by eating it; and 'competition' in which one species overcomes another without having resource to predation.

In many management practices it is the habit to exercise predator control. In many instances this control is undertaken without regard for the relationships existing between predator and prey species. For example, it is the practice to remove predatory fish, such as the pike, from waters in order to improve trout fishing or safeguard salmon smolts migrating through a lake containing these predators. However, it has been found (Mills, 1964a) that when pike were being removed from such waters the first thing that happened was for the average size of the pike to decrease and so the first effect of controlling the numbers of pike was to increase the rate of predation on young salmon because, as the size range of pike had altered, more smaller prey species (such as young salmon) and fewer large prey species (such as trout, char and other pike) were eaten. Furthermore large trout, previously taken by large pike, were no longer preyed on and were therefore available in greater numbers to prey on salmon smolts.

Another fish which is sometimes removed from game fish waters is the perch. However, the removal of perch may disturb the food relations of fish to the detriment of young salmon, as perch are an important forage fish for pike and, with a decline in the numbers of perch, the pike would be compelled to eat other fish species to a greater extent. This condition was anticipated by Worthington (1949) who, after three seasons of intensive perch trapping in Windermere, decided to start pike netting. Furthermore, perch and trout, having a similar diet, might compete with each other for the available food. Worthington has suggested that the decline in the trout and char populations in Windermere was due to the abundance of perch, and considers that the trout and char have increased after a number of years of intensive perch fishing.

Competition takes many forms, for example many salmonid fish show aggressive behaviour from an early age. Fry of both trout and salmon establish territories soon after starting to feed, and each territory consists of a central refuge from which sallies are made to catch food. When 250 trout fry were placed in an aquarium all obtained territories, but when more were put in some failed to establish a territory and these spent their time hiding or being chased from the territories of the dominant fry. Those without territories were soon smaller than the others. Symons (1968) suggested that an increase in aggression which has also been found to occur upon food deprivation could function to increase the size of feeding territories when food is scarce. This and the strengthening of hierarchies would cause emigration of some fish from the area.

It is said that young salmon rely on stylised threat posture to drive interlopers away and trout more on actual attack. For this reason, as well as a faster growth rate, trout are considered to be the more successful when the two species are in competition.

Nilsson (1955) found in Sweden two lakes in both of which char and trout occurred and a third where there were char only. When both occurred together, char were confined to deeper water, where they fed on bottom fauna in winter, on airborne insects in June, and then on waterfleas, whereas trout in the shallow water fed on bottom fauna all the year round and also on airborne insects in late summer. Both species appeared to be feeding on whatever was most readily available in their respective habitats. In the lake with no trout, char occupied the shallow as well as the deep water, and fed on much the same food as the trout in the other lakes. They grew large on this diet, and in shallow water these big fish appeared to belong to a distinct race from the smaller char occurring in the deeper water which behaved as all char did when trout were present. It has also been noted that trout regularly spawn both in running water and in the lakes themselves when living in the absence of char, whereas in the presence of char they spawn only in running water.

When new species are introduced to a country they may have to compete with species already present. When attempts were made to establish American brook trout and rainbow trout in French streams they were successful only in waters where brown trout were absent. Where they had to compete with brown trout they were unsuccessful. When the brown trout was introduced into North American waters it was more successful as its slightly higher thermal death point enabled it to establish itself in some places where the brook trout could not live.

Brown trout were successfully introduced into New Zealand lakes and grew to a large size, but when rainbow trout were also introduced to the same waters there were instances, such as Lake Taupo, where the brown trout numbers started to diminish. This was because the rainbow trout spawn in the spring and, in laying their eggs in the gravel of the streams running into the lakes, displace the autumn laid eggs of the brown trout which are then eaten or perish.

7.6 Ecological succession

Odum states that: "Ecological succession is the orderly process of community change; it is the sequence of communities which replace one another in a given area." Typically, in an ecosystem, community development begins with pioneer stages which are replaced by a series of more mature communities until a relatively stable community is evolved which is in equilibrium with the local conditions. The whole series of communities which develop in a given situation is called the sere; the relatively transitory communities are called seral stages or seral communities, and the final or mature community is called the climax.

Ecological succession is directional, so that in situations where the process is well known the seral stage present at any given time may be recognised and the future changes predicted. Succession in freshwater areas will vary in rate and pattern, depending upon the extent of the aquatic area and the net rate of movement. In lakes, ponds and swamps, where water does not exhibit any gross movement over long periods from one geographic locality to another, a silting-in process will determine the rate of succession. Silting-in refers to the soil which is introduced into a quiet body of water from outlying areas by rivers, brooks and small streams. The rate at which this process occurs depends upon the amount of erosion that will occur in the area's neighbouring streams, the types of soil in surrounding areas, the amount of precipitation and the type of precipitation. The number, size and rate of flow of streams introducing this soil into a lake, pond or bog will also affect the rate of silting-in. As this build-up of soil material continues uninterrupted over a period of years, the entire lake or pond will accumulate so much soil that the body of water becomes shallower. Eventually a bog or swamp type of habitat will appear, and finally some types of forest may become established in the area. Around the shoreline of any lake or pond there will be zones of vegetation. These concentric rings of vegetation change position relative to the original shoreline as silt accumulation continues and the water gradually becomes shallower. As the shoreline moves towards the centre of the lake or pond the vegetation moves in the same direction over a period of time.

Not all aquatic successions lead to land communities. Where the body of water is large or deep, or where there is strong wave action, succession may lead to a stable aquatic community which undergoes no further change, or else only a limited change. Gilson (1966) refers to the biological implications arising from impounding Morecambe Bay behind a barrage and states that he is inclined to predict a good trout fishery in the reservoir for the first few years. As time passes, however, and the salt leaches out, the weed would increase and the reservoir would become much more of a coarse fish habitat.

An interesting example of succession is that resulting from enrichment of water, or eutrophication as it is often termed, by domestic drainage. Hasler (1947) describes this process in the Zürichsee, a lake in the foothills of the Alps. The lake is composed of two distinct basins, the Obersee and the Untersee, separated only by a narrow passage. In the past five decades the deeper of the two, at one time a decidedly oligotrophic lake, became strongly eutrophic owing to urban effluents from a group of small communities. The shallower of the two received no major urban effluent and retained its oligotrophic characteristics. It was noticed that along with domestic fertilisation the Zürichsee changed from a whitefish (coregonid) lake to a coarse fish lake. Hasler lists further examples of Alpine and Finnish lakes in which the populations of whitefish have been replaced by coarse fish.

It can be seen that from a study of ecological succession we can predict the consequence of any developments which man may plan, or the situations which may occur naturally and we are therefore in a better position to manage the resource more efficiently.

7.7 Production

Having started this chapter with a description of the biochemical cycle and some of its components and followed on with a description of the aquatic environment and how the fauna are interrelated, it is useful to conclude by bringing all these aspects together with an account of production so as to complete our proper understanding of the freshwater ecosystem.

Allen (1947) defines annual production as the actual amount of new living matter of the kind under consideration which has been produced during the year, either by the growth of old individuals, or by the production and subsequent growth of new individuals, whether these individuals have survived to the end of the year or not. It is equal to the algebraic sum of the amount dying or otherwise leaving the area during the year and the increase in the standing stock. The annual production bears no fixed relation either to the standing stock at a particular time, or to any increase in the stock during the year. Where the stock is the same at the end as at the beginning of the year – the average case in a stable population – the annual production equals the amount dying or otherwise leaving during the year.

If the annual production of an invertebrate population is a given amount, then in the ideal case, which never occurs in reality, the annual production of a fish population living on it would be a similar amount. Fish do not consume the entire production of the invertebrates, and there is an incomplete conversion into additional fish material of that which is eaten. In the simple case of stable stocks, that portion of the annual production of invertebrates which is not eaten by fish dies in other ways. Either it dies while immature, through disease or as the victim of some predator, or else it survives to maturity and completes its life cycle. Completion of the life cycle does not necessarily mean that individuals concerned do not contribute to the production of the next stage in the chain, since fish may feed on the bodies of insects of aquatic origin which have returned to the water after breeding.

The food which is available to the invertebrates is utilised in the production of a great number of types, and these vary greatly in the extent to which they are consumed by fish. This is partly due to differences in the habits of the animals, which results in a varying availability to the fish as food. So the proportion of the original plant material which is ultimately converted into fish will vary according to the type of invertebrate through which it passes. The relative extent of consumption of different invertebrates varies not only from one species of fish to another, but also for fish of the same species according to their size and age. For related fish of similar habits, such as the salmon and trout, the differences between size groups of fish are generally greater than those between species.

Of the food actually consumed by the fish only a certain amount can be used for growth as some of the food consumed is required for maintenance, and it is only the surplus which is converted into additional fish flesh. The maintenance level varies considerably with temperature, and with the size of the fish. The normal maintenance requirements for brown trout may be about 5% to 10% of body wet weight per week. It is only food in excess of this amount which is available for growth. The weight of flesh produced in trout supplied with abundant food is normally about 10% to 25% of the total food intake.

The efficiency of conversion under natural conditions varies between very wide limits, since it depends primarily on the excess of the food intake over maintenance requirements. In addition to the physical and other environmental factors, such as temperature, which control feeding activity, it is also affected by the amount of food available to the fish; that is by the relation between the standing stock of the fish and the annual production of the invertebrate fauna. As a result of these factors the annual production of a fish population, feeding upon an invertebrate fauna with a given productivity, is held at a certain level.

Backiel and Le Cren (1967) have published a schematic representation of the production process in an animal trophic system. The figure (Fig. 37) has been designed to show the main processes which are as follows:

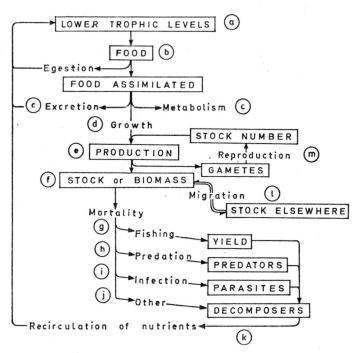

FIG. 37. Diagrammatic representation of some of the influences of population density on the production processes in fish (from Backiel and Le Cren, 1961).

(*a*) The production of food for the fish being considered, including the population and production dynamics of the food organisms.

(*b*) The feeding of the fish and the assimilation of some of this food, the remainder being egested as faeces.

(*c*) The loss of some of the matter and energy assimilated in metabolic processes including excretion.

(*d*) The growth of the individual fish.

(*e*) The sum of the growth of all the individuals in the stock, or the production, including the production of gonad products.

(*f*) The accumulation of this production as stock or biomass which in turn suffers loss through mortality of several kinds. The principal sources of mortality are:

(*g*) Fishing, giving yield to man.

(*h*) Predation, leading to production of predators.

(*i*) Infection by parasites and pathogens leading to the production of parasites. (Some parasites remove material and energy from the system at other stages, e.g. between the ingestion and assimilation of food or between the assimilation of food and growth. Many parasites may not cause the death of fish, but for the sake of simplicity in this scheme all parasites are considered as equivalent to predators.)

(*j*) Other causes of mortality including diseases not due to parasites or pathogens, accidents and pollution.

(*k*) Some of the organic matter in all the fish that die will return as either organic matter or mineral nutrients to the lower trophic levels.

(*l*) As well as mortality and natality, emigration and immigration will have similar negative and positive effects upon the stock.

(*m*) Reproduction or the replenishment of the stock with new individuals, is an essential process. Production contributes to this in the form of the matter (and energy) contained in the fertilised egg.

Chapter 8

MAN'S ACTIVITIES
AND THEIR EFFECTS ON
THE ENVIRONMENT AND RESOURCE

8.1 Pollution. 8.2 Forestry. 8.3 Agriculture.
8.4 Water abstraction. 8.5 Hydro-electric development.

Freshwaters and their associated flora and fauna may be affected in many ways by man's activities. The man-made changes having the most effect on the salmon and trout fisheries are those associated with the exploitation and development of other natural resources such as forestry, agriculture, water power and various industries such as mining. Many of these have, at some stage of their development or exploitation, similar effects on the aquatic environment, for example pollution. As pollution commonly results from so many man-made practices it will be considered first, after which the effects of other man-made changes associated with his other activities will be described in turn.

8.1 Pollution

The physical, chemical and biological effects of pollution can, from an ecological point of view, be divided into five categories, one or more of which may be characteristic of any one effluent. Sewage, for example, is capable of producing all five types of effect. These categories are: poisons, suspended solids, de-oxygenation, non-toxic salts and heating of the water. In practice these effects rarely occur singly, but for convenience they will be considered separately.

Poisons. Poisons in solution occur in waste waters from many industries. They include acids and alkalis; chromium salts from tanning and electro-plating and zinc from galvanising; phenols and cyanides from

chemical industries and mines, and insecticides from sheep dips and agricultural chemicals. The commonest toxic inorganic substances are free
chlorine, ammonia, hydrogen sulphide and salts of many heavy metals (e.g.
copper, lead, zinc, chromium, silver and mercury). Any appreciable
amounts of these compounds may kill fish or other aquatic life. Copper and
zinc affect the gills and cause respiration troubles. Phosphorus causes
haemolysis and rapid death. Some of these substances are rapidly precipitated in the waters into which they flow, but others are very persistent. A
few, such as ammonia are destroyed fairly rapidly by oxidation, while
others such as phenolic and cyanide compounds are similarly destroyed,
but much more slowly. Streams polluted by the heavy metals lead, zinc
and copper in concentrations measured in parts per million or less can be
rendered practically devoid of all animal life. From studies of lead pollution
in Wales and copper–zinc pollution in eastern Canada it has been shown that
biological conditions in the streams can be closely connected with the metallic content of the water (Carpenter, 1924). Poisons usually decrease steadily
in concentration. This is partly because the volume of diluting water in any
river increases as more tributaries join it, and partly because many poisons,
such as metals, are precipitated by chemical action, while others, particularly organic compounds, are oxidised and changed into non-toxic materials.
A number of toxic discharges also originate from agricultural chemicals
such as insecticides, herbicides, fungicides, sheep dip and chemicals used
for destroying rats and rabbits.

There are two main groups of synthetic insecticides, the chlorinated
hydrocarbons and the organo-phosphorus compounds. The former are
generally regarded as the more toxic to fish. This group includes benzene
hexachloride (B.H.C.), D.D.T., aldrin, dieldrin, endrin and heptachlor.
Some of these chemicals present an added danger in that they are resistant
to breakdown by the digestive processes of mammals, birds or fish and are
concentrated in the food chain. Residues of D.D.T., dieldrin and heptachlor have been found in various forms of wildlife, mainly in fatty tissues.
An example of the contamination of a trout population in a lake by a discharge of dieldrin from an industrial establishment is provided by Loch
Leven, Kinross-shire. This discharge, which had continued for several
years, ceased in 1964. The actual amount discharged into the lake is not
known, but dieldrin was found in fish long before it was realised that the
source was primarily industrial, rather than agricultural.

Large-scale spraying of forest areas with D.D.T. in Canada and the
United States has caused severe fish mortalities. In northern New Brunswick, which we have seen to be an important salmon area with rivers such
as the Miramichi, these spraying operations were directed against the
spruce budworm. Each spring since 1952 large forest areas were sprayed.

Some areas were sprayed at intervals of one, two or three years. In spite of this the budworm population continued to expand until in 1957 over 5 million acres of New Brunswick forest were sprayed, and nine years later, in 1966, 8·5 million acres or 56% of the province's forest were sprayed. In 1954 the effects of spraying one watershed were clearly seen and not one salmon fry was found in that year, the older parr were also reduced. In 1954 salmon parr were held in cages in several parts of the Northwest Miramichi and from 63% to 91% of those held within the spray area were dead in three weeks, while only 2% died in an unsprayed control stream during the same period. Brook trout were also reduced in numbers. Fish poisoned by D.D.T. are first excited and then exhibit ataxia and paralysis. The first symptom of D.D.T. poisoning is tremor of the skeletal muscles.

Saunders (1969) recorded a mass mortality of brook trout and young salmon in a Prince Edward Island stream after accidental spillage of a spray mixture containing the fungicide nabam and the chlorinated hydrocarbon endrin. The interesting feature of this pollution was that surviving trout and salmon showed abnormal behaviour including unseasonal downstream movements in summer and unusual response to an electric field. Saunders suggested that this abnormal behaviour could provide a useful biological indicator of pollution by these pesticides.

The second group of insecticides, the organo-phosphorus compounds, is greater in numbers than the first group, but at present is smaller in quantity produced. In this group are included malathion, parathion, phosphamidon, schradan and menazon. As a group they are generally less toxic to fish than the chlorinated hydrocarbons.

The main group of herbicides includes 2,4–D, 2,4,5–T, M.C.P.A., M.C.P.B. and mecoprop. They are generally less toxic to fish than insecticides although a few, such as 2,4–D and M.C.P.A., may constitute a potential danger in normal use.

The organo-mercury compounds are also very toxic to fish and humans. These include methyl mercury dicyandiamide and other alkyl mercurys. These compounds are used as fungicides to dress seeds. Phenyl mercury may enter the water from pulp factories and the chlorine-alkaline industry where it is taken up eventually by the fish.

Among other commonly used agricultural chemicals which are toxic to fish are the phenolic disinfectants, sheep dips, which may contain B.H.C. and dieldrin, rat poisons and sodium cyanide for rabbit destruction. The latter chemical is frequently used in some areas by poachers and, given low water conditions, is a swift and sure way of killing large numbers of salmon (Holden and Marsden, 1964). The observed lethal concentrations of selected chemicals in aquatic environments are given in Table 18.

Suspended solids. The effect of inert suspended solids is twofold. If they are light or very finely divided, as are some mine slurries, the waste water from china clay works and coal washing effluents, they do not settle rapidly but make the river opaque and prevent the penetration of sunlight and so prohibit plant growth.

When particles are large the deposits smother all algal growth, kill rooted plants and mosses and alter the nature of the substrate. Quantities of silt-like material destroy plants, and quite small amounts, such as those produced by gravel washing plants or by soil erosion or the regular washing of farm implements or root crops, may change the nature of the stream bed sufficiently to alter the flora. For example plants such as *Ranunculus* and *Myriophyllum*, which are found in silt-free conditions, may be replaced by *Potamogeton pectinatus* which is found in silty conditions. The coarser sand particles may have a scrubbing effect on the rocks and gravel of the stream. This tends to remove algal growth as well as the bottom fauna. Coarser rock particles may plug up the spaces in the gravel and hence reduce the habitat of the bottom fauna. Spawning of trout may be affected since they may avoid turbid water and will crowd into clear areas to spawn. If the clear area of the stream suitable for spawning is insufficient a reduction in the number of offspring could result. If eggs are already in the gravel when pollution occurs the compaction of the gravel with tailings will reduce circulation of the water through the redds and cause the eggs

TABLE 18

Observed lethal concentrations of certain chemicals in aquatic environments.

Chemical	Fish	Lethal concn. (mg/litre)	Exposure time (h)	Authority
Copper	Rainbow trout	0·5[a]–0·05[b]	48[c]	Brown (personal communication)
Lead nitrate	Brown trout	0·33 lead	—	Carpenter, 1927
Phenol	Rainbow trout	6	3	Alexander, Southgate, Bassindale, 1935
Potassium cyanide	Rainbow trout	0·13 cyanide	2	Bassindale, 1935
DDT	Rainbow trout	0·32–0·5	24–36	Mayhew, 1955 Hatch, 1957
DDT	Salmon	0·08	36	Hatch, 1957
DDT	Brook trout	0·032	36	Hatch, 1957
Dieldrin	Rainbow trout	0·05	24	Mayhew, 1955
Heptachlor	Rainbow trout	0·25	24	Mayhew, 1955
Toxaphene	Rainbow trout	0·05	24	Mayhew, 1955

[a] In water ≃ 300 mg/l as $CaCO_3$.
[b] In water ≃ 20 mg/l as $CaCO_3$.
[c] 48 hour median lethal concentration.

to suffocate. In Bluewater Creek in Montana the best survival of trout eggs (97%) was found where the stream discharge was stable and sediment concentrations were low. Fish eggs can become buried by suspended solids and the pressure caused by the weight of solids may even cause the less resistant eggs to burst. Fine silt and other sediments are said to cause the death of alevins by accumulating on the gill membranes.

Hamilton (1961) and others have found that the bottom fauna is unaltered by the presence of sand and silt in suspension except where the river bed is completely covered with sand and silt. Where the stones are partially free from the deposit animals typical of the unaffected part of the river are present.

Suspended solids decline in amount as one proceeds downstream from the source of pollution because they settle out of the water. The rate of settling depends on the density and size of the particles and the turbulence of the water, and is particularly rapid above weirs and in pools or where the current is slack. If the solids are completely inert, as are the wastes from sand and gravel washing and china clay works, the amount of deposit on the river bed slowly builds up and extends farther and farther downstream as it is stirred up and carried on by floods. Oxidisable solids on the other hand, such as those in sewage and dairy wastes, are steadily broken down by bacteria; a balance therefore results between the rates of settling and decomposition, and the deposits slowly tail off downstream.

De-oxygenation. This is usually caused by bacterial breakdown of organic matter, but it may be due to other reducing agents. Organic residues include the effluents from a great variety of activities including dairies, silage, manure heaps and cattle yards, slaughter houses, sugar beet factories, textile manufacture, canning plants, laundries, breweries, tanneries (Plate 15), fish-meal factories, paper mills and domestic sewage. Residues from all these sources contain complex organic compounds in solution and suspension, often together with toxic substances and various salts. The oxidation of sewage effluent uses up a considerable amount of dissolved oxygen, and the concentration can decrease below the necessary minimum required by fish, particularly at high water temperatures when there is less dissolved oxygen and the oxygen requirements of the fish are higher. This can be serious in rivers where food processing plants and other manufacturers use the city sewers for releasing their wastes. This situation can reach very serious proportions at the mouth of a river so much so that seaward migrating smolts may not be able to negotiate a belt of pollution at the river mouth.

Inorganic reducing agents, such as sulphides and sulphites, occur as constituents of the effluents of several types of industry. These substances use up the oxygen in the river water, and important among them are the ferrous salts which are present in many underground waters. These often reach the rivers quite naturally, but large volumes are pumped up from mines and can produce serious pollution. Ferrous waters are usually acid, but as the acid becomes neutralised, usually by loss of carbon dioxide to the atmosphere, the ferrous salts become oxidised, often by bacterial action, and ferric hydroxide ('ochre') is precipitated. This then takes on the role of an inert suspension which covers the bed of the river, blanketing all the bottom fauna.

The polluting effect of organic materials is correlated with the amount of oxygen taken up by micro-organisms bringing about the decomposition of the material. If large quantities of dissolved oxygen in the water are 'removed' as a result of this decomposition, conditions tend to become anaerobic causing foul smells and the death of all forms of plant and animal life. The intensity of pollution is estimated by determining the amount of oxygen taken up by 1 litre of the water or effluent at 20° C for 5 days, and is designated the Biochemical Oxygen Demand (B.O.D.). This is stated as mg per litre or parts per millilitre (p.p.m.) and a B.O.D. of 20 is considered a satisfactory level for effluent entering a watercourse. In addition to satisfying the B.O.D. standard, effluents in the British Isles must not contain more than 30 p.p.m. of suspended solids (S.S.). If the effluent on entering the water-course is not diluted at least eight times, then a correspondingly lower B.O.D. and S.S. standard would be required if satisfactory conditions are to be maintained. Crude domestic sewage may have a B.O.D. of about 400 p.p.m. In agricultural effluents B.O.D. values can be much higher. The B.O.D. of dairy effluent, including byre washings and equipment cleaning, can vary between 450 and 4,000. Piggeries produce an effluent with a much higher B.O.D. in the region of 1,200 to 13,000. Silage is the strongest type of polluting material produced on a farm with a B.O.D. varying between 12,000 and 60,000. Up to 40 gallons of effluent per ton of silage may be produced, and on this basis the effluent from 300 tons of silage has a polluting power equivalent to the domestic sewage of a town with a population of 60,000. In the paper industry pulp mill wastes consist of sulphite pulp wastes, kraft pulp wastes, bleach plant wastes and groundwood, woodroom and paper-machine wastes. Spent sulphite liquor (S.S.L.) comes from the sulphite process. It has high oxygen-consuming properties and, on a population equivalent basis, the oxygen consumption of effluent from a 500 ton per day sulphite mill may be equivalent to that of sewage from 2 million people (Waldichuk, 1962). Kraft mill and bleach plant effluents have not such a high B.O.D. as spent sulphite liquor. Wastes from mechanical pulping and other non-chemical wood processing are harmful to the aquatic environment because of the high concentrations of suspended particulate materials. There is a nominal B.O.D. associated

PLATE 16

A stream blockage caused by forest thinning operations. This can result in heavy deposits of silt immediately upstream of the blockage and also prevents the movements of migratory fish.

PLATE 17. Torr Achilty dam and power station, part of the Conon Basin Scheme, Ross-shire. The power station forms part of the dam structure. The entrance to the Borland Fish Pass can be seen as the smallest rectangle below the railings to the

with groundwood wastes arising from decomposition of raw organic constituents leached from the wood.

The rate at which a particular type of effluent is able, in the presence of
ample oxygen, to satisfy its oxygen demand depends on what it contains.
Industrial effluents which contain only chemical reducing agents, such as
ferrous salts or sulphides, take up oxygen by purely chemical action; they
do this very rapidly, exerting what is sometimes known as immediate
oxygen demand. Organic substances such as starch, sewage and milk waste,
become oxidised only by the activities of bacteria. The rate at which they
are broken down therefore depends at first on the presence of suitable
bacteria, and secondly on how satisfactory and balanced a food they are for
micro-organisms. Sterile effluents, such as phenols, take some time to
build up a suitable bacterial flora and, if they are very uniform in composition, they may contain inadequate amounts of some substances, such as
phosphates, which are needed for bacterial growth, even after they have
been mixed with river water. Sewage of course is well inoculated with
bacteria and is adequately supplied with a wide range of compounds, so it
gets broken down relatively easily. But some materials, such as wood pulp,
are very poor bacterial foods and are decomposed very slowly. They therefore exert a lower oxygen demand but for a long time, and in the aggregate
it may be very great.

The oxygen can only be returned to the water by aeration at the surface
or by the photosynthetic activities of green plants. This re-oxygenation of
the water may be slowed down by the presence of a thin film of oil on the
water surface and a thick film may prevent it. Synthetic detergents also
affect the uptake of oxygen by foam blankets on the water surface. The
same is true of foaming in effluents from chemical pulping.

Hynes (1960) has pointed out that weirs which isolate artificial by-
passes, and which allow water to pass only at times of flood, may exert
devastating effects on the oxygen regime of the river below them at certain
times. The isolated reach may become filled with water at flood time, and
this water is often more polluted than usual, because at times of heavy
rainfall many sewage works are unable to handle the extra run-off from
roads and roof drains and so pass quite untreated sewage out through
'storm overflows'. Normally this has little effect because the discharge is
at a time of high water and maximum dilution, but if such water is then
impounded and left to stagnate it rapidly putrefies. Because of the absence
of flow and turbulence its rate of oxygen uptake is low and the water becomes
totally de-oxygenated; anaerobic bacteria then take over and reduce the
nitrates to ammonia and then sulphates to sulphides. Thus a mass of water
is formed which is not only de-oxygenated but which contains poisons and
has a heavy oxygen debt and when a sudden flood, such as a summer

G

thunderstorm, occurs it is suddenly pushed into the river and passes down-stream as a more or less discrete 'plug'. The sudden death of thousands of fish (Plate 15), particularly in hot weather, can often be attributed to this sort of cause, and it may appear as if there has been a 'spill' or some other failure at a treatment plant when, in fact, everything is functioning normally.

Where conditions are so extreme that there is hardly any oxygen there may be no organisms present except bacteria, but generally the river bed is carpeted with sewage fungus and colonised by small red worms known as *Tubificidae* and red midge larvae (*Chironomidae*). As conditions become less severe algae grow among the sewage fungus and eventually replace it and leeches, water slaters and snails are present. As the effects of pollution diminish a fauna and flora similar to that of the unpolluted stream reappear and eventually replace the pollution tolerant organisms. This is the normal succession as one passes downstream from the source of pollution provided new sources do not occur on the way, and it indicates recovery of the river. Pentelow (1953) shows that the same succession occurs according to the quality of the effluent. A bad effluent allows only sewage fungus and worms to exist, a better effluent or greater dilution may produce algal growths, leeches and water slaters, a good effluent or considerable dilution may do no more than increase the productivity, in animal and plant life, of the stream into which it is discharged.

Non-toxic salts. Soluble salts, or dissolved solids, commonly found in streams and in discharges to streams include chlorides, sulphates, nitrates, bicarbonates and phosphates of sodium, potassium, calcium, magnesium, iron and manganese. In small concentrations these are harmless to fish. However, drainage from a salt works, for example, or brine from water softening plants using ion-exchange methods of softening, are liable to contain large amounts of sodium chloride which may pollute a freshwater stream by converting it to brackish water with harmful results for certain fish. Repeated re-use of river water for domestic purposes may also lead to an undesirably high sodium chloride content.

Mercer (1967) has pointed out that pollution by salts which are non-toxic, but which render the river water less suitable for subsequent use, is a form of pollution of increasing importance. The salts may be added to the river from sewage effluent, industrial discharges and run-off from agricultural land treated with fertilisers.

Heating of the water. The discharge of heated trade effluents from factories and mills and the large volumes of warm 'cooling water' from electricity generating stations may cause a temperature rise of several degrees. When a rise in temperature occurs in a stream polluted by organic matter, there is not only a reduction of dissolved oxygen, due to the lower solubility of oxygen at the higher temperature, but also an increased rate of utilisation of dissolved oxygen by biochemical reactions which proceed much faster at higher temperatures. For these reasons many rivers may be satisfactory as regards dissolved oxygen content in the winter but may contain little or none during the summer.

Fish are affected by a rise in temperature and there may even be mortality among those fish sensitive to temperature. Although fish can become acclimatised to high temperatures, at a certain point they will eventually die. Moreover, a rapid change in temperature, or the sudden transference of fish to warm water, may result in death at a temperature well below that regarded as lethal for the species. A rise in temperature also increases the lethal effect of compounds toxic to fish such as cyanide. Furthermore, although a rise in temperature lowers the dissolved oxygen content, the minimum critical concentration of dissolved oxygen for fish is greater when the temperature increases. Thermal death points for salmon and trout are given in Table 19. The brown trout shows very little capacity for adjustment to high temperatures. In the warm season of the year when river temperatures may rise to 24° C under natural conditions, a further rise of one or two degrees may be fatal. As Klein (1962) emphasises:

> the thermal tolerances determined experimentally define the extreme limits of existence. The temperature zone within which the life of the fish, in every way, including feeding, growth, reproduction and competition with enemies, can be said to be normal, may be very much more restricted. Maximum activity may be displaced at a temperature far below the thermal death point.

Alabaster (1966) has pointed out, from the results of his investigations of the effect of heated effluents on fish, that heated effluents in Britain, while potentially lethal to trout and the more sensitive coarse fish, seldom kill in practice. This is because of the ability of the fish to take avoiding action and also the tendency for the warm water to remain near the surface

TABLE 19

Thermal death points of some salmonid fish

Fish	Acclimatisation temperature °C	Thermal death point °C	Reference
Brown trout	14–18	25	Gardner, 1926
Brown trout	26	26	Brett, 1956
Brown trout fry	5–6	22·5	Bishai, 1960
Brown trout fry	20	23	Bishai, 1960
Atlantic salmon			
grilse	?	29·5–30·5	Huntsman, 1942
parr	?	32·5–33·8	Huntsman, 1942
Brook trout	15	25	Brett, 1956

of the recipient rivers, leaving water of almost normal temperature beneath. Where the temperature of the whole river is above normal because of mixing with a continuous discharge of heated effluent there will, depending on water temperature, be some local mortality.

Huntsman (1942) records the death of salmon in the Moser River, Nova Scotia. He found that freshly run grilse died at about 29·5° C and acclimatised grilse at about 30·5° C. Large salmon died first and salmon parr survived. In an experiment he found that salmon parr died between 32·9 and 33·8° C, the smallest parr died at the highest temperature.

Warm water also tends to encourage excessive growth of sewage fungus (*Sphaerotilus natans*) and water weeds which may in some cases interfere with stream flow and so cause flooding.

Natural pollution. Pollution of rivers may take place as a result of natural causes not necessarily associated with the activities of man. It is often associated with adverse weather conditions. For instance, it may consist of run-off from the land carrying silt, vegetable matter and manure washed into the river during a storm. Drainage from peaty areas is liable to contain much vegetable matter and organic acids and a cloudburst in the upper Eden valley in 1930 caused pollution by peaty matter downstream resulting in large numbers of trout being killed.

Pollution of lakes, ponds and reservoirs can be caused by excessive 'blooms' of algae, particularly the blue-green algae. This has caused a great deal of trouble in lakes into which sewage is discharged. The factors influencing the formation of algal blooms include climate, lake area and shape, prevailing winds, pH, presence of carbon dioxide and of inorganic nutrients such as nitrogen and phosphorus. Algal blooms are associated with the presence of fairly high concentrations of certain nutrient materials such as nitrates and phosphates, found in sewage effluents and the 'run-off' from rich agricultural areas, which stimulate the growth of algae particularly under conditions of excessive sunshine and warmth. These blooms can also occur in eutrophic lakes on which large concentrations of wildfowl occur, the excreta from the birds producing the required excess of nutrients. This situation occurs on Duddingston Loch in Midlothian where 8,000 pochard, in addition to other species, roost on this 20-acre water most of the winter. Eventually the algae undergo decomposition and cause fish mortality by depleting the water of its dissolved oxygen.

Recovery. All five of the main effects of pollution are to some extent transitory, and if they are not too severe, and if the river is long enough and receives enough extra water from tributaries and surface run-off it can 're-purify' itself. With the less persistent effects such as de-oxygenation, suspended solids or increase in temperature the alteration may be detectable only for a mile or two below the effluent outfall. But more usually the polluting load is heavier than this and the alteration may persist for a long way. It has been said that no river in Britain is long enough to recover completely from a load of organic matter sufficient to cause total de-oxygenation.

The effects of pollution are of the same type as 'natural phenomena', and if they are not so severe as to produce extreme conditions they serve merely to alter one sort of river environment into another. As Hynes says: "there is therefore a great difficulty in defining pollution and we must accept the fact that at least some man-made alterations to rivers closely resemble changes which, in other rivers, occur quite naturally".

The subject of pollution is a very large one and much has been written on the subject including standard works by Hynes (1960), Klein (1957, 1962 and 1966) and Jones (1964).

8.2 Forestry

Many of the habitat requirements of salmonid fish are to be found in streams running through areas of forest. The tree canopy provides shade and keeps down the water temperatures. For example, in a comparison of stream temperatures from two watersheds, one containing a farm and the other a forest, it was recorded that over a period of a year the farm stream, with little or no shade, had an average water temperature $11.5°$ F higher (ranging from 9 to 20° F) than the forest stream with its abundant shade. Abundant riverside vegetation contributes directly to the fish's food supply by insects falling into the water and indirectly by supplying leaf litter which soon becomes detritus in the streams and provides a food supply for many of the aquatic invertebrates. The trees and undergrowth also provide cover and shelter for the fish and give stability to the stream banks. This stability becomes less as the forest matures and the shade from the tree canopy inhibits growth of plants and shrubs, and in some fast-flowing streams there may be erosion of the banks and exposure of the tree roots. There is a slow run-off of water in forest areas as the soil is very permeable and has a high storage capacity. The trees also increase the area of surface available for the evaporation and interception of precipitation. Forest streams are therefore less susceptible to large floods and drought conditions.

After deforestation there is compaction of the soil and reduction of leaf litter followed by decreased permeability and storage capacity of the soil for water and therefore a greater fraction of the water runs off the soil surface. This results in an increase in the absolute amount of water flow from that area, an increase in the flood peak discharge and a decrease in the low water flow. Increased run-off and flood peak flows usually mean increased erosion of the watershed area and increased turbidity and sedimentation. With a decrease in low flow conditions with more frequent droughts many spawning and feeding areas will be left exposed. Tree removal also leads to an increase in water temperature due to lack of shade. A study in the Smoky Mountains of Tennessee showed that the migration of trout upstream followed logging of the watershed (Greene, 1950). Gray and Edington (1969) showed that felling of a woodland produced a large increase in the summer temperature of a small stream flowing through it; and Hall and Lantz (1969) found not only a substantial change in water temperature but also in the dissolved oxygen content of the stream water following logging.

During logging operations logs may be stranded and direct the water flow from gravel bars. This may result in the drying out of deposited spawn, or diversion of normal water flows from potential spawning areas. Log jams and logging debris often cause obstructions (Plate 16) and, where they hinder the migration of fish, are undesirable. Where log jams are directly attributable to the operation of a logging company, the operators, in certain countries, are obliged to clear the obstruction. In Canada, fisheries officers and stream-clearance personnel of the Fish Culture and Development Branch of the Department of Fisheries and Forestry clear jams other than those mentioned. Unless jams are impassable or at least a hindrance to fish passage, they may be a stream asset as the deep holes usually associated with jams afford places of refuge for salmon prior to spawning. Brushwood and thinnings that fall into small streams may cause a sufficient blockage to allow deposition of silt immediately upstream, resulting in the smothering of bottom fauna and the suffocation of eggs.

8.3 Agriculture

One of the main agricultural practices which has an adverse effect on streams and their fauna is land drainage. Land drainage causes a quicker run-off of water with an associated increase in bank erosion. This results in the transportation of a heavy silt load from the upper areas of streams and the deposition of this elsewhere in the river with a consequent smothering of spawning and nursery areas. Stewart (1963) refers to the drainage of the fells in the upper reaches of the Ribble in Lancashire. In 1947 small open channels 12 inches wide and 9 inches deep were cut in the hills in the form of a herring bone. By 1963 the main channels had eroded into large drainage channels varying in width from 6 to 12 feet with depths greater than 4 feet. Stewart found that the amount of suspended silt flowing down the River Lune during a January spate amounted to $1\frac{1}{2}$ tons for each 250,000 gallons of water. Land drainage also results in more 'flash-floods', the river rising and falling rapidly due to efficient drainage schemes.

Wolf (1961) has shown in the case of the Kävlinge River system in Sweden that, through ditching, canalising and cultivation of bad as well as good farm land over 150 years, the greater part of the surface water has disappeared (Fig. 38). The intensive cultivation of the area has caused every possible bit of land to be drained, ditched and ploughed.

Wolf also estimated the amount of top soil in the catchment area of the Kävlinge River system carried away by flood water. He found that 1 m³ of water contains about 50 gm of humus material and about 100 gm of minerals. This means that a stream carrying 60 m³ of water per second also carried with it 3 kilos of humus material and 6 kilos of mineral matter. Thus in 24 hours about 750,000 kilos of soil would be carried out to sea.

Silt also occurs in rivers from erosion from overgrazing, muir burn and crop production on steeply sloping land. In Scotland sheep cause a great deal of erosion by destroying the ground vegetation by grazing. They also contribute to the instability of hill ground and river banks by creating innumerable tracks and narrow paths and by using small knolls and irregularities in the ground and river banks for protection from the weather; these places are gradually worn down until a shallow soil profile is exposed which later increases in width and depth. Fairbairn (1967) and McVean and Lockie (1969) mention just how dangerous this erosion can be by drawing attention to the damage done in the south-east Scotland floods of 1948 and floods in the White Esk, Ettrick, Dulnain, and Lochaber areas in 1953.

Muir burn may contribute to erosion and to landslides in certain types of terrain. Muir burn is an age-long practice of rotational firing of heath land, used particularly on hill land to prevent tree regeneration and especially to promote new growth of ling heather (*Calluna vulgaris*) which provides part of the diet of sheep and grouse. The firing is usually carried out in the spring as a basic part of moorland management; as Fairbairn points out, repeated burning at close intervals may result in the disappearance of herbaceous species which, in turn, has an adverse effect on the soil, destroying the organic horizon, when erosion is inevitable and becomes accelerated.

Peat workings on peat mosses and moors can also lead to adverse effects. The Peat Silt Research Group in Ireland have found that high concentrations of peat silt in a river reduces the bottom fauna density. The silt may also eliminate certain invertebrate species by altering the habitat; increase the mortality of fish ova, and affect the growth rate of young fish. It was noticed that larger fish were not affected by the presence of peat silt except where concentrations were very high.

Another major agricultural practice which may affect fisheries is irrigation. Irrigation can affect fish and the river environment by the removal or storage of water, by the diversion of fish into irrigation channels or by silting arising from irrigation-caused erosion.

The surface waters in Kävlinge River system around 1950.

The excerpt of the map shows how much surface water there now is after the intensive cultivation that has taken place in 150 years. Only 41 km² remain which is 3.4 per cent of the whole drainage area. Through ditching, canalizing and cultivation of bad as well as good farm land, the greater part of the surface water has disappeared. If this continues, we shall end with an almost completely dried out area.

(10.134 acres)

The surface waters in Kävlinge River system at the beginning of the 18th century.

The excerpt of the map shows how much surface water there was before the land was altered to any appreciable extent by man. All black parts on the map indicate surface water. This comprised 356 km², which was 29 per cent of the whole drainage area.

(87.988 acres)

FIG. 38. Kävlinge river system (from Wolf, 1961c).

8.4 Water abstraction

The abstraction of water from a river system may be permanent, as in the case of a reservoir in the upper reaches of a large river which is remote from the city it is supplying with water for domestic use, or temporary when water is being 'borrowed' by industry sited along the river system to which the water will be returned. The use of water to generate electricity is dealt with under a separate heading.

The effects of water abstraction include: diversion of part of the river to a new drainage system; change in volume of flow; change in temperature regime of the stream; a change in the quality of the water; obstruction and delay to migratory fish and flooding of spawning and nursery grounds.

In many domestic water supply schemes large rivers, such as the Tweed, may have their upper tributaries dammed to form reservoirs. The water in the reservoir is then piped to the city which may be a considerable distance away. The formation of reservoirs may result in the flooding of salmon spawning and nursery grounds and also the barring of salmon to spawning areas upstream of the reservoir. The Fruid Reservoir, for example, on one of the Tweed's upper tributaries, has flooded some spawning and nursery ground and, because there is no fish pass in the dam, salmon are prevented from reaching spawning grounds upstream of the reservoir.

The storage of water will also affect the flow of the river for some distance downstream until other tributaries join the main channel. Immediately downstream of the dam the flow may be reduced to a minimum compensation flow or cut off completely, when the river bed will be left dry. Usually on migratory fish rivers a compensation flow is agreed upon by the authorities, with increases in the compensation flow to form 'freshets' at times of the year when fish are moving upstream to spawn. However, a fixed compensation flow usually implies a reduced flow and consequently the water temperature regime will be affected and this may mean that critical water temperatures for fish are reached during periods of warm weather. In addition the width of the river is reduced with a consequent reduction in space and food for the fish, an increased exposure to predators and the likelihood of the fish being more susceptible to disease.

Gudjonsson (1965) describes the effect of water removal on the catch of salmon in the River Ulfarsa in Iceland. A dam was built across the Ulfarsa in 1953 and from the reservoir thus formed water was piped at a continuous rate of 220 to 230 litres per second to a fertiliser factory. The average flow of the river lies between 800 to 1000 litres per second so that an appreciable amount of the water was being abstracted. The effect of this water abstraction resulted in a loss of 281 salmon (61·5% of the predicted average catch) on the average each year during the period 1954 to 1963. The explanations Gudjonsson gave for these losses were (1) impaired living conditions in the river caused by removal of water; (2) young salmon getting into the water pipes leading to the fertiliser factory, and thus being lost to the perpetuation of the salmon stock in the river and (3) the sudden drying up of the river bed below the dam in the winter time during snowstorms and frost. Loss of water to the fertiliser factory is likely to cause high mortality in the young salmon below the dam.

Water is also used in large quantities by industry for cooling purposes and process work. Among the largest industrial users or consumers of water are the chemical industry, steel plants, textile industries, tanneries, oil refineries, paper and pulp mills, power stations and atomic energy plants. Much of this water will come from the river along which the industry is sited, but other sources include the city's water supply which, as has already been mentioned, may have come from reservoirs some distance away. These industries use tremendous amounts of water, and Table 20 gives some idea of the quantities used by various industries. Most of this water is returned to the rivers, sometimes after treatment, but at other times very much changed from its state before use. As Klein (1962) mentions, much water can be saved in an industry by the adoption of proper water-conservation measures.

8.5 Hydro-electric development

Hydro-electric installations are of three main types: (1) a simple dam or barrage which diverts water for use in an adjoining water-course or in

TABLE 20
Approximate water requirements of some industries
(Figures given in Imperial gallons per unit of material).
(After Klein, 1962)

Industry	Water requirements
Steel	50,000 gal/ton
Paper	32,000 gal/ton
Wood pulp (sulphite)	50,000 gal/ton
Wool scouring	1,000 gal/1,000 lb wool
Tanning	8,000 gal/1,000 lb hide
Milk	4,500 gal/1,000 gal milk
Coal washing	100 gal/ton
Whisky	70,000 gal/1,000 gal whisky
Beer	10,000 gal/1,000 gal beer
Broiler (chicken) packing	5 gal or more/3lb bird

another catchment area; (2) a simple dam, normally larger than the diversion dam, integral with which is a generating station (Plate 17). The water passes from the reservoir through the turbines in the station and back to the river immediately downstream of the dam; (3) involves a storage reservoir some distance from, and usually at a much higher level than, the power station, thus providing a greater 'head' of water so that less water is required to produce the same amount of, or more, electricity as the situation described in (2). The adverse effects of these power developments (Fig. 39) include:

Obstructions to fish migration

Ascent. During periods of low discharge the ascent of fish in the estuary may be delayed and fish in the river deterred from moving upstream. As

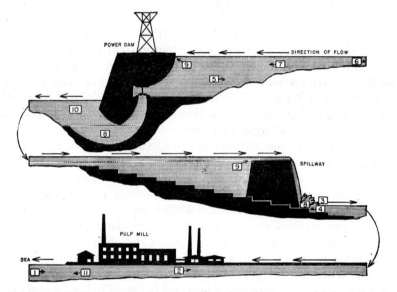

FIG. 39. Diagrammatic representation of problems created for salmon by multiple water use (from Brett, 1957. Reproduced with the permission of the Queen's Printer for Canada).

Upstream migrant	Downstream migrant
1. Delay from low water.	7. Passage through reservoir, and habitat limitations.
2. Pollution and raised temperature.	
3. Diverted 'home stream' water.	8. Mortalities in turbine or spill.
4. Blocked passage and by-pass delays.	9. Guiding and by-pass problems.
5. Passage through reservoir, and flooded spawning grounds.	10. Predator accumulation.
6. Final spawning efficiency.	11. Changed water quality.

Brett (1957) points out, the question which arises is, how long can delay in salt water or freshwater occur without affecting the ability to move up-stream and to spawn effectively. There may be a change in the quality of the freshwater from reduced flow, increased temperature and perhaps even pollution. For example, McGrath and Murphy (1965) describe a high mortality of adult salmon in the River Lee, Ireland, being probably partly due to a change in the quality of the water discharged from Inischarra Dam as the dissolved oxygen in the deeper parts of the reservoir had reached a dangerously low level. This was a transitory condition and arose because of the decay of organic matter in the reservoir basin following the first flooding with water and the situation had been aggravated by the fact that the turbines had not gone into operation for some time after the reservoir was filled, which permitted the quality of the water to deteriorate.

The dams will, initially at least, obstruct the ascent of adults. Most dams on migratory fish rivers have fish passes of one sort or another (Plate 18), but the problems associated with such structures involve the question whether the fish can find the entrance to the pass and, when they have found it, whether they will ascend readily. Fish not finding the pass immediately may attempt to 'fight' the spill water and even attempt to ascend the dam spillway, while others are occasionally injured by entering badly screened turbine draft tubes. However readily the fish ascend there must always be some delay at that point.

With diversion of water from one river to another there may be some 'straying' of fish due to their homing to their 'home waters' being dis-charged down another river channel. This may result in fish merely moving up a 'foreign' river or may result in their reaching an impassable source such as a power station. Pyefinch and Mills (1963) and Mills (1965d) refer to this problem on the Conon River system in Scotland, where some water from the River Meig is released from a power station on the River Conon.

Fish in the river below a power station may be subjected to a wide range of flows a number of times in a day. On the River Conon in Ross-shire the water level may rise to flood conditions and fall away to low summer flows as often as three times in the 24 hours. These rapidly fluctuating water levels may affect sport fishing by unsettling the fish and may affect com-mercial fishing by decreasing netting efficiency at high flows and making netting too effective for a satisfactory upstream escapement at reduced flows.

Descent of downstream migrants

Smolts. Young fish, particularly the seaward migrating smolts, may be delayed in the reservoirs either through not finding the entrance to the fish pass at the dam face or through being diverted into the power station tunnel. Although most power station tunnel intakes on Scottish hydro-electric schemes are screened, to prevent smolts and parr passing through the turbines, the screening is not always completely effective and smolts have been recorded passing through and under screens and being killed on them. The mortality of smolts passing through the turbines may vary widely. Munro (1965b) found that the mortality of smolts passing through Francis turbines at Clunie Power Station on the River Tummel was about 25% under normal operating conditions. At Invergarry Power Station, where kaplan turbines are installed, the mortality may be as high as 60% when the turbines are running at speed but producing no electricity, but under normal conditions is less than 20%.

Montén (1955) suggested that the factors likely to cause injury to the smolts were (1) water speed, (2) turbulence, (3) pressure, (4) cavitation and (5) collision with the machinery, particularly the runner vanes. He considered that because of the very short period of time that the smolt was subjected to factors (1), (3) and (4) it was less likely to be injured by them. In relation to pressure this held good for water heads up to 106 feet and Calderwood (1945) concluded that smolts would not be injured by a pressure equivalent to a head of about 100 feet. Montén considered that apparent mortality is caused by a combination of factors (2) and (5) and principally (5). This mortality was found to depend on the probability of collision, the force of impact and the possibility of the fish being struck in a vital spot. More recently a number of investigators have considered the effects of cavitation to be more serious than collision with the machinery. Normally smolts are excluded from both stations by appropriate screens.

If smolts cannot find their way out of an impoundment they may remain a further year in freshwater, and large, old smolts have been recorded from a number of Scottish reservoirs; although Koch, Evans and Bergström (1959), among others, record that there is a heavy mortality among smolts retained in freshwater due to the impairment of the osmotic capacity in freshwater at the time of transformation from parr to smolt. There is also increased predation in these reservoirs, the main predators being pike and trout.

Kelts. It has been found that kelts may be delayed by dams, and they are frequently to be seen swimming in the impoundment along the dam face, and Pyefinch and Mills (1963) have described the delay at dams on the Conon River system. On the Tay-Tummel system kelts have been observed passing downstream at the Faskally dam at the normal time (i.e. March to May).

Damage to, or elimination of spawning and nursery areas

Frequently large spawning and nursery areas are either eliminated by reservoir formation or are reduced by tapping of their water supply, which is diverted to a reservoir. There may also be some damage to other areas due to rapid fluctuations in water level below a power station resulting in exposure of redds during periods of frost and stranding of both spawning adults and young fish. In addition reduced flows may cut down the area available to fish.

Effects of impoundment on lakes and reservoirs

After impoundment, resulting in either reservoir formation or raising of the level of an existing lake, there is usually an increase in the general biological productivity due to leaching of salts from newly-inundated ground. Frequently the production of planktonic and semi-planktonic crustacea increases as a result of the leached nutrient salts and decaying terrestrial vegetation, and some of the important food sources for fish during the early impoundment period will be terrestrial invertebrates, such as earthworms and terrestrial insect larvae. The forage area of fish is usually greatly increased and therefore the population density of fish temporarily reduced. Immediately after impoundment the growth rates of fish such as trout, char and perch have been shown to improve substantially, but in almost all cases it has been found that these improved growth rates only last for a few years. However, if there is a greater area of shallow water after impoundment than before and water levels remain relatively stable the initial increase in fish production may be sustained and Campbell (1963) suggested that this might be the case with trout in Loch Garry, Invernessshire.

Elder (1966) has pointed out the effects on the littoral vegetation and fauna of fluctuating lake levels. Those species closely associated with the littoral vegetation will be greatly reduced or even eliminated, notably many of the larger insect larvae and crustacea, while chironomid larvae may increase. However, in terms of the production of fish food the net results of these changes are loss of the most valuable food organisms and survival of types which tend to be less available to fish.

PART IV

CONSERVATION AND MANAGEMENT
OF THE RESOURCE

Chapter 9

LEGISLATION AND ADMINISTRATION

9.1 History of Scottish salmon legislation. 9.2 Arrangements for water pollution control. 9.3 Water conservation. 9.4 Hydro-electric Development Act. 9.5 Miscellaneous Acts. 9.6 Canadian fisheries legislation.

9.1 History of Scottish salmon legislation

It is interesting to note that for 800 years the preservation of salmon has been the subject of some form of legislation in Scotland, England and Ireland. Most of the early legislation was designed to protect the stocks of fish from being overcropped as they entered the rivers to breed, from being taken off the spawning grounds, protecting them during the breeding season by creating close seasons and prohibiting the catching and killing of the young, particularly on their migration to sea as smolts. With regard to Statute Law it is interesting that in Scotland from very early times well-defined provisions have existed, and that the existing salmon Acts have, while adding much of value, continued the root principles of the early Scottish Acts. In the twelfth century a weekly close time was in force, and in an Act of 1424 reference is made to the annual close time. At this date it was from the Feast of Assumption of our Ladie till the Feast of St Andrew (15 August to 30 November).

In the time of David I (1124–1153) and of William the Lion (1164–1214) it was enacted that in dam dykes there should be a gap big enough to allow a three-year old swine, well fed, to stand in it.

Old Scottish Acts refer to the preservation of the 'reid fische' by means of a close time; to the removal of all standing obstructions to the run of fish, whether meant to capture, or only fitted to impede; and to the measure, weights, prices and other conditions of sale. Nothing better can be put than the reason given over and over again in the Scottish statutes 500 years

ago, for putting down unseasonable fishing and fixed engines – such practices 'destroy the breed of fish, and hurt the common profit of the realm'.
The vigour of these old statutes is as remarkable as their number. For
instance, an Act of the First Parliament of James I (of Scotland) 26 May,
1424, runs that:

> whosoever be convicted of slaughter of salmon in time forbidden by
> the law, shall pay forty shillings for the unlaw, and at the third time
> if he be convicted of such trespass, he shall lose his life, or pay for it.

In the whole mass of Scottish legislation on the protection of salmon there is
only one instance of exemption or relaxation of the restrictions and this was
in the Ninth Parliament of James I, 1429, when an Act passed – excepting
from the other Acts regarding salmon preservation, the waters of Solway
and Tweed which shall be available to Scotsmen at all times of the year,
as long as Berwick and Roxburgh are in the hands of the Englishmen. That
is to say, the Scottish king and his Estates solemnly passed an Act author-
ising and enjoining all Scotsmen to go a poaching in England, and in those
portions of the Border waters in which, though properly Scottish, the
English had or occasionally took an interest. Not only were Scotsmen legally
authorised to take English salmon, but if Englishmen wanted Scottish
salmon, then:

> it is ordained that no Scottish man sell to Englishmen, or in England
> beforehand or otherwaies, ony salmonde, bot that Englishmen bye
> them in Scotland for English gold, and none other contentation; And
> gif the Englishmen will not bye them; the Scottis merchandes may
> send them in Flanders or other places, quhair them thinkis; swa that
> of na wise they nouther send them nor sell them in England.

By the early statutes there was provision that fixed engines – which
may properly be interpreted as cruives – be done away with in the tidal
parts of the rivers. Cruives in fresh waters, although they are held under
special charter, have now been given up, since this method of fishing is
quite inconsistent with the proper ascent and distribution of fish, and materially interferes with the value of neighbouring fisheries.

The three main provisions of the early Scottish Salmon Acts were
thoroughly sound. By clearing the estuaries of fixed engines fish were
enabled to enter fresh waters; the fishing of fixed nets on the open coast
had in those early days not been thought of; by securing a gap in fixed
engines in freshwater, fish were able to distribute themselves over the
higher reaches, this being also assisted by the operation of the weekly close
time – which seemed at the same time the proper observance of the Sunday –
while the wisdom of protecting fish from all fishing during the breeding

season is exemplified by the creation of the annual close time.

The activity of the Legislature appeared to slow down for about two centuries and the next Act, known as Mr Home Drummond's Act, was the Salmon Fisheries (Scotland) Act of 1828 and this remained the governing Act for thirty years although another Act, the Salmon Fisheries (Scotland) Act, was passed in 1844. The Act of 1828 altered the commencement of close-time in all Scottish rivers north of the Tweed and Solway, from the 26 August to 15 September. From about that time excepting the Tweed, altered in 1857, and the Tay, altered in 1858 – the following were the legal fishing seasons of the Scottish rivers till 1863: all rivers north of the Tweed and Solway, from 1 February to 14 September; the waters flowing into the Solway Firth, from various periods between 1 January and 10 March to about 25 September, with a protraction in favour of rod fishing for various periods – in the case of the Annan, where there is a late run of salmon, till 1 November; and the Tweed and its tributaries from 15 February to 15 October, with three weeks more for rod fishing. Though these were the legal seasons, some of the chief fisheries in Scotland were, by the voluntary act of their owners, closed three or four weeks before the period fixed by law, during a considerable number of years before the recent Acts. This was not a good Act as, by adding to the length of the net fishing season, making the addition at the end of the season, and fixing no extended time for rod fishing after the removal of the nets, it killed a greater quantity of fish, and did not add to but lessened the inducements for the better protection, by the upper proprietors of the river, of the smaller number of fish that reached the breeding grounds. Because of this there was great ill feeling between those who had the fishing on the upper reaches of the river and those who had the fishing on the lower reaches. The upper proprietors felt that the lower proprietors were taking more than their fair share of fish which were destined for the upper waters and that few fish reached the upper part of the river until late in the year when they were not worth eating and at a time when it was illegal to fish for them.

The first successful attempt at reform was made in 1857 with the Tweed Fisheries Act, promoted by the majority of the Tweed Commissioners. One of its main objects was the suppression of certain fixed engines called stell nets and cairn nets (see pages 6–7). The fishing season was altered to run from 1 March to 1 October for nets and to 14 October for rod fishing. However, this did not give more fish time enough to reach the upper reaches after the nets had been taken off for successful rod fishing and the Tweed Amendment Act of 1859 altered the season, for nets, from 15 February to 14 September and for rods from 1 February to 30 November. The Tweed Act of 1857 abolished salmon spearing and the Act of 1859 rendered illegal even the possession of such a weapon within five miles of the river.

A number of other regulations set out in the Tweed Acts were to be incorporated in future Acts. These included making the weekly close-time begin six hours before and last six hours after the twenty-four hours of Sunday; prohibiting the killing of spawned fish even during the legal fishing season; restricting nets as to the size of meshes and attempts towards modifying or removing the obstructions caused by dams and dykes. The proprietors of the River Tay followed the good work of the Tweed Commissioners and in 1858 got a local Act taking the Tay fisheries out of the Home Drummond Act.

Within the next ten years two important Salmon Fisheries Acts were passed – the Salmon Fisheries (Scotland) Act of 1862 and the Salmon Fisheries Act of 1868. The first brought into being a small body of Commissioners whose duties were to fix the limits of fishery districts in Scotland; to fix a point on each river which would divide the upper from the lower proprietors; to determine the dates of the annual close-time for each district; and to make general regulations as to the observance of the weekly close-time, the construction and use of cruives, the construction and alteration of mill dams or lades or water-wheels, the meshes of nets, and respecting obstructions in rivers or estuaries. Eighty-seven fishery districts having been arranged, provision was made for the creation of District Fishery Boards to regulate local matters. These Boards are composed entirely of proprietors who hold rights of salmon fishing, the maximum number on the Board is seven, and the proprietor with the highest assessed rental acts as chairman. Members are elected at meetings of the upper and lower qualified proprietors so that each group is equally represented independently of the chairman. There are now 108 Salmon Fishery Districts, but Boards at present exist in only 45. These cover almost all the important salmon rivers.

By the Act of 1868 the powers and duties of District Boards were defined and extended. By section IX they are given power to petition the Secretary of State for Scotland:

(1) To vary the annual close-time, which must, however, always be 168 days.
(2) To vary the weekly close-time, which must, however, always be 36 hours.
(3) To alter the regulations with respect to the observance of annual and weekly close-times.
(4) To alter the regulation with respect to the construction and use of cruives and weirs.

Power is also given to purchase, for purpose of removal, dam dykes, cruives, or other fixed engines; to remove any natural obstruction or waterfall, by agreement, and to attach a fish-pass thereto, and generally to do such acts or execute such works as may appear expedient for the protection and improvement of the fisheries under their charge.

Almost 90 years elapsed before the passing of any more important salmon Acts, the next one being the Salmon and Freshwater Fisheries (Protection) (Scotland) Act, 1951. This made the weekly close-time from noon on Saturday to six on the following Monday morning. In addition it laid down methods of fishing in inland waters (i.e. by rod and line and net and coble); prohibitions against explosives, poisons; taking of dead salmon or trout; and set out the powers of water bailiffs employed by District Fishery Boards; set out the legal procedure for convictions against the Act. It also empowered the Secretary of State for Scotland to collect salmon and sea trout catch statistics for the purposes of protecting and developing stocks of salmon, although there are limitations on his power to publish the statistics collected.

This short account of the history of salmon legislation shows quite clearly how conscious Scotland has been of one of her valuable natural resources and how she has taken steps for over 850 years to protect the resource and not dissipate it as have a number of countries, such as France and Spain. Although in all fairness it must be said that it would have been difficult to enforce many such regulations over a considerable period in these two countries due to the state of turmoil which has existed throughout much of their history.

9.2 Arrangements for water pollution control

As long ago as the eighteenth century Coleridge wrote:

> The River Rhine, it is well-known,
> Doth wash your city of Cologne,
> But tell me, nymphs, what power divine,
> Shall henceforth wash the River Rhine?

The 'power divine' varies from country to country and a description of the development of the law relating to pollution in all the salmon countries would be a lengthy task. In certain instances pollution legislation has been described at some length, particularly by Pentelow (1953) and Klein (1966), and two reports describe water pollution control over a large area of the world, they are: *Control of Water Pollution: A survey of existing legislation* by the World Health Organisation in 1967 and published by Her Majesty's Stationery Office and, *Fresh Water Pollution Control in Europe* by the Council of Europe in 1967, also published by Her Majesty's Stationery Office. It is therefore not proposed to deal at length with the exceedingly numerous Acts concerning pollution, but simply to outline the position regarding pollution legislation in Scotland, England and Wales and how this came about.

To understand the legal position on pollution in the United Kingdom it is essential to appreciate the difference between 'Common Law' and 'Statute Law'. The former is based largely on rights and usages which have been acquired in past years, and any arguments in the Courts are based on references to previous cases. For Statute Law, the provisions of various Acts and the maximum penalties for infringement can be obtained in printed form. The law in Scotland is not necessarily the same as in the rest of the United Kingdom.

In Common Law a riparian owner (that is, in this case, an owner of land on the banks of the river or stream) is entitled to expect that the water in the river shall flow past his land neither diminished nor increased in amount without sensible alteration to its natural quality. A riparian owner is therefore entitled at Common Law (and quite apart from Statute Law) to take proceedings in the Civil Courts against any person or body causing interference with the flow of the stream or polluting its quality. In certain circumstances prescriptive rights to discharge an effluent into a stream may have been acquired, but in their absence a riparian owner aggrieved by pollution of the stream can normally apply for an injunction and/or damages. A discussion of the development and application of the Common Law with respect to pollution may be found in Taylor's book, *The Law Affecting River Pollution.*

There have been a number of statutes affecting water pollution. In a number of old Acts, both English and Scottish, there are enactments against the poisoning of rivers in other respects: for instance the Gas Works Clauses Act of 1847, which prohibited the discharge of gas wastes into streams, and the Scotch Removal of Nuisances Act of 1856. This Act imposed a penalty of £50 on:

> any person engaged in the manufacture of gas, naphtha, vitriol or dye stuffs, or in any trade in which the refuse produced in any such manufacture is used, who shall at any time cause or suffer to be brought or to flow into any streams, etc., any washing or other substance produced in any such manufacture, or shall willfully do any act connected with any such manufacture whereby the water in any such stream, etc., shall be fouled.

The fisheries Acts in both England (Salmon Fisheries Act, 1861) and Scotland (Salmon Fisheries (Scotland) Act, 1868) were the first to deal with pollution, the pollution Acts coming later. The Scottish Salmon Fisheries Act was stronger than the English Act for it enacted that "Every person who causes or knowingly permits to flow or puts into or knowingly permits to be in any river containing any salmon any liquid or solid matter poisonous or deleterious to salmon" is made liable to certain penalties. In England there was no remedy unless fish were actually poisoned whereas in Scotland the mere placing of any poisonous matter in a stream was an offence.

The first of the Acts, apart from certain purely local Acts, designed to prevent pollution was the Public Health Act of 1875 which dealt only with pollution from sewage works and gas works. The reports of the First Royal Commission on sewage, set up in 1857, led to the Rivers Pollution Prevention Act of 1876 which covered the whole of Great Britain and which gave local authorities, such as county councils and town councils, power to take criminal proceedings against polluters. In spite of this Act, as Pentelow (1953) points out, "the condition of our rivers generally did not improve and with the general adoption of the water closet system in the towns, sewage pollution increased greatly in the closing years of the last century".

After the passing of this Act many people were wrongly under the impression that the old Common Law rights had been superseded and thus if Local Authorities would not stop the pollution nobody else could do so. Another serious result of the Act of 1876 was that it discouraged research into methods of purifying trade effluents. So long as the polluter could escape liability under the Act by proving he was using the best-known means of purification which he could apply at reasonable cost there was no incentive to spend money on discovering any more effective purification treatment for his effluent.

Another Royal Commission, the Royal Commission on Sewage and Sewage Disposal was appointed in 1898 and continued to sit until 1915. It issued nine reports and they constituted a record of information and scientific investigation which became the standard work on all aspects of the problem. They recommended that standard of purity to be applied to effluents should be defined by law but these standards were confined to two qualities, suspended solids and to the oxygen absorbing power of the effluent. The standards, too, were to be related to the degree of dilution that the liquids would receive in the stream to which they were discharged. Although these standards were never given legal sanction they were constantly quoted in the Courts in pollution cases and obtained a general degree of acceptance.

The next advance, if it can be so termed, was the English Salmon and Freshwater Fisheries Act of 1923. Section 8 of the Act made it an offence to pollute waters so as to make them harmful to fish or their eggs or food. There was an 'escape clause' for any acts done by prescriptive right or in continuation of methods used at the time of the passing of the Act, provided that the best practical means within reasonable cost were used to prevent such discharges doing injury to fisheries.

This Act was comparatively successful and principally by using the powers given in Section 8 many fishery boards succeeded in preventing further deterioration and some, such as the Trent and Ribble, brought about a marked improvement in the waters under their care and both these rivers were in 1950, according to Pentelow, much better fishing rivers than they were in 1925.

According to some people this Act was in some ways ineffective in procuring conviction as it was necessary to prove that one particular effluent by itself had caused injury to fish or fish food. This alone made the Act useless for dealing with multiple pollutions. The only penalty imposed was a fine which was too small to be a real deterrent. It was a defence for the defendant to show that, although he was applying the best-known means, at reasonable cost, of purifying his effluent and no proceedings could be taken unless the water actually contained fish at the time of pollution. If one pollution wiped out all fish life in a river anyone might then pollute it as much as he liked and he could not be prosecuted under the Act.

In 1936 the Public Health Act was passed which rejected the recommendations of the Royal Commission and reasserted in effect that sewage effluents must comply with the common law rights of riparian owners. This Act was followed closely by the Drainage of Trade Premises Act of 1937 which entitled industries to discharge their effluents into the sewers, subject to certain safeguards, and threw the onus of purifying them on to the Local Authorities. Since then the position has been that most of the effluents still being poured into the rivers are being so discharged simply because they are too foul or poisonous to be accepted into the sewers or because there is no sewage system available.

At about this time the subject of River Boards was remitted for consideration to a Central Advisory Water Committee, set up in 1937 by the Minister of Health. They recommended the establishment in England and Wales of River Boards to be authorities with jurisdiction over a whole watershed or a group of watersheds and responsible for administering the law for the prevention of pollution, for the administration of fisheries and land drainage. This recommendation was given legislative effect by the River Boards Act of 1948 and thirty-two River Boards, covering the whole of England and Wales, except the Thames and Lee watersheds, which were already adequately provided for by local legislation, and certain areas in the County of London, were set up. Three years before this the Water Act of 1945 re-established the Central Advisory Water Committee. This Committee appointed a sub-committee to consider the law relating to river pollution. This Committee, known as the Hobday Committee, produced a comprehensive report, the Hobday Report and, assuming that the River Boards would be in existence to administer new legislation, proposed a complete new code which was embodied in the Rivers (Prevention of Pollution) Act, 1951. This Act, largely following the Brown-Lindsay Report (1950, Cmnd. 8111), made three important additions to the law: giving of river boards power to prescribe, in bye laws, standards for determining when effluents are to be regarded as poisonous, noxious or polluting; making it necessary for anyone proposing a new opening for the discharge of an effluent to obtain the consent of the river board; and enabling the provisions of the Act, or any of them, to be extended to tidal waters by order of the Minister of Housing and Local Government on general grounds and not only, as was the case before, on sanitary grounds. By these Acts the intentions of both Royal Commissions were at last given legislative effect.

At the same time as the English Rivers (Prevention of Pollution) Act, 1951, was passed a similar Act was passed in Scotland, the Rivers (Prevention of Pollution) (Scotland) Act. This Act was similar in many ways to the English Act but also set up administrative bodies to enforce it, these are the River Purification Boards, of which there are nine in all, all south and east of a line between Inverness and Fort William. North of this line the County Councils carry out these functions. It also dictated how the Boards were to be constituted, and gave the technical branch of these Boards, the River Purification Authority, powers of entry and inspection to any premises, subject to certain conditions. Nine years later the Final Report of the Trade Effluents Sub-Committee, 1960, suggested that the River Purification Authorities should test effluent samples, when application is made for consent, for:

(*a*) a 'sanitary analysis' of a composite sample of the following:

    (i) Suspended solids.
    (ii) B.O.D.
    (iii) Permanganate value or organic carbon.
    (iv) Nitrogen as free and saline ammonia, albuminoid or organic nitrogen and oxidised nitrogen.

(*b*) a chemical analysis of a composite sample for:

    (i) pH.
    (ii) cyanide.
    (iii) thiocyanate.
    (iv) phenols.
    (v) sulphides.
    (vi) metals.

Two-thirds of the membership of the Boards are made up of selected representatives of the county councils or large burghs whose districts are based wholly or partly in the Board's area. The remaining one-third is appointed by the Secretary of State for Scotland and the interests of angling, agriculture and industry must be represented.

The Clean Rivers (Estuaries and Tidal Waters) Act, 1960, gave river boards powers to control all new discharges to estuaries. In 1961 came the Rivers (Prevention of Pollution) Act for England and Wales, which introduced a licensing system for all purposes, superseding the area standards system. It also required that all effluents, including those occurring before 1951, should comply with consent discharges. The legislative machinery was slow and there was a minimum of two years permissible between changes in consent levels. Four years later the Rivers (Prevention of Pollution) (Scotland) Act was passed. This modified the 1951 Act in some respects, in giving the River Purification Authorities new powers to control all discharges including those into tidal waters and those existing prior to 1951. When making application for consent to discharge effluent into a river it was made necessary to state: (a) the nature and composition of the effluent concerned; (b) the maximum temperature of the effluent at the time of discharge; (c) the maximum volume proposed to be discharged on any one day and (d) the highest proposed rate of discharge. In granting consent the Authority may set conditions as to the above and also for sampling the effluent. These conditions operate after a period of three months, or after an appeal to the Secretary of State for Scotland has been dealt with. The Act also delineated the tidal waters to be considered, and proposed that the River Purification Authority responsible was the one from whose area the effluent discharge was made. It also set restrictions on the disclosure of information collected during routine´sampling. However, it still retained the minimum period of two years between changes in consent levels. Thus the legal means were available to control effectively the quality of the water both in the streams and in the tidal reaches of the rivers, the only real hindrance being the time-lag between changes of consent.

There have been some criticisms of the constitution of River Purification Boards in that the River Purification Board/River Purification Authority system is inefficient. Those people on the Board may have 'interests' in the industries causing pollution of the rivers in the Board's area. They may also be local authority members who are concerned at the cost of sewage purification. Usually these 'interests' are financial and may run directly contrary to the objectives of the Authority. There is thus considerable hindrance in the achievement of the goals of the Authority and much friction and ill-feeling between the technical officers of the Authority and members of the Board. Furthermore the Authority is frequently unable to enforce its powers against large concerns, such as city corporations and large industrial concerns, and it is only the small offender that is convicted.

In some situations there are industries which cannot afford to instal adequate treatment plant and the cost of installation of such equipment might reduce the profit margin of these firms to a level which would not allow them to continue in business. As this closure might affect the country's economy the Authority may not insist on the levels of the quality of the effluent until such time as a way is found of dealing with the effluent, for example its diversion to a trunk sewer which might be planned for that area in the near future.

There is also the criticism of the layout of the Board's area. These are not determined by natural boundaries with the result that one Board may be responsible for pollution prevention in a particular river, say the Forth, while another Board may be responsible for pollution prevention in the estuary of that river, in this case the Firth of Forth, and the latter can exert no influence over the former with regard to its pollution prevention policy.

Lastly, it should be noted that the River Purification Authorities are mainly dependent on Local Authorities for their finance, while in England the River Authorities are given direct Government aid as well.

9.3 Water conservation

There are certain Common Law rights to water in the United Kingdom. Briefly it is that nobody owns the water flowing in a river. Riparian owners, however, have rights to take and use the water and also are entitled to have the water flowing past or through their land undiminished in quantity and quality so long as it is consistent with the legitimate rights of other riparian owners. As Gregory (1967) states:

> At Common Law the riparian owner's right to abstract water from watercourses is therefore qualified. He is entitled to take it for his domestic purposes and for his livestock, even if in so doing he deprives lower riparian owners of sufficient water for these purposes. The lower riparian owners have no redress in this case, but if they are prejudiced by an upper riparian owner abstracting water for other purposes, and not returning it in sufficient quantity and quality, they can claim damages and an injunction.

An injunction is a court order restraining a person or body from doing something. Disobeying the order is Contempt of Court for which the court may commit the offender to prison.

In the Government white paper, *Water Conservation, England and Wales* (1962, Cmnd. 1693), the recent history of a national water policy is described. In this report water conservation is defined as meaning:

> the preservation, control and development of water resources (both
> surface and ground) whether by storage, including natural ground
> storage, prevention of pollution, or other means, so as to ensure that
> adequate and reliable supplies of water are made available for all
> purposes in the most suitable and economical way whilst safeguarding
> legitimate interests.

In this paper the Government outlined their proposals and mentioned their
intention to introduce legislation in due course. These included the formation of river authorities; assessment of resources and requirements; control and development of water resources, and a licensing system.

A year later the Water Resources Act was passed and this now controls
water abstraction in England and Wales by prohibiting the abstraction of
water from a source of supply "in a river authority area except in pursuance
of a licence under this Act granted by the river authority and in accordance with the provisions of that licence". The Water Resources Act substi-
tuted river authorities for river boards. The River Boards (mentioned in
9.2 under River Boards Act, 1948) had three main responsibilities in river
board areas – fisheries, land drainage and pollution prevention. The river
authorities have taken over these three, and additionally are charged with
water conservation duties.

In order to have a proper yardstick for determining applications for
abstraction licences, the river authority must fix 'the minimum acceptable
flow (M.A.F.)' for each water in the area that abstraction licences are
needed for. In deciding whether to grant a licence, or how much water to
allow to be abstracted the river authority must pay regard to the need to
secure that the flow will not be reduced below the minimum that has been
fixed, if a minimum has been fixed. At present no 'minimum acceptable
flows' have been fixed. Until this is done, the river authority must have
regard to the considerations which they must take into account when
fixing 'minimum acceptable flows'. These considerations include the requirements of fisheries, and also the character of both the water concerned
and its surroundings, in particular any natural beauty, the safeguarding of
public health, the needs of existing lawful uses, including those of agriculture, industry and water supply, and also the requirements of land drainage and navigation.

The Water Resources Act also established the Water Resources Board
which is charged with the duty of advising river authorities with respect to
the performance of their new functions.

Akroyd (1966) summarised the value of the Water Resources Act when
he said:

The abstractor will no longer be able to abstract regardless of the effect on others, and the fact that he will have to pay for his water means that he will probably value it in a way which he has never done before.

It means that good water will not be used when an inferior water will do, and it is already causing people to seek to explore the underground water over which they might be sitting and thus provide an additional supply, rather than take water from the public supply. It means that spray irrigators can no longer abstract regardless of the effect on other interests.

I think it might be said that the purpose of this Act is to ensure that we have, so far as is possible, streams which are in a condition fit to meet the demands which might be made on a good natural water, and it follows that that must be of benefit to fishery interests.

I believe that the industrial and water supply representation will not result in strife with fishing representation, but will lead to a better understanding of each others problems.

In 1964 the Spray Irrigation (Scotland) Act was passed to enable river purification boards in Scotland in pursuance of their functions (i.e. among other things the promotion of the cleanliness of rivers and the conservation of water resources) to control the abstraction of water for the purpose of spray irrigation. This granting of power to control the amount of water extracted by farmers was very much needed as there had always been the likelihood that so much water would be used in spray irrigation that, if all the pumps were in operation at the same time, some streams in low rainfall areas, during dry weather, might dry up completely. This type of situation might, but for control, easily have arisen in a few years' time on a number of rivers. However, before the purification board can enforce this Act it has to apply for an order which may take a long time to be granted.

When a reservoir is constructed for domestic supply in Scotland the Water Board has control over the water in the reservoir but the local purification board decides on the level of the compensation flow from the reservoir. In many cases the purification board will act in consultation with the local district fishery board if the river, from which water is being abstracted, holds migratory fish.

9.4 Hydro-electric Development Act

The Hydro-electric Development (Scotland) Act, 1943, makes it a duty of the Electricity Boards to "have regard to the desirability . . . of avoiding as far as possible injury to fisheries and to the stock of fish in any waters". The Secretary of State for Scotland is required by the Act to appoint a Fisheries Committee to give advice and assistance to the Electricity Boards and to himself. The Committee consists of a small group of members who between them contribute expert knowledge of fisheries, water engineering, electrical engineering and administration. Electricity Boards are obliged to consult the Fisheries Committee before and during the preparation of a constructional scheme and the Committee may, upon being consulted, or at any other time, make recommendations to the Board, who transmit copies to the Secretary of State and say whether or not they are prepared to accept the recommendations. The decision whether or not a disputed recommendation should be implemented rests with the Secretary of State. The board with which the Committee has been chiefly concerned is the North of Scotland Hydro-electric Board. This Board furnishes all information about the proposed scheme, the information about the fisheries has to be obtained by discussion with proprietors, District Boards, where they exist, and others having knowledge of the waters affected. Often only a few catch statistics are available and the Committee is further hampered by having no investigating staff. However, although the Committee have built up a fund of experience, as their field work is limited to on-the-spot inspections, their methods, by force of circumstance, are rather unscientific.

The proposals for hydro-electric schemes are normally made known to the Fisheries Committee at an early stage, and the North of Scotland Hydro-electric Board begin negotiation with District Boards and proprietors concerned. The scheme is later published and time allowed for objections. If an objection is taken to the stage of an inquiry, the views of the Fisheries Committee, which have been confidential to the Board and to the Secretary of State, are placed before the inquiry, and have often been stated in the Press notice announcing it. If there is no inquiry, the recommendations of the Fisheries Committee are first made public when the Secretary of State announces his decision and lays an explanatory memorandum before Parliament (*Scottish Salmon and Trout Fisheries*. Cmnd. 2691, 1965, p. 72).

In order to fulfil their obligations under the Act to avoid possible injury to fisheries, the North of Scotland Hydro-electric Board built salmon hatcheries in connection with certain schemes where spawning grounds were due to be flooded and installed fish-passes and fish-lifts where fish migrations would be hindered by dams. The Fisheries Committee informed the Secretary of State in May, 1956, that in the light of the information available to them they were not satisfied that fish-passes and lifts in operation at that time were allowing smolts and kelts to descend freely. They felt that the matter was of such importance in the interests of fish preservation that an independent investigation should be made. At that time a committee, the Salmon Research Committee, was already in existence to design, keep under review and have general direction of the census of ascending adult fish and descending smolts to be undertaken on the River Conon and its tributaries by the Scottish Home Department and North of Scotland Hydro-electric Board and to take cognisance of the related programme of salmon research in the same area. It was therefore decided to appoint a Pass Investigation Sub-Committee of the Salmon Research Committee to carry out an investigation into the descent of smolts and kelts at the fish passes and lifts in operation and this Sub-Committee was appointed in August, 1956. A report of the Sub-Committee on a preliminary inquiry into this question was published by Her Majesty's Stationery Office just over a year later entitled, *The Passage of Smolts and Kelts through Fish Passes*. In their report they recommended that a programme of research should be designed to cover: (*a*) factors influencing smolt behaviour; (*b*) experimental modifications of the fish-passes and (*c*) a further study of the environmental conditions of parr and smolts particularly in the Bran and Meig. Much of this research has now been carried out and is described in Chapter 10.

In Sweden the Water Law is administered by a Water Court. The country is divided into six areas, each having a Water Court consisting of a chairman, who is a lawyer with the standing of a judge, assisted by two engineers and two lay members. Any sizeable development proposed which is likely to affect a river or lake must be submitted to the local Water Court who not only consider the promoter's case and any objections thereto, but may also initiate investigations on their own account. In this way independent expert evidence on fisheries may be obtained. The Water Court consider the case against the background of the Water Law, which is a comprehensive code describing in detail the circumstances in which development may be allowed, the compensation payable and other requirements. If a hydro-electric scheme is going to harm property, the Water Court assess in money terms the benefits and disadvantages of the scheme and applies a formula given in the Water Law. This decision is determined by the results of this assessment and calculation. There is also provision for appeals against decisions of local Water Courts.

9.5 Miscellaneous Acts and Reports

Diseases of Fish Act, 1937. In order to prevent the spreading of disease among salmon and freshwater fish in Great Britain the Diseases of Fish Act was passed in 1937. This enables the Minister of Agriculture and Fisheries and the River Authorities in England, and the Secretary of State for Scotland and the Scottish District Fishery Boards to take measures to check the spread of disease among fish in much the same ways as diseases of farm animals are checked.

The Act prohibits absolutely the importation into Great Britain of any live fish of the salmon family which is defined to include all fish of whatever genus or species belonging to the family Salmonidae.

Live freshwater fish, or live eggs of fish of the salmon family, or of freshwater fish, may not be imported into Great Britain except under a licence issued by the Minister, or Secretary of State, to the person they are consigned to.

If at any time the Minister is satisfied that waters in any area are infected with furunculosis, or any disease of fish, such as U.D.N., which the 1937 Act may be extended to by Order in Council, he may make an order declaring the area to be an infected area. This enables him to use special powers to prevent the spreading of disease.

The Bledisloe Report, 1961. A committee was set up in October, 1957, by the Minister of Agriculture, Fisheries and Food "to review the English Salmon and Freshwater Fisheries Acts, 1923–35, and their operation, taking into account the provisions of the River Boards Act, 1948; and to make recommendations". A comprehensive report, known as the Bledisloe Report, after the chairman of the Committee the Rt. Hon. the Viscount Bledisloe, was published in 1961.

This report, among other things, outlined the history of local fishery administration, the conservation of fisheries, obstruction to the passage of migratory fish, water abstraction, pollution, constitution and function of river boards, fishery finance and licences and penalties and legal procedure. One of the useful appendices gives details of salmon and trout catches, going back to the late nineteenth century in some cases, on twenty-three English and Welsh rivers. The report (Cmnd. 1350, 1961) made a number of suggested alterations of the law and some of these alterations were made in the Salmon and Freshwater Fisheries Act (Amendment), 1965. Many of the other suggested recommendations have not yet been implemented and it is understood that no action was to be taken on these until such time as the Hunter Committee Report was published.

The Hunter Committee Report, 1963 and 1965. A committee, under the chairmanship of Lord Hunter, was set up in 1962 "to review the law relating to salmon and trout fisheries in Scotland, including the Tweed, and its operation, with special reference to the constitution, powers and functions of District Boards, and the responsibilities of the Secretary of State, and to consider in the light of current scientific knowledge the extent to which fishing for salmon and trout by any method, whether in inland waters or in the sea should be regulated, and to recommend such changes in the law as might be thought desirable".

First Report (Cmnd. 2096, 1963). The Committee was asked to give priority to that part of their remit which dealt with the regulation of fishing for salmon and migratory trout, and if possible to submit an interim report. The Secretary of State pointed out that although the question related to all forms of fishing, it had been thrown into prominence by the problem of drift-netting (pp. 7 and 8); and that it was his intention to make a Prohibition Order when the power to do so became available on the passage of the Sea Fish Industry Bill, which was then before Parliament.

It became apparent to the Committee that they could not deal adequately with the regulation of all forms of salmon fishing until they had taken evidence on the whole of their remit. They therefore decided to concentrate in the first place on the issue of drift-net fishing for salmon as it seemed possible that they might be able to prepare an interim report on that subject. This they did and the subject was dealt with at length in their interim report published in 1963.

After reviewing the development of drift-net fishing, and reviewing some of its effects and its possible extension, the Committee considered possible interim measures. At the time of the report there were available a number of powers of control. Section 7 of the Sea Fish Industry Act, 1959, as amended gives the Ministers powers to make Orders prohibiting fishing for salmon and migratory trout in any area within or outside territorial waters adjacent to Great Britain. The methods of fishing that are prohibited must be stated in the Order, which would apply within the limits of territorial waters to all fishing boats and outside those limits to British boats. Section 2 of the White Fish and Herring Industries Act, 1948, was amended in 1962 to give the Ministers power to prohibit fishing for salmon and migratory trout in any part of the sea specified in the appropriate Order except under licence. In other words, fishing boats working in the sea for the capture of salmon and trout could be controlled by a scheme of licensing. The report goes on to say:

> Powers to prohibit the landing in the United Kingdom of salmon and migratory trout are conferred on Ministers by Section 2 of the Sea-Fishing Industry Act, 1933, as amended. Under these powers, Ministers may prohibit the landing in the United Kingdom of salmon and migratory trout taken in waters specified in the Order, subject to such limitations as they may impose regarding the method of fishing and time of capture and to such exceptions as are mentioned in the Order.
>
> The Acts of 1933, 1948, 1959 and 1962 apply only to sea fisheries and although the point could be settled only by a court, we understand that Departmental legal advisers take the view that the provisions of these Acts which we have briefly described could not be used to regulate fixed engines on the coast, nor net and coble fisheries in estuaries and rivers. Any change in the weekly close time, any country-wide change in annual close times and any restriction on traditional

H

methods of fishing would require an Act of Parliament and would not be classed as interim measures in the way we regard them. All that could be achieved by Order would be to prevent the holders of coastal salmon fishing rights as well as others from using drift nets or other methods of sea fishing from boats in those parts of their fisheries which are in the sea.

Some of the main findings summarised at the end of the Report were as follows:

1. Any problem of the salmon fisheries must be considered in the light of the life history of the fish.
2. Since the Acts of 1862 and 1868 there have been great changes in the fishing gear and in the salmon's environment. The salmon fishing law of Scotland is partly outdated, but the fundamental assumption that control of fishing is necessary for the preservation of the fisheries remains true.
3. Salmon are faced with man-made hazards arising from exploitation of the species and interference with its habitat as well as from naturally occurring changes. If all netting rights were exercised in full the strain on the stocks would be substantially increased.
4. Drift-net fishing has already had some effect on the structure of the coastal and river netting industry.
5. An unregulated drift-net fishery could quickly deplete salmon stocks in some rivers.
6. None of the following methods of regulation would by themselves or in combination be a successful means of control of the drift-net fisheries: annual and weekly close-times, restriction on the length and mesh of nets, licensing of boats, catch quotas, length of boats and licensing of nets.
7. Drift-net fishing does not have such merits as a means of exploitation that its development should be encouraged.
8. Drift-net fishing has introduced a serious risk of overfishing and has the added disadvantage that a permanent drift-net fishery on any material scale would frustrate or prevent scientific management of individual salmon rivers and their most economic exploitation.
9. Other methods of salmon fishing as well as drift-netting have their disadvantages and this aspect will be considered in the second stage of the inquiry.

Second Report (Cmnd. 2691, 1965). Many of the points considered by the Hunter Committee will be discussed in the final chapter of this book. Perhaps two of the most important statements made in this report were that:

If Scottish salmon fisheries are to be used to produce the maximum benefit for the country, the methods of controlling the fisheries must be capable of something more positive than maintaining the spawning stock, vital though that is. The existing methods of regulation, which have the survival of the stock as their main objective and thus always tend to err on the safe side, must be replaced by a system of management under which the right numbers of fish are caught in the ways which bring the greatest advantage. It should be capable of dividing the run between the commercial catch on the one hand and the angling stock and breeding escapement on the other, in such proportions as are required. It should ensure that the breeding escapement is sufficient without being excessive. It should provide a way of measuring as accurately as possible the effect of any changes which have occurred naturally or by design.

We believe that commercial fishing should be permitted only in the river and by methods that allow the catch and escapement to be measured with reasonable accuracy.

This latter statement referred to a recommendation that the commercial catch of a river should be made at a single point, preferably by a trap, or failing that, by concentrated net fishing associated wherever possible with a counting device.

Two of the many recommendations which could have far-reaching effects on Scottish salmon and trout administration were (1) the formation of Area Boards and (2) a licensing system whereby all anglers should be required to hold rod licences for both salmon and trout.

None of the recommendations made by the Hunter Committee have as yet been implemented.

Forest Act, Forest Management (Canada). There is little in the way of legislation to control the effects of various forestry practices in Great Britain. However, we may in time adopt some of the steps taken by the Canadian Department of Fisheries and Forestry in this respect.

Many of the recommendations concerning fisheries in the Canadian Sloan Commission on Forestry, 1956, have now been implemented and Pennell (1959) refers to the arrangements in the Prince Rupert area, British Columbia, between the forestry and fisheries departments. As soon as an application for logging is received at the district forester's office the files are consulted to see if a salmon stream is within the area to be logged – the salmon streams within forestry areas having been indicated on forestry maps by the fisheries inspectors of each sub-district. If a salmon stream or a portion of a stream is involved, the district supervisor is advised and he notifies the fisheries inspector in charge of the district involved requesting that he recommend the most suitable clause of the Forest Act, Forest

Management, that would provide adequate protection to the salmon stream involved. The clause is then inserted in the logging contract and once the licence is granted the fisheries inspector can carry out periodic checks to ensure that the conditions of the contract are not being violated. The forest management clauses most applicable are:

[L30]: The licensee shall at all times keep all streams and stream beds free from logging debris, sawdust and slabwood, and shall cause no interference with, or obstruction to, stream flow at any time. All trees felled within . . . . . . feet of the . . . . . . stream shall be felled away from the creek.

[L30A]: It is understood and agreed that it is a condition of this contract that no slash or other logging debris is to be placed in any stream channel, neither are earthfilled stream crossings to be used, nor are logs to be skidded within any stream channel whether containing water at the time or not.

[L30B]: All streamside trees within . . . . . . chains of any stream or stream bed on the sale area, which are required to be cut under contract shall be felled away from the stream even though this may require special measures.

[L30C]: All logging and road building debris shall be kept out of streams at all times and out of reach of high water. Such logging and road building debris as does get into the streams shall be removed by methods as directed by the forestry officer in charge.

9.6 Canadian fisheries legislation

Under the British North America Act of 1867 the federal government was given blanket legislative authority over all fisheries matters in Canada. In years to follow several of the provinces were granted rights to administer their own fisheries in whole or in part, but the power to legislate with respect to management and control of the fisheries remains a federal power which is exercised on the recommendation and with the concurrence of the province concerned.

Federal responsibility for the administration of fisheries also carries with it certain responsibilities for the control of pollution in fish-bearing waters. Pollution laws were first embodied in the Fisheries Act of 1868. Today the Department of Fisheries and Forestry acts under the Fisheries Act of 1932 which has a section devoted to the "Injury of fishing grounds and pollution of waters." This section was revised a few years ago but it has changed little from pollution sections of the first Fisheries Act of 1868. The control of pollution has now, however, been extended to several other Canadian Government departments.

Chapter 10

CONTROLLING THE EFFECTS
OF MAN'S ACTIVITIES

10.1 Pollution control. 10.2 Water abstraction and river flow
arrangements. 10.3 Fish facilities at hydro-electric schemes.

10.1 Pollution control

One of the first questions to ask when the problem of pollution control is
raised is, what is the acceptable minimum river water quality standard?
Lester (1967) gives perhaps the best answer when he says:

> The minimum river quality standard which is acceptable to River
> Authorities, which are also fishery authorities, is one that requires the
> river to support a fishery. Fish are excellent indicators of pollution,
> for they often demonstrate with their lives when the dissolved oxygen
> level approaches zero, due to organic pollution, or when the river
> becomes toxic due to ammonia, cyanide, phenol or non-ferrous metals.
> Such a water is unlikely to be suitable as raw water for potable water
> supplies, or for many industrial processes without very extensive
> treatment.

Standards are of great value in that they permit self-control by dis-
chargers; furnish a historical documented story of an event and thus assist
in controlling the future, and they make possible the definition of a problem.
McGauhey (1968) tabulates the standards of water quality currently used
in relation to public supply, agriculture and industry.

Classification of rivers. The Royal Commission on Sewage Disposal, in
the course of investigations on the quality of the water of a number of
rivers in England, suggested a classification of river waters into groups (very
clean, clean, fairly clean, doubtful and bad) based on the general visible
condition of a stream as indicated by such characteristics as smell, degree of

turbidity, presence or absence of fish, presence of suspended matter, nature of algal growth, etc. The observed physical and biological condition of the stream was correlated with the average analytical figures of the water above and below a sewage outfall and results produced by the Royal Commission Reports are given in Tables 21 and 22.

TABLE 21

Classification of rivers in accordance with their visible degree of cleanness, based on riverside observations under normal summer conditions. From 8th Report of Royal Commission on Sewage Disposal, Vol. II, Sect. 6, Cd. 6943, H.M.S.O. (1913)

Observed condition of river water	Very clean	Clean	Fairly clean	Doubtful	Bad
Suspended matter	Clear	Clear	Fairly clear	Slightly turbid	Turbid
Opalescence	Bright	Bright	Slightly opalescent	Opalescent	Opalescent
Smell on being shaken in bottle	Odourless	Faint earthy smell	Pro- nounced earthy smell	Strong earthy or wormy smell	Soapy, faecal or putrid smell
Appearance in bulk	Limpid	—	Slightly brown and opalescent	Black looking	Brown or black and soapy look- ing
Delicate fish	May be plentiful	Scarce	Probably absent	Absent	Absent
Coarse fish	—	Plentiful	Plentiful	Scarce	Absent
Stones in shallows	Clean and bare	Clean	Lightly coated with brown fluffy deposit	Coated with brown fluffy deposit	Coated with grey growth and deposit
Stones in pools	Clean and bare	Covered with fine light brown deposit	Lightly coated with brown fluffy deposit	Coated with brown fluffy deposit	Coated with brown or black mud
Water weeds	Scarce	Plentiful. Fronds clean ex- cept in late autumn	Plentiful. Fronds brown coloured in places	Plentiful and covered with fluffy deposit	Scarce
Green algae	Scarce	Moderate quantities in shallows	Plentiful in shallows	Abundant	Abundant in pro- tected pools
Grey algae	—	—	—	Present	Plentiful
Insects, larvae, etc.	—	—	—	Plentiful in green algae	Abundant in green algae

Another useful classification is that given by the then Trent River Board, now the Trent River Authority, in their Annual Report for 1958 and based upon the 4-hour permanganate value, the 5-day B.O.D., the ammoniacal nitrogen content, the summer dissolved oxygen concentration, the prominent animal life present and the use to which the river is put (Table 23a).

TABLE 22

Average analytical figures for river waters above and below sewage outfall: Royal Commission on Sewage Disposal. From 8th Report of Royal Commission on Sewage Disposal Vol. I, Cd. 6464. H.M.S.O. (1912)

Observed condition of stream	5-day B.O.D. 18.3° C p.p.m.	4 hours O.A. from N/80 KMnO$_4$ at 80° F p.p.m.	Ammoniacal N p.p.m.	Albuminoid N p.p.m.	Nitric N p.p.m.	Susp. solids p.p.m.	Chloride, as Cl p.p.m.	Oxygen in solution when analysed ml/l	p.p.m.
Very clean	1	2	0.04	0.1	0.5	4	10	7.8	11
Clean	2	2.5	0.24	0.25	2	15	25	6.5	9.3
Fairly clean	3	3	0.67	0.35	2.2	15	30	6.2	8.6
Doubtful	5	5	2.5	0.6	5	21	50	4.6	6.6
Bad	10	7	6.7	1.0	4	35	> 50	Low	Low

TABLE 23a

Approximate classification of quality and use of River Trent and 69 tributary streams by the Trent River Authority. (Source: *Annual Report of the Trent River Board, 1958*)

Class of Stream	Prominent Animals	Total River Miles = 975		Average Chemical Analyses in parts per million				Approximate 'Use' Classification	Biotic index[a] (approximate)
		Miles	Percentage	P.V. (4 hour)	B.O.D. (5 day)	A.N.	D.O. (summer)		
I	Trout Grayling Stoneflies Mayflies	230	23½	0 to 3	0 to 3	0 to 0.5	10 to 8	Domestic Water Supply.	8–10
II	Chub Dace Caddis Shrimps	300	31	3 to 6	3 to 10	0.5 to 1.0	9 to 7	Agriculture, Industrial processes and wash waters.	6–7
III	Roach Gudgeon Hog-lice (Asellus) and Leeches	260	26½	6 to 10	10 to 15	1 to 4	7 to 5	Condenser Water Irrigation.	4–5
IV	No fish Red Chironomids (bloodworms)	105	11	10 to 20	15 to 30	4 to 10	5 to 2	Very little. Unsuitable for any amenity use.	2–3
V	Barren or with fungus or small worms (Tubifex)	80	8	over 20	over 30	over 10	below 2	None.	0–1

P.V. Permanganate value.
B.O.D. Biochemical oxygen demand.
A.N. Ammoniacal nitrogen.
D.O. Dissolved oxygen.

[a] Biotic index does not appear in the original table but has kindly been added by Mr Woodiwiss of the Trent River Authority.

Table 23b
Classification of Biological Samples

Clean			Total number of groups present				
			0–1	2–5	6–10	11–15	16+
					Biotic index		
	Plecoptera nymph present	More than one species	—	7	8	9	10
		One species only	—	6	7	8	9
	Ephemeroptera nymph present	More than one species[1]	—	6	7	8	9
		One species only[1]	—	5	6	7	8
	Trichoptera larvae present	More than one species[2]	—	5	6	7	8
		One species only[2]	4	4	5	6	7
	Gammarus present	All above species absent	3	4	5	6	7
	Asellus present	All above species absent	2	3	4	5	6
	Tubificid worms &/or Red Chironomid larvae present	All above species absent	1	2	3	4	—
polluted	All above types absent	Some organisms such as *Eristalis tenax* not requiring dissolved oxygen may be present	0	1	2	—	—

Organisms in order of tendency to disappear as degree of pollution increases

[1] *Baetis rhodani* excluded.
[2] *Baetis rhodani* (Ephem.) is counted in this section for the purpose of classification.

Groups

The term 'Group' here denotes the limit of identification which can be reached without resorting to lengthy techniques. Thus the Groups are as follows:
Each known species of Platyhelminthes (flatworms).
Annelida (worms) excluding genus Nais.
Genus Nais (worms).
Each known species of Hirudinae (leeches).
Each known species of Mollusca (snails).
Each known species of Crustacea (Asellus, shrimps).
Each known species of Plecoptera (stone-fly).
Each known genus of Ephemeroptera (may-fly) excluding *Baetis rhodani*.
Baetis rhodani (may-fly).
Each family of Trichoptera (caddis-fly).
Each species of Neuroptera larvae (alder-fly)
Family Chironomidae (midge larvae) except *Chironomus Ch. thummi*.
Chironomous Ch. thummi (blood worms).
Family Simulidae (black-fly larvae).
Each known species of other fly larvae.
Each known species of Coleoptera (beetles and beetle larvae).
Each known species of Hydracarina (water-mites).

PLATE 18

The Faskally dam at
Pitlochry, Perthshire,
showing the salmon
ladder. This fish pass
is 1,020 feet long.
There are 34 pools,
including three large
resting pools, all con-
nected by underwater
pipes. The rise from
pool to pool is 18
inches. The pass has
two observation
chambers, one where
the public can watch the
fish and one where the
fish are recorded by a
watcher.

PLATE 19

Untreated sewage from Edinburgh is discharged into the Firth of Forth at the rate of 53 million gallons a day. A large sewage slick is very much in evidence from the air.

Woodiwiss (1964) of the Trent River Authority describes a biological system of stream classification and Table 23b depicts this classification of biological samples. Many authorities have adopted the Royal Commission classification of streams based upon B.O.D. (Table 24). This classification can only be used as a rough guide and is only fairly satisfactory if the pollution is predominantly of an organic nature measurable by the B.O.D. test and so long as toxic substances are not present in sufficient concentrations to cause material interference with the test.

Disposal and treatment. There are various ways of disposing of or treating effluents depending upon the industry and the nature of the waste. Effluents may be disposed to rivers, sewers, tidal waters, to the land or to disused mines or mine shafts. The various forms of treatment include biological treatment, chemical precipitation, screening, lagooning, settling, floatation, spreading on the land, aeration and filtration. However, Klein (1966) stresses that:

> before a satisfactory method of dealing with a particular industrial waste problem can be recommended, it is essential to make a thorough preliminary survey of the volumes and characteristics of the various waste waters over a sufficiently long period. . . . It must be emphasised that each trade effluent must be considered on its merits and the best and most economic method of treatment must be determined for each type of waste after exhaustive laboratory experiments have been carried out, followed by extensive pilot plant tests, and finally full-scale plant tests.

Before construction of a trade waste purification plant advisers on their construction usually require to know: (1) the nature of processes and materials used; (2) chemical composition of the effluents, including suspended solids, total solids, permanganate value, B.O.D., pH value, alka-

TABLE 24

Extended Royal Commission classification of rivers used by Mersey and Weaver River Authority

5-day B.O.D. of river (20° C) p.p.m.	Classification
1 or less	Very clean
About 2	Clean
About 3	Fairly clean
About 5	Doubtful
About 7·5	Poor
About 10	Bad
20 or more	Very bad

linity or acidity, temperature, as well as any special constituents such as oil, free chlorine, sulphide, cyanide, phenols and metallic contaminants; (3) maximum, minimum and average volumes of discharges in gallons per hour, and the number of hours per day during which the discharges occur.

Disposal to sewers. Trade wastes are often disposed of by discharge into sewers where they pass on to the sewage disposal works for biological treatment along with the domestic sewage. This is not always possible and is avoided if the trade waste is likely to interfere with the efficiency of the biological filters or is too large in volume. Even after the reception of trade wastes to the sewers, the final effluent discharging from the sewage works to the river must still comply with any standards set by the river authority. In some areas wastes may be passed into trunk sewers which often discharge directly into the sea without any form of treatment.

Disposal to tidal waters. More industries are now sited on estuaries as there is an abundant supply of water suitable for industrial purposes and good facilities for discharging relatively untreated effluents without affecting other water users. Edinburgh, for example, at present discharges all its sewage and trade wastes directly into the Firth of Forth (Plate 19). However, the idea that effluents can be discharged into tidal water without having any harmful effects is erroneous. The practice of discharging large volumes of untreated trade effluents into many estuaries has led to increased pollution often resulting in fish mortalities. Even as long ago as 1935 large numbers of salmon and sea trout smolts were killed in the polluted Tees and Tyne estuaries when they migrated through the pollution barrier.

Settling. The usual method of removing settleable solids by gravitation is by the use of lagoons or settling tanks. These are particularly useful for waste waters from sand, gravel and coal washing plants which require little other treatment than settlement. They are also used in the paper industry to remove pulp wastes, phosphate reduction plants and in meat and poultry processing. Tanks should be frequently cleaned and the accumulated sludge removed.

Floatation. Floatation is a method used to get rid of suspended solids which do not settle easily, and also oil, grease and fat. This process involves causing the matter to rise to the surface of a liquid as a floating sludge, usually by aeration.

Biological treatment. Biological treatment of sewage effluent is simply an artificial intensification and acceleration of the ordinary aerobic processes of natural purification that go on in rivers polluted by limited amounts of organic wastes. The modern biological methods of sewage treatment are described in some detail by Klein (1966) and others.

Very briefly, they are (1) Activated sludge, which incorporates digestors to treat the sludge. The methane gas produced is frequently used to supply power at generating stations. (2) Biological percolating filtration system, where the sewage effluent, after primary sedimentation to remove grosser solid materials, is filtered through biologically active beds of filtering medium before final discharge.

Percolating filters require high initial costs but low running costs, they work well in the summer but are liable to clog and freeze in winter. Some of the other drawbacks of this process are that they are unsuitable for strong and difficult industrial wastes, a large area of land is necessary, there is a smell and fly nuisance and it produces a highly nitrified effluent with much suspended solid. One aid to the natural biological purification of sewage is fish ponds. Such ponds have been in use in Germany for many years (Waddington, 1963).

Removal of synthetic detergents (Syndets). Attempts have been made to remove detergents from sewage effluents by the use of activated carbon, ion exchange, chemical precipitation and foam fractionation but all these methods are expensive. However, it may be unnecessary soon to have to remove syndets from effluents, as some biologically soft detergents have already been tested and used on a large scale in some areas.

10.2 Water abstraction and river flow arrangements

The question of minimum acceptable flows and the problem of how much water to allow to be abstracted from the river has already been raised (p. 169). Before it is possible to decide what is the minimum acceptable flow in any river certain basic information on the river flow is required, for example one needs to know the yearly river flow pattern, the frequency, size and duration of peak floods, the frequency and length of droughts and the average daily flow. It is also essential that this information is collected over a fairly long period of time (e.g. 5 to 10 years). Then there are a number of other factors to be taken into consideration when deciding what is an acceptable flow and these include: (1) existing abstractions, and returns of surface and ground water, including the effect of land drainage and land use all over the catchment area. (2) quality of the water, including its chemistry, temperature, silt load in flood and drought conditions and the influences of pollution. (3) the fisheries. (4) the use for navigation, and (5) the amenity of the river and its use for recreational purposes.

The procedure for fixing a Minimum Acceptable Flow is laid down in section 19 of the Water Resources Act and its object is to ensure that consideration is given to all these factors.

Up until recently there were very few, if any, rivers for which a complete record of annual flow pattern was available, with the exception of rivers harnessed for hydro-electric power. River flow data are now being collected by the English river authorities and the Scottish purification boards.

From a fishery point of view it is essential to know, in terms of water supply, what are the minimum needs of fisheries. It is the migratory species particularly for which this information is required, as while a discharge may be sufficient to maintain the survival of non-migratory species it may be insufficient to encourage movement of migratory species and facilitate their capture by rod and line. However, the minimum acceptable flow for these requirements is not needed for the whole of the year and a smaller flow may be sufficient at other times for spawning requirements and the survival of the progeny.

A number of investigations have been undertaken to determine the effects of river discharge on migratory fish. Brayshaw (1967) states that evidence so far available indicates that migration and successful angling reach a peak of intensity over a discharge range of 0·7 to 1·5 times average daily flow.

Attempts are made on rivers where water abstraction schemes exist to induce fish to move upstream by means of artificial floods or 'freshets'. This has been shown to be successful in at least one case on a river unaffected by water abstraction and that was on the Grimersta River in the Outer Hebrides. A small impounding dam was removed so as to create an artificial spate in order to bring up salmon which had gathered in the tidal waters because of drought conditions in the river. This was so successful that three anglers caught over 400 salmon in the following ten days. However, not all artificial freshets are so successful.

The work of Hayes (1953) on the La Have River, Nova Scotia, has probably supplied most information on the effects of artificial freshets on the upstream migration of salmon, and the following conclusions were reached:

1. Large or small natural freshets are capable of moving fish when other factors like wind and tide are favourable, otherwise they have no effect.
2. Major runs can occur without the aid of natural or artificial freshets and can be maintained by a steady flow of water during the 'run' season.
3. Artificial freshets can move fish, which happen to be at the head of tide, into fresh water, but are unable by themselves to move fish into the estuary, but if they are timed with wind and tides they could probably bring fish into the estuary as well (Fig. 40).
4. The reverse of a freshet, that is, cutting down the river level and then increasing it again, may also act as an effective stimulus in moving fish.
5. Temperature appeared to have little effect in initiating runs.

6. Fish move out of tidal waters into freshwater at dusk and light change could be the operating factor.

7. Strong onshore winds, approaching 20 m.p.h., induce salmon to concentrate in the river estuary and eventually ascend.

8. Peaks in the tidal cycles representing daily increasing difference between high and low tides seem to be effective in concentrating salmon in the estuary and initiating a run into fresh water.

Baxter (1961) examined the water requirements for migratory fish on a number of British rivers and produced a plan of water control which took account of the likely needs of the fish at all stages in their life history. He strongly advocates the use of freshets in any river system which has been regulated by man.

From a number of considerations Baxter produced a schedule of flows (Table 25) as a guide which could be changed to meet the needs of individual rivers. For small rivers this schedule represents an annual mean of 18·5% of the average daily flow and for larger rivers 15%. This basic schedule is intended to provide adequate flow and bottom coverage, for example at times when these are needed for spawning, and during the early summer when large areas of water-covered river bottom will allow greater food production used during the growing season of the parr. This schedule does not provide adequate conditions for the ascent of migratory fish, but it is intended that sufficient stored compensation water should be available to provide freshets.

On rivers where a dam is well downstream, so that there will be little natural augmentation to the compensation water, Baxter considered that

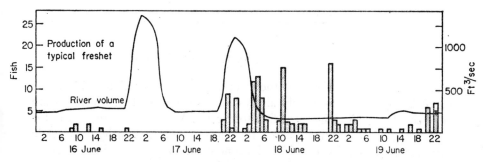

FIG. 40.   Example of the type of freshet production which appeared to be most successful on the La Have River, Nova Scotia in 1950. Two freshets were produced on successive days. Apparently the first one brought salmon some distance up into estuary, and the second one took them into fresh water. Observations were made at a head-of-tide trap (from Hayes, 1953. Reproduced with the permission of the Queen's Printer for Canada).

weekly freshets should be provided from the time that fish are expected to enter the river until spawning time. Where the dam is well upstream a few freshets in summer to bring fish through the fish-pass may be all that is needed if there is adequate spate water entering below the dam.

Banks (1969) has produced a very good review of the literature on the upstream migration of adult salmonids and he considers that for British rivers the general conclusions of Baxter (1961) regarding the volume and number of freshets, and of Hayes (1953) regarding their timing, would seem a reasonable working basis. However, as more data from current investigations are available some modifications to the working plans of Hayes and Baxter will no doubt be possible.

TABLE 25

Schedule of flows, exclusive of freshets (Baxter, 1961)

Month	Smaller rivers % A.D.F.	Larger rivers % A.D.F.	Remarks
October	15 to 12½	15 to 12½	in alternate weeks
November	25	15	
December	25 to 12½	15 to 10	25 and 15 normally only in first 2 weeks
January	12½	10	
February	12½	10	
March	20	15	
April	25	20	
May	25	20	
June	25 to 20	20 to 15	in alternate weeks
July	20 to 15	15 to 12½	in alternate weeks
August	15	15 to 12½	in alternate weeks
September	15 to 12½	15 to 12½	in alternate weeks

10.3 Fish facilities at hydro-electric schemes

On any hydro-electric scheme the river flows have been changed to some extent but provision is nearly always made to ensure that the flows are sufficient to enable migratory fish to ascend. Where spawning areas for salmon and sea trout remain above the dams constructed for hydro-electric purposes it is usually considered economical to provide fish-passes to enable them to complete their upstream journey and breed.

Fish-passes. Some of the earliest fish passes in use at dams were what are known as pool passes. These consist of a series of pools so that the rise from water level below the dam to water level above is broken up into a number of steps which can be negotiated by salmon or sea trout by either swimming or jumping. The pool passes are of two general types, one where the water passes from one pool to the next by falling over a weir and one where the water passes through an orifice in the bottom of the dividing wall between two pools (Plate 18). A development of the normal pool-type pass was the construction of pools spirally inside towers close to the face of the dam (Aitken, Dickerson and Menzies, 1966).

Pool passes are relatively expensive and, owing to site conditions, may present design difficulties in relation to the main dam structure. A pass working on the principle of a canal lock and designed by Borland reduced construction costs considerably. The pass, or fish-lift, provided a design which is readily adaptable and proves to be very effective. The Borland pass consists of two pools, one totally enclosed at river level at the foot of the dam and the other at the level of the impoundment above. The pools are joined by a sloping shaft located in the dam structure. The fish are attracted into the pool at the foot of the shaft. The outlet to the pool is then closed. As the water continues to pour in from the reservoir via the upper pool (Fig. 41), the level rises and the fish rise with it until they reach the top pool and then jump or swim over the sluice into the reservoir. This type of pass is designed to work automatically on a two- or four-hour cycle but, at most of the dams where they are installed in Scotland, they are worked manually as some adjustments to the flow over the top sluice are often found necessary in order to stimulate the fish into jumping or swimming out of the reservoir.

Since in impoundments the water level is often liable to great variations it is necessary to ensure that a pass of any type can be fed with water at any upstream level to enable fish to escape from, or to enter, the pass. For this reason some of the Borland fish passes have two shafts, one coming into operation when the water in the impoundment drops below a certain level. In the Orrin Dam in Ross-shire there are four steel-lined vertical shafts to cater for the seasonal draw-down of this storage reservoir.

One of the chief difficulties experienced with fish-passes is that of ensuring that the entrance will be readily found by the fish and the flow attractive enough to induce them to enter in preference to passing on to other more attractive flows close by. This problem has been discussed at some length by McGrath (1959) who considered that the problem stemmed from the fact that the unidirectional flow of the river downstream from the dam which exerts a directive influence on the fish, is replaced by a many-directional flow caused by the discharge from the turbines. The outflow from the fish-pass which, in many cases, forms a very small proportion of the total discharge has to be found by the fish and be such that the fish are encouraged to move against it into the pass. Because of this it has been found desirable to introduce extra water to form a more attractive flow to the bottom of the pass. This is done by passing an auxiliary flow through a

208

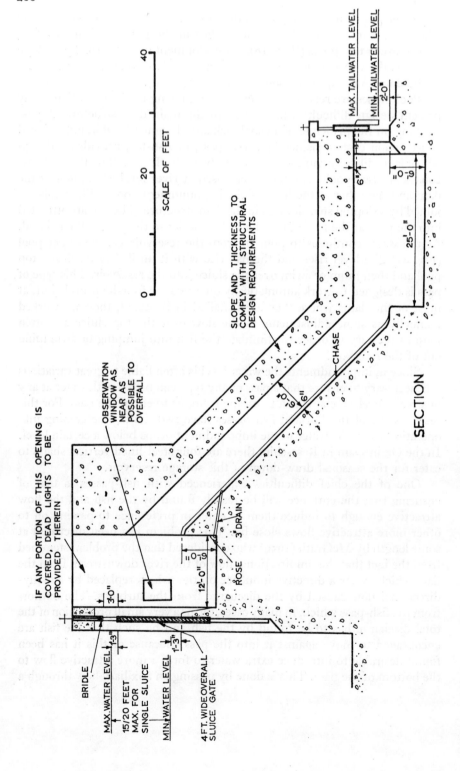

SCALE OF FEET

0   20   40

SECTION

SLOPE AND THICKNESS TO
COMPLY WITH STRUCTURAL
DESIGN REQUIREMENTS

CHASE

3" DRAIN

ROSE

OBSERVATION
WINDOW AS
NEAR AS
POSSIBLE TO
OVERFALL

IF ANY PORTION OF THIS OPENING IS
COVERED, DEAD LIGHTS TO BE
PROVIDED THEREIN

BRIDLE

MAX. WATER LEVEL

15/20 FEET MAX. FOR SINGLE SLUICE

MIN. WATER LEVEL

4 FT. WIDE OVERALL
SLUICE GATE

3'-0"

1'-3"

1'-3"

12'-0"

9'-0"

6"

9'-0"

6"

25'-0"

9'-0"

6"

2'-0"

MAX. TAILWATER LEVEL

MIN. TAILWATER LEVEL

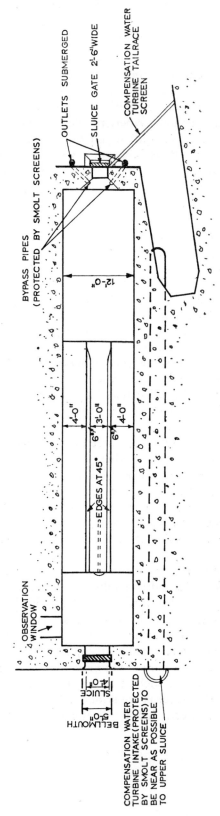

FIG. 41. Parameters for a Borland Fish Pass (from Aitken, Dickerson and Menzies, 1966).

Each site for a Borland Pass or Lock has its own particular characteristics. Where the difference between upstream and downstream level is low, the sloping shaft can be eliminated, in which case the pass in effect becomes a vertical shaft.

For large reservoir operating ranges (e.g. 70 ft) as many as four individual passes or locks have been constructed, as at the Orrin dam, Ross-shire.

small turbine to use the energy in the water; the flow from the draft tube is then directed upwards through the floor of the bottom pool of the pool-type passes or towards the outflow of the Borland passes. Because of these arrangements there have been few problems in getting fish to ascend fish-passes at Scottish hydro-electric installations. Where problems have arisen solutions have soon been found. Mills (1965d) found that more of the salmon passing upstream of a trap on the River Meig in Ross-shire ascended the Borland pass after pools had been constructed below the pass. These allowed the fish to remain in the vicinity of the entrance to the pass until they were inclined to move upstream. Experience has shown that fish do not ascend the fish-pass at all times of the year with equal readiness. Sometimes fish will run freely and ascend a pass continuously. At other times, for reasons seemingly unconnected with the arrangements, few will ascend for a week or more. Where there is a series of dams in the course of a river, fish may ascend one fish-pass, but not, for the time being, the next, so that there is a temporary accumulation between them. McGrath (1959) made an interesting point when he said that reports of the first year's working of fish-passes at hydro-electric dams were not very favourable, whereas the reports of later years were quite favourable. He suggested that this seemed to indicate that there may be some factor in a new pass which deters fish until it has been in operation for some time.

The greatest problem associated with fish-passes has been in encouraging smolts and kelts to descend, and again much depends on the correct siting of the pass and the provision of a surface exit. For example, Mills (1965d) showed that at Meig Dam in Ross-shire, where the pass had been built at one end of the dam, close to the shore, there was little delay of smolts; but at Luichart Dam, where the fish-pass lies to one side of a structure which projects about 25 yards into the reservoir, delay was considerable. At some Scottish hydro-electric installations alternative means for smolt and kelt descent have been provided, such as chutes constructed down the face of the dam, spillways and even bag nets set in the reservoir at the dam face.

Screens. Fish have to be excluded from the turbines and this is done by the introduction of screens or hecks. Ascending adults are excluded from the tailraces to turbines while smolts and kelts are excluded from intakes to turbines or from diversion aqueducts. For ascending fish the screens may be mechanical, providing an actual physical barrier; or electrical, providing a field with intermittent pulses which fish avoid. Aitken, Dickerson and Menzies (1966) suggest that where screens are used to exclude fish from a tailrace channel, the alignment should be such as to lead the fish up the main channel. It has been found that screens are seldom required where turbine draft tubes discharge either directly into the river channel or do so through a very short tailrace. Where screens are not provided, fish may be able to get into the draft tubes of the turbines while they are starting or operating at light load. The best way to avoid this is to run the turbines at flows which will give adequate deterrent velocities. The permissible clear spaces between the vertical bars of the screens, the mesh sizes and velocities through them for installations at Scottish hydro-electric works are given in Table 26.

Because of their mesh construction and the small clearances, smolt screens cannot be cleaned *in situ*. Two sets of guide channels are, therefore, provided so that a spare set of clean screens can be placed in the downstream guide channels before the upstream dirty screens are removed. At large intakes cleaning work has been mechanised by the provision of lifting and washing gantries which deal with complete bays of panels.

There is now ample evidence (Pyefinch and Mills, 1963 and Mills, 1965d) that smolts, unlike kelts, which move away from an obstruction, are extremely persistent in trying to find a way through or around a screen. It is, therefore, essential that all screens fit tightly on the sill and in the guides. The maximum clearance in the guides should be $\frac{1}{4}$ in. This small clearance may make the movement of frames difficult and can best be effected by a rubber seal. Particular care must always be taken in replacing frames after cleaning to ensure that they fit tightly to the sill. The presence of an obstruction, large or small, can prevent the frames resting properly on the sill and so provide a gap through which the smolts can pass. It is of assistance if

TABLE 26

Mechanical screens: The allowable clear spaces and velocity are:—

	Clear space between vertical bars (in.)	Velocity
For ascending salmon	$1\frac{5}{8}$	no limit
For ascending sea trout	$1\frac{1}{4}$–$1\frac{1}{2}$	no limit
For descending salmon kelts	2	$2\frac{1}{2}$–3 ft/s
For descending sea trout kelts	$1\frac{1}{2}$	$2\frac{1}{2}$–3 ft/s

	Mesh screens Clear space between		Velocity
	Vertical wires (in.)	Horizontal wires (in.)	
For descending salmon smolts	1	$\frac{1}{2}$	1 ft/s
For descending parr	$\frac{1}{2}$	$\frac{1}{2}$	1 ft/s

(From: Aitken, Dickerson and Menzies, 1966).

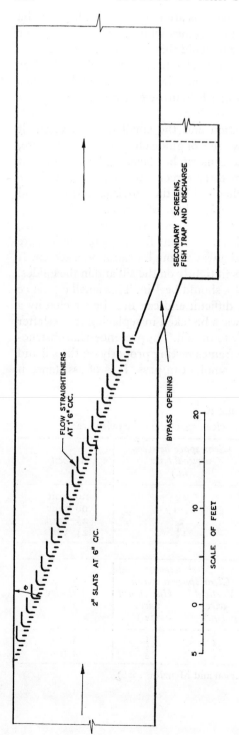

SECONDARY SCREENS,
FISH TRAP AND DISCHARGE

FLOW STRAIGHTENERS
AT 1'6" C/C.

2" SLATS AT 6" C/C.

BYPASS OPENING

20

10

SCALE OF FEET

0

5

FIG. 42

Plan of a louver screen (from Aitken,
Dickerson and Menzies, 1966).

the bottom of the screen frame is fitted with a sharp edge to cut through any soft debris. The sill should be set above the river bed to allow debris to fall away from it. Screens should be kept clean at all times, particularly during the period of the smolt migration. Severe smolt mortalities have occurred when the screens have become clogged with debris with a resultant increase in water velocity through those areas of screen which are relatively clean, the smolts becoming pinned at that point in these areas.

One type of screen which has been used successfully to divert juvenile Pacific salmon from intakes is the louver screen (Fig. 42). These consist of a row of vertical louvers through which water passes inducing small turbulent eddies by the angle at which they are set and through which small fish will not apparently pass. Although these screens are not in use at Scottish hydro-electric installations Munro (1965c) has tested them in an experimental flume in Scotland. The results were encouraging and suggested that, in suitable situations, diversion efficiencies of more than 90% can be expected at velocities of from 2·25 to 3·75 ft/sec with gaps between louvers of up to 6 inches and that, even with 12-inch gaps, the efficiency may be as high as 90%. The screens were equally effective in daylight and darkness.

Electric fish screens for upstream migrants only require to dissipate sufficient power to prevent fish swimming against the water flow. For this reason, alternating current or rectified alternating current can safely be used in this case as, even if fish are tetanised, they are immediately washed downstream into safety and recover at once; in general, Hartley and Simpson (1967) have found that the fish avoid the screen without being incapacitated at all. The situation is not so simple where an electric screen is required to keep descending smolts away from the water flow into a power station, as any interference with the swimming ability of the fish will cause them to be washed farther into the electric field and thus prevented from escaping from the danger which the screen is meant to guard. A pulsed current should be used to avoid interfering with the swimming ability of the fish, and the screen must be located where it can be used to guide the fish into a safe by-pass channel.

Transportation. Instead of constructing fish-passes at some dams, facilities for the trapping and transporting of migrants have been installed. The transportation may, in some cases, involve no more than lifting the trapped adults over the dam and releasing them in the reservoir, while in other cases it may involve the 'trucking' of the trapped adults some distance and releasing them many miles upstream of the installations. For example, at the Mactaquac Dam on the St John River in New Brunswick the ascending salmon are led into trapping or collection pools and guided into submerged hoppers. They are then transferred to large tank trucks and transported overland to release points above the dam site.

In addition to the transporting of adults upstream, the transporting of downstream migrants has also been attempted with some success. Smolts have been transported from the lower reaches of the River Bran, a tributary of the Conon, and released at a point below all the dams on this river system (Mills, 1966). The numbers transported ranged from 180 in 1964 to 9,090 in 1966. The percentage recapture of adult fish, tagged as smolts, from these transport experiments ranged from 2·2 to 4·0 (Fig. 43).

Results from the transport of kelts in Scottish waters have not been so encouraging albeit transport of kelts was tried in only one year. The surprising result of the kelt transport experiment carried out in December on the Inverness-shire Garry was that, although the 280 fish were transported from Loch Poulary, on the upper reaches of the Garry, to the mouth of the

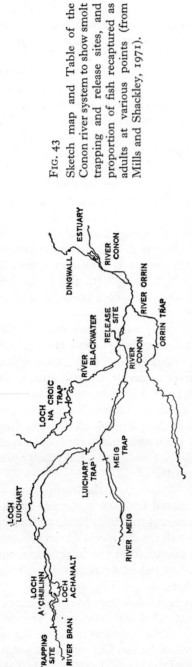

FIG. 43

Sketch map and Table of the Conon river system to show smolt trapping and release sites, and proportion of fish recaptured as adults at various points (from Mills and Shackley, 1971).

Details of transportation experiments, 1963–1966

Year	No. smolts transported	No. tagged	% of smolts recaptured as adult fish	Greenland	Coastal waters	Estuary	Rod & line	River Kelt nets	Traps	Site unknown
						No. recaptured in:				
1963	649	649	2·8 (18)	2	1	2	5	0	7	1
1964	207	180	2·2 (4)	2	0	0	2	0	0	0
1965	536	534	2·2 (12)	1	1	0	5	0	5	0
1966	9090	3347	4·0 (134)	14	4	3	29	15	68	1

Figures in brackets denote numbers of fish.

No. of tagged smolts recaptured in traps as adults.

Year	Luichart	Meig	Loch na Croic	Orrin
1963	6	0	1	0
1964	0	0	0	0
1965	3	1	1	0
1966	45	16	7	0

River Ness, a distance of some 55 miles, some fish were recaptured upstream in Loch Ness, and even in the Garry, a few weeks later. The fish had been stripped of their eggs and milt and this may have had some effect on their behaviour, but even so one of these fish was caught in the Ness as late as May in the following year, which seems to suggest that spent fish may take a considerable time to return to sea.

Artificial propagation. It is the usual practice on rivers affected by hydro-electric schemes to provide facilities for the upstream passage of spawning migrants and the downstream movement of their progeny and the spent spawners so as to ensure that the spawning grounds on the affected river systems are fully utilised and that the angling is not restricted only to the waters below these schemes. However, in some instances, where nursery grounds have been flooded, either alternative areas in the river system have been made available as compensation by liberating young salmon, reared in specially-built hatcheries (Plate 20), in suitable areas previously inaccessible to spawning fish and making arrangements for their return as adults, or supplementing the numbers of young resulting from the reduced spawning stock with hatchery-reared young. These are the type of arrangements that have been made in the United Kingdom and Canada where salmon angling is so important that all efforts to maintain the sport fishery are considered economically worthwhile. As a consequence a number of hatcheries have been built at the same time as the hydro-electric installations and provision for the trapping of adult salmon has been made near these installations so as to ensure the collection of brood stock for the hatcheries. Mills (1964a and 1965c) has given a detailed account of the smolt production resulting from the stocking of ten miles of previously inaccessible spawning and nursery grounds in the River Bran, Ross-shire, which was made available to fish with the advent of the Conon Basin hydro-electric scheme as compensation for the flooding of traditional spawning grounds on one of the other tributaries of the Conon River.

In Sweden artificial propagation has played a much larger part in compensating for the effects of hydro-electric development. While fishways and transportation facilities were used at first, later, as more and more power plants were built, the natural spawning areas, which, in Sweden, usually occur in the main river and not in the small tributaries, were either very much reduced or, in many rivers, completely destroyed. For this reason the few fishways built in later years and many old ones were taken away, and the salmon stock maintained completely by hatcheries (Plate 22). Natural smolt recruitment to the Baltic area from Swedish rivers is now less than 50% of its original value. However, the greatest part of this loss is compensated for by releasing smolts from these hatcheries (Fig. 44). By 1970, according to Lindroth (1965b), the hatcheries will contribute about 50%

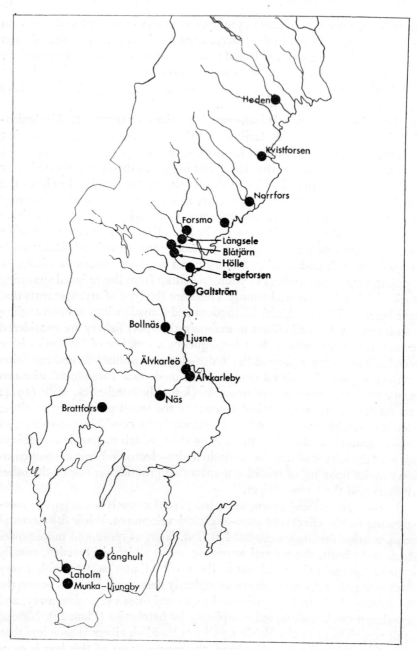

Heden

Kvistforsen

Norrfors

Forsmo
Långsele
Blåtjärn
Hölle
Bergeforsen

Galtström

Bollnäs
Ljusne

Älvkarleö
Älvkarleby

Näs

Brattfors

Långhult

Laholm
Munka–Ljungby

FIG. 44.   Map of Sweden showing salmon hatcheries (from Carlin, 1966).

216

PLATE 20. A vertical tray hatchery. Jars, holding malachite green, are sited at the top of the tiers of trays. This is drip fed into the trays to prevent fungus developing on the eggs. For details of operation see Menzies and Curtis (1966).

PLATE 21. Egg counting trough and perspex counter. The counter has 200 countersunk holes (see text for description). The small plastic boxes are Vibert boxes for holding salmon or trout eggs which can then be planted out in the stream gravel, on hatching the alevins escape through the slots.

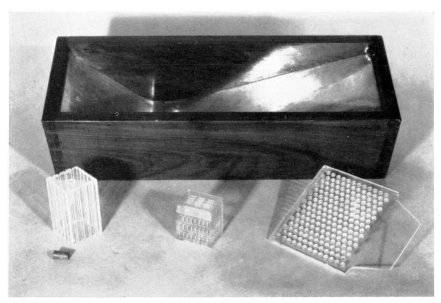

PLATE 22

The Bergeforsen salmon rearing station. The wires stretched across the ponds are to prevent predation by ospreys.

of the original Swedish recruitment to the Baltic salmon stock. The change over to artificial propagation was a relatively uncomplicated situation for the Swedes as they had no sport fishery to consider because the salmon in their northern rivers do not take anglers' lures very readily. However, other problems beset the Swedish authorities and when the decision to maintain the Baltic salmon stock by artificial propagation was considered several questions arose:

1. Is it biologically possible to release artificially reared salmon and to expect them to survive and grow up normally in the sea?
2. Is it technically possible to do so, that is: can one, with a reasonable effort, produce a sufficient number of smolts to maintain the Baltic salmon stock at its former level?
3. Is it economically sound, that is: can the cost of producing the salmon smolts be kept in reasonable proportion to the value of the resulting salmon caught in the fishery?
4. Which methods should be employed in producing the young salmon?

From the results of smolt tagging experiments (since 1950 over 1 million tagged smolts have been released into the lower reaches of Swedish rivers) some of the answers have been obtained for some of these questions. It has been shown that it is quite possible to stock the Baltic by releasing artificially-reared salmon. From the tagging experiments alone 100,000 adult salmon have been recaptured with a total weight of 400 tons. The average return is about 1,000 lb of salmon per 1,000 smolts. The answer to the second question is also in the affirmative and the Swedes now have about 20 major rearing stations with an output of over 1,600,000 salmon smolts and over 140,000 sea trout smolts. Since the total number of smolts entering the Baltic each year has been estimated to be about 5 or 6 millions this means that about 25% of the total number of salmon caught in the Baltic is now artificially reared. According to Carlin the third question is a little more difficult to answer. Before the Swedes started this vast annual production of smolts in their modern hatcheries they assumed that a recapture of 5% of the smolts as adult salmon should be enough to make salmon rearing a paying proposition. The average recapture has turned out to be 10% or more so that the value of the resulting salmon is therefore definitely higher than the cost of producing the young salmon. However, the Swedish share of the catch is not more than 50% of the total catch based upon Swedish salmon rearing, and consequently salmon rearing from the point of view of the Swedish economy alone is a little more doubtful.

The answer to the fourth question is dealt with by Carlin (1966) in some detail. The fish are reared in concrete or fibre glass tanks. The summer stocking density in these tanks is kept up to 3 kg/m² but in the winter can be more than 10 kg/m². At the beginning of this smolt cultivation, mainly fresh food was used, such as liver, spleen blood, fish and fish eggs supplemented with yeast and other vitamin-rich substances. However, in recent years the fresh diet has been almost completely replaced by pelleted dry food. Apart from its nutritional value, the pelleted food has the advantage of reducing the labour employed in the hatchery and also of reducing the contamination of the water. Eklund (1963), in a review of feeding costs of salmon cultivation at Bergeforsen Hatchery showed that the moist feeding costs worked out at 29·91 kr per kg of fish while the dry feeding costs were only 17·03 kr per kg of fish, a saving of 12·88 kr per kg of fish produced. To cut down on the cost of labour all rearing stations have automatic feeders. A strict disease control is also practised at all stations. A comprehensive report giving a complete record of fish culture within the Swedish State Power Board (Vattenfall) from 1950 to 1968 is given by Montén (1969).

Spawning channels. In order to replace several miles of natural spawning grounds lost due to water diversion on the Indian River, Newfoundland, the Canadian Department of Fisheries built a salmon spawning channel. Controlled flow spawning channels are used extensively for Pacific salmon but were, until this occasion, untried for Atlantic salmon. The channel, constructed in 1962–1963, is designed to provide 10,000 square feet of spawning area, capable of accommodating about 300 to 400 adult salmon. Since its construction favourable incubation conditions have resulted in an annual egg to fry survival rate of 40 to 50%. This is not as high as it might be and the problem of the eggs being smothered by a fine suspension of silt has not yet been completely overcome because these channels have not the required hydraulic characteristics of spawning beds described by Stuart (1953b).

Chapter 11

MANAGING THE ENVIRONMENT
AND THE RESOURCE

11.1 Increasing the food supply – fertilisation. 11.2 Population control. 11.3 Removal of unwanted species. 11.4 Stream improvement. 11.5 Increasing spawning and nursery areas. 11.6 Artificial propagation. 11.7 Construction of trout ponds. 11.8 Control of aquatic plants. 11.9 Control of parasites and disease.

11.1 Increasing the food supply – fertilisation

Having considered the means of controlling man's activities, or ameliorating their effects, it is now time to consider ways of controlling or managing the environment and the resource under natural conditions. Most of the methods involve either increasing the food supply or the fish population, both resulting in an increased production of fish flesh. Probably one of the methods that is given the most attention, because of its successful use for land crops, is fertilisation. Fertilisers used most frequently are lime, potassium, phosphorus and nitrogen. To understand their importance and when they should be applied it is useful to know how they act in water.

Lime produces an alkaline reaction and acts as a buffer in the presence of all acids. A weakly alkaline reaction (pH 7 to 8) has been found most productive and very acid waters unproductive. At pH 5·5 fish develop hypersensitivity to bacterial parasites and are not generally able to survive a reaction lower than pH 4·5. Apart from a direct effect on fish, acidity impedes the recirculation of nutrients by reducing the rate of decomposition and inhibiting nitrogen fixation. The calcium in lime will displace certain other fertilising substances from organic colloidal systems, thus making available greater quantities of nutrients such as potassium and phosphate when they are applied during the same season. In the presence of calcium carbonate, colloidal humus gels are flocculated thus increasing the mean particle size of the soil and giving it a loose 'crumb' structure thereby improving permeability and aeration. At the same time, the ability of these colloids to liberate hydrogen by interacting with neutral salts is reduced, resulting in conditions more favourable for rapid bacterial decomposition of organic matter accumulating in the bottom.

Potassium is taken up readily by plant tissues and is particularly effective in stimulating the growth of the soft underwater flora; thus the control of potassium in a pond is associated with the management of aquatic plants. During rapid plant growth potassium from the water and soil is stored in the tissues to be released later when the plants die back and decompose, and then held in the bottom by adsorption. Ponds with sandy, non-adsorptive soils are usually potassium-poor and respond well to fertilisation.

Phosphorus is the most important single fertiliser. It is never present in large quantities naturally and is easily 'lost' from the trophic cycle. According to Neess (1949), it has frequently appeared to assume the role of a limiting factor, and competition for it has been ascribed a reason for periodicity of plankton blooming.

Phosphorus, as phosphate, is removed from the water by the bottom deposits and Brook and Holden (1957) have measured the rate of uptake of phosphate by the mud surface in Loch Kinardochy. Rooted aquatic plants benefit from fertilisation with phosphorus. Neess suggests that since the transpiration stream of plants is upward from the roots, mineral nutrients are probably absorbed from the bottom even though the whole plant is immersed in a dilute nutrient solution. This fact may explain why phosphorus is able to stimulate rooted vegetation without affecting, or even at the expense of, planktonic algae.

Nitrogen. It has been said that bacterial fixation can provide most, if not all, of the nitrogen content of a pond, and Demoll (1925) suggested that additions of nitrogen may stimulate denitrification and may thus be actually detrimental.

Fertilisation of trout waters is often done at random without fishery managers considering the possible effects of their work other than that they hope to produce an increase in fish flesh. In some instances the result is a lake covered with an algal scum and a depleted oxygen content. Hasler and Einsele (1948) have pointed out that these detrimental effects may outweigh the biological gains in pounds of fish and they strongly emphasise designing an experiment to test the effect of lake fertilisation. The type of experiment they recommend is not always possible for many fishery managers but, by considering the general aspects of fertilisation it is possible to know what sort of water responds favourably to fertilisation.

In ponds conditions of productivity differ widely from lakes. In a pond dead organisms readily decompose and enter the food chain immediately

while in a lake they deposit under the thermocline and are kept from entering the plant nutrition cycle for long periods or become permanently
sedimented. However, the littoral zone of a lake, where there is no thermocline, resembles pond conditions. The chief gains in pond productivity
result from the addition of phosphorus. So lakes with an extensive littoral
area and no thermocline will also respond best to fertilisation with phosphorus (P).

The amount of P, as superphosphate, to apply depends upon the extent
of growth of large aquatic weeds such as pond weed (*Potamogeton*) and
lilies. If these are not abundant and the water is fairly hard a fertilisation
rate of about 12 kg/hectare (10·7 lb/acre) is sufficient when considering one
dose in the spring. However, it must be borne in mind that where large
aquatic plants are abundant the benefit of fertilisation to fish may be masked.
This is because these plants take up large quantities of P which stimulate
growth resulting in extensive beds of weed. Therefore, prior to fertilisation,
it is wise to cut and remove the weeds. If the cut weed is left in the lake the
organic matter produced may induce growths of unwanted blue-green
algae.

The addition of P to lakes with a muddy littoral zone encourages rapid
assimilation of elemental nitrogen (N). In a lake with a sandy or stony littoral zone and with few aquatic plants the bottom is not suitable for nitri-
fying bacteria and therefore the addition of P by itself is of little use and
a low productivity will result unless N is also added. However, care should
be taken in controlling the $P:N$ ratio at about 1:2. With the addition of two
fertilisers fertilisation becomes more costly without any assurance that one
can get as good a yield as from a lake whose littoral zone is muddy.

Phosphorus should not be added to acid lakes such as dystrophic or
bog lakes before lime has been added. Lime makes these peat-coloured acid
lakes more transparent as they become neutralised and the pH is raised
producing a medium more suitable for algal production. Lime in the form
of ground limestone is recommended as there is a danger with quick-lime
that the pH value may become too high and the toxic nature of the quick-
lime may prove harmful to the fish population.

There have been numerous experiments on the fertilisation of trout
lakes in Australia (Weatherley and Nicholls, 1955), Canada (Langford,
1950 and Smith, 1948), Ireland (Twomey, 1956), Scotland (Holden, 1959)
and the United States (Ball, 1948). The results of only two of these experiments, one in Scotland and one in Ireland, will be described.

In Scotland four acid and neutral lochs (pH range from 5·6 to 7·3 and
alkinity from 1·0 to 12·0 mg $CaCo_3/l$) were fertilised with phosphate-
containing fertilisers. Two of the lochs were fertilised with a mixed fertiliser (N.P.K.) at the rate of 100 lb/acre with additional sodium nitrate to

raise the nitrogen approximately to the proportion required; the other two lochs were treated with superphosphate at the rate of 60 lb/acre. The amounts added were sufficient to produce roughly the same distribution of phosphorus per unit area in all four lochs (25–30 lb P/acre). Two of the more acid lochs, one treated with N.P.K. and one treated with superphosphate, were also treated with ground limestone at the rate of 10 cwt/ acre. The fertilisers as limestone were spread over the water from a boat. In the year following the first application of fertiliser the percentage conversion of added phosphate to organic forms of phosphorus in the water was greater in the lochs treated with N.P.K. than in those treated with superphosphate. In the former lochs dense populations of phytoplankton were produced. During the two years following the last fertilisation, the organic phosphorus concentrations in the fertilised lochs were significantly higher than in the two unfertilised lochs used as controls, and were comparable with those found in lochs of higher productivity in Scotland. Holden found no evidence for the utilisation of the added potassium by the planktonic algae. He attributed the greater development of this section of the flora, when N.P.K. was used, to the presence of both nitrogen and phosphorus in the fertiliser. There were indications that the attached algal flora increased to a greater extent than the planktonic flora in the absence of added nitrogen.

Morgan (1966) found no change in the biomass of bottom fauna in these lochs until two years after fertilisation when, in one loch, it reached a maximum of 25 times the immediate pre-treatment biomass. He considered the two-year delay in the higher production of bottom fauna following the addition of fertiliser might well have been because the fertilisers were taken up by phytoplankton, the mud and macrophytes and only later released to become available to the algae of the mud and the attached algae, which are important foods of the bottom fauna. Most of the response to fertiliser was produced by a big increase in the number of chironomid larvae.

Although there was this two-year delay in an increased production of bottom fauna the trout showed an immediate response to fertilisation (Munro, 1961) with a much improved growth rate (Figs. 45 and 46), although the timing of its appearance and its duration differed in the various lochs. In one loch, however, a marked change in the growth rate of the trout did not occur until two years after the initial treatment with fertiliser. The increased production of chironomids was not utilised efficiently by the trout and this may have been because the chironomid larvae and pupae were only available to trout for a limited period of the year. There appeared to be no distinct difference between the improvement in trout growth rate produced by the two phosphatic fertilisers and there therefore appears to be no

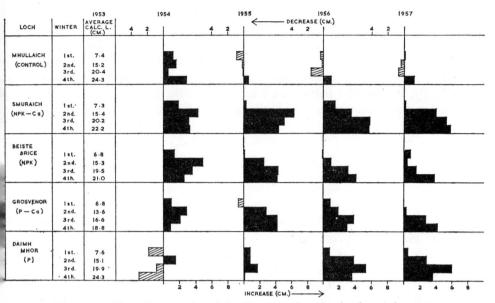

FIG. 45. The effect of mineral fertilisers on the growth of trout in some Scottish lochs, showing decrease or increase in calculated length of fish (from Munro, 1961).

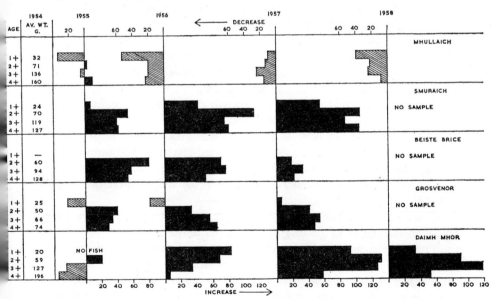

FIG. 46. The effect of mineral fertilisers on the growth of trout in some Scottish lochs, showing percentage decrease or increase in weight of fish (from Munro, 1961).

justification for the greater expense of the mixed type.

Morgan made the useful suggestion that it might be profitable to introduce suitable food organisms such as *Gammarus* spp., *Asellus* spp. and *Limnaea pereger* following the application of fertiliser. He also made the point that, rather than attempt to produce a dense phytoplankton bloom initially, it would be better to try to stimulate the growth of algae of the mud and the attached and epiphytic algae which form a part or the whole of the diet of many members of the bottom fauna. This might be achieved by the use of a pelleted fertiliser, formulated so that the phosphate is released more slowly, or by the use of organic fertilisers. He considered that the culms or draft from whisky distilleries might prove to be a useful organic fertiliser which is locally available in Highland areas of Scotland.

Twomey (1956) describes the effects of fertilising four Irish acid or bog lakes with ground limestone (8 cwt/acre in 3 lakes and 1 ton/acre in 1 lake), superphosphate ($1\frac{1}{2}$ cwt/acre) and commercial potassium chloride (Muriate of Potash) ($\frac{1}{2}$ cwt/acre). The applications were made each April and August for three years. One lake received 60 tons of ground limestone in three applications during the spring, summer and autumn of one year. The artificial fertilisers were added a fortnight after the additions of ground limestone. The addition of ground limestone to all of these lakes had the effect of making the water clearer. During the first year of fertilisation the lakes became 'cloudy' with plankton, the cloudiness lasting until late summer. This condition continued during the three seasons of fertilisation. However, a year after the last fertilisation the phytoplankton in one lake was replaced by filamentous algae which caused an unsightly and malodorous condition. The addition of fertilisers had little or no effect on the growth rate of trout during the first year of application, but in the second and third year the growth rate showed a marked increase in three of the lakes, but in the lake which received the large applications of ground limestone no increase in growth rate was observed. The growth rate of the one- and two-year-old fish prior to and after fertilisation is given in Fig. 47 and it can be seen that there is an appreciable increase in length of the young fish. There was also an increase in the weight increments of the trout (Fig. 48).

The cost of fertilising a lake with superphosphate at the rate of 1 cwt/ acre is in the region of £1 to £3 per acre per annum.

There is also some evidence that, under certain conditions, fertilisation of a stream may produce beneficial results. Mills (1969b) found that there was a substantial increase in the standing crop of young salmon in a moorland stream ($2 \cdot 8$ g./m^2 to $4 \cdot 2$ g./m^2) after the addition of mineral fertiliser to the loch at the head of this stream and an increased discharge from a faulty septic tank. There was no sign of an improvement in the standing crop of a similar moorland stream when fertiliser was added to the stream itself. However, Huntsman (1948) placed bags of fertiliser on the shores of a barren stream in Nova Scotia and found that the effects

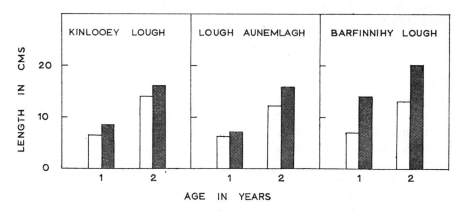

AVERAGE   LENGTH   IN   CENTIMETRES   OF   ONE   AND   TWO - YEAR - OLD TROUT   BEFORE   AND   AFTER   FERTILISATION

☐ BEFORE and

▨ AFTER FERTILISATION

FIG. 47. Average length in centimetres of one- and two-year-old trout before and after fertilisation (from Twomey, 1956).

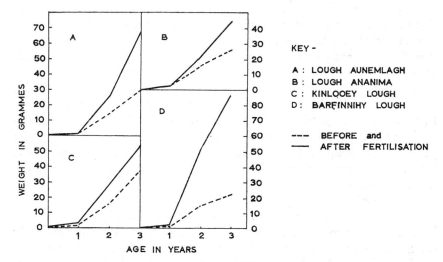

FIG. 48. Average weight increments made during the first three years of life before and after fertilisation (from Twomey, 1956).

I

were beneficial with a resulting growth of algae, rooted plants in the mud and an increased survival of planted salmon fry when previously few had survived. Jones (1957) points out that before this experiment the stream, which was shallow, was not overcrowded with fish, and it carried very little fauna and flora. Whether the effects of such fertilisation would be apparent on fertilising a normal stream is very doubtful.

11.2 Population control

Many trout waters, particularly in moorland and high ground areas, carry large populations of small trout. It had often been suggested that the growth of brown trout might be directly influenced by the chemical nature of the water and that acid water conditions which usually prevail in these areas directly inhibit the growth of brown trout. However, it has been shown earlier (p. 117) in reference to the work of Pentelow and Campbell that populations of large, fast-growing trout are found in acid waters, while populations of small, stunted trout are also found in markedly alkaline waters. Campbell suggests that the growth rate of individual trout is affected primarily by the relative abundance of the food supply. In an acid lake of low biological productivity supporting a low population density of trout, because of restricted spawning facilities, there may be relatively more food available per fish than in a highly productive alkaline lake with good spawning facilities supporting a large population of trout. Many moorland lakes, however, usually have good spawning facilities which result in a large population of small trout. Many anglers and fishery managers also believe that individuals in populations of small trout are stunted owing to genetic factors and that fish of this stock cannot therefore increase their rate of growth significantly even when an abundant supply of food is made available. That this effect, if it exists, is of negligible importance has been demonstrated from the results of fertilisation experiments. It has also been shown in recent years in hydro-electric reservoirs where the newly-inundated land has provided established trout populations with abundant terrestrial food, spectacular increases in growth rate have resulted in all but the youngest age groups of trout (Campbell, 1965). It would appear therefore, that an effective way of improving sport fishing is to adjust the size of the population in relation to the available food supply in such a way that the growth rate of fish is adequate to provide fish of acceptable size.

One way of controlling the fish population is to remove some of the fish by netting. However, this may not have much effect as the netting may only remove some of the larger fish and so allow more of the smaller ones to survive and grow. In addition, netting many moorland lochs some distance from a road is a difficult task and labour costs may make the operation

uneconomical. A more certain way of controlling the population is by restricting the recruitment of young fish to the stock. This is done by either trapping the adults as they ascend the spawning streams and by allowing only a
limited number to spawn, or preventing the adults from ascending the
streams by installing screens. It may be easier to trap all the ascending
adults and strip them of their eggs, some of which can then be planted in
the unused spawning grounds above in Vibert type boxes (Plate 21).
Campbell (1967a) describes a barrier and trap in use for this purpose on
Fincastle Loch in Perthshire (Fig. 49).

While the methods described help to control the fish population the
fishing effort must be sufficient to prevent the water from becoming overpopulated once more. The fishing effort is often insufficient to have much
influence on the fish population, but by dispensing with a size limit it may
be possible to remove a proportion of the excess of small fish. As Pyefinch
(1969a) stresses, it is not always clearly understood that the adjustment of a
fish population is, unless circumstances are exceptional, a long-term project
and, if remedial measures are undertaken, full and careful records of catches
must be kept since otherwise it is difficult, or impossible, to detect the
changes which are taking place. Further, it is rarely, if ever, possible to
produce significant and permanent changes in the fish population in one
operation and, once modifications have been made, the management effort
must also be maintained or else the water will soon revert to its initial state.
If success is achieved, however, it must be remembered that the trout
population is now not in a state of natural equilibrium, and if any of the
remedial measures are relaxed, the trout population will quickly revert to
its natural state of balance.

11.3 Removal of unwanted species

It is often necessary to control or eliminate coarse or rough fish in salmon
and trout waters. This is usually necessary when fish such as pike, perch
and roach accidentally find their way into the water when a pond or lake
containing them bursts its banks, as sometimes happens. At other times it
may be decided to remove them from a lake in order to develop a trout
fishery or to re-establish a trout fishery.

In some waters control, and even elimination, can be carried out with
nets, floating lines and traps, but these procedures must be applied regularly and continually. Sometimes it is possible to control the numbers of
pike and perch by destroying the spawn. This is done by either lowering the
level of the lake or reservoir, where this is possible, immediately after the
fish have spawned in the spring; or by anchoring bundles of brushwood in
the lake. These are attractive to spawning perch, which deposit their eggs

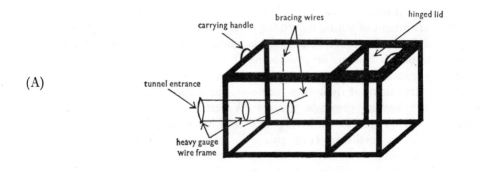

(A)

carrying handle

bracing wires

hinged lid

tunnel entrance

heavy gauge
wire frame

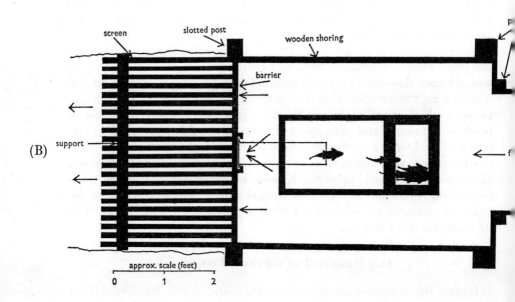

(B)

screen

slotted post

wooden shoring

barrier

support

approx. scale (feet)

0   1   2

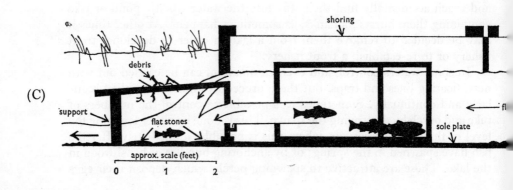

(C)

shoring

debris

support

flat stones

sole plate

approx. scale (feet)

0   1   2

on them. Large quantities of spawn can be collected and destroyed by this method.

Probably the most effective way of destroying unwanted fish species is to use a poison such as derris extract ($2\frac{1}{2}\%$ rotenone). Eradication of coarse fish by means of rotenone is practicable only where a lake is either isolated, or is at the top of a lake system. Where a lake is connected to others containing coarse fish then it should be effectively screened after treatment to prevent re-colonisation. It is important, too, that the outflow from the treated lake does not discharge directly into an important fishing water or a salmonid nursery stream unless it is so diluted that it will not prove lethal. Rotenone is harmless to warm-blooded animals, it has only a limited and transient effect on other aquatic organisms and breaks down quickly, so that stocking can be safely carried out within a few months of treatment. Derris extract can be applied in a liquid form or as a powder. The concentrated liquid extract ($2\frac{1}{2}\%$ rotenone) is applied at a rate of $1\frac{1}{2}$ lbs of powder, of a minimum of 5% rotenone content, per acre/ft of water. Beausang (1966) suggests that where it is economically feasible, and the discharge is unlikely to do damage elsewhere, this dosage rate could be doubled in special cases. Derris powder is more effective as a fish poison in warm than in cool water and the treatment of lakes should be carried out in summer. Only shallow lakes can be properly treated, since thermal layering of the water may delay or prevent diffusion of the poison and, in Canadian lakes at least, the experience has been that some fish survive the poisoning and soon repopulate the lake. The poison is often sprayed over the water by means of pumps and is sometimes pumped down to deeper levels to aid diffusion. Special attention should be paid to marshy areas and backwaters where pike fry are likely to be present. Even when this precaution is taken, however, some pike fry

FIG. 49

(A) Trap; $\frac{3}{4}$ in mesh wire netting on wooden frame 36 × 18 × 18 in with netting tunnel trap 5 in in diameter.

(B) Plan of barrier with trap in position. Screening laths 30 × $\frac{3}{4}$ × $\frac{3}{4}$ in laid with $\frac{3}{4}$ in gaps.

(C) Sectional side view of barrier with trap in position, flat stones below outfall prevent scouring of streambed (from Campbell, 1967a).

nearly always survive the treatment. This means that spraying has to be repeated within two years.

The cost of poisoning a water is often prohibitive and works out at 30s per acre/ft (the concentrated liquid extract costs £3 a gallon). A 20-acre loch therefore, with an average depth of 10 feet, would cost £300. However, it may in some cases, be possible to carry out spot-rotenone-treatment in big lakes to keep coarse fish populations down.

It must be stressed that poisoning is illegal and permission is only given if all the authorities concerned are satisfied that no harm will result to other fisheries or other interests. Under the Salmon and Freshwater Fisheries (Protection) (Scotland) Act, 1951, it can be done for research purposes and for management, when permission is granted, under supervision. Permission is required from: (i) the local river purification board; (ii) a local district fishery board or from a person holding rights for fishing for migratory fish when there is no district fishery board. If contamination of drinking water is likely the public health officer may have to be approached. (iii) The Secretary of State for Scotland, once permission from the other two authorities has been granted. The Secretary of State will then contact the Freshwater Fisheries Laboratory, Pitlochry, the staff of which may be required to carry out the work or supervise the operations. In Canada poisoning of fish can be carried out only with the permission of Federal and Provincial fisheries authorities, and Provincial health authorities.

Unwanted fish species are also sometimes removed from rivers by nets and traps. In certain cases they may be poisoned. For example, in the Great Lakes, sea lamprey control is achieved by the chemical treatment of spawning streams using a selective chemical or 'lampricide' known as T.F.M. which kills lamprey larvae without harming fish.

Burnet (1968) describes the control of two species of eel (*Anguilla dieffenbachii* and *A. australis*) in a New Zealand trout stream. Control brought a three to tenfold increase in the number of yearling trout. However, following the increase in the trout population numbers, the growth rate of the trout decreased markedly and there was a decline in the condition of the fish from good to poor. So while more trout were being produced as a result of control of an unwanted species their size and condition made them less acceptable to the angler.

11.4 Stream improvement

The physical nature of streams may, as a result of one sort of disturbance or another, change drastically and result in a reduction in the fish population. One of the results of various forms of disturbance is erosion. This may be caused by a flood which strikes directly at a soft place in a bank and scours out a large quantity of land, or by diversion of the main axis of the stream resulting from the deposit of a new gravel bed thrown up, usually at the tail of a pool where the width increases and the speed of water diminishes. In some instances pools are filled with gravel and silt.

There are a number of ways of preventing this erosion: (1) protecting or reinforcing the area of bank (normally the outer bank) being scoured by the stream with large stones, brushwood staked in with trees, concrete, tree trunks or boarding secured with piling. (2) diverting the current with croys or groynes, or with boards secured to stakes. Once the banks are stabilised the character of the stream may be slightly altered and deeper pools may be formed. Where there has been reinforcement, particularly on a sharp bend, it is advisable to ensure that the bank on the inside of the bend allows even a moderate flood to flood over it so as to take the pressure off the reinforcements.

One type of structure which is proving very useful in countering erosion is the Maccaferri gabion. These are large, steel wire-mesh baskets, rectangular in shape, variable in size, and galvanised to insure long life in, under and around water, and frequently covered with a P.V.C. plastic coating. These baskets are filled while in tension with hand size (larger than the mesh openings), clean boulders. These gabions are permanent, flexible and maintenance free. Being wire baskets they are easily transported to the site and can be filled with stones from the river or from the neighbouring area. The gaps between the stones in the gabions may also increase the aquatic insect life in the stream. A natural appearance can easily be achieved by covering them with vegetation. The ways in which these gabions can be used to protect banks from erosion is seen in Fig. 50. They also be used to check the erosion which occurs near weirs on torrential streams. Where the river runs through wide and often multiple channels gabion groynes can play a useful role in controlling the watercourse. The groynes are usually required on concave bends and in straight channels, rarely on convex bends.

Many salmon and trout rivers flow over shale, sand and loose gravel and are consequently unstable. Frequently many long stretches of water occur with few or no holding pools. In some instances holding pools are filled in by flood action and others formed. Obviously any method which can create pools and protect existing ones will be of value. Tétreault (1967) describes a rock ballasted crib angled approximately 45° upstream, and placed in a position so as to deflect and accelerate the current at a chosen location. The new force and the direction of the current causes a new pool to be dug downstream, from the crib, during floods. The pointed front end of the pier, which is floorless and filled with large boulders, is undermined and the boulders are washed out and deposited in the newly-excavated pool and presumably form 'lies' for fish. Figs. 51 and 52 show how properly placed

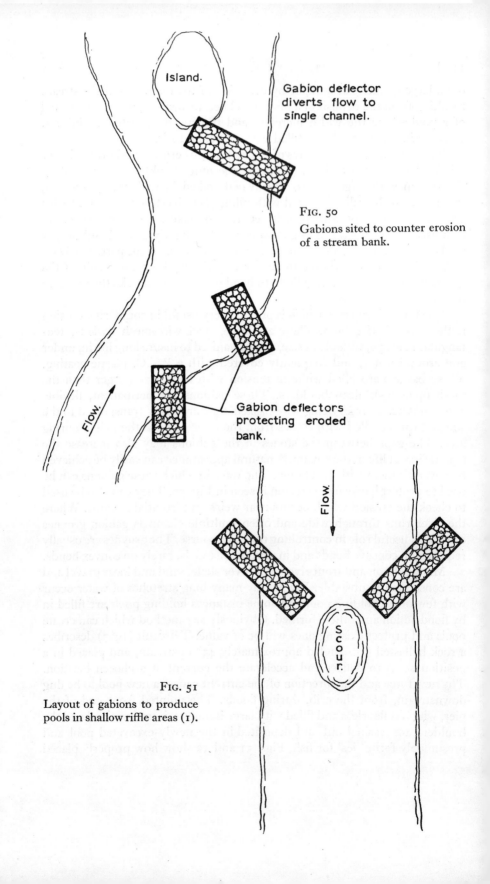

Island.

Gabion deflector
diverts flow to
single channel.

Fig. 50
Gabions sited to counter erosion
of a stream bank.

Flow.

Gabion deflectors
protecting eroded
bank.

Flow.

Scour.

Fig. 51
Layout of gabions to produce
pools in shallow riffle areas (1).

PLATES 23–24. A series of gabions increase the river's surface area and help to stabilise the stream bed.

Plate 25

Plate 26

Plate 27

PLATES 25–27

Stages in the construction of the streambank devices used to narrow and deepen section A of Lawrence Creek. The pattern of the device has been staked out and the longitudinal oak plankings have been installed beneath the surface of the water. The planks are nailed to oak pilings which have been forced into the stream bed.

gabions, producing increased stream velocity can also scour out pools in shallow riffle areas and Plates 23 and 24 show the effect of such a lay-out of gabions.

The effects of stream improvement has been studied in great detail by Hunt (1969) who extensively altered a mile-long section of Lawrence Creek in Wisconsin by the addition of bank covers and current deflectors. The procedures of construction consisted of:

1. Sinking pairs of 5-foot-long oak pilings into the stream bottom to a depth that left their tops below water.
2. Nailing 3-inch-thick boards (stringers) to each pair of pilings at a right-angle to the stream bank.

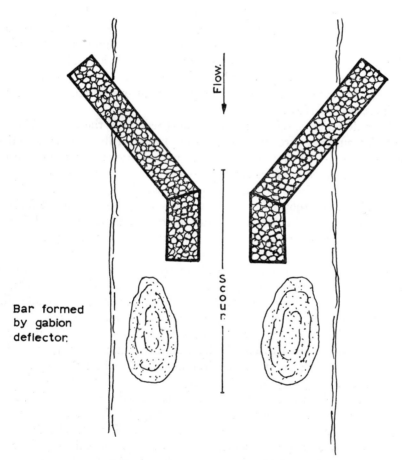

Fig. 52.　Layout of gabions to produce pools in shallow riffle areas (2).

3. Nailing 3-inch-thick oak planks to the stringer boards and parallel to the stream bank.

These wooden substructures, completely under water, provided platforms extending 1–3 feet out from the natural stream bank.

4. Covering the substructure platforms with rocks and filling in a wall of rocks between the inner edge of the platforms and the old stream bank.

5. Covering the protruding wood and rock structures with grassy sod to stabilise the devices and restore the aesthetic appearance of the stream (Plates 25–27).

These alterations reduced the surface area by 50% and increased its average depth by 60%. The cubic configuration (acre/ft) of the altered channel was reduced by only 20%. The amounts of sand bottom and silt bottom were reduced by 40% and 70% respectively. Stream bottom classified as gravel was increased by 11%, and gravel accounted for 10% of the bottom area as compared to only 4% prior to alteration. The number of pools was increased by 52% and the area of stream bottom in pools was increased by 170%. The amount of permanent overhanging bank cover was increased fourfold.

After alteration of this section of stream (Section A) the average biomass of brook trout over three years (1965–1967) was 231 lb or 50% more than the average of 165 lb for the three-year period prior to alteration. In the lower unaltered section (Section B) of stream, used as a reference zone, the standing crops of brook trout increased in weight by an average of only 11% during 1965–1967 as compared to 1961–1963. Both angling effort and yield nearly tripled in Section A after alteration. Yield increased from a maximum of 27 lb per season during 1961–1963 to 44, 82 and 79 lb during 1965–1967 respectively and the number of trout creeled increased from an average of 103 to an average of 300. The average yield of 23 lb per season during 1961–1963 was equivalent to 9% of annual production. During 1965–1967, average yield increased to 68 lb which was 196% greater than the 1961–1963 average and 23% of annual production (Fig. 53).

Similar alterations to a quarter of a mile section of stream in Prince Edward Island were carried out by Saunders and Smith (1962). The devices used to alter the stream environment consisted for the most part of dams, deflectors (groynes) and covers. The dams were constructed of poles or rocks. Alternate layers of spruce boughs and cobble were laid at the face of each dam to make the structure watertight. A small spillway was made in each dam to facilitate upstream passage of trout. The deflectors were designed to dig new pools, enlarge or re-shape existing pools, or remove silt from the stream bed. The deflectors also acted to raise water levels at their upstream faces and thus served as small dams. Alders and spruce or fir were used to create covers. Alders were intertwined and held together by nails and wire to form a tangle in shallow areas and in pools. Debris floating downstream became enmeshed in these additional tangles and created additional cover. In the year following that in which alterations were made to the stream the standing crop of brook trout yearlings was above average, and the numbers of 1-year old and older trout were approximately doubled. The alterations had no noticeable effect on the growth of trout.

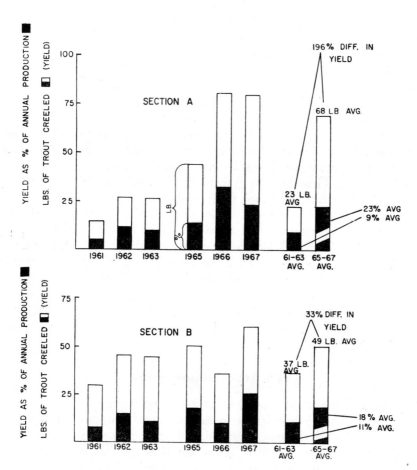

FIG. 53.   Yield (angler harvest) of brook trout from sections A and B of Lawrence Creek during 1961–1963 and 1965–1967 and yield as a percentage of annual production of those years (from Hunt, 1969).

11.5 Increasing spawning and nursery areas

There are many miles of river and stream which would make suitable spawning and nursery areas for salmon that, for one reason or another, are barred to these fish. In 1885 there were about 800 miles of rivers in Scotland which were barred to salmon by a variety of obstacles. Smart (1965) referred to two such obstacles caused by falls on the River North Esk System in Angus which, though not impossible for salmon to ascend, presented considerable difficulty unless river levels were suitable. There was, therefore, a hold-up of fish at each fall which prevented the proper spread of fish to the spawning areas and, at times, led to severe outbreaks of disease due to overcrowding of fish below the falls. Over a period of four years (1947–1950) these two obstacles were cleared and passes installed on two weirs downstream. After the completion of these main improvements the North Esk District Fishery Board continued to improve minor obstacles on some of the spawning tributaries by blasting on a small scale and, where this has not been possible due to falls which could not be economically dealt with, many miles of inaccessible streams have been planted with ova and fry and at times ripe spawning fish have been transported above these obstacles. As a result there has since been a marked increase in the salmon catch and a spectacular rise in the grilse catch (Fig. 54).

In America it has been found that lack of suitable conditions for spawning is a limiting factor in brook trout production. This has been overcome to some extent by constructing two kinds of spawning area: (1) replacing the unstable bottom material with gravel on or near known natural spawning areas and (2) piping and dispersing water through a gravel-filled box.

An obvious development from the latter method has been the artificial spawning channels for Pacific and Atlantic salmon which have already been described (p. 218).

Streams, in which spawning grounds have become consolidated, silted or overgrown, may be rehabilitated by the introduction of new gravel of suitable size for spawning.

11.6 Artificial propagation

Supplementing natural reproduction by artificial propagation is usually necessary when: (1) there is a deficiency in natural reproduction; (2) where the species has in the past been reduced or eliminated, as on the River Rheidol in south-west Wales (Jones and Howells, 1969); (3) where the species, for one reason or another, has not existed previously or (4) to by-pass natural mortality. It is also carried out in sport fisheries on a 'put and take' basis where the aim is to introduce fish of catchable (legal-sized)

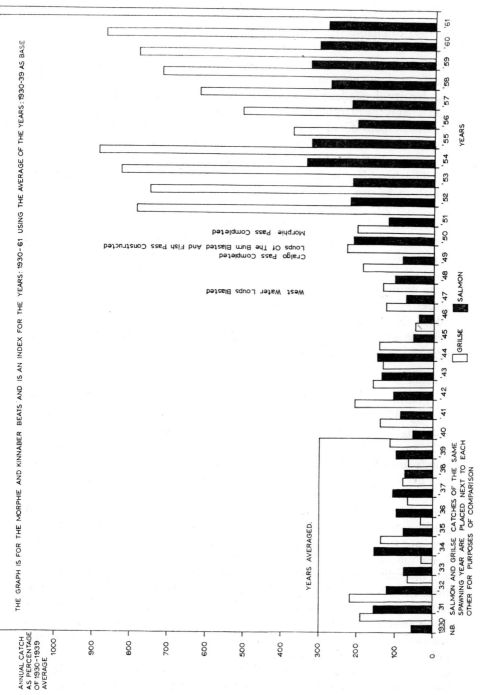

FIG. 54. Salmon and grilse catches by rod and net in the River North Esk, Angus (from Smart, 1965).

or near catchable size with a view to catching them within a very short time.

Some of the questions to be asked before considering artificial propagation are: will stocking work in this situation, is the population regulated by density-dependent factors or limited by density independent factors, and what is the carrying capacity of the environment? The carrying capacity is usually considered to be the ability of the environment to support a population in good condition indefinitely, and not the number of animals it can physically hold for a short time.

The 'stocking' of a river should be done in the first place by means which make use of the river's own production capacity, whenever it can be restored or when lost production areas can be replaced by stream improvement or by opening up new grounds to the fish. Where natural spawning occurs there is little advantage gained by introducing eggs, fry or parr. Unless the number of spawners is obviously too low for the area to be adequately occupied by their progeny, the number of fry and parr resulting from natural spawning will in most cases very soon adjust itself to a level corresponding to the amount of space and food available. If more fish are added the competition is increased and many of either the introduced fish or those already present will die, the equilibrium will be restored and little or nothing will be gained.

Salmon

Planting salmon can be done at either the egg, fry, parr or smolt stage.

Egg. Planting at the egg stage is ideal for those who have either no hatching facilities or else very limited facilities. Spawning fish are netted or trapped and either held in 'corffs' (wooden-slatted boxes) or holding ponds until ripe. The hen fish is stripped of her eggs which are collected in a dry basin. The milt from a cock fish is then used to fertilise the eggs. Milt is mixed well with the eggs which are then covered with water. The water becomes cloudy with the milt and this must be poured away and freshwater added. The procedure is repeated until the water is clear. The eggs are then allowed to swell up and harden for about two hours before being moved. Any sudden jolting of the egg container may result in a high egg mortality. It is the practice of some fishery managers to strip two or three hens before fertilising the eggs. This is risky and may result in many of the eggs being unfertilised. A large number of unfertilised eggs may also result from stripping the eggs into a basin of water, a practice sometimes resorted to in frosty weather, as the micropyle in the egg closes before the milt has been added. It is often not until the eggs have reached the eyed stage that it becomes apparent that many of the eggs are infertile, the 'eyeless' infertile eggs being very conspicuous on the hatching trays.

Many managers plant the eggs at the newly-fertilised stage when the eggs are known as 'green' ova. The eggs being placed under the gravel in slatted perspex boxes of various design (Plate 21) at a depth of about 18 inches (50 cm). The eggs can be counted beforehand by pouring them into a trough and then transferring them to a basin of water using a perspex tray in which 100 or 200 countersunk holes have been drilled for holding the appropriate number of eggs (Plate 21).

Shearer (1961b) has recorded the survival rate of young salmon in streams stocked with 'green' eggs. Over three years the percentage hatching was 90·9, 87·6 and 84·6 respectively. The majority of the eggs which died were infertile and it was found that if a large number of eggs are present in a box and become infected with fungus, this infection can spread to the fertile eggs and kill them.

Where a hatchery is available the 'green' eggs can be held on hatching trays (Plate 20) until they have become 'eyed', after which they can be planted selectively when water conditions are most suitable. Eyed eggs can withstand rough handling and can travel safely for 24 hours or more if they are kept on damp moss and can be planted out in the same way as green eggs.

Sedgwick (1960) describes an efficient method of planting a very large quantity of eggs over great distances of river with a minimum of effort, as follows: A hole is dug in fist-sized gravel roughly 18 inches across and 6 inches deep. A piece of stiff polythene pipe of $1\frac{1}{2}$-inch to 2-inch diameter bore is placed upright in the hole and held in position by a helper while a second hole is dug immediately upstream of the first. The gravel from the second hole is passed back to fill the first hole round the polythene pipe and piled up until the pipe stands embedded in gravel. A second pipe length is put into the upstream hole. Several holes can be dug and filled in with standing pipes, moving upstream. A similar series can be set out parallel a yard or so away to one side. This is repeated until the assessed capacity of the area both as redd and potential rearing ground is reached.

The eggs are transferred from the container to a plastic jug with a broad lip which is filled with water. The eggs are then poured into a standing pipe through a plastic filter funnel. The operator should then raise the pipe slightly and blow down it. This pushes the eggs out into the crevices between the gravel in bottom of the redd. The pipe is then gently withdrawn and at the same time the gravel pushed inwards to fill the small hole that is left. By this method a very large quantity of eggs can be planted over great distances of river with the minimum of effort.

The number of eggs to plant will depend on the type of stream. Elson (1957c) calculated that to get maximum smolt production on the Pollett River a potential egg deposition of 200 per 100 square yards was required.

However, he considered that the number of eggs required in various streams depended, to some extent, on the density of the eel population.

Unfed fry stage. Although the planting of ova would seem to be the best way of introducing hatchery stock from the point of view of ease, time and effect on the young, many Scottish District Fishery Boards prefer to keep the eggs in the hatchery until the young have reached the unfed fry stage, that is, the immediate post-alevin stage when yolk sac absorption is almost complete. However, there is more urgency in the planting out of unfed fry as the stage at which these fry are liberated is important. If the nutrients in the yolk sac have been completely used up before the fry are liberated mortality could well be high. While there may be no intention to keep the young in the hatchery longer than necessary their retention may be governed by the water level of the streams and, if floods prevail over the critical time in their development and so prevent their liberation, mortality in the hatchery may well be high (Marr, 1966).

It has been shown by Mills (1969b) that the movements and survival of salmon fry in some Scottish moorland streams is affected by stocking density (Table 27). However, stocking density was not considered to be the only factor affecting survival as the presence of older salmon parr and trout also appeared to have some effect (Table 28). In Scottish moorland streams a high stocking rate (12·0 to 15·0 fry/m²) is wasteful of fry and a similar production of young fish can be achieved by introducing a lower rate (2·0 to 5·0 fry/m²), thus allowing the hatchery production to be used to better advantage. Lowland streams running through agricultural land will tend

TABLE 27

Trap catches of fry in Allt a' Chomair and Allt dos Mhuicarain, in relation to stocking density and population density of older fish in the streams

Year	Stocking density (no./m²)	Density of salmon parr and trout at census (no./m²)	Percentage of fry planted entering traps
		Allt a' Chomair	
1960	12·73	0·07	24·6
1961	12·42	0·08	15·5
1963	13·23	0·03	5·9
1964	3·09	0·15	3·3
1965	3·00	0·10	1·4
		Allt dos Mhuicarain	
1960	15·24	0·28	18·0
1963	15·52	0·07	9·0
1964	3·43	0·18	2·5
1965	3·53	0·15	3·1

(From: Mills, 1969b.)

to support a much higher density of salmonids and higher stocking rates (10·0 to 15·0 fry/m^2) can be used. The stocking rates should never be so low as not to provide a reasonable insurance against natural incidents. Owing to the variation in survival due to the population density of older fish it is less easy to provide a reliable guide to the numbers of fry to be released in an area to give a certain survival. Obviously where no other fish are present hatchery planting in the first year will be uncomplicated. Where the only species are salmon and trout it may be decided to remove the trout before fry planting to reduce predation, although salmon parr are also predators. However, a reduction in the trout population may only be temporary and recolonisation can take place quite quickly, so while trout reduction may be worthwhile in limited areas, to attempt a large-scale reduction in a river system would probably be less successful. In situations where it is known that older fish are present it would be more useful to reduce stocking rates in alternate years. Where several fish species are present the inter-relationships may be so complex that no hard and fast rule can apply.

TABLE 28

Disposition of salmon fry after planting

	1960	1961	1962[b]	1963	1964	1965	1966
Allt dos Mhuicarain							
Stocking density (unfed fry/m^2)	15·24	—[a]	—[b]	15·52	3·43	3·53	3·65
Density at census (fry/m^2)	0·20	—[a]	—[b]	0·93	0·80	0·36	0·39
Percentage surviving in stream at census	1·3	—[a]	—[b]	6·0	23·3	10·2	10·6
Density of salmon parr and trout at census (no./m^2)	0·28	—[a]	—[b]	0·07	0·18	0·15	0·11
Standing crop of fish (g/m^2)	2·70	—[a]	—[b]	2·94	4·25	2·81	2·83
Allt a' Chomair							
Stocking density (unfed fry/m^2)	12·73	12·42	—[b]	13·23	3·09	3·00	3·02
Density at census (fry/m^2)	0·18	0·11	—[b]	0·61	0·15	0·22	0·39
Percentage surviving in stream at census	1·4	0·8	—[b]	4·6	4·9	7·3	12·9
Density of salmon parr and trout at census (no./m^2)	0·07	0·08	—[b]	0·03	0·15	0·10	0·07
Standing crop of fish (g/m^2)	1·17	0·96	—[b]	1·04	1·18	1·34	1·66
Allt Coire nan Laogh							
Stocking density (unfed fry/m^2)		5·5	5·5	1·7	1·7		
Density at census (fry/m^2)	No	0·07	0·16	0·54	0·15	No	
Percentage surviving in stream at census		1·3	2·9	30·3	8·5		
Density of salmon parr and trout at census (no./m^2)	Stocking	0·20	0·12	0·19	0·23	Stocking	
Standing crop of fish (g/m^2)		1·27	1·09	1·95	1·93		

[a] Samples of fry collected at weekly intervals for feeding studies (see Egglishaw, 1967).
[b] Severe flooding occurred at time of release of fry.
(From: Mills, 1969b).

Underyearlings. In order to avoid a high mortality by releasing hatchery fish at the unfed fry stage some hatcheries hold their fish for a few months and feed them until they reach a length of two or three inches and then release them as 'underyearlings' or 'fingerlings'.

To know how many fish to plant it is first necessary to know how many smolts an area can produce. Mills (1964a) found that survival from the unfed fry to the smolt stage on the River Bran was of the order of 3%, which implied a smolt producing capacity of 3·5 smolts/100 sq. yd. Elson (1957b) has produced figures for the numbers of underyearlings to plant in eastern Canadian salmon streams. In addition, he has noted how many should be planted in the presence and absence of fish-eating birds such as mergansers and kingfishers. For streams on which mergansers will not greatly exceed the figure of one per 10 miles of stream of 10 yards width, and which flow through geologically fertile areas the maximum number of smolts likely to be produced is around 1,000 per mile of stream 10 yards wide. To get this number of smolts about 7,000 underyearlings should be planted, per similar area, in streams with mostly 2-year smolts and about 10,000 in streams with mostly 3-year smolts.

For streams with no bird control or those in geologically infertile areas, these figures should be reduced to about 2,500 and 3,500 for a maximum expectancy of 400 smolts.

When liberating underyearlings at planting sites nothing is gained by scattering them more widely than at a rate of 5,000 fish in an area of 100 sq. yd. These fish will move in some numbers about one mile up- and down-stream from planting sites. So planting sites should ideally be about two miles apart. Some fish will disperse to as much as several miles away, so that partial use of intervening water will be made even if sites have to be further apart. Fry and underyearlings are best liberated in shallow riffles above gravel and small stones rather than in deep pools where large trout may be present.

Smolts. Hatchery-reared smolts are usually liberated in a river in order to supplement the natural reproduction of a salmon population without affecting the natural situation. This is possible because the smolts will migrate to sea shortly after being liberated and yet will return, as adults, to the rivers in which they were released. Release of hatchery smolts into the lower reaches of rivers is the general practice in Sweden where the remainder of the rivers, harnessed for hydro-electric power, is no longer available to salmon.

Hatchery smolts have been shown to give poorer returns as adult fish, both in numbers and weight than 'wild' smolts. Shearer (1965) found from two experiments that the proportion of wild smolts recaptured (5·1 and 3·1%) on return was much greater than that of hatchery smolts (1·9 and

0·28) in both experiments. It was also noticed that hatchery-reared smolts could be distinguished on return by their external appearance. They were more heavily pigmented and seemed to be in poorer condition and many retained physical deficiencies such as deformed or missing fins or short gill covers.

This impression of poorer condition in returning hatchery fish would appear to be confirmed by the findings of Österdahl (1969) in Sweden. He showed that, while the percentage returns of tagged hatchery smolts were practically as good as those for wild fish, the size of the hatchery fish at recapture (expressed as kilogram salmon recaptured per 1,000 smolts released) was less than that of wild fish.

It has been suggested that the unnaturally 'easy' conditions under which smolts are reared reduces their viability because it leaves them inexperienced in dealing with natural conditions. Possible reasons for decreased viability include a reduction in swimming ability, inability to use natural food and inability to evade predators.

Lakes as rearing grounds for young salmon. In recent years in Wales, Scotland, Ireland, Sweden and Norway a number of investigations have been started to see whether small lakes could be used as rearing grounds for young salmon. Probably some of the earliest experiments on rearing young salmon in virgin lakes were those carried out by Evans of the Gwynedd River Authority in Wales. In Llnau Dyrnogydd, a small lake of 5 acres, 1,400 feet above sea-level, Evans planted varying numbers of salmon fry (20,000 to 120,000). The majority of these fish became smolts in the spring of the following year at the age of 1 +. He estimated that 35% of the fry planted reached the smolt stage (Evans, 1958 and Jones and Evans, 1962). With plantings of only 12,000 fry Evans found that 80% 'smolted' the year after planting. This work has been extended, with similar success, to another lake, Llnau Cilan (Sinha and Evans, 1969). The success of this work has been demonstrated in the production of seaward migrating smolts which, it has been claimed, have resulted in improved salmon catches. In Scotland, Munro (1965d) planted 40,000 unfed salmon fry into Loch Kinardochy after removing the existing pike population with rotenone. By the end of two years over 6,000 had migrated out of the loch and 85% of them were 10 cm or more long. This suggests that this type of natural rearing of young salmon might be quite feasible. The only problem in the Kinardochy experiment was that although 60% of the migrants were smolts a high proportion of them left the loch in late summer or in the autumn, outside the normally accepted period for smolt migration.

Trout

Before commencing stocking waters with trout it is necessary to con-

sider a number of points, these include: (i) the character of the water concerned; (ii) the state of the existing trout population; (iii) the way in which
the water is fished or will be fished in the future; (iv) the level or quality of
fishing available or intended; (v) the practical and economic actions involved; and what future measures will be necessary in attempting to achieve
a particular set of results.

Many estates and trout clubs are guilty of overstocking, not realising
the number of factors to be considered before introducing additional trout
to their waters. Sometimes of course, they are advised badly and, if taking
the advice of a local trout hatchery out to sell its product, are told to introduce very many more fish than are required.

Stocking at the unfed fry stage is fraught with danger. Le Cren (1961)
has shown that above a certain stocking density the survival rate of brown
trout dropped (Fig. 55). Introductions of unfed fry into waters with trout
already present is rarely successful. Only in virgin waters is stocking with

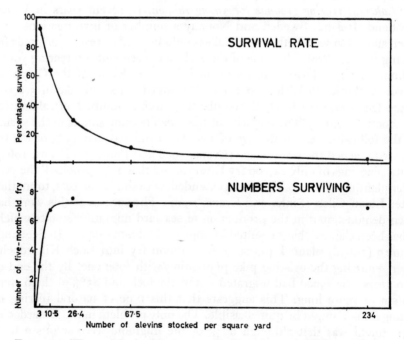

FIG. 55.   The survival of brown trout fry when stocked at different
densities. *Upper graph:* The percentage surviving from starting to feed
(beginning of May) until the beginning of September. *Lower graph:* The
actual numbers per square yard recovered in September; both plotted
against the numbers of alevins stocked per square yard (after Le Cren,
1961. Reproduced by permission of the Association of River Authorities).

unfed fry worthwhile. The Irish Inland Fisheries Trust, however, have found that brown trout stocked in the autumn as underyearlings have had a consistently high survival, whether stocked in lakes or rivers, and whether or not wild fish were present. However, Beausang (1966) says that:

> whether this is due to Irish ecological conditions or to the conditions under which the fish are reared, or both, is not quite clear; but the fact is that the autumn fingerling brown trout gives a good return for the money invested in rearing it – and it is a 'wild' fish in quality and behaviour by the time the angler catches it.

Beausang gives no survival rates for these fingerlings and it may be that the planting in the autumn, when adult trout are not feeding intensively, is their salvation. For this reason there is some advantage in stocking in the autumn. Yearlings can also be planted at this time and with the advent of spring are ready to feed, being already acclimatised to their new environment. The summer growth of hatchery trout, of the same age, planted in the spring, will stop or slow down temporarily until the fish become acclimatised.

Anglers wanting immediate results in terms of catchable fish may be tempted to introduce fish of much larger size and adopt the put-and-take philosophy.

Generally speaking it can be said that there are three problems which can be solved simultaneously by this put-and-take philosophy of supplementing natural reproduction: (a) there is a big demand for sport fishing near urban areas, (b) this demand cannot be met by the number of fish supportable by the carrying capacity of the environment, (c) if young fish are stocked most will die from natural mortality before anglers have a chance to catch them. Thus the answer is to raise fish until they are old enough to be beyond the age when losses to natural mortality are greatest, and release them close to the beginning of the fishing season and expect to catch them that season. Jensen (1958) provides data on trout streams where more than half the released 'catchable' rainbow trout were caught within 9 to 12 days of release. This is such a highly artificial situation that, as the fish are in the water such a short time, 'carrying capacity' is irrelevant.

Introducing large trout is very expensive and Campbell (1967b) estimates that if 12-ounce brown trout were introduced to fishless ponds and the recapture rate was 75% each trout landed would cost about 10s. (50 new pence).

Cuinat (1962) refers to the work of Needham who summarised the results of 240 releases of marked trout in the United States (Table 29).

From this table four conclusions emerge:

1. The percentages of recapture are on average fairly small.

2. The returns increase when the size of the trout released increases; that is not to say that the return is necessarily better, since the price per head of the fish released increases at the same time.

3. The returns are greater in a lake than in a river.

4. The release of trout of more than 13 cm in the river produce the best returns to the basket when they are carried out during the fishing season.

According to Oliver (1963 and 1968) the aim of a trout fishery manager is to get the best fish to be caught on a fly at the most economical cost. Oliver gives a Table (Table 30) to give alternatives in methods of stocking a

TABLE 29

Summary of the results of 240 releases of marked trout in the United States

		Percentages of recaptures obtained		
		Av.	Min.	Max.
In lakes	Alevins or small trout (less than 13 cm long)	7	0	37
	Trout over 13 cm long	35	1	90
In rivers	Alevins or small trout	2	0	21
	Larger trout – in autumn	17	0	88
	shortly before the opening of the season	29	1	80
	during the fishing season	41	2	90

TABLE 30

In order to catch 14,000 fish per annum, over 12 inches, in a 400-acre reservoir, it is necessary to stock with the number of fish given below

						Brown		Rainbow	
Number	Age	Length inch	Season	Recovery Rate (%)	Average Weight (lb)	Price /1000 (£)	Cost (£)	Price /1000 (£)	Cost (£)
14 Million	0+	1	Spring	0·01	Large Fish	5	70,000	6–10	91,000
280,000	1–	6	Autumn	5·0	2	111	31,000	96	27,000
140,000	1+	7–8	Spring	10	2	181	25,000	150	21,000
28,000	2–	11	Autumn	50	1	423	12,000	351	9,800
18,750	2+	12	Spring	75	1	535	10,000	380	7,100

400-acre fertile reservoir, such as Eye Brook, so as to catch 6,000 fish each year. His policy now is to stock 12-inch (30 cm) fish, as he finds, in the case of Eye Brook, that it is cheaper to stock with large expensive fish. It should be added that this reservoir is full of millions of small roach and these large fish serve to keep the roach within bounds.

As has already been mentioned, the time of stocking can be important and preliminary results of a study on the growth of hatchery-reared 2 + years trout released into a Yorkshire reservoir by the Yorkshire Ouse and Hull River Authority in autumn and late winter (February) tend to show: (1) that the growth rate of the fish released in February increases sooner and more quickly during the current season that that of the autumn-planted fish, although these latter fish reach the same size as the fish released in late winter by the end of the season and (2) there are better angling returns from the trout released in February (Templeton, personal communication).

In any water which is stocked artificially a close watch should be kept on the growth rate of the trout so that the population can be manipulated to some extent so as to produce either fewer larger trout or more slightly smaller trout. So often owners of trout waters keep few if any data on the fish they catch and rarely take scale samples; it is only when things appear to be going wrong that they sit up and pay attention.

One method of obtaining trout for stocking purposes, rather than depending on hatcheries, is to remove fish from small streams incapable of supporting or producing large trout, or from lakes where the population is too large and the growth of the fish retarded.

Frequently there is some debate as to which trout to introduce to waters, the brown or the rainbow. A number of factors are involved which have a bearing on the choice of species (p. 150). Rainbows stocked as autumn fingerlings have been found by Beausang to survive in large numbers to the end of the following season (1 +), but survival to 2 + is small. Browns, on the other hand, have a very high survival to 2 +, 3 +, and 4 +, whether they are stocked alone or in combination with rainbows. Against this, the rainbow grows faster than the brown trout. So in rich waters, where rainbows become big fish at 1 +, they are an excellent proposition and give a high yield to anglers. Where, however, trout need two seasons' growth to attain a good size the slower growing brown trout, because of its high survival rate over a number of years, is much the better fish to stock.

11.7 Construction of trout ponds

One method of providing some, or more, trout fishing is through the construction of ponds varying in size from small waters of less than an acre to large ponds of a few acres. Ponds to be used for trout fishing normally require a constant supply of cool, clean water and this can be obtained from springs or, better still, small feeder streams. The surface run-off from drainage areas is also a good source of water. For example, one estate in the north of Scotland, in order to prevent erosion from surface drainage after clear-felling a hillside of trees, bulldozed a series of ponds down the hill. Each pond was fed from the one above and the upper one collected the surface run-off channelled to it. The ponds were stocked with small trout collected from an overpopulated loch. Various types of aquatic vegetation were planted in and around the ponds to which were introduced a variety of aquatic invertebrates such as shrimps (*Gammarus* spp.) and snails (*Limnaea* spp.).

An alternative method of constructing a pond is to excavate an area with suitable surrounding terrain, for example, land bordered by high ground on one side and a flood bank along a neighbouring stream on the other and by-passing water flowing in the near-by stream. There is also the situation where a small stream runs into a marshy area and meanders through the marsh before joining the main river. In this situation the marshland can be partially excavated and the top soil used for forming banks and impounding, any local seepage can often be eliminated by using plastic sheeting covered with earth. A sluice can be installed on the opposite side of the site to which the stream enters. These are only two examples of many situations which may occur where, by a little excavation and diversion, a pond can be formed.

Ponds with a continuous outflow of water should have an average depth of 6 to 8 feet, with some deeper water. In ponds with a low or intermittent flow, part of the pond should be at least 12 feet deep. The margin of the pond should slope as steeply as possible to a water depth of 3 to 4 feet. The pond capacity can be approximately determined from the following relationship:

$$\text{Volume (gallons)} = 325{,}850 \, A \times d$$

Where A = area of the pond in acres, and
d = mean depth of water in feet.

For example, a pond of 2 acres in surface area with a mean depth of 5 feet will have a capacity of:

$$\text{Volume} = 325{,}850 \times 2 \times 5 = 3{,}258{,}500 \text{ gallons.}$$

A useful addition to the pond site is a small plantation of trees to provide shelter and an additional source of food. A suitable tree for this purpose is the alder (*Alnus* spp.). The pond will soon become colonised by invertebrates from the inflowing stream, and where it is convenient to take gravel from a near-by stream or river this is worthwhile as the addition of beds of

PLATE 28

Electro-fishing a small stream. A stop net helps in the capture of small fish.

PLATE 29

A fry trap on a small Highland burn. The horizontal screen, which consists of bronze wire gauze (10 meshes to the inch), is partly covered with roofing felt to allow more water to pass over the screen at low stream flows.

gravel in shallow water will help to vary the substrate and provide more living space for various types of invertebrate.

A restocking programme for these ponds should be planned carefully. Ponds managed on a put-and-take basis generally present less of a management problem than those in which it is planned to have a spawning stock with some supplementation by hatchery fish.

Prospective pond owners would be well advised to read *Construction and Management of Farm Ponds in Ontario* by Ayers, McCrimmon and Berst.

Two works which deal thoroughly with various aspects of fish culture are those by Huet (1970) and Leitritz (1959).

11.8 Control of aquatic plants

One part of the management of the aquatic environment is that of weed control. Partial control rather than complete elimination is preferable in most cases as in many instances plants are essential to the well-being of the water and the maintenance of some important aspect of the river or lake. The main functions of aquatic weeds are: aeration of the water (during the process of photosynthesis); shelter for animals; consolidation of the bed and banks of the stream; provision of food for other aquatic organisms, and interception of silt and plant debris. Because aquatic plants have these functions and make an important contribution to the maintenance of environmental conditions suitable for other forms of aquatic life the objective of water weed control measures, as Robson (1968) points out, should seldom be that of total eradication. The degree to which weeds are to be controlled will depend upon local conditions of land drainage and water use.

Water weeds can be divided into four categories:

Emergent weeds. Emergent plants have erect aerial leaves arising from open water or mud. They grow in situations where the water level ranges from just below ground level to about half the maximum height of the plant. They are generally large and erect plants and most of the important ones have long, narrow leaves like grasses and are commonly called reeds, e.g. common reed (*Phragmites communis*), bur-reed (*Sparangium erectum*), reedmace (*Typha latifolia*), reed grass (*Glyceria maxima*) and bulrush (*Schoenoplectus lacustris*). Other erect plants in this category are similar to broad-leaved plants and include water plantain (*Alisma plantago-aquatica*) and arrow head (*Sagittaria sagittifolia*).

Floating-leaved weeds. Most of these plants are rooted in the stream or lake bed and have long pliable stems, although a few, such as duckweed (*Lemna minor*), drift about on the water surface. Many of the rooted plants in this category also have submerged leaves (e.g. water crowfoot, *Ranunculus aquatilis*; starwort, *Callitriche stagnalis*; yellow water lily, *Nuphar lutea*).

Submerged weeds. The submerged water plants are only found where there is permanent water and soon die if exposed. They are commonly rooted in the mud as is the case of Canadian pondweed (*Elodea canadensis*) and water milfoil (*Myriophyllum* spp.), but a few are free-floating below the water surface such as hornwort (*Ceratophyllum demersum*). They are all completely submerged except at flowering when most extend their flowering shoots above the water, e.g. water milfoil (*Myriophyllum spicatum*) and mare's tail (*Hippuris vulgaris*).

Algae. These are microscopic plants which can occur as single cells or filaments. The green, threadlike, filamentous algae are usually the most troublesome in drainage channels and ponds, forming scums on water surfaces, slime on rocks or stones, or growing in characteristic entangled mats and known as 'blanket weeds' or 'cott'. The single-celled microscopic forms, known as diatoms and desmids, float about in the water and give rise to 'blooms' when conditions are suitable for their rapid growth. In addition to the green algae there are the blue-green algae; these produce substances toxic to fish and other organisms and may cause serious trouble in sluggish or stationary water.

In very overgrown and neglected waters control of the aquatic vegetation is not enough and it is often necessary to remove the silt and detritus. This can be done by means of dredges and draglines. Sometimes the lakes can be drained and the silt and detritus removed by means of a powerful jet of water. The silt so liquefied runs into the depression of the lake where it is pumped out. Where it is not possible to drain the lake the silt and detritus are detached and broken up by means of a high speed propeller. The propeller is linked to a suction pump by which the silt and detritus, mixed with water, are evacuated to the outside of the lake by floating pipes. Obviously only the smaller waters can be dealt with in this way.

The methods used in general day-to-day management of lakes and streams fall into three groups: (i) biological methods, (ii) mechanical methods, and (iii) chemical methods. Timmermans (1961) has pointed out that an abnormal enrichment with organic and mineral matter coming from water from sewers, industries and drainage of agricultural land, cattle yards and piggeries can strongly accelerate the invasion, by vegetation, of slow-moving or still waters. Purification of used waters must therefore be considered as an indirect means of attack.

Biological methods. Although some fish, such as the common carp and grass carp (Cross, 1969), are used to control weeds in certain waters their use will rarely apply to trout waters. However, swans on a lake can contribute to the control of submerged vegetation in shallow areas. The coypu (*Mycastor coypus*), which does not feed on fish, but emergent plants, can be useful in the control of the latter. Timmermans quotes the replacement of a detrimental plant, Canadian pondweed, with a useful one, starwort. The starwort has the advantage of spreading towards the surface while leaving enough space free towards the base. Its superficial rooting habit further allows of a much easier removal than that of Canadian pond weed.

Mechanical methods. Cutting of aquatic vegetation can be done by means of a single or double-bladed hand scythe. Articulated scythes, made up of several blades, are towed in a zig-zag course along the bottom and worked by two people from a boat, from the bank, or while wading in the water. Special saws can be employed in the same way. Cutting by hand is laborious work which is only employed for small areas where the use of motorised machines is not practicable. Numerous models of weedcutters worked and propelled by motors exist, provided for the most part with horizontal and vertical cutting bars. For cutting submerged vegetation articulated cutters, driven by motor from a boat, are also used.

Emergent plants, such as bulrushes and reeds, are cut two or three times a year, a first time in May–June when the tissues have not yet hardened, then when the plants grow again. They should be cut as far under water as possible. If this operation is carried out thoroughly work in subsequent years becomes lighter. Once the cut vegetation is brought into the shores by the wind it is removed to prevent decomposition in the water with a resultant build-up of anaerobic conditions.

Cutting of the floating-leaved and submerged weeds gives poorer results and in general it is more effective to remove them with a rake which pulls up the superficial roots.

Filamentous algae, forming blanket weed on the surface of the water, can be pulled on to the bank by hand or dragline.

One method of weed control attempted by Mayhew (1962) was to float large sheets of black polythene plastic over weed beds and leave them for a predetermined number of days. Adequate control of all species of *Potamogeton* was achieved in 10 to 18 days. *Ceratophyllum demersum* was eliminated in the control plots in 18 to 28 days. Control was unsuccessful for *Chara vulgaris* and *Sagittaria*. However, all control plots were colonised by filamentous algae within 30 days of the plastic sheets being removed.

Chemical methods. The herbicides to be used and the techniques of application vary, and depend upon whether the plants are emergent, floating, semi-immersed or immersed. Moreover, it is necessary to consider the end in view, the chemical composition of the water, the toxicity for the fish and invertebrate fauna, and the use of the treated water for cattle or irrigation.

Total or selective herbicides can be distinguished according to whether they are effective against most plants or against only certain plants. Sodium chlorate, for example, is in the first category, copper sulphate, at certain concentrations, in the second. According to their mode of action herbicides are said to be contact herbicides if they kill the tissues at the point of contact (e.g. benechlor), or translocatory herbicides if their effect is felt in the whole plant of which only a part has been touched (e.g. phytohormones – 2,4-D; 2,4,5-T; M.C.P.A.).

The best time for the treatment of aquatic vegetation is that which corresponds with their active growth, during which the herbicides are best taken up. The use of translocatory herbicides should be made during sunny weather and in the absence of wind when the air temperature reaches at least 10° C. The water must be at a temperature of at least 16° C if copper sulphate and sodium arsenite are used against algae or other submerged plants. Active growth of the plants, and a high water temperature increase the action of the herbicide but these conditions also coincide with a greater activity of aquatic animals, particularly fish. The result of this is a greater susceptibility of the latter to the possible toxicity of the herbicide employed.

If it is necessary to take account of the toxicity of herbicides employed, it must not be forgotten either that the rapid death and decomposition of a large quantity of plants, particularly of algae and submerged plants, can result in a shortage of oxygen, and consequently the death of fish.

For the control of reeds and other grass-like emergent weeds Dalapon is usually used. It is one of the herbicides cleared under the Pesticides Safety Precaution Scheme (1968). It is a translocatory herbicide and is most successful against the common reed and reedmaces. Sedges (*Carex* spp. and *Scirpus* spp.) usually receive a top-kill but re-grow rapidly the same season. Rushes (*Juncus* spp.) and the bulrush (*Schoenoplectus lacustris*) show little effect and are not considered susceptible. Dalapon is applied at the rate of 15–20 lb/acre as a foliar spray in 50–100 gallons of water. Dalapon is sold, at 7s a lb, in a powder form as the sodium salt and is readily dis-solved in water (10 lb can easily be dissolved in 10 gallons). The plants can be sprayed early in the year, when it will be necessary to repeat the treat-ment annually, but over three or four years re-growth will gradually dimin-ish. However, Dalapon is most effective if sprayed when the reeds are flowering. At this time much of the chemical is moved from the leaves to the roots. With some plants this late treatment will mean that the hard flower stems remain erect over the winter following treatment. The longer the reeds can be left before they are cut, the better will be the control over re-growth in subsequent seasons. It is usually advisable to leave them stand-ing for at least six weeks after spraying.

The only herbicide cleared under the Pesticides Safety Precaution Scheme which is of any use against submerged and floating-leaved weeds is Diquat. It is absorbed rapidly by the leaves and kills the foliage within a few days. Certain weeds are very susceptible to Diquat and are usually killed, although some re-growth may sometimes occur. They include water crowfoot, spiked water milfoil, Canadian pondweed, duckweed and frogbit. Other plants are defoliated but usually re-grow the next year, e.g. starworts and some pondweeds (*Potamogeton* spp.). Water lilies, some pondweeds (*Potamogeton* spp.) and most filamentous algae are either not affected or re-grow very rapidly.

Diquat (Reglone) is recommended at a concentration of 0·5 to 1 p.p.m. It is sold in the form of a liquid concentrate which diffuses very rapidly in water. It can be either injected below the surface through a sprayer lance or poured into the water in measured quantities at regular intervals from a boat. May or June is the best time to use Diquat. When the treatment of a heavy growth of weed cannot be avoided only part of the lake ($\frac{1}{2}$ acre plots) should be treated at one time to reduce the risk of de-oxygenation, leaving an interval of 14 to 21 days between the treatment of each part. Diquat is very expensive. The cost is approximately £5. 5s a gallon and, with the suggested dosage of two gallons per acre foot (£10. 10s), the cost of treating a 40-acre lake for the elimination of Canadian pondweed, say, with a mean depth of five feet may be as much as £2,100.

If a shallow depth is taken, for example $1\frac{1}{2}$ feet, as is sometimes recommended, the cost can be reduced considerably although the treatment may be less effective.

Best weed control is obtained when the water is completely still and, therefore, ideally it should be carried out in ponds and lakes in which there is no water movement. Because Diquat is inactivated on contact with soil particles treatment is unlikely to be successful in muddy water and for the same reason Diquat-treated water should not be stirred up or agitated.

Great care should be taken to avoid accidental spillage of the concentrate into any water-course.

Copper sulphate is the cheapest and most effective herbicide for algae. Although some writers (Hasler, 1949) claim that its use is dangerous for fish, good results can be obtained without prejudice to fish. The concentrations depend on the hardness of the water, the water temperature and on the means of treatment of the stretch of water, either complete or partial. In acid water 0·5 to 1·0 g. of copper sulphate per m³ is sufficient, while in alkaline water 1·5 to 2 g. is necessary. The results are best when the water temperature is above 16° C. The treatment may need repeating in warm weather. The copper sulphate is applied as a solution. Before applying copper sulphate it is advisable to have the lake accurately surveyed by engineers experienced in treating reservoirs so that the correct amount of copper sulphate can be added. The shore line may be pegged out in 100-foot lanes and the amount required for each lane is estimated, after which the solution can be added by rowing up each lane.

11.9 Control of parasites and disease

Very little has been achieved in attempts to control fish parasites and disease under natural conditions. In hatcheries malachite green has been success-fully used as a fungicide to control *Saprolegnia parasitica* on salmon eggs, and antibiotics have been used to control furunculosis. In addition, attempts have been made to deal with 'whirling disease' in hatcheries using Osarsol (Bauer, 1959), but the only effective means of eradication of this disease is to kill all fish with disease symptoms and drain and disinfect the ponds with calcium cyanide at a rate of 4,000 kg per hectare, or quicklime, although the latter is less effective. Davis (1961) gives a very full account of the diseases of game fish in his book *Culture and diseases of game fish.*

Under certain conditions it might be possible to control an outbreak of furunculosis in a wild population of adult salmon by treating them with chloramphenicol at a strategic point on a river system; for example a trap. The aim in the treatment is to use an intramuscular depot injection so as to maintain the highest blood levels of antibiotic for the longest time after a single injection. Leaman (1965) describes this treatment on a population of impounded adult salmon in northern Scotland. The preparation used was 'Intramycetin' which contains 15% chloramphenicol in aqueous suspension. It was used successfully at a rate of 1 ml/15 lb of fish. At this rate, a single intramuscular injection of this preparation should supply effective blood levels of chloramphenicol for 24 to 48 hours. This treatment is inexpensive, 50 fish could be treated for less than £5, so that it would not be too expen-sive to treat a run of three or four hundred fish.

In cases where a maturing female fish is seen near spawning time to be dying from disease, for example in impoundments where fish are being held for stripping, or even in a river, the eggs may still be saved. The maturing fish is injected with gonadotrophin to help advance ovulation. This will bring a fish into 'stripping condition' within 18 to 27 hours after injec-tion, so allowing the eggs to be removed and fertilised before the fish dies. Mr Elson of the Marine Laboratory, Aberdeen, has had a fair measure of success (one-third) with this method.

The control of ectoparasites has also been possible in certain circum-stances, for example the concentration of copper sulphate required for the destruction of algae is also lethal for the fish leech (*Piscicola geometra*). However, the larvae are not killed and after three to four months repetition of the treatment is necessary. There have been a number of recommen-dations for the control of *Argulus*. The most important control measure in ponds is the prevention of direct and indirect contact between young pond fish with older individuals and with wild fish. Thorough drying out of the pond bottom, which kills the egg batches, is also very important. The most effective control measure against *Argulus* in lakes and natural reservoirs, according to Bauer, is by an increase in the flow which raises the oxygen content of the water.

Recently some measure of success has been achieved by Shell in their attempt to eliminate the eye fluke *Diplostomum spathaceum* from a population of wild trout with the molluscicide Frescon.

A field trial was carried out at Lodge Reservoir, Essex, to test the effectiveness of chemical control of the snails, *Limnaea pereger*, which are the first intermediate host of the parasite. The molluscicide was applied in the first instance to give a concentration of 0·025 p.p.m. in the water using a motorised applicator mounted at the rear of a small boat. A second treatment was carried out when only the periphery of the lake was sprayed to a distance of 5 metres from the banks to give a concentration of 0·1 p.p.m.

No *L. pereger* were found in samples taken 10 days after the second application of Frescon and it is concluded that this snail had been virtually eliminated from the reservoir. No mortality of trout was observed. Some sticklebacks were killed and this may be attributable to uneven distribution of molluscicide near the margin of the reservoir. There were no apparent side-effects on aquatic invertebrates or other wild life.

Five months after treatment some re-population of the shoreline by *L. pereger* was observed, and applications of Frescon may therefore need to be repeated on several occasions during the season to maintain an effective level of control. However, where snail pests are confined mainly to the margin of water bodies, peripheral treatment may be effective and would be relatively inexpensive (Crossland, personal communication).

Chapter 12

MANAGEMENT TECHNIQUES

12.1 Methods for the collection of water samples and their analysis. 12.2 Sampling general fish habitat characteristics of streams. 12.3 Bottom fauna assessment. 12.4 Capture and examination of fish. 12.5 Marking and tagging. 12.6 Estimation of fish populations. 12.7 Growth studies. 12.8 Production estimates.

12.1 Methods for the collection of water samples and their analysis

It has been shown in earlier chapters how the chemistry of the water plays an important role in the distribution of organisms and in the productivity of waters.

Water samples are usually collected in routine surveys and care should be taken with their collection. In streams it is advisable to collect the sample close to the stream bed. The water container should be washed out once or twice with the stream water before a sample is collected. The most suitable container is a polythene bottle. In cases of pollution a label on the sample bottle should include details of the stream, where the sample was taken, the temperature of the water or effluent, the time of taking the sample and the state of the tide, if an estuary.

It may be necessary to collect samples at regular intervals over a period of 24 hours, or longer, and automatic water samplers (Holden, 1962) are available. Water bottles are made which collect samples from various depths in a lake, the bottle being lowered on a wire rope from a winch to the required depth and then being closed with the aid of a messenger which is sent down the wire to trigger off the mechanism to close the bottle.

The most usual analysis of water samples, collected on routine surveys is for the pH, total alkalinity and conductivity (total dissolved solids). In certain cases the chemical analysis may be extended to include nitrogen and phosphorus. Where pollution surveys are being carried out a much more detailed analysis of the water has to be made to include suspended solids, ammoniacal nitrogen, nitrous and nitric nitrogen, chloride, alkalinity, pH dissolved oxygen and B.O.D. A physical analysis of the water will include a record of temperature and light penetration, both of which affect the distribution of organisms. Electronic thermistors permit rapid measurement of temperatures at various depths, while the Secchi disc is used to measure light penetration, although it provides only an index of visibility.

Most laboratories of fishery departments, water authorities and city analysts will analyse samples sent in to them. Samples can be analysed rapidly with such sophisticated apparatus as auto analysers and atomic absorption spectrophotometers. Gas liquid chromatography extends the analyses to the pesticides – organo-chlorine, organo-phosphorus and organo-mercury compounds and to the polychlorinated biphenyls.

A number of works describe the chemical analysis of freshwaters at some length (Mackereth, 1963 and Golterman and Clymo, 1969).

12.2 Sampling of general fish habitat characteristics of streams

It is frequently necessary to assess the fishing potential of streams and, as this is strongly related to the condition of the fish habitat, it is essential to record the habitat characteristics. Herrington and Dunham (1967) describe a useful sampling technique for taking measurements along selected transects across streams. When tested on three streams in Utah the results provided acceptably precise estimates of stream length and width, surface area, pool and riffle area, depth and stream-bed composition, as well as of the stability and vegetative cover of the stream banks. The characteristics measured which were recorded on the form depicted in Fig. 56 were:

Width. The width of the water surface was measured to the nearest foot. Protruding rocks, stumps or logs were included as part of the total width. Whether the channel was at high or low-water level at the time of sampling was noted on the form.

Depth. Depth was measured to the nearest inch at three points along each transect at intervals of one-quarter, one-half and three-quarters of the distance across each channel.

Pools and riffles. Those parts of the stream channel where the water flowed more slowly and was deeper than in surrounding portions were called pools. The faster moving more shallow portions were called riffles.

K

Five pool-quality classes were designed on the basis of pool size, water depth and fish shelter (Table 31). The deeper and larger pools with abundant shelter were considered better fish habitat than the smaller, shallower and more exposed pools.

Bottom composition. Five types of bottom material were defined as follows:

> Boulder – Rocks over 12 inches in diameter.
> Rubble – Rocks 3 to 11·9 inches in diameter.
> Gravel – Rocks 0·1 to 2·9 inches in diameter.
> Sand-silt – Particles less than 0·1 inch in diameter.
> Other – Other matter (sunken logs or other debris).

Bank stability. Bank conditions at each end of a transect were rated either as 'stable' or as 'unstable'. An unstable rating was given if there was any evidence of soil sloughing within the past year. The number of stable banks for each transect was recorded as 0, 1 or 2. On multiple channels, only the two outermost banks were rated.

Streamside vegetation. Three types of streamside vegetation were recog-

Drainage Unit No. ——————   Field Crew ——————————————

Sample No. ——————   Date ——————————————

Photo No. ——————————————

Transect No.	Channel No.	Total width	Riffle width	Pool width	Width										Vegetative bank cover			Bank stability		Stream channel depth				Average gradient
					Pool quality					Bottom material					F	B	O	·S	U	A	B	C	Av.	
					#1	#2	#3	#4	#5	B	R	G	S-S	O										
					Feet										No. of banks					Inches				Percent
Total																								

FIG. 56. Stream sampling record as used by Herrington and Dunham (1967).

nised: 'forest', 'brush' and 'open'. Forest was defined as stands of trees. Other woody vegetation was defined as 'brush' and banks without woody types of vegetation were rated as 'open'.

Channel gradient. Two gradient readings were taken using a hand level: one reading, one hundred feet upstream from the sample point and the other, one hundred feet downstream. The average of these two readings (ignoring the minus sign of the downstream reading) was recorded as the gradient of the sample point.

Perhaps to these characteristics could be added the distribution and abundance of weed and the type of stream flow. Four types of flow were distinguished by Allen (1951), i.e. cascade, broken, turbulent and smooth. A broken flow is described as having surface waves equal to at least half the depth of the water; a turbulent flow produced either with small waves or distorted vision, while a smooth flow allowed clear vision. Cascade is the irregular flow found among large protruding stones in sections of steep gradient and is often accompanied by some white water. Classification, which is done visually, is carried out at normal water level.

TABLE 31

Pool quality recognition guide. (From: Herrington and Dunham, 1967.)

Quality class no.	Length or Width	Depth	Shelter[1]
1	Greater than a.c.w.[2]	2 ft or deeper	Abundant[3]
	Greater than a.c.w.	3 ft or deeper	Exposed[4]
2	Greater than a.c.w.	2 ft or deeper	Exposed
	Greater than a.c.w.	<2 ft	Intermediate[5]
	Greater than a.c.w.	<2 ft	Abundant
3	Equal to a.c.w.	<2 ft	Intermediate
	Equal to a.c.w.	<2 ft	Abundant
4	Equal to a.c.w.	Shallow[6]	Exposed
	Less than a.c.w.	Shallow	Abundant
	Less than a.c.w.	Shallow	Intermediate
	Less than a.c.w.	<2 ft	Intermediate
	Less than a.c.w.	2 ft or deeper	Abundant
5	Less than a.c.w.	Shallow	Exposed

[1] Logs, stumps, boulders, and vegetation in or overhanging pool, or overhanging banks.
[2] Average channel width.
[3] More than $\frac{1}{2}$ perimeter of pool has cover.
[4] Less than $\frac{1}{4}$ of pool perimeter has cover.
[5] $\frac{1}{4}$ to $\frac{1}{2}$ perimeter of pool has cover.
[6] Approximately equal to average stream depth.

12.3 Bottom fauna assessment

There are very many methods of sampling bottom fauna and, depending on the purpose for which they are required, the methods may yield either qualitative or quantitative results. For example, if only a qualitative sample is required, the simplest of hand nets will serve the purpose. However, if quantitative samples are needed more critical techniques have to be used. Quantitative bottom fauna samples can be collected from lakes by means of various types of spring-loaded grabs closing, either on contact with the bottom or with the aid of a messenger, and scooping up a known area of substrate. Core sampling is also used to sample lakes with a muddy substrate.

In stony streams various methods of sampling the bottom fauna have been devised and these have been reviewed by Macan (1958). These methods have been divided into five categories:

(i) Lifting by hand of individual stones. One way of doing this is to lift individual stones gently off the bottom and enclose them in a net before taking them out of the water. Animals that have not dropped off into the net are scraped off into a dish. The area of the stones is then measured. Another way of carrying out this method is on a time rather than on a surface-area basis. Collecting is carried out for 5 or 10 minutes during which the collector works slowly up and across the stream lifting stones and holding the net in such a way that anything beneath each stone is swept into it. Animals clinging to a stone are dislodged by vigorous washing in the mouth of the net and then the stone is discarded. This is scarcely a quantitative technique but does yield useful comparable figures and is used by some River Purification Boards.

(ii) Provision of a known area of removable substrate for colonisation. An area of bottom is reconstructed on a tray and lowered into the water and left until it has been recolonised by the animals from the substrate around it. This is not a satisfactory method in fast-flowing streams as the tray tends to get washed out or gravel from upstream is washed on to it. Furthermore, organisms frequently congregate under it and not on it.

(iii) Boxes and cylinders. From a box without a bottom and of a definite area, which has been placed on the stream bed, the larger stones are picked out by hand, smaller material is dug out with a shovel and sieved, and any animal that may leave the substrate and swim is caught by baling the water out into a sieve. One criticism of this method is that when the box is immersed in the stream it deflects the current downstream before it reaches the bottom and scours the area that it is intended to sample.

(iv) Fixed nets. A known area upstream is disturbed and the animals dislodged from it are washed into the net. Morgan and Egglishaw (1965) in their survey of the bottom fauna of streams in the Scottish Highlands tried a number of methods but, for one reason or another, discarded them in preference for a method they devised whereby a standard number of kicks are given in front of a net to provide the sample. A hand net is used which consists of a pyramid-shaped net, 30 cm deep, made of grit gauze, 12 meshes per cm, which is attached to a square frame with 24 cm sides. The net is held against the downstream side of the area to be sampled and the substrate disturbed with the investigator's boot. A given number of kicks (four was the number eventually decided upon) are made in an upstream direction for a distance of about 18 inches (46 cm), each kick digging deeper into the substrate. Morgan and Egglishaw decided, in view of the versatility, speed and good replication of results, to use this technique during their stream survey. Three four-kick samples were taken in each stream, one in a pool, one in a run and a third in a position where conditions were intermediate between those at the other two sampling sites.

(v) Nets that are pushed forward through the substrate. The net most commonly used in this method is the shovel sampler. The net is rather like a shovel open at the back and carrying a bag. The net frame in the model used by Mills (1964a) is 12 inches wide and 18 inches high and the lower part of the frame, which is in contact with the substrate, has a cutting edge. To the frame is attached strong, small-meshed netting to prevent the inner net from being worn and torn by the stony substrate. Most of the organisms collect in the inner net which is made of 60 meshes to the inch grit gauze. Over this net is attached an inner metal frame with a large mesh net of thick twine. This prevents the larger stones falling into the gauze net. This shovel sampler is pushed forward into the substrate a given distance, say a foot, to sample, in this case, a square foot of bottom. Any stones collected on the inner frame of large-meshed netting are lifted out and washed in a basin of water. An addition to this sampling technique is a wooden three-sided sampling frame with raised sides. The two arms are of solid wood while the upstream side is made of weld-mesh. The purpose of the frame is to outline the sampling area and to prevent gravel and small stones, together with some of the fauna, being pushed ahead of the net. The shovel net is of limited use in streams where a considerable proportion of the bottom is composed of large stones or bedrock.

A quantitative sampler used in rivers too deep to wade has been devised by Allan (1952). This is a type of grab which consists of a long steel tubular handle at the end of which is a box fitted with toothed jaws operated, from the end of the handle, by means of a steel operating rod moving within it. The body and open jaws form a box with a toothed edge, which, when lowered on to the substrate and pushed into the extent of the teeth, forms a complete trap, the entire contents of which are lifted into the body of the grab as the jaws are closed, the closing action being effected by a downward pressure on the operating rod.

A number of people studying bottom fauna have found that the distribution of aquatic insects in a stream is not random. Furthermore, there has been found to be considerable variation between adjacent samples; seasonal variations in numbers are also considerable.

When comparisons between rivers are needed the value of grading is of some use in broad terms. Madden (1935) classified Arizona streams on a numerical basis. Those with more than 2,152 organisms/m^2 were 'rich', those with 1,076 organisms/m^2 were 'average' and those with less than 1,076 organisms/m^2 were 'poor'. However, Allen (1941b) found that while the value of the bottom fauna as a source of food corresponds approximately to its density the correspondence is by no means exact and considerable discrepancies occur. He noticed that while there was a considerable difference in average population density between the bottom fauna of the Halkirk Burn (3,016/m^2) and the Sleach Burn (4,060/m^2) on the Thurso system there was no significant difference between them as sources of food for first-year salmon. He showed that this arose from the fact that the fauna of the Halkirk Burn was proportionately richer in the more available food animals. Furthermore, drifting fauna and wind-blown organisms of terrestrial origin are also available and are taken by fish. These are valuable supplements at certain times of the year and should be taken into account when any assessment of stream fauna is made.

12.4 Capture and examination of fish

Capture. As Lagler (1968) points out, the key to the assessment of fish production is knowledge of the fish stock, its specific taxonomy, number of individuals, sex- and year-class composition and the rates of growth, mortality and recruitment. "Such knowledge derives from the study of captured individuals."

Some of the methods used for the capture of salmonid fish have already been described in the earlier chapters of this book. Most fish capture methods are selective with respect to size and maybe species and sex as well. So if it is desired to sample all ages of a trout population in a lake, say, then various types of fishing gear may be needed. For example, if the fish are to be caught in gill or hang nets then nets of various mesh sizes will be required. However, few of the youngest age classes will be captured in these and so a sweep-net or shore seine with a bag of very small mesh ($\frac{1}{2}$ inch) will be required. Even these methods may still not produce a representative sample of the population. For example, the young fish may remain in the nursery streams for two years or more before entering the lake, and will therefore have to be caught by electrical fishing methods, or the fish distribution may be seasonal, with mature fish congregating at the mouths of the spawning streams in the early autumn and spawning in the streams in the early winter. All these aspects of fish size, distribution and state of maturity, etc., have to be taken into consideration when attempting to sample any fish population adequately. As Lagler says: "there is no substitute for operational experience in fish capture".

One of the least selective of all methods of fishing is electrical fishing, which is best adapted for use in streams although electrical 'seines' can be used in lakes. It involves producing an electrical field in the water by passing a current between two electrodes. The types of apparatus one can use vary from heavy stationary to light, highly portable sets. Using alternating current (A.C.) of correct strength, fish in its field are stunned with their muscles in a cramped state and rapidly become unconscious, remain unconscious for a short time after the current is switched off and may be netted from the water. Direct current (D.C.) induces 'galvanotaxis' so that the fish move towards the anode, generally without loss of consciousness, but should the field attain a sufficient intensity they will turn over. In this condition their bodies are entirely relaxed, and the fish tend to recover instantly when the current is switched off.

When alternating current is used, fish are stunned close to the electrode or further from it, according to their size. It is therefore necessary to collect the passive fish, and in a stream this is conveniently accomplished by allowing them to drift down into a stop net. However, not all the stunned fish float on the surface; commonly they make a dash to the top, become unconscious and begin to sink at once and may get caught up in underwater vegetation.

With direct current, the fish swim actively towards the positive electrode and remain there. In ordinary circumstances they do not lose consciousness at any stage and show no signs of distress. This system has the advantage that it avoids losing fish which are stunned and caught in obstructions; on the contrary, they swim out of weed beds and out of the mud.

The relative effectiveness of the two systems depends on the circumstances. Alternating current produces a much more powerful effect on fish than direct current; it is therefore much more efficient electrically, and can be used at lower voltages than D.C. On the other hand, if it is desired to remove as many fish as possible from a stream D.C. should be used; it is also effective round the banks of pools and in weed beds. A.C. is not very popular with many salmon fishery managers as it can cause fracture of the spine in adult salmon (Stewart, 1965).

When different water and soil conditions are encountered there may be disconcerting differences in the behaviour of the apparatus. This is most noticeable when D.C. is used, as it is more sensitive than A.C. If the con-

ductivity of the water increases, the effective electric field around the electrode will contract. Conductivity is increased by rise of temperature and by
dissolved salts. For this reason, fishing in waters receiving domestic or
industrial wastes is frequently difficult, as the current demand is considerable and the behaviour of a D.C. set in particular may alter substantially.

Considerable economies in power may be made if the available current
is used in short separate pulses instead of continuously. The effect of such
an interrupted current on a fish resembles that of a powerful D.C.; the
fish are collected at the anode, rapidly stunned and paralysed. They recover
after a short interval.

The stop nets used in conjunction with electrical fishing (Plate 28) may
also be used on their own for netting small pools and can be very effective
samplers. Elson (1962b) has designed a stop net, which he refers to as the
Pollett apron seine, which has a modification which prevents fish, falling
back into the belly of the net, and escaping upstream (Fig. 57).

Various aspects of electrical fishing, electrophysiology and electric
screens are dealt with fully in the F.A.O. publication *Fishing with Electricity* edited by Dr Vibert (1967).

Finally, it should be stressed that in many countries electric fishing is
illegal. In Scotland, electrical fishing is governed by the Salmon and
Freshwater Fisheries (Protection) (Scotland) Act, 1951, (Section 4), and requires the prior written permission of the Secretary of State or of the District Board (Section 9). In England and Wales, the use of electrical methods
of fishing is legal unless the River Authority or Conservancy responsible for
the waters concerned is administering a bye-law which, directly or by
inference, makes the method unlawful. If the method is not illegal in the
area where it is proposed to work, the necessary licence for the apparatus
will be issued by the local River Authority.

Traps are another means of sampling fish populations and the type
most effective for sampling migratory fish is the Wolf trap. This consists of

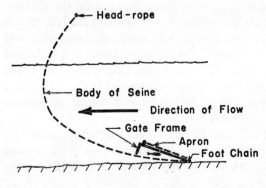

Head - rope

Body of Seine

Direction of Flow

Gate Frame

Apron

Foot Chain

FIG. 57

Profile diagram of the Pollett
apron seine in action (from
Elson, 1962. Reproduced with
the permission of the Queen's
Printer for Canada).

PLATE 30

A salmon counting fence, Indian River, Newfoundland, 1967.

PLATE 31. Female grilse (52.5 cm long) bearing a silver wire tag at the anterior end of the dorsal fin. The fish was tagged as a hatchery-reared smolt, the slightly distorted dorsal fin is characteristic of hatchery fish.

PLATE 32. Female grilse showing regenerated left pelvic fin which had been clipped at the smolt stage.

a horizontal framework covered with wire mesh or a wooden grid. The water flows through this horizontal screen leaving a small film of water to flow into a trough attached to the downstream side of the screen. Fish 'sieved' out of the water flop into the trough and swim down it, in water fed into the trough from one end, to a holding pool. These traps can be of various sizes, from some only a few feet wide, built on small nursery streams (Plate 29), to large structures built across a river 50 feet or more wide. Fig. 58 depicts traps of the latter size built on the rivers Meig and Conon in Ross-shire. There is a grid trap for descending fish and a series of holding pools for ascending fish.

The traps used for migratory fish in Canada consist of vertical screens with box traps sited along them and are known as counting fences (Plate 30).

Another type of trap, which is a useful sampling device, is the box trap (Fig. 59). This consists of a square wooden frame, covered with small-meshed netting, with a V-entrance and an inclined ramp. The fish can be lead into and up the 'funnel entrance' by means of a leader. On entering the trap the fish can drop to the bottom of the trap a foot or more below the opening and so find it difficult to escape.

Examination. Examination of fish includes recording their length, weight and sex, although it is rarely possible to identify the sex from external appearances outside the spawning season. During the spawning season it is always possible to distinguish the sex of the salmon. The sex of trout that are ready to spawn can also be found by gentle pressure of the 'belly'. With pressure the genital papilla at the vent is apparent, and even a few eggs may be shed; similar pressure on male fish will cause some milt to be shed. If the fish being examined are to be killed, the sex, stage of maturity and condition of the gonads can also be noted.

Scales are usually taken at the time of examination and placed in a small envelope on which is recorded the other data. Scale samples are best taken above the lateral line on the 'shoulder' of the fish (i.e. between the head and dorsal fin). It is usually necessary to take at least 20 scales in order to be sure that some of the scales are normal. This is because some populations of brown trout have many regenerated (replacement) scales.

Length is best measured by using a measuring board in which the head of the fish is placed against a stop at the beginning of the measuring scale. A large fish is best placed on a board which has a canvas or rubber hood at the top, under which the head is placed, to keep the fish from moving (Fig. 60). Length measurements are usually taken from the metric scale. The fineness of measurement depends mainly on the use to which the data are to be put. Anything finer than the nearest millimetre is rarely attempted. The two length measurements normally taken are either: fork length – from the tip of the nose to the tip of the median rays of the tail, or total length,

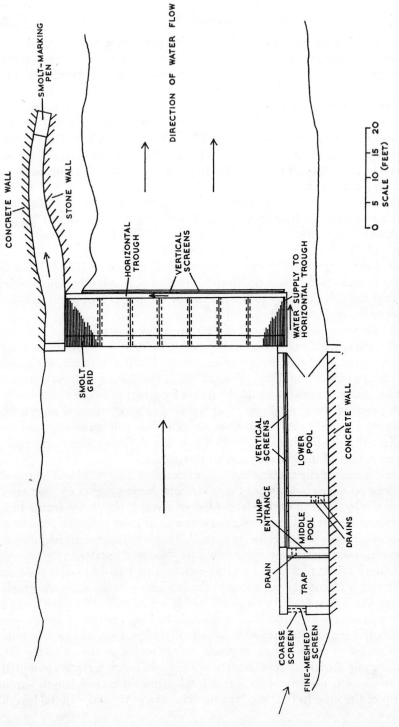

FIG. 58. Diagram of a Wolf grid-type trap (from Pyefinch and Mills, 1963).

which is the greatest length of the fish – from the tip of the nose to the end of the tail fin. Errors in fish measurement are due to muscular tension in live fish and relaxation after death, and shrinkage due to preservation, including freezing.

FIG. 59.   Box trap, designed for catching migrating smolts.

Another method of measuring is by the use of a board, with a stop at one end, covered with sheet cork. Over this is placed a sheet of white paper and a sheet of non-shrinkable tracing paper; modern plastic tracing material is best. The fish is laid on this with its head against the stop and its length pricked out on the paper. For those measuring and weighing a large number of fish without help, a tape recorder is most useful.

Weight can be taken from live fish, if anaesthetised, on a spring balance or better still a shop-counter style balance. The smaller fish can be weighed individually on a balance which has a crocodile clip which is attached to the tail of the fish. Larger fish can be weighed by either placing a hook, on the end of the spring balance, under the operculum of the fish, or, to avoid possible damage to the gills, placing the fish in a polythene bag and then deducting the weight of the bag from the total weight. Much more reliable readings of length and weight are obtained if the fish is first anaesthetised. The anaesthetic most commonly used is MS–222 (tricaine methanesulphonate). The concentrations to use, which vary with water temperature among other things, are given in a pamphlet published by Sandoz in Basle, Switzerland, who are the manufacturers of this chemical.

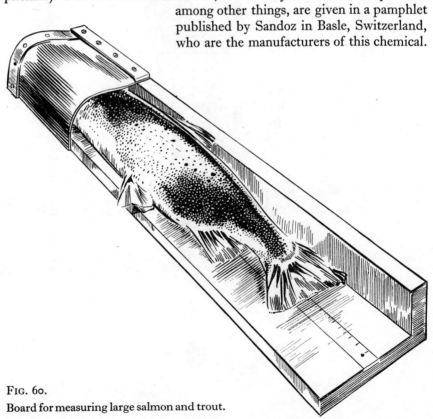

FIG. 60.
Board for measuring large salmon and trout.

Length–weight relationship. From an adequate number of paired measurements of length and weight, it is possible to derive conversion factors to obtain one of the measurements when the other is known. The length–weight relationship can nearly always be represented by:

$$w = al^b$$

where b is an exponent with a value nearly always close to 3. The form can be transformed to:

$$\log w = \log a + b\,(\log l)$$

Log weight is plotted against log length and the regression line calculated by the method of least squares. The regression coefficient is b, while $\log a$ is the intercept of the line with the y-axis.

Length–weight relationships can also be estimated by plotting length and weight for each fish on double logarithmic paper. Approximate regression lines are then drawn by eye: by using a transparent ruler with a line scratched down the lower surface (Fig. 61). In calculating length–weight relationships it is important to use samples of fish that are unbiased in respect to length and weight. For example, a sample from a gill net of a particular size is unsuitable, because the net tends to select fat fish among the

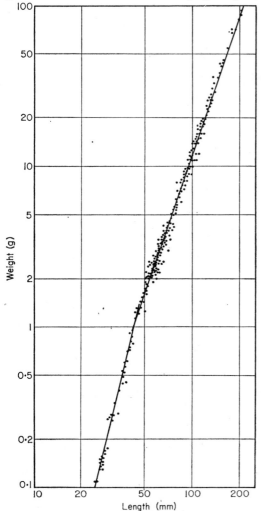

FIG. 61.

A 'dot diagram' of weight against length, plotted on double logarithmic axes. Two lines are drawn by eye, to represent the length–weight relationship below and above a length of 42 mm. Data are from a population of brown trout, supplied by E. D. Le Cren (in Ricker, 1968).

shorter ones and thin fish among the larger ones, thus introducing a strong bias in *b* (Kipling, 1962). Samples should also cover as wide a range of lengths and weights as possible.

Condition factor. The coefficient of condition or condition factor (*CF*) can be calculated from the formula:

$$CF = \frac{w}{l^3}$$

Comparisons of condition factors are useful for investigating seasonal and habitat differences in 'condition'.

Stomach contents. Frequently it may be desired to study the feeding habits of the fish being examined, but because they have to be returned to the water, particularly if it is a sport fishery that is being surveyed, this

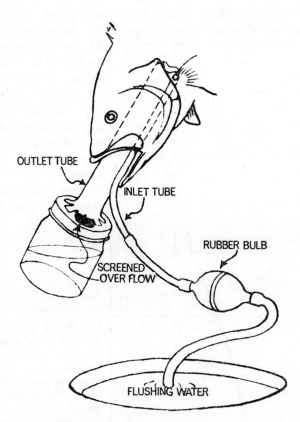

FIG. 62.   Stomach sampler (rubber bulb of the type used on syringes). (After Seaburg, 1957.)

study has to be ignored. There is also sometimes the difficulty of obtaining a sufficient number of stomachs for an adequate study of feeding habits. This is because most of the waters being surveyed are either sport fisheries or nursery areas and to kill a large number of fish is not in the interest of all concerned. Seaburg (1957) appreciated this problem and has designed a stomach sampler for live fish (Fig. 62). Referring to the figure, the procedure is as follows: the fish is held with its head downward. The tube of the sampler is placed in the open mouth and then inserted slowly into the oesophagus. The rubber bulb (which is connected by a short piece of rubber tubing to a supply of water) is squeezed, and water is forced through the inlet tube into the stomach. If the tip of the sampler is not completely enclosed by the oesophagus, a spray of water will be released through the gills. Flushing water and stomach contents pass through the large tube and into the attached specimen jar. It is sometimes necessary to use forceps to extract from the stomach food particles too large to pass through the outlet tube.

Fecundity. The eggs of salmon and trout are large and therefore easy to count. However, the eggs are also valuable, so that if any fecundity study is to be made it may be necessary to do the work during the stripping operations at a hatchery or trap. Pope, Mills and Shearer (1961) used some of the following methods for their study of the fecundity of salmon: (1) The eggs were stripped from ripe females, fertilised, washed and allowed to harden. Then the total volume of water (v_1) displaced by all the eggs (n_1) poured into a large measuring cylinder was noted, then a known number of eggs (n_2) that displaces a unit volume of water (v_2) is also recorded. It is then possible to find n_1, which is the only unknown. (2) By counting all the eggs in a sloping trough by means of a plastic plate in which there are 200 countersunk holes. The plate is pushed down the trough and lifted up under the eggs. The eggs run into the holes and the excess run off with the water. The eggs are gently washed out into a basin of water and the process is repeated until all the eggs are counted (Plate 21). (3) By counting the eggs in the ovaries of dead fish. The ovaries are first placed in Gilson's fluid (Simpson, 1951), which dissolves the ovarian tissue, for a few days. The loosened eggs are then shaken in a jar to separate them from the remaining tissue and then poured into a plastic sieve and washed. They can then be laid out on blotting paper to dry and then counted like dried peas.

Parasites. The following parts of the fish should be examined for parasites: (1) External surfaces of body and fins, (2) Body cavity, inner surface of body wall and surfaces of viscera, (3) Stomach, (4) Intestine, (5) Liver and gall bladder, (6) Heart and pericardium, (7) Gonads, (8) Swim bladder, (9) Kidney and urinary ducts, (10) Gills and gill cavities, and (11) Eyes.

Some of the parasites will be seen by the naked eye while others will have to be found by microscopical examination. All these organs can be located by reference to Plate II.

Chubb and Powell (1966) give a very useful guide to the examination of fish for parasites and describe the methods for preserving parasites of different types:

Ectoparasites – lice, leeches and certain flukes, those on the gills, should be freed from mucus and preserved by shaking in 5% formaldehyde (one part of commercial 40% formalin to seven parts of water).

Endoparasites – (i) Flukes – these should be killed by plunging in hot water, at a temperature of about 60° C and preserving in alcohol-formol-acetic (A.F.A.) (Absolute alcohol – 720 ml., 40% formaldehyde – 100 ml., glacial acetic acid – 50 ml. and distilled water – 130 ml.).

Tapeworms – for general studies, they should be relaxed in cold water until they do not contract when touched and preserved in 5% formaldehyde.

Roundworms – these should be killed in either hot 70% alcohol or in glacial acetic acid.

Spiny-headed worms – each worm should be relaxed in cold water until the proboscis is fully extended and does not contract when it is touched. A.F.A. should be used as a preservative.

Lastly, as Chubb and Powell state:

Before one begins to look for parasites as the primary cause of death of animals, an important point must be driven home. It must be remembered that every natural population of animals or plants is infected by a range of species of parasites. Few, if any of these parasites will be pathogenic in normal circumstances. Indeed, from a teleological viewpoint, successful parasites are those which cause least disturbance to the life of the host.

The occurrence of parasites, therefore, cannot necessarily be regarded as a primary factor in the death of an animal. The parasites may contribute towards the general stress leading to death, but in the majority of cases, only in a secondary manner.

12.5 Marking and tagging

Marking fish is an important technique in the study of fish populations. Marks, such as fin-clips and tags, are used to study (i) the various population parameters such as density and mortality rate, (ii) movements and

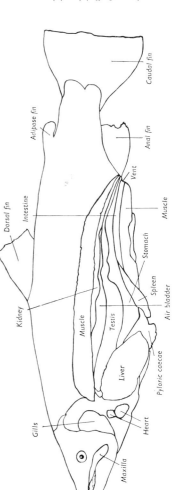

Dorsal fin

Adipose fin

Caudal fin

Anal fin

Vent

Intestine

Muscle

Kidney

Stomach

Spleen

Air bladder

Muscle

Testis

Pyloric caecae

Liver

Gills

Heart

Maxilla

migrations, (iii) growth and age determinations, and, (iv) behaviour studies where individuals have to be recognised. As Arnold (1966) points out, an ideal fish mark should have some of the following characteristics: It should be retained in essentially unaltered condition for the lifetime of the fish; it should have no effect on the fish's behaviour, reproduction, life span, growth, feeding, movement or vulnerability to predation, angling and other external factors; it should not entangle in vegetation or nets; it should be inexpensive; it should be easy to apply to fish in the field without the need for anaesthetic; it should be easily detected in the field by untrained personnel or the public; there should be enough possible variations of the mark so that many individuals or many small groups can be identified separately; the mark should not cause adverse public relations by spoiling edible parts of the fish. No mark or tag at present satisfies all these requirements.

The types of mark, fin-clip and tag that are used in these studies are so numerous that a detailed description would become an inventory. However, those types most commonly used will be described.

Staining. Stains are most commonly used for identifying batches of fish. Young salmonids have been mass-marked by forcing fluorescent pigment into the dermal tissue with compressed air from a small sandblast gun. It is particularly useful in short-term studies of the dynamics and distribution of fish populations.

Another method of staining is to immerse the fish, usually fry, in stains such as Bismarck brown Y. Arnold (*loc. cit.*) describes the relative merits of over 100 dyes that have been tried on fish and reference to this paper is well worthwhile before any stains are tried. His conclusions are that at present the most promising methods of marking with chemicals are use of radio-isotopes, subcutaneous injection and tattooing. Materials that appear most promising for injection and tattooing include cadmium sulphide, chromium green, National fast blue 8 GXM, mercuric sulphide and 'Panjet'. For immersion staining, neutral red, Bismarck brown Y, acridine orange and rhodamine B appear most useful.

Branding. Branding appears to be a satisfactory way of doing short-term marking by which individual fish may be identified for varying periods. The branding tool has a handle of copper tubing with a marking tip of silver, smoothly polished to facilitate heat transfer. The mark is cut according to the desired pattern from a quarter-inch-thick silver plate to form a flat surfaced figure which is mounted and soldered in reverse on to a matching piece of one-eighth-inch-thick silver. This in turn is soldered to the end of the copper tube. This physical continuity maintains a relatively uniform heat flow from the handle to the marking surface when applied to a fish. The handle is insulated by polyvinyl tubing which covers the copper

except for the first two inches from the marking tip. The fish is anaesthetised and the branding tool, which is removed from the heating water, is
applied to the skin surface between the lateral line and the dorsal fin.
Groves and Novotny (1965), who describe this technique, had no mortalities
and the fish are easily identified upon recovery after varying intervals up to
45 days. Freeze-branding can also be done in the same way, with the
branding tool cooled in dry ice.

Fin-clipping. This is the most popular of all marking methods. There is
some fin-regeneration after clipping but it is possible for trained personnel
to detect this even when regeneration is complete. There is little or no
regeneration of the adipose fin, and, for this reason, it is the fin most
frequently removed on salmonids. Pelvic fins are also used for marking
experiments and, while there may be considerable regeneration, it is usually
possible to identify the fin-clip (Fig. 63 and Plate 32).

Tagging

The advantage of using tags is that they can be used either for batch
marking (Plate 31) or for identifying individual fish. A description of the
main types of tags used follows.

Plastic or metal discs and labels. (Fig. 64b and c.) Plastic tags can be
in various colours. The metal plates may be rather bright but they can
be darkened chemically. The tags are usually attached by means of a wire
loop usually made of either soft-annealed silver wire or stainless steel. One
arm of the wire is threaded through the dorsal musculature slightly anterior
to the base of the dorsal fin by means of a hypodermic needle and the other
arm of wire is brought over the back of the fish and twisted with the other
arm thus bringing the disc or label close in to the side of the fish (Plates
33–37).

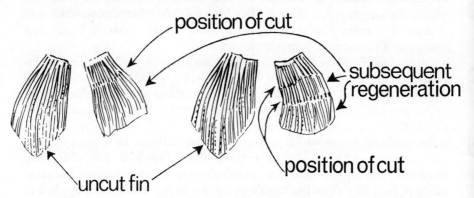

FIG. 63. Diagram of fins after being clipped, showing subsequent regeneration.

Double attachment trailer tag or Carlin tag. (Fig. 64d.) This consists of articulated links of stainless steel fastened to a strip of cardboard in celluloid and bearing a message. It is attached by two wires passing through the internal bones under the dorsal fin. A modification of this is the replacing of the stainless steel with polyethylene filament.

Hydrostatic tag (Lea tag). (Fig. 64a.) This tag is attached in the same way as are the tags in (i), or else by means of a bridle. It consists of a plastic cylinder plugged at both ends and contains a piece of paper bearing a number and message. This tag is used chiefly on adult salmonids.

The Petersen tag. This is one of the earliest tags and is still one of the most successful. It consists of two metal or plastic discs or plates connected by a wire or polyethylene filament passing through the dorsal musculature of the fish immediately below the dorsal fin.

Jaw tag. These are usually made of monel metal and are used for larger fish which have a strong jaw. The lettering is easy to read and the tags are easy to apply with a pair of long-nosed pliers. However, they may affect feeding and growth.

Internal anchor tag. There are a number of variations of these tags which are secured internally with a plastic anchor. The tag itself is usually made of plastic tubing on which lettering can be printed. Dell (1968) describes the application of these tags by means of a cartridge fed tagging gun.

The criticism of all tags is that they may affect the growth of the fish

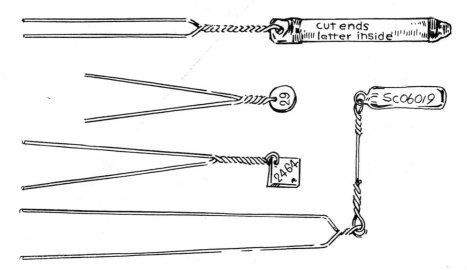

FIG. 64. Tags: (a) Lea hydrostatic, (b) plastic disc, (c) Ivorine disc, and (d) Carlin.

(De Roche, 1963) and a number of tagging tests have been carried out, with varying results, to test the efficiency of various types. Mills (1959) found that the lighter tags (plain silver wire with or without coloured plastic tubing) remained in hatchery smolts longer than the heavier plastic discs and hydrostatic tags.

12.6 Estimation of fish populations

There are a number of methods used for the estimation of population size and these have been reviewed by Jones (1964).

The simplest method, which is known as the Petersen estimate or Lincoln index, consists of marking animals on one occasion, and sampling

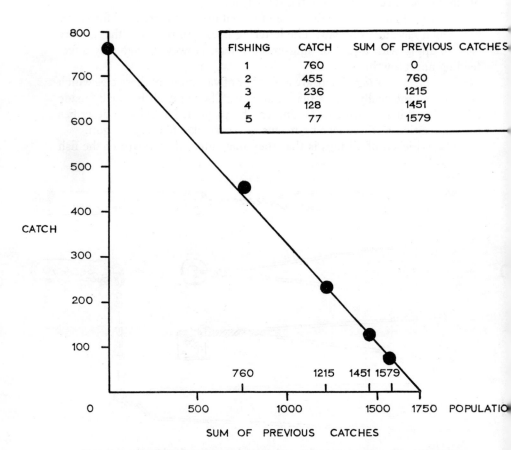

FISHING	CATCH	SUM OF PREVIOUS CATCHES
1	760	0
2	455	760
3	236	1215
4	128	1451
5	77	1579

FIG. 65. Graphical method used by De Lury for estimation of a fish population by means of successive units of fishing effort.

for recaptures on a single occasion or over a single period of time. Thus, out of a population of N individuals suppose that T are marked. The probability of subsequently recapturing one of these marked individuals will depend, in the first place, on how they are distributed throughout the population and on the way the recapture effort is deployed. If one of these is random, the probability that a sampled animal is marked is $\dfrac{T}{N}$.

Out of a sample of n animals one would therefore expect to get exactly $\dfrac{nT}{N}$ marked ones.

If this number is denoted by m, then

$$m = \frac{nT}{N}$$

and, rearranging terms, one gets

$$N = \frac{nT}{m}$$

This is a first estimate of population size (N) in terms of the number marked (T), the number recaptured (m) and the number sampled (n) in the process of obtaining these recaptures. A better approximation is obtained from a model in which the number of marked animals per sample is treated as a random variate. This can be done by considering the probability distribution of numbers of marked animals out of a sample size n and this is the approach used by Bailey (1951).

Bailey derived the formula:

$$\hat{N} = M \frac{(n + 1)}{(m + 1)}$$

where $\hat{N}$ = total population size
M = number taken in first sample, marked and released
n = number taken in second sample
m = number of marked individuals recaptured in second sample

A sufficiently accurate estimate of the variance of $\hat{N}$, also given by Bailey, is

$$\text{var } (\hat{N}) = \frac{M^2(n + 1)\,(n - m)}{(m + 1)^2\,(m + 2)}$$

To give an example: 3,851 trout were netted (in the first sample) and marked and released; 2,072 were caught in the second netting, a week later say, and 428 were marked fish, then:

$$\hat{N} = 3851 \cdot \frac{2073}{429} = 18,609$$

$$\text{var}\,(\hat{N}) = 638,653$$

The square root of this quantity, ± 799, is the standard error (S.E.) of the estimated number of fish. According to standard statistical techniques the approximate 95% confidence limits for the number of fish in the population are given by $18069 \pm (1 \cdot 96)\,(799)$; which are $17,011 - 20,207$.

Seber and Le Cren (1967) describe a method where two successive catches, c_1 and c_2 are taken with the same effort from a population, and an estimate of the size of the population, $\tilde{n}$, is given by

$$\tilde{n} = c_1^2/(c_1 - c_2)$$

with a variance

$$\text{var}\,[\tilde{n}] = [c_1^2 c_2^2 (c_1 + c_2)]/(c_1 - c_2)^4$$

A third method of estimating population is by De Lury's method (1947, 1951). This is based upon the assumption that the number of fish caught in the course of successive units of fishing is a function of the available population. When in the population the number of individuals diminishes, the catches per unit fishing effort are expected to diminish in the same proportion.

Captures made in the course of successive units of fishing effort are shown on a graph whose ordinate indicates the number or the weight of fish caught per unit of fishing effort, the abscissa the cumulative total of the preceding captures. (Fig. 65.) The line about which the points are grouped is located by eye. By extrapolation, this straight line is continued to its point of intersection with abscissa, that is to say to a theoretical point corresponding with the complete removal of the fish, where the unit of fishing effort would not permit any further catch at all. To this point of intersection corresponds the estimate of the number or the weight of the total population.

This method of estimation requires two conditions:

(1) During the successive fishings, the migration and natural mortality of the fish must be negligible.
(2) The possibility of capture must remain identical during the successive fishings, that is to say the proportion of the number of fishes captured to the number of fishes remaining must remain the same for each unit of fishing effort. The coefficient of capture must therefore remain invariable.

If these two conditions exist, the following formula can be deduced:

$$C = k(N - S) \text{ in which}$$

$C = $ catch per unit of fishing effort.
$N = $ total population present before the first unit of fishing effort.
$S = $ sum of the catches made in the course of preceding units of fishing effort.
$k = $ coefficient of capture.

If successive values of C are placed along the ordinate, and successive values of S along the abscissa, the points so obtained and joined up give a straight line, k being constant. At the point at which this line crosses the abscissa, C is equal to o and N is equal to S. Instead of making an estimate of the total number of individuals present, separate estimates for different classes of age or size can be made.

Having obtained an estimate of the population of fish of various age classes it is useful to estimate the mortality between these age classes. Cuinat and Vibert (1963) give a formula to estimate mortality according to the age pyramid. The formula is:

$$S = \sqrt[n]{\frac{R(a + n)}{Ra}} \text{ in which:}$$

$S = $ Average level of annual survival between age a and age $a + n$
$R = $ Number of subjects of age a
$R(a + n) = $ Number of subjects of $a + n$

Assuming a trout population with the following distribution per age group:

$$o + - 2136; \ 1 + - 862; \ 2 + - 352; \ 3 + - 60; \ 4 + - 6.$$

Then of age o+ to the age 4+ :

$$S = \sqrt[4]{\frac{6}{2136}} = \sqrt[4]{0 \cdot 002809} \simeq 0 \cdot 23 \text{ or } 23\%$$

The level of annual mortality: $Z = 1 - S = 77\%$

This of course assumes that the recruitment has varied little in the course of the preceding years, and that the migrations of trout have been of little importance.

A more mathematical approach to the estimation of population numbers and mortality rates is described by Robson and Regier (1968).

12.7 Growth studies

Salmon and trout scales carry a particularly good record of the age and

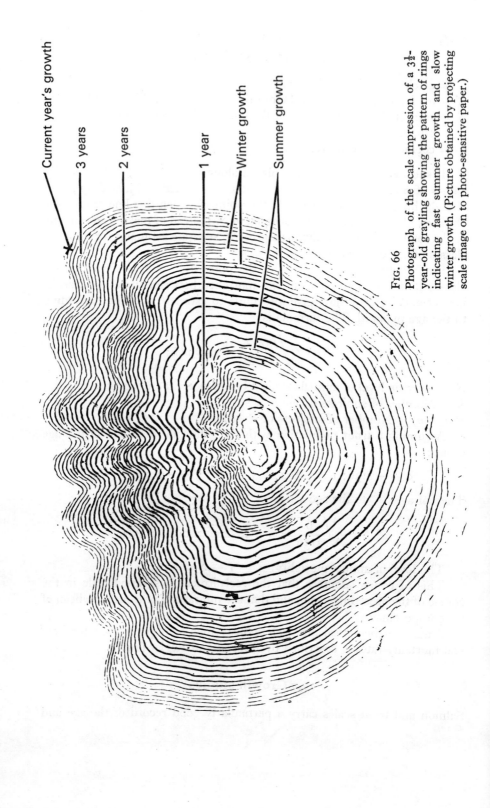

Current year's growth

3 years

2 years

1 year

Winter growth

Summer growth

Fig. 66
Photograph of the scale impression of a 3½-year-old grayling showing the pattern of rings indicating fast summer growth and slow winter growth. (Picture obtained by projecting scale image on to photo-sensitive paper.)

TAGGING OPERATIONS

Plate 33

A hypodermic needle is inserted into the base of the dorsal fin at its anterior end.

Plate 34

One arm of the silver wire attached to the tag is threaded into the needle which is then withdrawn from the fish.

Plate 35

The other arm of the silver wire is brought over the back of the fish and the two arms of silver wire are twisted together.

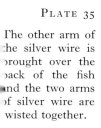

Plate 36

The excess silver wire is cut off.

Plate 37

The wire and the tag are pressed close to the sides of the fish.

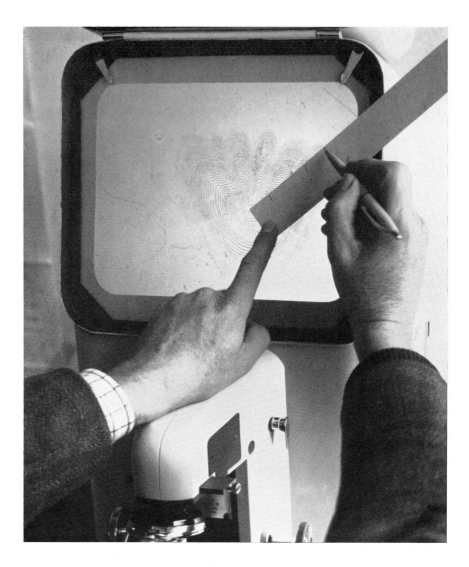

PLATE 38

Reading a grayling scale from the image produced on a micro-
projector. A strip of cardboard is laid from the centre of the
scale image to the edge of the scale image and then a pencil mark
is made on the cardboard at the end of each 'band' of winter
rings. (See text.)

growth of these fish, as do the scales of some other members of the salmon family. Fig. 66 depicts the scale of a grayling on which has been indicated the areas of fast and slow growth and the annual rings or annuli.

The method most commonly used for reading scales is to obtain an impression of the scale. This is done by laying the scales between two pieces of celluloid strip and then passing them between two metal rollers. The impressions are formed on one of the pieces of celluloid. The celluloid strip bearing the impressions is then placed on a microscope stage under a microscope lens and the magnified image projected on to a screen. There are several ways of projecting the image, one of the most sophisticated is with the aid of a Scale Projector which produces a magnified image on a built-in screen (Plate 38). The scale impressions on the strip are examined and the one showing the clearest scale pattern selected, first making sure that it is not a regenerated scale, which does not give the complete age as its centre is filled with regenerated scale material. The annuli (or "bands" of winter rings) are marked off on a strip of cardboard laid on the image from the centre of the scale to its edge. The strip of cardboard is then laid on a piece of graph paper on which the expected range of fish lengths has been marked along the ordinate (Y-axis). With the zero of the scale measurement at the origin, the strip is rotated until the scale-edge mark is opposite the observed length of the fish. Intermediate lengths corresponding to the annuli can then be read on the ordinate side of the graph paper. The data from such scale readings can then be incorporated into the construction of growth curves, such as those depicted in Fig. 67. This procedure is possible when there is a direct proportionality between the rate of growth in length and that of the scales, as is the position in salmon and trout.

The back-calculations of length frequency may exhibit a tendency for computed lengths at a given age to be smaller, the older the fish from which they are computed the smaller would be the calculated length. This is known as 'Lee's phenomenon'. Four possible causes have been suggested: (a) incorrect procedure for back calculation, (b) non-random sampling of the stock, (c) selective natural mortality, favouring a greater survival of the smaller fish of a given age and (d) selective fishing mortality, similarly biased.

A simple method for age determination is the analysis of size frequency distributions, known as the Peterson method. This method uses the individual lengths of a large number of fish of a population. It requires a unimodal size distribution of all fish of the same age, and is easy to employ if there is no large overlap in the size of the individuals in the adjacent age groups or difference in the growth rates of males and females. In principle, it is more generally useful than all the other methods, but usually it can be applied only to the youngest age groups of a population. Even when age determination from scales is possible, using the length composition may make it possible to reduce greatly the amount of age determination needed. Close to the modes, all or nearly all of the fish may be expected to be of one age group, age determinations can then be concentrated on those that lie between the modes, and on the bigger fish whose length distribution overlaps.

12.8 Production estimates

There are a number of ways in which fish production can be estimated. Perhaps the most satisfactory and simplest is the graphical method used by Allen and described in some detail by Chapman (1968). Very simply, in

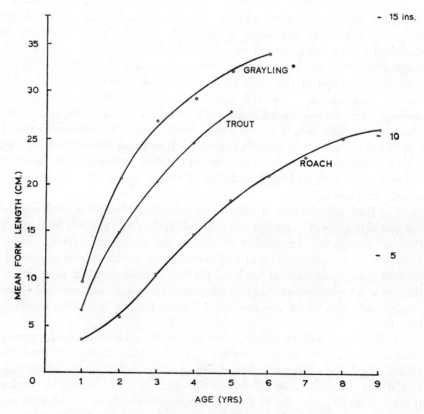

FIG. 67.   Growth rates of roach, trout and grayling in the Eden Water, Roxburghshire (from Mills, 1970).

Allen's method the number of individuals (N) in the population at successive time instants is plotted against the mean weight ($\overline{w}$) of the individual at the same instants. With data for a single age group over 12 months one can

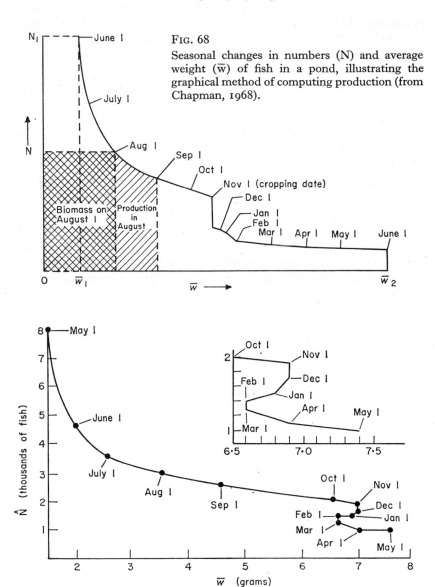

FIG. 68

Seasonal changes in numbers (N) and average weight ($\overline{w}$) of fish in a pond, illustrating the graphical method of computing production (from Chapman, 1968).

FIG. 69. Graphical estimation of production for a population from data for a single age group over 12 months (from Chapman, 1968).

compute production or estimate it graphically by plotting the weight survivorship curve (Figs. 68 and 69), which is known as an Allen Curve. Using a planimeter or by counting the squares on the graph paper, one can measure the area beneath the curve which is equivalent to the annual production. The inset enlargement of the Allen curve in Fig. 69 includes a period of negative production. Production in October is the area between the curve and weight axis or about 0·8 kg. Because no growth occurred in November, there is no area to add for production in that month. In December and January, weight loss occurred, and the area (production) beneath the curve in these months should be subtracted. No production took place in February. Subsequently tissue was elaborated by the population and the area beneath the curve for March and April should be added. Chapman deals with estimation of production in detail in *Methods of Assessment of Fish Production in Fresh Waters* edited by Ricker (1968).

For those with computer facilities, a Fortran programme can be obtained from Dr Hunt of the Department of Natural Resources, Division of Conservation, Waupaca, Wisconsin. The 'input' statistics are the numbers of fish of each age present and their mean individual weights at the beginning of each month. 'Output' sheets contain monthly tabulations of instantaneous growth rate, production, stock biomass and mean biomass at the start of the month, and the instantaneous rate of biomass increase or decrease.

Part V

THE FUTURE

Chapter 13

DEVELOPMENT AND REGULATION

13.1 The high seas salmon fishery

In considering the future of this resource we have to bear in mind the effect future exploitation is likely to have on our stocks of salmon and trout as well as the effects of man's other activities. Salmon are of particular concern in this respect as, however much action one takes in managing and conserving the stocks on their breeding and nursery grounds, conservation will count for little if they are overfished on their feeding grounds. It might be argued that providing the nursery grounds are kept filled, even if it means supplementing natural reproduction, and there are sufficient young to provide an exploitable stock of maturing adults and a reasonable spawning escapement, it matters little where they are caught. This is probably sound in theory, but who catches them is more important because, as has been described in the earlier chapters of this book, vast sums of money are tied up in salmon fishing, be it for commerce or sport. No one is likely to pay for the upkeep of the stocks (the seed) and consider sound management practices (cultivation) if the future crop is harvested by another 'farmer' who is unlikely to worry as he is not paying for the 'seed'. The analogy can be taken further if the farmer harvesting the crop does not consider the future source of seed, but sells all his crop, retaining none for seed. In other words he does not limit his catch to allow for a reasonable spawning escapement. This sort of situation has arisen with the development of a high seas salmon fishery. Ever since the development of an autumn salmon fishery off the west coast of Greenland in 1956–1957 there has been a growing concern for the future stocks of salmon. At first the concern was slight as the fishery was inshore and was operated by local Greenland fishermen who were more interested in catching cod if these were plentiful. However, concern grew when the numbers landed rose each year (Table 2b) and more and more evidence from a number of countries was produced, in the form of tagged fish being recaptured in Greenland waters, that the fish were not of Greenland origin, there being only one small salmon river in Greenland. Between 1960 and 1966 about 220 tags were returned from fish caught in this inshore fishery. About 60% came from Canadian fish, 15% from Scottish, 15% from English and Welsh and 2% each from fish from Ireland, Sweden and the United States. Furthermore the number of tag recaptures off Greenland rose and Pyefinch (1969c) records 316 tags from fish tagged in Canada and Scotland between 1963 and 1966. Even so in the early years of the development of this fishery there was some hope that the fishery could be controlled. Some of the countries concerned, in particular Scotland, approached Danish fishery authorities and set up a fishery research programme. The programme started in 1965 with Scotland and Greenland and continued in 1966, with England included, and in 1967 with Canada included and has since continued.

In addition in 1965 a Joint Working Party on North Atlantic salmon was established by the International Commission for the Exploration of the Sea and the International Council for the Northwest Atlantic Fisheries. This is composed of representatives of the governments of Canada, Denmark, England, Wales, Ireland, Scotland, Norway, Sweden and the United States. The primary object of the research programme was to try to discover whether the salmon in that area returned to home rivers, as it had been alleged by Danish authorities that they never would have returned even if they had not been caught. The indications are that this is not true, since nine salmon tagged in Greenland by the research teams from Scotland, Denmark, England and Canada have already been caught in home rivers on both sides of the Atlantic.

The situation has been further complicated by the development of a Greenland offshore fishery by Danish, Norwegian, Faroese and Swedish vessels using drift nets. Another high seas fishery developed almost simultaneously off the north-west Norwegian coast with Danish, Swedish and Faroese vessels participating and using drift nets and long-lines. The fishery in the northern part of the area around the Lofoten Islands has a season from April to mid-July and long-lines are used; further south, from April to mid-July, drift nets are used. This fishery has produced salmon tagged in Norway, Sweden, and England. In addition fish have returned to Norwegian rivers carrying line hooks indicating that they had escaped from the line fishing gear being used at sea. Another fishery in existence is that off the Faroes and this fishery too has produced fish carrying Scottish and Swedish tags.

These high seas fisheries have therefore resulted in a 'free for all' without any apparent thought of regulations, voluntary or otherwise, governing type of gear, size of mesh or quota to ensure an adequate escapement of stock for breeding. Fraser (1968) (Table 32), showed that the spawning stocks of salmon in three Canadian rivers were already declining reputedly as a result of the Greenland fishery. However, Elson (1969) states that: "If half of the salmon caught in Greenland are of Canadian origin and would return home, that fishery places a substantial drain on Canadian fishermen. But the present state of our knowledge scarcely seems to warrant fears that the Greenland fishery, at present levels, spells extinction for Canadian stocks." There has also, so far, been no apparent decline in the stocks of salmon in some other countries, and the combined Scottish salmon and grilse catches from 1952 to 1969 by all methods (Table 33) show no indication of any effect. Furthermore, the weight of salmon landed has shown a slight upward trend since 1960 (Table 34).

The Danes were quick to point this out when stating in a Press release that no one had produced any scientific evidence to show that Danish netting of Atlantic salmon had been responsible for a decline in the number of salmon caught in British rivers.

This reaction from the Danes came after a proposal had been drawn up by the International Commission for the Northwest Atlantic Fisheries at a meeting in Warsaw in June, 1969, for a ten-year ban on drift netting in the known salmon feeding grounds. The Danish government went on to say that:

> It would thus seem indisputable that no case can be made for the imposition of a ban on high sea fisheries on the ground that the present high sea catches threaten the survival of the Atlantic salmon. In fact, no such contention has been advanced by any responsible spokesman of any country. The British authorities, when proposing the ban, stated that they did not contend that catches at their present level endangered the propagation of the species. The grounds advanced in favour of a ban were that in the view of the British authorities there is

TABLE 32

Spawning stocks of three adult salmon rivers in relation to the Greenland exploitations in numbers of adult fish

Year	Grande Cascapedia		Bonaventure		Ste. Marguerite		Combined		Greenland and Davis Strait
	Catch	Spawners	Catch	Spawners	Catch	Spawners	Catch	Spawners	
1954–63 10-yr av.	290	781	363	644	435	1332	1088	2757	140,000 (63)
1964	277	860	1146	767	749	1173	2172	2376	465,000
1965	288	893	653	575	554	742	1495	2210	265,000
1966	271	1000	452	604	388	516	1111	2120	405,000
1967	266	423	353	354	341	715	960	1492	460,000
Reduction of 10-year average		46%		45%		46%		46%	

The increasing commercial catches in Greenland waters and in Canada combined with equal or greater angling pressures are taking a greater toll of our salmon stocks and decreasing the number of fish left to spawn. (From: Fraser, 1968.)

L

TABLE 33

SCOTTISH

SALMON

	ROD AND LINE		NET AND COBLE		FIXED ENGINE		TOTAL
Year	Number	% of Total	Number	% of Total	Number	% of Total	
1952	35383	15·0	93618	39·6	106684	45·4	235685
1953	44247	20·9	73432	34·6	94256	44·5	211935
1954	53504	20·9	113011	44·1	89886	35·1	256401
1955	46494	18·4	108074	42·9	97541	38·7	252109
1956	49374	24·6	72064	35·9	78987	39·4	200425
1957	62748	28·8	85119	39·1	69705	32·0	217572
1958	62023	27·6	86111	38·6	76686	33·8	224820
1959	47551	17·6	123727	45·8	98728	36·5	270006
1960	53210	26·4	87365	43·3	61218	30·8	201793
1961	49108	27·3	72468	40·3	58310	32·4	179886
1962	62155	29·1	90836	42·6	60445	28·3	213436
1963	69991	26·2	108122	40·4	89182	33·4	267295
1964[a]	69644	25·8	100319	37·2	99603	36·9	269566
1965	68433	29·3	85461	38·3	72814	32·4	226708
1966	64208	28·1	87077	38·1	77078	33·8	228363
1967[b]	62898	24·7	123168	47·1	75468	28·8	261534
1968	45675	21·3	103079	48·2	65239	30·5	213993
1969	42754	20·3	107675	51·2	59536	28·5	209965

[a] = 'Greenland' first reached high figures (1500 tons)
[b] = Majority Scottish rivers affected by U.D.N.

Note: Grilse can only be separated from salmon by Scale reading. As it is impossible for this to be carried out by either anglers or commercial concerns this table suffers from errors. Recent surveys have shown that many rod-caught fish which are recorded as salmon are, in fact, grilse.

(Source: *Department of Agriculture and Fisheries for Scotland, Fisheries of Scotland, Annual Reports*)

a danger that if the catches of salmon on the high seas increase sharply in the future (which the British authorities consider likely) this could endanger the North Atlantic salmon and that remedial action then might prove too late.

The view expressed by the Danish authorities in opposing the ban is that the present level of high seas fishing does not justify a ban. In their view consistently with the principles that have so far always governed international co-operation in this field, a ban should only be introduced on the basis of reasonably convincing evidence, it being accepted that absolute proof would be too stringent a requirement.

In opposing a complete ban, the Danish authorities have also referred to the fact that intensive fishing on the high seas has been going

TABLE 33

SALMON CATCHES

GRILSE

| ROD AND LINE | | NET AND COBLE | | FIXED ENGINE | | TOTAL | |
Number	% of Total	Number	% of Total	Number	% of Total		Year
6066	4·0	61014	40·4	84077	55·6	151157	1952
6273	4·4	51631	36·4	83878	59·1	141782	1953
4856	4·1	46742	39·6	66318	56·2	117916	1954
4045	3·0	51643	38·0	80327	59·0	136015	1955
7971	6·8	46019	39·2	63265	54·0	117255	1956
9996	5·1	76721	38·9	110257	56·0	196974	1957
10114	5·0	72989	36·4	119600	58·6	202703	1958
3439	3·0	51958	44·8	60565	52·2	115962	1959
11259	6·1	80108	43·4	93324	50·5	184691	1960
6245	4·0	73165	46·8	76861	49·2	156271	1961
10497	3·7	146222	52·1	124071	44·2	280790	1962
9625	5·4	61139	36·9	96142	57·6	166906	1963
12685	4·4	115723	40·4	158054	55·2	286462	1964[a]
9036	4·1	99713	46·4	108752	49·6	217501	1965
8474	3·8	95202	43·1	117344	53·1	221020	1966
14450	4·2	161227	47·1	166920	48·7	342597	1967[b]
6701	3·1	98861	46·2	108317	50·6	213879	1968
8090	2·3	169559	48·6	171132	49·1	348781	1969

[a] = 'Greenland' first reached high figure (1500 tons)
[b] = Majority Scottish rivers affected by U.D.N.

TABLE 34

Scottish salmon catch (excluding grilse), 1960–1967

	(metric tons)
1960	945
1961	807
1962	999
1963	1266
1964	1197
1965	1048
1966	1049
1967	1223

on in the Baltic for many years without causing any dwindling of the salmon stock.

The representatives of Denmark and Germany, as well as Sweden, are against a ban on salmon fishing on the high seas of the North Atlantic on the strength of present evidence. The Dutch and Portuguese representatives have taken an intermediate position. The Dutch at the last conference voted with the majority, with Portugal abstaining.

However, Hr Einar Wøhni, Director-General of the Directorate for Game, Wildlife and Freshwater Fisheries in Norway, said at the Salmon and Trout Association Conference in 1969 that it would only be a matter of time before all the feeding areas of the salmon in the Atlantic would be so well pin-pointed that they could be fished at all stages of maturity and during the whole year with obvious repercussions on the salmon stocks. At present very few grilse have been present in the high seas catches and nearly all the fish caught are potential 'salmon'.

The proposal put forward in Warsaw was vetoed by Denmark, Sweden and West Germany. Denmark felt that there was not enough evidence to attribute falling catches to drift-netting activity – mainly by Faroese and Norwegian boats. But they indicated that they would be prepared to consider measures less drastic than a total ban.

The nations proposing the ban had hoped that it would allow time for detailed research on the stocks of salmon in the high seas. Such studies would help to determine whether stocks from various countries could be identified through an examination of blood characteristics, including variations in the haemoglobins, blood groups and serum proteins; variations in lactic dehydrogenases, eye lens proteins, and variations in the liver esterases. In addition a study of the parasite fauna in the fish might reveal differences in the species harboured by the various stocks, as was the case in the Asian and North American sockeye salmon stocks of the North Pacific (Margolis, 1963). Pippy (1969), for example, has already shown that a freshwater parasite, an acanthocephalan, *Pomphorhynchus laevis*, seems to be useful for indicating the tributary of origin of salmon smolts in several Irish rivers. Its usefulness as a tag for Irish salmon on the high seas, however, is not yet established.

Such studies, together with tagging of salmon on the high seas, might lead to a mapping of the distribution of salmon from the various countries and reveal when and where the sea mortality occurs, which we've seen is very high. With such information available some consideration could be given to the feasibility of a high seas fishery in relation to existing inshore fisheries in home waters. Even so, the ban could not be everlasting. A more controlled cropping of the various stocks at different times of the year with gear of various mesh and hook size to conform with the size of fish in the various areas, might have to be considered in the light of the data collected.

As it is, the Danes and Faroese, with no domestic salmon problems to concern them, no doubt intend to continue their high seas fishery and collect a higher (× 3 to 4) price per pound for top quality salmon they land in Denmark and the European markets than Canadian fishermen do on their home markets. Obviously discussions at international level must continue with a view to finding a compromise. A quota system could be considered whereby all nations with salmon interests allow the Danes and Faroese to engage in a restricted high seas fishery, without engaging in it themselves, but impose a levy on the Danish and Faroese landings. A quota system is difficult to control and satisfactory inspection is virtually impossible. However, the landings could all be made at co-operative associations based at certain points through which all the salmon are marketed. Canada, Japan, the United States and Russia came to a similar sort of agreement with the Alaska fur seal fishery with the North Pacific Fur Seal Convention agreement whereby Canada and Japan each receive 15% of the sealskins taken commercially by the United States and Russia.

Another form of regulation would be by either limiting the fishing effort by restricting the number of vessels entering the fishery, or imposing an upper limit on the catch and laying down a close season as was done in the Pacific halibut fishery. Some effort could also be made to conserve the salmon stocks by treaty. There are at least three treaties to restrain North Pacific high seas fisheries. The most successful is the treaty between the United States and Canada for regulation of the halibut fishery. There is a treaty between Russia and Japan limiting the catch of salmon in the western Bering Sea, and one between the United States, Canada and Japan regarding the salmon fishery in the eastern Bering Sea and along the North American coast.

One salvation might be a fall in the world price of salmon, due to the supply being greater than the demand. This could conceivably result in either a reduction in fishing or a levelling off of fishing effort.

Two very valuable studies of the economic, legal and political aspects of the Pacific salmon fisheries have been made by Cooley (1963) and Crutchfield and Pontecorvo (1969) and they are well worth considering in relation to our own problems with the Atlantic salmon high seas fisheries.

Any pig-headedness between nations might only place the salmon in the position the whaling industry is in at the moment. The whale fishery being a classic example of where research, conventions, commissions, regulations, quotas and systems of inspection amounted to nothing in the face of sheer greed. In the meantime research will continue and further consideration will no doubt be given to the position of salmon exploitation in home waters.

13.2 Regulation of salmon fishing in home waters

Many of the methods employed to catch salmon around the coasts of their home countries are outdated and in many countries the salmon fishing industry is geared to these methods. More often than not the methods are inefficient and costly to maintain. For example, the description of fishing a bag net given in the first chapter of this book indicates the difficulties involved. In bad weather the nets may not be fished for some days and the start of the fishing season is usually delayed because of stormy weather preventing the setting of the nets. Furthermore coastal nets tend to be unselective, catching fish still on migration as well as those moving into neighbouring rivers. In addition it is not always possible to 'slap' (remove the leader) the nets during the weekly close-time because of rough weather, with the result that they remain fishing. There is, therefore, little control over the escapement of fish into the rivers for angling and spawning. Furthermore, appreciable runs of salmon may enter the river during the annual close season. As only 5% of the Scottish Atlantic salmon stock in any one year can be expected to return to the river more than once, there is only one chance to crop most of the stock and it is therefore imperative that the stock is cropped wisely. That the salmon will return to the river to spawn is an established biological fact, so it should be possible to utilise this phenomenon by catching them at one point only – in the river – with a trap. With a knowledge of the fecundity of the fish, the survival of the eggs and young and the carrying capacity of the river system, it should be possible to regulate the numbers of fish passing upstream for sport fishing and for breeding purposes. There are difficulties in building traps of the dimensions that would be required on the larger rivers in Scotland, such as the Tweed, although on the smaller rivers these difficulties have been surmounted. Traps have been built on some rivers for trapping fish for hatchery purposes, and cruives or fish-weirs are still in existence on others although not in use. However, with rapid development in the field of electronics it may soon be possible to count ascending and descending fish, and even divert them, without needing a trap. In their final report (Scottish Salmon and Trout Fisheries, Cmnd. 2691) the Hunter Committee recommended that commercial fishing should only operate in the river and that it should be done, where possible, by means of a trap. Where this was not possible then all net fishing should be concentrated at a single point on each river and that such a fishery should be associated with a count of the escapement. A similar recommendation was made by the Digby Committee in Ireland, over thirty years ago.

A number of social complications are likely to arise out of such a scheme, particularly in relation to the long-established salmon netting companies up and down the coast. However, such methods would give the Scottish salmon industry, and other countries that followed suit, a more rigid control over their salmon stocks, a control which they will most certainly need if the resource is to remain viable in the face of additional exploitation elsewhere. As Allan (1965b) states:

> We are at present, almost completely in the dark about how the numbers of one generation are linked to those of preceding and subsequent generations. We don't yet know how salmon numbers are regulated, from year to year, by natural conditions or how the stocks respond to the variations in even such river conditions as we can measure quite easily, such as water levels, temperature and incidence of floods. We are still further from knowing exactly how the stocks respond to artificially created conditions such as reduced or levelled river flows. We still cannot answer, for our rivers, such questions as "How many salmon are needed to maintain the stock from year to year?" or "How many salmon can we catch from the stock each year without causing damage to the stock in subsequent years?" And yet these are indeed crucial questions both for the protection of the resource and for its correct management and for its exploitation, for there is no benefit in possessing a resource if you don't make use of it.

13.3 Sea trout

The role of the sea trout could grow in importance. At present it is not as valuable as the salmon but if the yields of salmon decline many more anglers will turn their attention to sea trout. Hr Einar Wøhni pointed out at the Salmon and Trout Association Conference in 1969 that it was technically and biologically possible to produce sea trout instead of salmon in the Norwegian rivers. Furthermore the sea trout is a coastal and fjord fish which does not leave Norwegian territorial waters and which is, therefore, not liable to uncontrolled catches. As Wøhni emphasises "Economically the sea trout will probably be less profitable than the salmon, but when there is a choice of something or nothing one tends to choose something."

There is much still to be learnt about the sea trout; its stream life, for example, has received little attention. As yet no one can distinguish young sea trout from young brown trout, although present studies of blood characteristics may help to elucidate this problem.

13.4 Brown trout

Brown trout too will have an important role to play, both recreationally and commercially, in the future. There are numerous trout waters in Scotland, Canada, Norway, Sweden, Finland and Iceland which are relatively un-exploited. Many in northern Scotland will need intensive management before they produce worthwhile trout, but the potential is there. In addition many salmon rivers hold good trout which are ignored by salmon anglers, the only fishermen to visit the water in many cases.

In the industrial midlands of England, although the rivers are re-duced in quality, trout angling is taking on a new lease of life with the proliferation of large reservoirs to meet the needs of the towns and in-dustries in this heavily-populated area. Many of the more fertile of these English reservoirs, such as Grafham Water and Eye Brook, are noted for the phenomenal growth of their trout, with brown trout reaching 12 inches in length in their third year of life and rainbow trout attaining that length in their second year. Much further north in Scotland, Norway and Sweden, hydro-electric reservoirs have provided additional trout and char fishing for the increasing number of tourists visiting these remote areas.

However, the development of trout angling in Scotland is hindered by the absence of any legal system governing its control. At present trout fishing proprietors cannot in practice stop unauthorised fishing on their waters and, for this reason, take no steps to improve them as much as they could. The Hunter Committee were told by many interested parties that if the proprietors are given statutory protection, the result will be either that they will keep the angling to themselves and their friends, or will make the price of permits so high that trout angling becomes a rich man's sport. This fear has probably little real foundation. Many estates already lease the fishings they are trying to improve, in spite of unauthorised fishing, to the public at reasonable prices. Some estates also advertise trout fishing in with the lease of holiday chalets. Furthermore, there are far and away too many lochs in the Scottish Highlands for the proprietors to keep all the fishing to themselves and their friends, and the economics of management will pre-vent them from putting too high a price on the many waters that could become available.

The Final Report of the Hunter Committee states:

Trout fisheries need proper maintenance if they are to give good angling. It must be recognised clearly that unrestricted fishing eventu-ally means no worthwhile fishing for anyone. The aim should be to make available an adequate supply of fishing of a reasonable standard at a price the ordinary angler can afford, together with some higher quality fishing which would often be expensive.

We recommend that as the necessary basis for improving quality, fishing for brown trout without the appropriate permission should be made a statutory offence.

It is likely that many proprietors won't take very great pains to improve their fishings until they get this assurance that 'illegal' fishing will, in fact, become illegal.

13.5 Salmon and trout cultivation

Stocks of salmon and trout can be supplemented by artificial rearing, as has already been shown earlier in this book. The sophisticated rearing techniques of the Swedes have already been described. It is partly the high survival rate of smolts in the Baltic which makes their production economic. Smolt rearing in other countries is, at present, far from economic. Piggins (1969) estimated the cost of producing two-year-old smolts, in his hatchery in Ireland, at 3s 6d each, so that each adult which returns to the fishery has cost £8. 15s, at the current recapture rate of 2%. Each rod-caught fish is worth at least £10 to the fishery, or if used to provide ova for hatchery work, each pair of fish is worth at least £10. 10s.

The future of smolt rearing, in the countries whose salmon feed in the Atlantic, appears to be, as Piggins points out, in reducing one's costs by improvements in hatchery techniques (use of automatic feeders, anti-fouling paint, production of cheaper high protein food) and the development of selectively bred strains of fish which grow faster and survive better in both the freshwater and marine stages of their life history. Both Menzies (1967b) and Piggins (1969) mention the considerable saving in costs by rearing one-year-old smolts. However, Piggins found that their survival rate in the sea has been poorer than that of two-year-old smolts, possibly because of their smaller size (less than 6 inches). Piggins has now started selective breeding which is beginning to show an effect in a faster growth rate in freshwater. In 1968 he was able to release 22% of the yearling fish as one-year-old smolts averaging 6 inches in length, compared with 5 to 10% of the stock in previous years. With hormonal treatment, in the form of thyroid feeding at the pre-smolt stage, it is possible to secure an increase in the smolt transformation rate but it is an expensive procedure at present. Piggins found until recently, as did Österdahl in Sweden, that hatchery-reared fish returning as adults tended to be small and thin. The quality of these fish is now equal to those of wild fish in both length and condition. This shows that, with continuous efforts to improve hatchery techniques, artificial propagation is likely to prove economic with obvious advantages to our salmon stocks.

Sweden, too, is considering the population genetic aspects of salmon culture. Rasmuson (1968) considers that:

Artificial culture implies a relaxation of selection during the young stages. Further, the heavy fishing and international rivalries in the

Baltic may lead to an unwanted direction of the selection among the fish which are captured when returning to their native rivers and are used for breeding purposes. These drawbacks have to be counteracted by breeding disposition, which also ought to aim at a more efficient salmon production. At present the most promising method seems to be a breeding which uses recaptured females and artificially reared males.

Another important salmon-rearing development is that undertaken by Vik in Norway in 1959. Vik kept adult salmon in a sea water pool in Sykkylven Fjord after they had been stripped, and fed them until the following season until they were again ready for stripping. He was able to do this again the year after and in this way some were stripped four times. This confirmed earlier Norwegian work quite clearly that Atlantic salmon could be bred artificially and also reach maturity without going on a sea migration. Between 1961 and 1962 40 trout-rearing stations were built on the west coast of Norway. The technique of rearing adult salmon is, at present, in its infancy, but the potential is there and its feasibility on a small scale suggests its possibility on a larger scale in the future. Until such time as this happens we must be satisfied with large-scale trout farming. Rainbow trout farming is increasing rapidly in many countries. The Danes are now producing 15,000 tons annually, France 10,000 tons and Italy about the same. Yugoslavia has at least 12 trout farms and there are at least 15 in Spain. So far, however, Scotland has been slow to develop trout farming. However, the Highlands and Islands Development Board are aware of Scotland's potential and are anxious to assist financially in trout rearing in the crofting counties.

However, one problem which at present exists in the field of Scottish trout farming generally is the lack of any Government aid in the form of grants, and absence of any regular form of inspection for the certification of fish as disease free. This is now being required for fish exports to Canada and the United States.

The results of experimental farming of rainbow trout in small highly productive lakes in progress in Manitoba at present have been most encouraging. One lake under study yielded more than 100 lb of trout per acre. Five thousand rainbow trout fingerlings were planted in this 25 acre lake at the end of April and the catch some six months later amounted to some 3,390 fish with a total weight of 2,570 lb. The harvesting of trout has to be done in the late autumn of the same year in which they are introduced as fingerlings. The reason for this is that the basic requirements of the lakes being used is that they produce conditions in the winter months, when covered with ice and snow, that result in a total lack of oxygen. This would cause a complete mortality (i.e. a winter-kill) of any fish present. The lakes, to produce these conditions, need to be less than 25 feet deep and have no in-flowing water during the winter. The best results have been obtained from trout fingerlings, $2\frac{1}{2}$–3 inches in length, introduced as soon as possible after the ice goes in late April, at a rate of 200 per acre of water surface. Harvesting with gill nets is done as late in the year as possible.[1]

13.6 Angling associations and trusts

Little has been said in this book concerning angling associations and trusts. It has been purposely avoided because there are so many in the salmon and trout countries of the world that even to list them in an appendix would be a mammoth task. The more important laboratories, institutions and associations have been listed in Appendix 2.

Associations and councils tend to proliferate and some are politically inclined. The trouble with many is that they tend to lessen the value of others and also themselves. At present, in the United Kingdom, there is the Salmon and Trout Association, the Anglers' Co-operative Association (which is set up to fight pollution and help affected angling clubs in legal actions), the National Federation of Anglers, the National Anglers' Council, the Scottish Anglers' Association, the Scottish National Angling Clubs' Association and the Scottish Salmon Angling Federation, to name but a few.

The Hunter Committee suggested the formation of a Scottish Anglers' Trust which would be a co-operative of anglers administering such facilities as there are and seeking to improve and add to them generally to develop trout angling in Scotland. This trust could conceivably take the place of many of those listed above.

Two of the most important trusts to be formed recently, because of the high seas salmon fishery, are the Atlantic Salmon Research Trust and the International Atlantic Salmon Foundation. The most important role these trusts can fulfil is to serve as a voice for the many interested parties and to make representations at Government level, to convene meetings at which experts would be invited to speak and, most important of all, to sponsor and give financial aid to specific research projects, rather than engage in research directly. Research is already being actively carried out by a number of research laboratories and university departments and what is required is more money and staff for existing institutions rather than new institutions.

13.7 Hydro-electric development

This is one of man's activities which, in the future is likely to have less

[1] Johnson, L., Lawler, G. H. and Sunde, L. A. 1970. Rainbow trout farming in central Canada. Fisheries Research Board of Canada. Technical Report No. 165.

effect on salmon and trout than many of his others. Hydro-electric development is likely to continue in Norway and eastern Canada but is unlikely to expand to any great extent in Scotland. An inquiry into the future of hydro-electric projects in Scotland has shown that they cost too much to build and it is estimated that the cost is £150 for every kilowatt of generating capacity compared to £60 for thermal stations. The future of the conventional hydro-scheme in Scotland is therefore doubtful, particularly with nuclear power stations becoming commercially practicable in the 1970s. The only way round this cost barrier is to use a pumped storage scheme where one gets more power out of the same tonnage of water. The Loch Awe pumped storage scheme produces 400 megawatts during the day for Glasgow's factories, at night there is spare power from the south which aids in pumping the water up to the storage reservoir again. The cost in this case is about £40. However, further pumped storage schemes are likely to cost only £30–£35 for every kilowatt of generating capacity.

13.8 Pollution

Much could be said further about the problem of pollution in the future and the loopholes in the present systems of control. Standards are still needed for (1) chlorinated hydrocarbons, polychlorinated biphenyls and mercury compounds in the aquatic environment, (2) the transparency of the water, (3) nutrients in the water, (4) safety in freshwater recreation, (5) safety of reclaimed water, and, (6) growth stimulants in water.

The problem of eutrophication is due for more attention. The Great Lakes are the best example of the problem, where excessive over-enrichment has caused a tremendous growth of algae. A need for a phosphorus control programme to reduce this adverse effect on water quality and water use resulting from excessive growths of algae has already been stressed in a report submitted to an International Joint Commission set up by Canada and the United States.

A great deal of attention should also be given to the chlorinated hydrocarbons. Vast fish mortalities occurred in 1969 in the Rhine and the Elbe. The former pollution was believed to be due to the dumping of Endosulvan, a chlorinated hydrocarbon. While these are direct and evident cases of pollution there are the more insidious ones to which no mortality can at present be attributed. D.D.T. is spread over the earth by wind and water in much the same way as radioactive fallout. It can also be carried great distances by migrating fish and birds and ocean currents. D.D.T. has only a low solubility in water, but as algae and other organisms absorb the substance in fats, where it is highly soluble, they make room for more D.D.T. to be dissolved into the water. So that water that never contains more than a trace of D.D.T. can continuously transfer it from deposits on the bottom to organisms. D.D.T. is an extremely stable compound that breaks down very slowly in the environment. So with repeated spraying, the residues in the soil or water basins accumulate. The Baltic has been polluted by D.D.T. to such an extent that it is dangerous to eat certain fish regularly. Salmon for instance have an average of 31 milligrams of D.D.T. per kilogram weight of fish. Sweden has now banned the use of D.D.T. for two years until scientists have attempted to establish how much is carried by winds and rain. The coho salmon, introduced to Lake Michigan to feed on the alewives, are now being affected. The eggs of the coho survive but the fry do not. This is because the D.D.T. concentrated through the food chain, has appeared in high concentrations in the coho eggs. Then, as the yolk sac is absorbed after the young fish has emerged, the D.D.T. becomes lethal. Furthermore, a consignment of coho salmon from Lake Michigan was recently seized by the Food and Drug Administration in the United States. They discovered that the fish contained 19 parts in a million of D.D.T. They declared the fish unfit for human consumption. Canada banned the use of D.D.T. in January 1970 and the United States is following suit, with a total ban in 1971.

An interesting finding from the study of the sub-lethal effects of D.D.T. on Atlantic salmon is that the learning capacity of the fish is shown to be retarded by minute quantities of D.D.T. (2 parts per 100 million of D.D.T. for 24 hours). Whether or not such a mild dosage will affect the ability of salmon smolts to recognise their home stream when they return from the sea is the subject of an experiment now being conducted in Canada.

There is a lot more we do not know. Reason must prevail in any international disagreement over a renewable resource. The reason for it not being renewed may not be the one under consideration at the time. For example, in December, 1970, vast stocks of canned tuna were withdrawn from American food stores because of the high levels of methyl mercury found in this fish. Lake Winnipeg has recently been closed to fishing for the same reason. The methyl mercury in this case came from a pulp mill discharging effluent into the Saskatchewan River which drains into the lake.

When will a similar situation arise with Atlantic salmon – a sobering thought?

APPENDIX 1

Currency conversion rates. (Source: *FAO Yearbook of Fishery Statistics.*)

United States Dollars per unit of national currency:

	1964	1965	1966	1967	1968
Canadian dollar	0·9279	0·9269	0·9274	0·9255	0·9280
Danish kroner	0·1447	0·1447	0·1447	0·1435	0·1335
New Finnish markka	0·3125	0·3125	0·3125	0·2900	0·2386
New franc	0·2026	0·2026	0·2026	0·2026	0·2019
Deutsche mark	0·25	0·25	0·25	0·25	0·25
Irish pound	2·80	2·80	2·80	2·75	2·39
Netherlands guilder	0·2762	0·2762	0·2762	0·2762	0·2762
Norwegian kroner	0·14	0·14	0·14	0·14	0·14
Polish zloty	0·25	0·25	0·25	0·25	—
Portuguese escudo	0·0347	0·0347	0·0347	0·0347	0·0346
Swedish krona	0·1932	0·1932	0·1932	0·1932	0·1932
Pound sterling	2·80	2·80	2·80	2·75	2·39
USSR new rouble	1·111	1·111	1·111	1·111	—

APPENDIX 2

List of laboratories, institutions, universities and associations
concerned with salmon and trout research.

AUSTRALIA

Inland Fisheries Commission,
Hobart, Tasmania.

Department of Fish and Game,
Melbourne, Victoria.

Department of Fish and Game,
Sydney, New South Wales.

AUSTRIA

Bundesinstitutet für Gewässerforschung
und Fischereiwirtschaft,
Scharfling am Mondsee.

BELGIUM

La Station de Recherches des Eaux et
Forêts,
Section d'Hydrobiologie,
2 Avenue Dubois,
Groenendaal – Hoeilaart.

CANADA

Atlantic Salmon Association,
Shell Tower,
1255 University Street,
Montreal, Quebec.

Department of Biology,
Queen's University,
Kingston, Ontario.

Department of Fisheries,
Halifax, Nova Scotia.

Department of Fisheries,
Saint John, New Brunswick.

Department of Fisheries,
Vancouver, British Columbia.

Department of Natural Resources,
Fisheries Laboratory,
University of Saskatchewan,
Saskatoon.

Department of Zoology,
University of Guelph,
Guelph, Ontario.

Department of Zoology,
University of Toronto,
Toronto, Ontario.

Department of Zoology,
University of Western Ontario,
London, Ontario.

Fish and Game Branch,
Department of Tourism, Fish and
Game,
Parliament Buildings,
Québec City.

Fish and Wildlife Branch,
Department of Recreation and Con-
servation,
Victoria, British Columbia.

Fisheries Branch,
Department of Mines and Natural
Resources,
Winnipeg, Manitoba.

Fisheries Research Board,
Arctic Biological Station,
P.O. Box 400,
Ste. Anne-de-Bellevue.

Fisheries Research Board,
Biological Station,
Nanaimo, British Columbia.

Fisheries Research Board,
Biological Station,
St. Andrews, New Brunswick.

Fisheries Research Board,
Biological Station,
St. Johns, Newfoundland.

Fisheries Research Board,
Freshwater Fisheries Institute,
Winnipeg 19, Manitoba.

Institute of Animal Resource Ecology,
University of British Columbia,
Vancouver.

International Pacific Salmon Fisheries
Commission,
New Westminster,
Vancouver, British Columbia.

Ontario Department of Land and
Forests,
Southern Research Station,
Fisheries Research Branch,
Maple, Ontario.

Station de Biologie Marine,
Grand-Rivière,
Gaspé,
Quebec.

CZECHOSLOVAKIA

Fisheries Research Institute,
Lipno.

Fisheries Research Institute,
Vodňany.

Institute of Vertebrate Zoology,
Department of Ichthyobiology,
Czechoslovak Academy of Sciences,
Květná 8, Brno.

DENMARK

Danish Trout Research Station,
Brøns.

Danmarks Fiskeri-og Harundersøgelser,
Charlottenlund Slot,
Charlottenlund.

Freshwater Biological Laboratory,
University of Copenhagen,
Hillerød.

ENGLAND and WALES

Atlantic Salmon Research Trust, Ltd.,
c/o Fishmongers' Hall, London, E.C.4.

Avon and Dorset River Authority,
3 St. Stephens Road,
Bournemouth.

Cornwall River Authority,
St. Johns,
Western Road,
Launceston.

Cumberland River Authority,
256 London Road,
Carlisle.

Dee and Clwyd River Authority,
2 Vicar's Lane,
Chester.

Department of Zoology,
University of Exeter.

Department of Zoology,
University of Liverpool.

Department of Zoology,
University of Salford.

Devon River Authority,
County Hall,
Exeter.

Freshwater Biological Association,
River Laboratory,
East Stoke,
Wareham, Dorset.

Freshwater Biological Association,
Windermere Laboratory,
Ambleside, Westmorland.

Gwynedd River Authority,
Highfield,
Caernarvon.

Institute of Fisheries Management,
Springfield,
Wallington,
Surrey.

Lancashire River Authority,
48 West Cliff,
Preston, Lancashire.

Northumbrian River Authority,
110 Oxborne Road,
Newcastle-upon-Tyne.

Salmon and Freshwater Fisheries
Laboratory,
Ministry of Agriculture, Fisheries and
Food,
Whitehall Place,
London, S.W.1.

Salmon and Trout Association,
Fishmongers' Hall,
London.

Severn River Authority,
Portland House,
Church Street,
Great Malvern,
Worcestershire.

South-west Wales River Authority,
Penyfai House,
Llanelli.

Usk River Authority,
The Croft,
Goldcroft Common,
Caerleon, Newport, Monmouthshire.

Water Pollution Research Laboratory,
Stevenage, Hertfordshire.

Yorkshire Ouse and Hull River
Authority,
21 Park Square South,
Leeds 1.

FINLAND

Bureau of Fishery Investigations,
Fabianink, 32,
Helsinki.

Department of Zoology,
University of Turku.

Institute of Limnology,
University of Helsinki.

FRANCE

The French National Association for
the Protection of Trout, Grayling and
Salmon (T.O.S.),
5 Rue Maurice Loewy,
Paris – 14e.

Station D'Hydrobiologie Continentale
Centre Scientifique,
64 Biarritz.

GERMANY

Democratic Republic

Institutet für Binnenfischerei,
1162 Berlin-Friedrichshagen.

Federal Republic

Institutet für Hydrobiologie und
Fischereiwissenschaft der Universtitat
Hamburg, 2 Hamburg-Altona 1.

Limnologisches Inst. der University
Freiburg i Br.,
7821 Falkau (Schwarzwald).

Bundesforschungsanstalt für Fischerei,
Institut für Küsten – und
Binnenfischerei, Labor Kiel,
Kiel – Seefischmarkc.

ICELAND

Institute of Freshwater Fisheries,
P.O. Box 754,
Reykjavik.

IRELAND

Northern

Ministry of Agriculture,
Small Farms and Fisheries Division,
2–4 Queen Street,
Belfast.

Southern

Electricity Supply Board,
27 Lower Fitzwilliam Street,
Dublin 2.

Department of Lands,
Fisheries Division,
3 Cathal Brugha Street,
Dublin 1.

Inland Fisheries Trust,
11 Westmorland Street,
Dublin.

Salmon Research Trust of Ireland,
Newport,
Co. Mayo.

ITALY

Instituto Italiano di Idrobiologica,
Pallanza (Novara).

Associazione Piscicoltori Italiani,
via Indipendenza 5,
31100 Trevisó.

JAPAN

Freshwater Fisheries Research Laboratory,
Nikko City.

River and Lake Division,
Freshwater Fisheries Research Laboratory,
Hino-shi,
Tokyo.

NEW ZEALAND

Department of Internal Affairs,
Wellington.

Department of Marine,
Wellington.

Department of Zoology,
University of Otago,
Dundedin.

New Zealand Limnological Society,
Marine Department,
Christchurch.

NORWAY

Freshwater Fisheries Research Department,
Inspektoren for ferskvannsfisket,
Vollebek.

Viltstell og Ferskvannsfiske,
Elgeseter Gt. 10,
Trondheim.

POLAND

Department of Fish Biology,
Faculty of Fisheries,
Wyzsza Szkola,
Rolnicza,
Olsztyn-Korotowo.

Department of Zoology,
University of Cracow.

Inland Fisheries Institute,
River Research,
Warsaw.

ROUMANIA

Academia R.S. România,
Institutel de Biologie "Tr. Savulescu",
Bucharest, 17.

RUSSIA

Department of Ichthyology,
Moscow State University.

SCOTLAND

Department of Forestry and Natural Resources,
University of Edinburgh.

Department of Zoology,
University of Glasgow.

Department of Zoology,
University of Stirling.

Freshwater Fisheries Laboratory,
Faskally,
Pitlochry, Perthshire.

Marine Laboratory,
Victoria Road, Torry,
Aberdeen.

Nature Conservancy,
12 Hope Terrace,
Edinburgh.

SPAIN

Servicio de Pesca Fluvial y Caza,
Goya, 25,
Madrid.

SWEDEN

Department of Fisheries,
Kastellg 4,
Harnösand.

Department of Zoology,
University of Umeå.

Fishery Board of Sweden,
Institute of Freshwater Research,
Drottningholm.

Institute of Zoology,
University of Lund.

Institute of Zoology,
University of Uppsala.

Salmon Research Institute,
Älvkarleo.

South Swedish Fishery Association,
Institute of Research,
Adeboda,
Lummhult.

UNITED STATES

Atlantic Sea Run Salmon Commission,
Fisheries Building,
University of Maine,
Orono,
Maine.

College of Fisheries,
University of Washington,
Seattle, Washington 98105.

Department of Conservation,
Fernow Hall,
Cornell University,
Ithaca, New York.

Department of Entomology, Fisheries and Wildlife,
University of Minnesota,
St. Paul.

Department of Fisheries and Wildlife,
Oregon State University,
Corvallis,
Oregon.

Department of Natural Resources,
Division of Conservation,
Waupaca,
Wisconsin.

Eastern Fish Disease Laboratory,
Leetown,
Route 1,
Kearneysville,
West Virginia 25430.

Fish Disease Unit,
Grayling Research Station,
State Fish Hatchery,
Grayling,
Michigan.

Idaho Co-operative Fishery Unit,
Moscow,
Idaho.

Institute of Fisheries,
University of Washington,
Seattle,
Washington.

Maine Atlantic Salmon Federation,
36 Pitt Street,
Portland,
Maine.

Institute for Fisheries Research,
Michigan Department of Natural
Resources,
Ann Arbor.

Michigan Department of Conservation,
Lewiston,
Michigan 49756.

School of Natural Resources,
University of Michigan,
Ann Arbor,
Michigan 48104.

Two institutes which have been recently opened in Canada are the:

Huntsman Marine Laboratory,
Brandy Cove,
St. Andrews, New Brunswick.

International Atlantic Salmon
Foundation,
P.O. Box 346,
Gaspé, Quebec.

Another Association recently opened in Scotland is:

The Scottish Fish Farming Association,
35 Melville Street,
Edinburgh.

Details of ministries, administrative services and other research institutes and organisations dealing with freshwater fisheries in Europe are described by Gaudet in Technical Paper No. 5 entitled *Organisation of Inland Fisheries Administration in Europe* published by the European Inland Fisheries Advisory Commission in 1968.

APPENDIX 3

A list of some scientific and semi-scientific journals
publishing papers and articles on salmon and trout.
Journals prefixed by an asterisk are those containing
articles for the general reader.

AUSTRALIA:

Australian Journal of Marine and Freshwater Research

BELGIUM:

Travaux de Station de Recherches des Eaux et Forêts

CANADA:

Atlantic Salmon Journal
Bulletin of the Fisheries Research Board of Canada
Bulletin of the International Pacific Salmon Fisheries Commission
Canadian Field Naturalist
Canadian Fish Culturist
Canadian Journal of Zoology
Contributions Departement des Pecheries
Fisheries of Canada
Journal of the Fisheries Research Board of Canada
Naturaliste Canadien
Transactions of the Royal Society of Canada

CZECHOSLOVAKIA:

Bulletin of the Fisheries Research Institute, Vodnany
Zoolgické Listy
Věstník Cěskoslovenskí Spolěčnosti Zoologické

DENMARK:

Journal du Conseil Permanent International pour l'Exploration de la Mer
Oikos
Rapports et Procès-Verbaux des Réunions
Annales Biologiques Conseil Permanent International pour l'Exploration de la Mer

FINLAND:

Annales Zoologici Fennici

FRANCE:

Annales de la Station Centrale d'Hydrobiologie appliquée
Bulletin Francaise Pisciculture

GERMANY:

Mitteilung der International Vereinigung für theoretische und angewandte limnologie (Communications of the International Association of Theoretical and Applied Limnology)
Verhandlungen der International Vereinigung für theoretische unde angewandte limnologie (Proceedings of the I.A.L.)

GREAT BRITAIN:

British Journal of Animal Behaviour
Fishery Investigations (Series I. Salmon and Freshwater Fisheries)
Freshwater and Salmon Fisheries Research Series (Scotland)
Journal of Animal Ecology
Journal of Applied Ecology
Journal of Fish Biology
Journal of the Institute of Fisheries Management
Marine Research Series (Scotland)
Proceedings of the Linnaean Society of London
Proceedings of the Royal Society of Edinburgh
Proceedings of the Zoological Society of London
*Salmon Net
**Salmon and Trout Magazine*
**Scottish Fisheries Bulletin*

HOLLAND:

Hydrobiologia

IRELAND:

**Inland Fisheries Bulletin*
Irish Fisheries Investigations. Series A (Freshwater)
Irish Naturalists' Journal
Proceedings of the Royal Irish Academy
Report of the Salmon Research Trust of Ireland
Scientific Proceedings of the Royal Dublin Society

ITALY:

**Rivista Italiana di Piscicoltura e Ittiopatologia*

JAPAN:

Bulletin of the Freshwater Fisheries Research Laboratory, Tokyo
Japanese Journal of Ecology

Journal of the Tokyo University of Fisheries
Memoirs of the College of Science of Kyoto University, Series B

NEW ZEALAND:

Fisheries Bulletin of New Zealand
New Zealand Journal of Marine and Freshwater Research
Technical Reports of the New Zealand Marine Department

NORWAY:

Acta Borealia
Fisk og Fiskestell

POLAND:

Acta Hydrobiologica
Roczniki Nauk Rolniczych

RUSSIA:

Zoological Zhurnal

SWEDEN:

Report of the Institute of Freshwater Research, Drottningholm
Swedish Salmon Research Institute Report

UNITED STATES:

American Naturalist
California Fish and Game Journal
Copeia
Ecology
Ecological Monographs
Fisheries Bulletin of the U.S. Fish and Wildlife Service
Journal of Wildlife Management
Limnology and Oceanography
New York Fish and Game Journal
Progressive Fish Culturist
The American Fish Farmer
Transactions of the American Fisheries Society

REFERENCES

AASS, P. 1956. Sil-andens naering i ferskvann. *Norg. Jeg.–og Fisk Forb. Tidskr.*, **85**, (1), 8–14.

AITKEN, P. L., DICKERSON, L. H., and MENZIES, W. J. M. 1966. Fish passes and screens at water power works. *Proc. Instn. civ. Engrs.*, **35**, 29–57.

AKROYD, D. S. 1966. The fishery implications of the Water Resources Act. *Proc. 3rd British Coarse Fish Conf.*, 7–11.

ALABASTER, J. S. 1966. The effect on coarse fish of heated effluents from power stations. *Proc. 3rd British Coarse Fish Conf.*, 109–110.

ALEXANDER, W. B., SOUTHGATE, B. A. and BASSINDALE, R. 1935. Survey of the River Tees. Pt. II. The estuary – chemical and biological. Technical Paper No. 5, Water Pollution Research, London.

ALLAN, I. R. H. 1952. A hand-operated quantitative grab for sampling river beds. *J. Anim. Ecol.*, **21**, 1, 159–160.

—— 1965a. Counting fences for salmon and sea trout, and what can be learned from them. Salm. Trout Assn., Lond. conf., 1965, 1–16.

—— 1965b. Towards logical conservation policies for our salmon and sea trout stocks: The River Axe Research. *Association of River Boards Year Book*, 1964, 1–7.

ALLAN, I. R. H. and BULLEID, M. J. 1963. Long-distance migration of Atlantic salmon. *Nature*, **200**, 4901: 89.

ALLEN, K. R. 1940. Studies on the biology of the early stages of the salmon (*Salmo salar*). 1. Growth in the River Eden. *J. Anim. Ecol.*, **9**, 1–23.

—— 1941a. Studies on the biology of the early stages of the salmon (*Salmo salar*). 2. Feeding habits. *J. Anim. Ecol.* **10**, 47–76.

—— 1941b. Studies on the biology of the early stages of the salmon (*Salmo salar*). Growth in the Thurso River system, Caithness. *J. Anim. Ecol.*, **10**, 273–295.

—— 1944. Studies on the biology of the early stages of the salmon (*Salmo salar*). 4. The smolt migration in the Thurso River in 1938. *J. Anim. Ecol.*, **13**, 63–85.

—— 1947. Some aspects of the production and cropping of freshwaters. *N.Z. Science Congress*, 1947, 222–228.

—— 1951. The Horokiwi Stream. A study of a trout population. *Bull. Mar. Dept. N.Z. Fish.* **10**, 1–238.

ALLARD, W. 1962a. British river flow gauging – A jubilee retrospect – I. *Salm. Trout Mag.*, **165**, 77–85.

—— 1962b. British river flow gauging – A jubilee retrospect – II. *Salm. Trout Mag.*, **166**, 175–186.

ALM, G. 1934. Salmon in the Baltic precincts. *Rapp. Cons. Explor. Mer.*, **92**, 1–63.
—— 1955. Artificial hybridisation between different species of the salmon family. *Rep. Inst. Freshw. Res.* Drottningholm, **36**, 13–56.
—— 1958. Seasonal fluctuations in the catches of salmon in the Baltic. *J. du Conseil*, XXIII, **3**, 399–433.

ANON. 1963. Scottish Salmon and Trout Fisheries. H.M.S.O. Cmnd. 2096.

ANON. 1965a. Scottish Salmon and Trout Fisheries. H.M.S.O. Cmnd. 2691.

ANON. 1965b. Water quality criteria for European freshwater fish: Report on finely divided solids and inland fisheries (Eifac Technical Paper No. 1). *Int. J. Air Wat. Pollut.* **9**, 151–168.

ANON. 1967. Salmon disease in Irish rivers. *Salmon Net*, III, 44–49.

ALLPORT, M. 1870. Brief history of the introduction of salmon (*S. salar*) and other salmonidae to the waters of Tasmania. *Proc zool. Soc. London*, 14–30, 750–752.

ARNOLD, D. E. 1966. Marking fish with dyes and other chemicals. Technical Paper of the Bureau of Sport Fisheries and Wildlife. Washington.

AYERS, H. D., McCRIMMON, H. R. and BERST, A. H. *The Construction and Management of Farm Ponds in Ontario*, 39 pp. Ontario Department of Agriculture.

BACKIEL, T. and LE CREN, E. D. 1967. Some density relationships for fish population parameters, in Gerking, S. D. (Ed.) *The Biological Basis of Freshwater Fish Production.* Oxford and Edinburgh: Blackwell.

BAILEY, N. T. J. 1951. On estimating the size of mobile populations from recapture data. *Biometrika*, **38**, 293–306.

BALL, J. N. 1961. On the food of the brown trout of Llyn Tegid. *Proc zool. Soc. Lond.*, **137**, 599–622.

BALL, R. C. 1948. Fertilization of natural lakes in Michigan. *Trans. Amer. Fish. Soc.*, **78**, 144–155.

BALMAIN, K. H. and SHEARER, W. M. 1956. Records of salmon and sea trout caught at sea. *Freshwat. Salm. Fish. Res. Scot.*, 11, 12 pp.

BAMS, R. A. 1969. Adaptations in sockeye salmon associated with incubation in stream gravels. Symposium on salmon and trout in streams. H. R. MacMillan Lectures in Fisheries, 1968. University of British Columbia, Vancouver, Canada.

BANKS, J. W. 1969. A review of the literature on the upstream migration of adult salmonids. *J. Fish Biol.*, **1**, 85–136.

BAUER, O. N. 1959. The ecology of parasites of freshwater fish. *Bull. State Scientific Res.*, Inst. of Lake and River Fisheries. XLIX – Parasites of freshwater fish and the biological basis for their control. Translation: Israel Program for Scientific Translations. Jerusalem, 1962.

BAXTER, G. 1961. River utilisation and the preservation of migratory fish life. *Proc. Instn. civ. Engrs.*, **18**, 225–244.
—— 1962. The preservation of fish life, amenities and facilities for recreation. In *Conservation of Water Resources in the United Kingdom.* Symp. Instn. civ. Engrs., 59–65.

BEAK, T. W. 1957. How Britain regulates salmon fishing. *Atlantic Salmon Journal*, **3**, 19–22.

BEAUSANG, T. J. 1966. The work of the Inland Fisheries Trust with particular reference to brown trout. *Salm. and Trout Assn. Lond. conf.*, 1–10.

BELDING, D. L. 1934. The cause of the high mortality in the Atlantic salmon after spawning. *Trans. Amer. Fish Soc.* **34**, 219–224.

BELDING, D. L. and HYDE, D. M. 1932. Notes on the ocean feeding grounds of the Atlantic salmon. *Trans. Amer. Fish. Soc.*, **62,** 304–306.

BELDING, D. L. and PREFONTAINE, G. 1938a. Etudes sur le saumon de l'Atlantique (*Salmo salar*). I. Organisation et resultats generaux des recherches dans le golfe Saint-Laurent en 1937. *Contr. Inst. Zool. Univ. Montreal*, no. 2, 50 pp.

—— 1938b. Studies on the Atlantic salmon. II. Report on the salmon of the 1937 Port-aux-Basques (Newfoundland) drift-net fishery. *Contr. Inst. Zool. Univ. Montreal*, no. 3, 58 pp.

—— 1939. Studies on the Atlantic salmon. III. Report on the salmon of the 1937 Miramichi (New Brunswick) drift-net fishery. *Contr. Inst. Zool. Univ. Montreal*, no. 4, 63 pp.

BENNIKE, S. A. B. 1943. Contributions to the ecology and biology of Danish freshwater leeches. *Fol. Limnol. Scand.* **2,** 1–109.

BERG, L. S. 1932. *Les poisson's des eaux douces de l' U.R.S.S. et des pays limitrophes*. 3–e Edition, Partie 1. Leningrad.

—— 1935. Evidence on the biology of *Salmo salar*. Izv. VNIORKh, 20.

BERG, M. 1953. A relict salmon, *Salmo salar* L., called 'småblank' from the River Namsen, North Trondelag. *Acta Borealia*, **6,** 1–17.

—— 1961. Pink salmon (*Oncorhynchus gorbuscha*) in northern Norway in the year 1960. *Acta Borealia*, **17,** 1–24.

—— 1964a. *Nord-Norske Lakseelver*. Oslo: Johan Grundt Tanum Forlag. 300 pp.

—— 1964b. Utsettinger av laksyngal: vatn og tjern. (English summary). *Fisk og Fiskestell*, **4,** 63 pp.

BERGERON, J. 1962. Bibliographie du saumon de l'Atlantique. Contrib. du Ministere de la Chasse et des Pêcheries, Québec. 88, 64 pp.

BERRY, J. 1932. Report of an investigation of smolts in the River Tay during spring, 1931. *Fisheries, Scotland, Salmon Fish.*, 1931, IV, 21 pp.

—— 1933. Notes on the migration of salmon smolts from Loch Ness, summer, 1932. *Fisheries, Scotland, Salmon Fish.*, 1933, **1,** 12 pp.

—— 1936. British mammals and birds as enemies of the Atlantic salmon (*Salmo salar*). Avon Biological Research, Annual Report, 1934, **35,** 31–64.

BISHAI, H. M. 1960. Upper lethal temperatures for larval salmonids. *J. Cons. int. Explor. Mer.*, **25,** 129–133.

BLAIR, A. A. 1968. Pink salmon find a new home in Newfoundland. *Fisheries of Canada*, **21,** 4, 9–12.

BRANNON, E. L. 1965. The influence of physical factors on the development and weight of sockeye salmon embryos and alevins. *Int. Pacific Salmon Fish Comm. Prog. Rep.*, **12,** 1–26.

BRAYSHAW, J. D. 1967. The effects of river discharge on inland fisheries, pp. 102–118 in Isaac, P. C. G. (Ed.) *River Management*, London: MacLaren.

BRETT, J. R. 1956. Some principles in the thermal requirements of fishes. *Quart. Rev. Biol.*, **31,** 75–87.

—— 1957. Salmon research and hydro-electric power development. *Bull Fish Res. Bd. Canada*, 114, 26 pp.

BROOK, A. J. 1956. Changes in the phytoplankton of some Scottish hill lochs resulting from their artificial enrichment. *Verh. int. Ver. Limnol.*, **13,** 298–305.

BROOK, A. J. and HOLDEN, A. V. 1957. Fertilization experiments in Scottish hill lochs. I. Loch Kinardochy. *Freshwat. Salm. Fish. Res.*, **17,** 30 pp.

BULL, H. O. 1931a. The smolt descent on the River Tyne. *Rep. Dove Mar. Lab.*, 1930, 37–66.

—— 1931b. The smolt descent on the River Tyne, 1931. *Rep. Dove Mar. Lab.* 1931, 32–43.

BURDICK, G. E. 1961. Chemical control of aquatic vegetation in relation to the conservation of fish and wildlife. *Proc. N. East Weed Control Conf.*, **15**, 485–492; Weed Abstracts, 12, 2, Abst. No. 514. 1963.

BURNET, A. M. R. 1968. A study of the relationships between brown trout and eels in a New Zealand stream. Fisheries Technical Report No. 26, New Zealand Marine Dept.

BURROWS, R. E. 1949. Prophylactic treatment for control of fungus (*Saprolegnia parasitica*) on salmon eggs. *Prog. Fish Cult.*, 97–103.

CALDERWOOD, W. L. 1901a. Water temperature in relation to the early annual migration of salmon from the sea to the rivers in Scotland. *19th Ann. Rept. Fish. Board Scotl.*, 57–76.

—— 1901b. Note by the Inspector of Salmon Fisheries on the range of the salmon spawning season in Scotland. 19th *Ann. Rept. Fish. Board Scotl.*, App. 2: 53–56.

—— 1903a. Water temperature in relation to the early annual migration of salmon from the sea to rivers in Scotland. 21st *Ann. Rept. Fish. Board Scotl.*, II: 71–76.

—— 1903a. The temperature of the River Tay and its tributaries in relation to the ascent of salmon. 21st *Ann. Rept. Fish. Board Scotl.*, III: 77–82.

—— 1906a. Autumn migration of smolts in Scotland. *Rep. Fish Bd. Scotl.*, 1905, Part II, 70–74.

—— 1906b. The white spot disease in salmon in the Island of Lewis. 24th *Ann. Rept. Fish. Bd. Scotl.*, App. 5: 78–79.

—— 1909. *The Salmon Rivers and Lochs of Scotland*. London: Edward Arnold, 442 pp.

—— 1927a. Atlantic salmon in New Zealand. The salmon of Lake Te Anau. *Salm. Trout Mag.*, **48**, 241–252.

—— 1927b. The salmon of R. Grand Cascapedia, Canada. *Proc. roy. Soc. Edinb.*, **47,** 142–147.

—— 1930. *Salmon and Sea Trout*. London: Edward Arnold, 242 pp.

—— 1931. *Salmon Hatching and Salmon Migrations*. London: Edward Arnold, 95 pp.

—— 1940. Thirty years of salmon marking. *Salm. Trout Mag.*, **88**, 207–213.

—— 1945. Passage of smolts through turbines: effect of high pressures. *Salm. Trout Mag.*, **115**, 214–221.

CALHOUN, A. (Ed.) 1966. *Inland Fisheries Management*. California Dept. of Fish and Game, 546 pp.

CAMINO, E. G. 1929. The sea life of Spanish salmon. *Fish. Gaz.*, **99**, 422.

CAMPBELL, R. N. 1961. The growth of brown trout in acid and alkaline waters. *Salm. Trout Mag.*, January, 47–52.

—— 1963. Some effects of impoundment on the environment and growth of brown trout (*Salmo trutta* L.) in Loch Garry (Inverness-shire). *Freshwat. Salm. Fish. Res.*, **30**, 37 pp.

—— 1965. Anglers' lore. *New Scient.*, **26**, 45–46.

—— 1967a. A method of regulating brown trout (*Salmo trutta* L.) populations in small lakes. *Salm. Trout Mag.*, **180**, 135–142.

—— 1967b. Improving highland trout lochs. *Flyfishers' Journal*, **56**, 221, 61–69.

CARBERRY, J. T. and STRICKLAND, K. L. 1968. Resistance of rainbow trout to ulcerative dermal necrosis. *Nature*, **217**, 5134, 1158.

CARLANDER, K. D. and LEWIS, W. M. 1948. Some precautions in estimating fish populations. *Prog. Fish Cult.*, **10** (3), 134–137.

CARLIN, B. 1953a. Märkning av lax på Norrbottenskusten. *Vandringsfiskutredn. Meddel.*, **2**, 1–4.

—— 1953b. Märkning av utvandringsfardiga laxungar. *Vandringsfiskutredn.*, **3**, 57–59.

—— 1959. Results of salmon smolt tagging in the Baltic area. *Rapp. et Proc.-Verb.*, **147**, 89–96.

—— 1962. Märkt lax återfångad vid Grønland. *Laxforskningsinstitutets, Meddelande*, No. 8, 5 pp.

—— 1966. Salmon rearing in Sweden. Swedish Salmon Research Institute – Report LFI Medd. 5/1966.

—— 1969a. The migration of salmon. Swedish Salmon Research Institute – Report LFI Medd. 4/1969.

—— 1969b. Salmon Conservation in Sweden. Swedish Salmon Research Institute – Report LFI Medd. 2/1969.

CARPENTER, K. E. 1924. A study of the fauna of rivers polluted by lead mining in the Aberystwyth district of Cardiganshire. *Annals of Applied Biology*, **11**, 1–23.

—— 1927. The lethal action of soluble metallic salts on fishes. *Brit. J. Exp. Biol.*, 4.

CARTER, W. M. 1962. A 5-point programme to multiply salmon. *Salm. Trout Mag.*, **165**, 93–101.

—— 1964. Quebec's salmon rivers. A glance at the past. A plan for the future. *Atlantic Salmon Journal*, Winter 64/65: 18–22, 36, 37.

CHANCELLOR, R. J. 1962. The identification of common water weeds. *Bull.* 183. London: H.M.S.O.

CHAPMAN, D. W. 1962. Effects of logging upon fish resources of the west coast. *J. Forest.* **60**, 533–537.

—— 1967. Production in fish populations. *The Biological Basis of Freshwater Fish Production*, p. 3. Shelby D. Gerking (Ed.) Blackwell, Oxford.

—— 1968. Production in *Methods for Assessment of Fish Production in Fresh Waters*. Ricker, W. E. (Ed.) Oxford and Edinburgh: Blackwell.

CHOATE, J. 1964. Use of tetracycline drugs to mark advanced fry and fingerling brook trout (*Salvelinus fontinalis*). *Trans. Amer. Fish. Soc.* **93**, (3), 309–311.

CHUBB, J. C. and POWELL, A. M. 1966. The examination of fish for parasites. *Proc. 2nd British Coarse Fish Conf.*, 87–93.

COLDWELL, C. 1939. The feeding habits of American mergansers. *Canad. Field-Nat.*, **52**, 55.

COOLEY, R. A. 1963. *Politics and Conservation: The Decline of the Alaska Salmon.* New York: Harper and Row.

CORBETT, R. W. 1963. The improvement of a midland trout stream. *Salm. Trout Assn. Lond. conf.*, 1963, 1–15.

COULL, J. R. 1969. Salmon-fishing in the north-east of Scotland before 1800. *The Salmon Net*, IV, 51–58.

CRICHTON, M. I. 1935. Scale absorption in salmon and sea trout. *Fisheries Scotland, Salmon Fish.*, IV, 8 pp.

CROSS, D. G. 1969. Aquatic weed control using grass carp. *J. Fish Biol.*, **1**, (1), 27–36.

CRUTCHFIELD, J. A. and PONTECORVO, G. 1969. *The Pacific Salmon Fisheries: A Study of Irrational Conservation*, vii + 220 pp. Baltimore: Johns Hopkins.

Cuinat, R. 1962. What can be expected from re-stocking? The latest French and foreign experiments answer. Toute la Pêche, 6: 30–33. 7: 28–31. Plaisirs de la Pêche 82/83–205–210.

Cuinat, R. and Vibert, R. 1963. Demographic diagnosis on fish populations in trout streams. Stud. Rev. gen. Fish. Coun. Medit., (Eng.) (21), 26 pp.

Curtis, B. 1949. The Life Story of the Fish, pp. viii + 284. New York: Harcourt, Brace & Co.

Cutting, R. E. 1964. Atlantic salmon report. Maine Fish and Game, 6 (I): 21.

Dahl, K. 1911. The age and growth of salmon and trout in Norway as shown by their scales. (English translation). Salm. Trout Assn. London, 1–141.

—— 1919. Studies of trout and trout waters in Norway. Salm. Trout Mag. 18, 16–33.

—— 1928. The dwarf salmon of Lake Byglands-fjord. Salm. Trout Mag. 51, 108–112.

—— 1938. A review of recent marking experiments in Norway. Rapp. Cons. Explor. Mer, 108, 3–15.

—— 1939. Homing instinct in salmon. Salm. Trout Mag. 94, 19–26.

Dahl, K. and Somme, S. 1936. Experiments in salmon marking in Norway, 1935. Skr. norske Vidensk Akad., 1935, no. 12, 27 pp.

Davidson, F. A., Vaughan, E., and Hutchinson, S. J. and Pritchard, A. L. 1943. Factors influencing the upstream migration of the pink salmon (Oncorhynchus gorbuscha). Ecology, 24, 149–168.

Davis, H. S. 1961. Culture and diseases of game fishes. Univ. California Press, Berkeley and Los Angeles, Calif. 332 pp.

Davis, R. M. 1967. Parasitism by newly-transformed anadromous sea lampreys on landlocked salmon and other fishes in a coastal Maine Lake. Trans. Amer. Fish. Soc., 96, (I), 11–16.

Dawes, B. 1947. The Trematoda of British Fishes. Ray Society. London: Quaritch. 364 pp.

Dell, M. B. 1968. A new fish tag and rapid cartridge-fed applicator. Trans. Amer. Fish. Soc., 97, (I), 57–59.

De Lury, D. B. 1947. On the estimation of biological populations. Biometrics, 3, 145–167.

—— 1951. On the planning of experiments for the estimation of fish populations. J. Fish. Res. Bd. Can., 8, 281–307.

Demoll, R. 1925. Teichdungung (In: Demoll, R. and Maier, H. N. Handbuch der Binnenfischerei Mitteleuropes, Vol. 4, 53–160, Stuttgart: Schweitzer-bart'sche Verlagsbuchhandlung.

Department of Agriculture and Fisheries for Scotland, 1963. Scottish Salmon and Trout Fisheries: First Report. Cmnd. 2096. H.M.S.O.

Department of Agriculture and Fisheries for Scotland, 1965. Scottish Salmon and Trout Fisheries: Second Report. Cmnd. 2691. H.M.S.O.

Department of Health for Scotland, 1950. Prevention of Pollution of Rivers and other Waters. Report of the River Pollution Prevention Sub-committee of the Scottish Water Advisory Committee. H.M.S.O. Cmnd. 8111.

DeRoche, S. E. 1963. Slowed growth of lake trout following tagging: Trans. Amer. Fish. Soc. 92, 185–186.

Dill, L. M. 1967. Studies on the early feeding of sockeye salmon alevins. Can. Fish Cult., 39, 23–34.

—— 1969. The sub-gravel behaviour of Pacific salmon larvae. Symposium on salmon and trout in streams, H. R. MacMillan Lectures in Fisheries, 1968. University of British Columbia, Vancouver.

DIX, T. G. 1968. Helminth parasites of brown trout (*Salmo trutta* L.) in Canterbury, New Zealand. *N.Z. J. Mar. Freshw. Res.*, **2**, 363–374.

DOGIEL, V. and PETRUSHEVSKI, G. K. 1935. An ecological study of the parasites of the salmon. (In Russian). *Publ. Ecol. & Biocenol.* Leningrad **2**, 137–169.

DOGIEL, V., PETRUSHEVSKI, G. K. and POLYANSKI, YU. I., 1961. *Parasitology of Fishes*. Edinburgh and London: Oliver and Boyd, 384 pp.

EARP, B. J., ELLIS, C. H. and ORDAL, E. J. 1953. Kidney disease in young salmon. State of Washington, Department of Fisheries, Special Report Series No. 1, 74 pp.

EGGLISHAW, H. J. 1967. The food, growth and population structure of salmon and trout in two streams in the Scottish Highlands. *Freshwat. Salm. Fish. Res.*, **38**, 32 pp.

EKLUND, G. 1963. Review of feeding costs of salmon cultivation at Bergeforsen for the period 1959–62. Swedish Salmon Research Institute. LFI Medd. 2/1963.

ELDER, H. Y. 1966. Biological effects of water utilization by hydro-electric schemes in relation to fisheries, with special reference to Scotland. *Proc. Roy. Soc. Edin*, B, LXIX, Pt. III/IV, 246–271.

ELLIOTT, J. M. 1966. Downstream movements of trout fry (*Salmo trutta*) in a Dartmoor stream. *J. Fish. Res. Bd. Canad.*, **23** (I), 157–159.

—— 1967. The food of trout (*Salmo trutta*) in a Dartmoor stream. *J. appl. Ecol.* **4**, 59–71.

ELLIS, M. M. 1936. Erosion silt as a factor in aquatic environments. *Ecology*, **17**, 29–42.

ELLIS, R. J. and GOWING, H. 1957. Relationship between food supply and condition of wild brown trout, *Salmo trutta* L. in a Michigan stream. *Limnology and Oceanography*, **2** (4), 249–308.

ELSON, K. R. 1968a. Salmon disease in Scotland. *The Salmon Net*, **4**, 9–17.

—— 1968b. Salmon disease in Scotland. *Scottish Fisheries Bull.* **30**, 8–16.

—— 1969. Whirling disease in trout. *Nature*, **223**, 5209, p. 968.

ELSON, P. F. 1950. Increasing salmon stocks by control of mergansers and kingfishers. *Fish. Res. Bd. Canad. Prog. Repts.* (Atlantic) No. 51, 12–15.

—— 1957a. The importance of size in the change from parr to smolt in Atlantic salmon. *Can. Fish Cult.*, **21**, 1–6.

—— 1957b. Using hatchery-reared Atlantic salmon to best advantage. *Can. Fish Cult.*, **21**, 7–17.

—— 1957c. Number of salmon needed to maintain stocks. *Can. Fish Cult.*, **21**, 19–23.

—— 1957d. The role of hatcheries in assuring maritime stocks of Atlantic salmon. *Can. Fish Cult.*, **21**, 25–32.

—— 1962a. Predator-prey relationships between fish-eating birds and Atlantic salmon. *Bull. Fish. Res. Bd. Canad.*, **133**, 87 pp.

—— 1962b. The Pollett apron seine. *J. Fish. Res. Bd. Canad.*, **19**, (I): 93–100.

—— 1969. Threat of industrialization to Canada's Atlantic salmon. *Fisheries of Canada*, **22** (5), 3–9.

EUROPEITSEVA, N. V. 1957. Transformation to smolt stage and downstream migration of young salmon. Vehenyi Zapidski Leningradskova Gosudarstvennova Universitata (LGV), 228, *Seria Bioloioheskikh Nauk*, **44**, 117–154.

EVANS, H. E. 1958. Hatcheries and their uses in fisheries developments. *Association of River Boards Yearbook*, 1957.

FABRICIUS, E. and GUSTAFSON, K.-J. 1955. Observations on the spawning behaviour of the grayling, *Thymallus thymallus* L. *Rep. Inst. Freshw. Res. Drottning-holm* **36**, 75–103.

FAIRBAIRN, W. A. 1967. Erosion in the Findhorn valley. *Scott. geogr. Mag.* **83** (1), 46–52.

FENDERSON, C. N. 1954. The brown trout in Maine. Maine Dept. of Inland Fisheries and Game, Fishery Research and Management Division, *Bulletin* no. 2, 16 pp.

FENTON, A. 1968. Scottish salmon fishing spears. *Salmon Net*, IV, 31–46.

FISH, G. R. 1968. An examination of the trout population of five lakes near Rotorua, New Zealand. *N.Z. J. Mar. Freshw. Res.*, **2**, 333–362.

FLETCHER, R. L. 1965. Constitutionality of limiting the number of fishermen in a commercial fishery. In *The Fisheries.* in *Problems in Resource Management*, Crutchfield, J. A. (ed.) Univ. Wash. Press.

FLOWERDEW, 1871. *The Parr and Salmon Controversy*. Edinburgh: Peddie, 147 pp.

FOERSTER, R. E. 1968. The Sockeye salmon, *Onchorhynchus nerka*. *Bull. Fish. Res. Bd. Can.*, **162**, 422 pp.

FONTAINE, M. 1951. Remarques sur certain comportements du saumon. *Bull. Francais de Pisciculture*, no. 160, 85–88.

FORT, R. S. and BRAYSHAW, J. D. 1961. *Fishery Management*, 398 pp. London: Faber.

FRASER, P. G. 1960. On *Diphyllobothrium medium* (Falmy, 1954) parasitic in trout in Great Britain. *J. Helminth.*, **34**, 193–204.

FRASER, T. B. 1968. The Greenland and Davis Strait Fisheries. *Salm. Trout Mag.*, **184**, 152–163.

FRIEND, C. F. 1941. The life history of the salmon gill-maggot *Salmincola salmonea* (L.) (Copepod crustacean). *Trans. roy. Soc. Edinb.*, **60**, 503–541.

FROST, W. E. 1939. River Liffey Survey II. The food consumed by the brown trout (*Salmo trutta* Linn.) in acid and alkaline waters. *Proc. R. Irish Acad.* **45B**, 139–206.

—— 1963. The homing of char *Salvelinus willughbii* (Günther) in Windermere. *Animal Behaviour*, **11**, 1, 74–82.

—— 1965. Breeding habits of Windermere char, *Salvelinus willughbii* (Günther), and their bearing on speciation of these fish. *Proc. Roy. Soc., B*, **163**, 232–284.

FROST, W. E. and SMYLY, W. J. P. 1952. The brown trout of a moorland fish pond. *J. Anim. Ecol.*, **21**, 62–86.

FROST, W. E. and BROWN, M. E. 1967. *The Trout*. London: Collins, 286 pp.

FURUNCULOSIS COMMITTEE. 1933. Second Interim Report (June 1933) 81 pp. H.M.S.O. London.

GARDNER, J. A. 1926. Report on the respiratory exchange in freshwater fish, with suggestions as to further investigations. Min. Ag. Fish., Fish. Invest. Ser., I, 3, 1–17.

GERKING, S. D. (Ed.) 1967. *The Biological Basis of Freshwater Fish Production*. Edinburgh and Oxford: Blackwell.

GIBSON, R. J. and KEENLEYSIDE, M. H. A. 1966. Responses to light of young Atlantic salmon (*Salmo salar*) and brook trout (*Salvelinus fontinalis*). *J. Fish. Res. Bd. Canad.* **23**, 7, 1007–1024.

GILSON, H. C. 1966. The biological implications of the proposed barrages across Morecambe Bay and the Solway Firth. pp. 129–137 in *Man-Made Lakes* by R. H. Lowe-McConnell (Ed.) London and New York: Academic Press.

GODBY, M. H. 1925. *Salmo salar*: at home and abroad. History of its acclimatization in New Zealand. *N.Z. J. Sci. Tech*, **8**, 19–27.

GOLTERMAN, H. and CLYMO, R. S. 1969. *Methods for Chemical Analysis of Fresh Waters*. (I.B.P. Handbook) Oxford and Edinburgh: Blackwell.

GRASBERG, E. 1956. *Economic benefits of the Atlantic salmon to the province of New Brunswick*. Fredericton, N.B., 14 pp.

GRAY, J. R. A. and EDINGTON, J. M. 1969. Effect of woodland clearance on stream temperature. *J. Fish. Res. Bd. Canad.*, **26** (2), 399–403.

GREENE, G. E. 1950. Land use and trout streams. *J. Soil and Water Conserv.* **5** (3), 125–126.

GREGORY, M. 1967. *Angling and the Law*. xvi + 196 pp. London: Knight.

GROVES, A. B. and NOVOTNY, A. J. 1965. A thermal marking technique for juvenile salmonids. *Trans. Amer. Fish. Soc.*, **94** (4), 386–389.

GUDJONSSON, P. 1965. The effect of water removal on the catch of salmon in the River Ulfarsa, Iceland. International Council for the Exploration of the Sea. C.M. 1965, No. 171.

HADOKE, G. D. F. 1967. An examination of the fishing effort of a selected number of anglers during the 1966 season. *Salm. Trout Mag.*, **181**, 245–249.

HAIG-BROWN, R. L. 1952. Canada's Pacific Salmon. Department of Fisheries of Canada, Ottawa. (Reprinted from *Canad. Geographical J.*, 5–23.)

HALL, G. H. 1930. *Life of the Sea Trout*. London. Seeley Service.

HALL, J. D. and LANTZ, R. L. 1969. Effects of logging on the habitat of coho salmon and cutthroat trout in coastal streams. Symposium on Salmon and Trout in Streams. H. R. MacMillan Lectures in Fisheries, University of British Columbia, 355–375.

HAMILTON, J. D. 1961. The effect of sand-pit washings on a stream fauna. *Verh. Internat. Verein. Limnol.*, XIV, 435–439.

HARDIE, R. P. 1940. *Ferox and Char in Lochs of Scotland. Part I.* Edinburgh: Oliver and Boyd, 266 pp.

HARRIMAN, P. 1960. The black salmon controversy. Maine Atlantic Salmon Federation. Document No. 1, 8 pp.

—— 1961. Water control + artificial freshets = Atlantic salmon. Maine Atlantic Salmon Federation Document No. 2, 14 pp.

HARRISON, A. C., SHORTT-SMITH, K. E., YATES, J. H., JUBB, R. A., RUSHBY, G. and FLAMWELL, C. T. 1963. *Fresh-water Fish and Fishing in Africa*. Johannesburg: Thomas Nelson, vi + 210 pp.

HARTLEY, W. G. and SIMPSON, D. 1967. Electric fish screens in the United Kingdom, pp. 183–197, in Vibert, R. (Ed.) *Fishing with Electricity – its applications to biology and management*. pp. xxviii + 276. London: Fishing News (Books) Ltd.

HASLER, A. D. 1947. Eutrophication of lakes by domestic drainage. *Ecology*, **28** (4), 383–395.

—— 1949. Antibiotic aspects of copper treatment of lakes. *Trans. Wisconsin Acad. of Sciences, Arts and Letters*, **39**, 97–103.

—— 1954. Odor perception and orientation in fishes. *J. Fish. Res. Bd. Can.*, **11**, 107–129.

HASLER, A. D. and EINSELE, W. G. 1948. Fertilization for increasing the productivity of natural inland waters. *Trans. N. Amer. Wildl. Conf.*, **13**, 527–51.

HASLER, A. D. and WISBY, W. J. 1951. Discrimination of stream odors by fishes and its relation to parent stream behaviour. *Amer. Nat.*, **85**, 223–238.

HATCH, R. W. 1957. Relative sensitivity of salmonids to DDT. *Progve. Fish Cult.*, **19**, 89–91.

HAYES, F. R. 1953. Artificial freshets and other factors controlling the ascent and population of Atlantic salmon in the La Have River, Nova Scotia. *Bull. Fish. Res. Bd. Can.*, **99**, 47 pp.

HAYES, F. R. and ANTHONY, E. H. 1964. Productive capacity of North American lakes as related to the quantity and the trophic level of fish, the lake dimensions, and the water chemistry. *Trans. Amer. Fish Soc.*, **93**, 53–57.

HEARD, W. G. and CURD, M. R. 1959. Stomach contents of American mergansers, *Mergus merganser* Linnaeus, caught in gill nets set in Lake Carl, Blackwell, Oklahoma. *Proc. Okla. Acad. Sci.*, **39**, 197–200.

HECTOR, J. 1966. The bag net. *The Salmon Net*, **2**, 27–29.

HEITZ, A. 1918. *Salmo salar*, seine Parasitenfauna und seine Ernährung im Meer und im Süsswasser. *Arch. Hydrobiol.*, XII, 2–3.

HELLAWELL, J. M. 1966. Coarse fish in a salmon river. *Proceedings of the Second British Coarse Fish Conference*, 43–48.

HERRINGTON, R. B. and DUNHAM, D. K. 1967. A technique for sampling general fish habitat characteristics of streams. U.S. Dept. Agr., Forest Serv., Intermountain Forest and Range Exp. Sta., Ogden, Utah.

HEWETSON, A. 1962a. Furunculosis in salmon kelts. *Nature*, London, **194**, 312.

—— 1962b. Furunculosis in salmon kelts. *Nature, London*, **196**, 1009.

—— 1963. Salmon rearing experiments in Lough Knader, a small lake in Co. Donegal, Ireland. Rep. Sea inlnd. Fish. Ire.

HOFFMAN, G. L. 1967. *Parasites of North American Freshwater Fishes*. Univ. of California Press, viii + 486 pp.

HOLCIK, J. and MIHÁLIK, J. 1968. *Freshwater Fishes*. Spring Books: Feltham, Hamlyn, 128 pp.

HOLDEN, A. V. 1959. Ferlilization experiments in Scottish freshwater lochs II. Sutherland 1954. I. Chemical and botanical observations. *Freshwat. Salm. Fish. Res.*, **24**, 42 pp.

—— 1962. A simple automatic water sampler. *Effluent and Water Treatment Journal*, June.

HOLDEN, A. V. and MARSDEN, K. 1964. Cyanide in salmon and brown trout. *Freshwat. Salm. Fish. Res.*, **33**, 12 pp.

HORTON, P. A., BAILEY, R. G. and WILDSON, S. I. 1968. A comparative study of the bionomics of the salmonids of three streams. *Arch. Hydrobiol.*, **65**, 187–204.

HUBBS, C. L., GREELEY, J. R. and TARZWELL, C. M. 1932. Methods for the improvement of Michigan trout streams. *Bull. Mich. Cons. Dept., Inst. Fish. Res.*, No. 1, 54 pp.

HUET, M. 1959. Profiles and biology of western European streams as related to fish management. *Trans. Amer. Fish. Soc.*, **88**, 155–163.

—— 1970. *Traité de Pisciculture*, xxiv + 718 pp. Brussels: Wyngaert.

HULT, J. 1947. Nogra resultat av markning av Luleälvslax sommaren 1946. *Svensk Fisk-Tidskr.*, **1**, 5–8.

HULT, J. and JOHNELS, A. 1949. Predators on salmon fry in the River Mörrumsa in 1948. *Rep. Inst. Freshw. Res. Drottningholm*, **29**, 45–48.

HUNT, R. L. 1969. Effects of habitat alteration on production, standing crops and

M

yield of brook trout in Lawrence Creek, Wisconsin. Symposium on Salmon and Trout in Streams. H. R. MacMillan Lectures in Fisheries, University of British Columbia, 281–312.

HUNTER, J. G. The Arctic Char. *Fisheries of Canada* (formerly *Trade News*) **19**, (3): 17–19.

HUNTSMAN, A. G. 1931. The maritime salmon of Canada. *Bull. Biol. Bd. Can.*, **21**, 99 pp.

—— 1933. St. John salmon – the earliest run known. *Biol. Bd. Can. Progr. Rept. Atl.*, **25** (6): 7–10.

—— 1936. Return of salmon from the sea. *Bull. Biol. Bd. Can.*, **51**, 20 pp.

—— 1937. The cause of periodic scarcity in Atlantic salmon. *Trans. roy. Soc. Can.* (v), **31**, 17–27.

—— 1938. Sea behaviour in salmon. *Salm. & Trout Mag.*, **90**, 24–28.

—— 1941. Cyclical abundance and birds versus salmon. *J. Fish. Res. Bd. Can.*, **5**, (3): 227–235.

—— 1942. Death of salmon and trout with high temperature. *J. Fish. Res. Bd. Can.*, **5**, 485–501.

—— 1948. Fertility and fertilization of streams. *J. Fish. Res. Bd. Can.*, **7**, 248–253.

—— 1952. Wandering versus homing in salmon. *Salm. Trout Mag.*, 130, 227–230.

HUTTON, J. A. 1923. The parasites of salmon. *Salm. Trout Mag.*, 34, 302–312.

—— 1924. *The Life History of the Salmon.* Aberdeen University Press.

—— 1947. Salmon scarcity. An attempt to get the real facts. *Salm. Trout Mag.*, Advance Rept.: 1–8.

HUXLEY, T. 1882. Saprolegnia in relation to salmon disease. *Quar. J. Micr. Sc.*

HYNES, H. B. 1960. *The Biology of Polluted Waters.* Liverpool: University Press, 202 pp.

IVANFI, E. 1927. A pontytetii (*Argulus foliaceus* L.) morphologiaja es biologiaja. *Archivum balatonicum*, v, 1, N2.

JANKOVIC, D. 1964. Synopsis of biological data on European grayling *Thymallus thymallus* (Linnaeus) 1758. FAO Fisheries Synopsis No. 24, Flb/S24 (Rev. 1).

JENKINS, J. T. 1925. *The Fishes of the British Isles.* London: Warne, viii + 408 pp.

JENKINSON, D. W. and SUTHERLAND, R. 1966. A portable press for making impressions of salmon scales. *J. Fish. Res. Bd. Can.*, **23** (7), 1089–1093.

JENSEN, J. M. 1967. Atlantic salmon caught in the Irminger Sea. *J. Fish. Res. Bd. Can.*, **24** (12): 2639–2640.

JENSEN, K. W. 1963. Farming trout and salmon in Norway. *Salm. Trout Mag.*, **168**, 86–96.

JENSEN, P. T. 1958. Catchable trout studies in Region II. 1957. California State Inland Fisheries, Administrative Report No. 58–1, 1–39 (Mimeo).

JOHNSON, H. E., ADAMS, C. D. and McELRATH, R. J. 1955. A new method of treating salmon eggs and fry with malachite green. *Progve. Fish Cult.*, **17**, 76–78.

JOHNSTON, H. W. 1904. The scales of Tay salmon as indicative of age, growth and spawning habit. 23rd Ann. Rep. Fish. Board Scot., App. II.

JOHNSTON, R. M. 1888. Results of the various attempts to acclimatise *Salmo salar* in Tasmanian waters. *Proc. Roy. Soc. Tasmania*, 27–46.

JONES, A. N. and HOWELLS, W. R. 1969. Recovery of the River Rheidol. *Effluent and Water Treatment Journal*, November, 1969.

JONES, J. R. E. 1964. *Fish and River Pollution.* viii + 203 pp. London: Butterworth.

JONES, J. W. 1949. Studies of the scales of young salmon *Salmo salar* L. (juv.) in relation to growth, migration and spawning. *Fish. Invest., Lond.*, Ser. I, **5** (1), 23 pp.

—— 1950a. Salmon of the Cheshire Dee. *Fish. Invest., Lond.*, Ser. I **5** (5), 11 pp.

—— 1950b. Salmon studies. *Fish. Invest., Lond.*, Ser. I, **5** (2), 23 pp.

—— 1957. Fertilization of waters. *Trout and Salmon*, **2** (8), 11–12.

—— 1959. *The Salmon*. London: Collins, xvi + 192 pp.

JONES, J. W. and BALL, J. N. 1954. The spawning behaviour of brown trout and salmon. *Brit. J. Anim. Behav.* **2**, 103–114.

JONES, J. W. and EVANS, H. 1962. Salmon rearing in mountain tarns – a preliminary report. *Proc. zool. Soc. Lond.*, **138**, 499–515.

JONES, J. W. and KING, G. M. 1949. Experimental observations on the spawning behaviour of the Atlantic salmon (*Salmo salar* Linn.). *Proc. zool. Soc. Lond.*, **119**, 33–48.

JONES, R. 1964. A review of methods of estimating population size from marking experiments. *Rapp. et Proc. – Verb.*, **155**, 202–209.

—— 1965. A review of methods of estimating population size from marking experiments. FAO Fish. tech. Pap. No. 51, App. 2, p. 39–46.

KALLEBERG, H. 1958. Observations in a stream tank of territoriality and competition in juvenile salmon and trout (*Salmo salar* L. and *S. trutta* L.) *Rep. Inst. Freshw. Res. Drottningholm.*, **39**, 55–98.

KEENLEYSIDE, M. H. A. and YAMAMOTO, F. T. 1962. Territorial behaviour of juvenile Atlantic salmon (*Salmo salar* L.) Behaviour, 19 (**1**): 139–169.

KENDALL, W. C. 1931. The question of salmon (*Salmo salar*) feeding in freshwater and taking of bait. *Copeia*, **2**, 33–38.

KENNEDY, W. A. 1956. The first ten years of commercial fishing on Grest Slave Lake. *Bull. Fish. Res. Bd. Can.*, **107**, 58 pp.

KERSWILL, C. J. 1955a. Recent developments in Atlantic salmon research. *The Atlantic Salmon Journal*, January, 26–30.

—— 1955b. Effects of black salmon angling on Miramichi salmon stocks. *The Atlantic Salmon Journal*, January, 30–31.

KERSWILL, C. J. and KEENLEYSIDE, M. H. A. 1961. Canadian salmon caught off Greenland. *Nature*, **192**, 279.

KESTEVEN, G. L. (Ed.) 1960. *Manual of field methods in fisheries biology*. FAO Man. Fish. Sci., No. 1, 152 pp.

—— 1969. Ethics and ecology. Ceres, FAO Review, II, 3, 53–56.

KIPLING, C. 1957. The effect of gill-net selection on the estimation of weight–length relationships. *J. Cons. Internat. Explor. Mer*, **23** (1): 51–63.

—— 1962. The use of the scales of the trout (*Salmo trutta* L.) for the back-calculation of growth. *J. Cons. int. Explor. Mer*, **27** (3): 304–315.

KING-WEBSTER, W. A. 1969. The Galloway Dee – a short history of a salmon river. *The Salmon Net*, V, 38–47.

KLEIN, L. 1957. *River Pollution 1: Chemical Analysis*. 215 pp. London: Butterworth.

—— 1962. *River Pollution 2: Causes and Effects*. xiii + 470 pp. London: Butterworth.

—— 1966. *River Pollution 3: Control*. xv + 484 pp. London: Butterworth.

KOCH, H. J., EVANS, J. C. and BERGSTRÖM, E. 1959. Sodium regulation in the blood of parr and smolt stages of Atlantic salmon. *Nature*, **184**, 283.

KOCH, H. J. A., BERGSTRÖM, E. and EVANS, J. C. 1964. The microelectrophoretic separation on starch gel of the haemoglobins of *Salmo salar* L. *Mededel. Vlaamse Acad. Kl. Wet.*, **26,** (9), 1–32.

KOCH, H. J. A., WILKINS, N. P., BERGSTRÖM, E. and EVANS, J. C. 1967. Studies of the multiple components of the haemoglobins of *Salmo salar* L. *Mededel. Vlaamse Acad. Kl. Wet.*, **29,** (7), 1–16.

KOHLER, L. 1966. *The Treasury of Angling.* 252 pp. London: Hamlyn.

KOZHIN, N. I. 1964. Atlantic salmon in the U.S.S.R. *Atlantic Salmon Journal*, **2,** 3–7.

LACK, D. 1966. *Population Studies of Birds.* Oxford, University Press, 341 pp.

LAGLER, K. F. 1956. *Freshwater Fishery Biology.* 421 pp. Iowa: Brown.

—— 1968. Capture, sampling and examination of fishes. in Ricker, W. E. (ed.) *Methods for Assessment of Fish Production in Fresh Waters.* Edinburgh and Oxford: Blackwell Scientific Publications.

LANGFORD, R. R. 1950. Fertilization of lakes in Algonquin Park, Ontario. *Trans. Amer. Fish. Soc.*, **78,** 133–144.

LARSEN, K. 1951. Om geddens (*Esox lucius* L.) føde i van dløb. (English summary: On the food of the pike (*Esox lucius* L.) in streams). *Sportsfiskeren* No. 2: 17–25.

—— 1965. The pike (*Esox lucius* L.) as a food competitor and a predator of trout in Danish streams. I.C.E.S./C.M., 1965, No. 29, 3 pp.

LATTA, W. C. 1965. Relationship of young-of-the-year trout to mature trout and groundwater. *Trans. Amer. Fish. Soc.*, **94** (1), 32–39.

—— 1969. Some factors affecting survival of young-of-the-year brook trout in streams. Symposium on salmon and trout in streams. H. R. MacMillan Lectures in Fisheries, University of British Columbia, pp. 229–240.

LEAMAN, A. C. 1965. Control of furunculosis in impounded Atlantic salmon. *Nature*, **208,** 5017, p. 1344.

LE CREN, E. D. 1961. How many fish survive? *Association of River Boards Year Book*, **9,** 57–64.

—— 1965. Some factors regulating the size of populations of freshwater fish. *Mitt. int. Ver. Limnol.*, **13,** 88–105.

—— 1969. Estimates of fish populations and production in small streams in England. Symposium on salmon and trout in streams. H. R. MacMillan Lectures in Fisheries, University of British Columbia, pp. 269–280.

LEE, R. M. 1920. A review of the methods of age and growth determination in fishes by means of scales. Fishery Invest. Lond. Ser. 2, **4,** (2), 32 pp.

LEIM, A. H. and SCOTT, W. B. 1966. Fishes of the Atlantic coast of Canada. *Bull. Fish. Res. Bd. Canad.*, **155,** 485 pp.

LEITRITZ, E. 1959. *Trout and Salmon Culture*, (*Hatchery Methods*). State of California, Dept of Fish and Game. Fish Bulletin No. 107, 169 pp.

LESTER, W. F. 1967. Management of river quality, 178–192, in Isaac, P. C. G. (ed.) *River Management*, x + 258 pp. London: MacLaren.

LINDROTH, A. 1950. Fluctuations of the salmon stock in the rivers of northern Sweden. (English summary). *Svenska Vattenkr. Fören. Publ.* 415, 99–224.

—— 1952. Salmon tagging experiments in Sundsvall Bay of the Baltic in 1950. *Rep. Inst. Freshwat. Res. Drottningholm*, **44,** 105–112.

—— 1955a. Mergansers as salmon and trout predators in the River Indalsälven. *Rep. Inst. Freshwat. Res. Drottningholm*, **36,** 126–132.

—— 1955b. Distribution, territorial behaviour and movements of sea trout fry in the River Indalsälven. *Rep. Inst. Freshw. Res. Drottningholm.*, **36,** 104–119.

—— 1965a. The Baltic salmon stock. *Mitt. int.Verein. Limnol.*, **13**, 163–192.

—— 1965b. The effect of hydro-electric power developments on salmon in the Swedish rivers. I.C.E.S. C.M. 1965. No. 11.

LOCKIE, J. D. 1962. Grey seals as competitors with man for salmon, pp. 316–322, in Le Cren, E. D. and Holdgate, M. W. (Eds.) *The Exploitation of Natural Animal Populations*, Edinburgh and Oxford: Blackwell Scientific Publications.

MACAN, T. T. 1958. Methods of sampling the bottom fauna in stony streams. *Mitt. int.Verein. Limnol*, **8**, 1–21.

—— 1963. *Freshwater Ecology*, pp. x + 338. London: Longmans, Green and Co.

MACAN, T. T. and WORTHINGTON, E. B. 1951. *Life in Lakes and Rivers*, pp. xvi + 272, London: Collins.

MACEK, K. J. 1968. Growth and resistance to stress in brook trout fed sub-lethal levels of DDT. *J. Fish. Res. Bd. Can.*, **25** (11): 2443–2451.

MACKERETH, F. J. H. 1963. Some methods of water analysis for limnologists. Freshwater Biological Association, Scientific Publication No. 21.

McCORMACK, J. C. 1962. The food of young trout (*Salmo trutta*) in two different becks. *J. Anim. Ecol*: 305–16.

McCRIMMON, H. R. and MARSHALL, T. L. 1968. World distribution of brown trout, *Salmo trutta*. *J. Fish. Res. Bd. Can.*, **25** (12): 2527–2548.

McCRIMMON, H. R. and CAMPBELL, J. S. 1969. World distribution of brook trout, *Salvelinus fontinalis*. *J. Fish. Res. Bd. Can.*, **26** (7): 1699–1725.

MacEACHERN, N. J. E. and MacDONALD, J. R. 1962. The salmon fishery in Nova Scotia. *Can. Fish Cult.*, No. 31, 43–57.

McFADDEN, J. T. 1961. A population study of the brook trout, *Salvelinus fontinalis*. *Wildl. Monogr.*, No. 7, 73 pp.

—— 1969. Dynamics and regulation of salmonid populations in streams. Symposium on salmon and trout in streams. H. R. MacMillan Lectures in Fisheries. University of British Columbia, pp. 313–329.

McFADDEN, J. T., ALEXANDER, G. R. and SHETTER, D. S. 1967. Numerical changes and population regulation in brook trout *Salvelinus fontinalis*. *J. Fish. Res. Bd. Can.*, (24), (7): 1425–1459.

McGLASSON, A. T. 1965. A history of salmon fishing on the Solway. *The Salmon Net*, **1**, 38–41.

McGAUHEY, P. H. 1968. *Engineering Management of Water Quality*, vi + 295 pp. London and New York: McGraw-Hill.

McGRATH, C. J. 1959. Dams as barriers or deterrents to the migration of fish. *Athens Proceedings of the I.U.C.N. Technical Meeting*, Vol. IV, 81–92.

McGRATH, C. J. and MURPHY, D. F. 1965. Engineering investigations into the effects of the harnessing of the River Lee, Co. Cork, Ireland, for hydro-electric purposes on the habitat and migration of salmonid stocks. I.C.E.S. C.M. 1965. Salmon and Trout Committee, No. 41.

McVEAN, D. N. and LOCKIE, J. D. 1969. *Ecology and Land Use in Upland Scotland*. x + 134 pp. Edinburgh: University Press.

MADDEN, N. J. 1935. A biological survey of streams and lakes in Fort Apache and San Carlos Indian Reservations, Arizona. U.S. Bur. Fish., 16 pp.

MADSEN, F. J. 1957. On the food habits of some fish-eating birds in Denmark. *Danish Rev. of Game Biology*, **3**, 2, 19–83.

MAGRATH, T. A. 1963. Fishing in Canada in 1873. *Atlantic Salmon Journal*, **4**, 26–27.

MAHEUX, G. 1956. Le saumon de l'Atlantique dans l'économie de la province de Québec, Canada. Laval Univ. Forest Res. Foundation, 30 pp.

MAITLAND, P. S. 1965. The feeding relationships of salmon, trout, minnows, stone loach and three-spined sticklebacks in the River Endrick, Scotland, *J. Anim. Ecol.*, **34** (1): 109–133.

—— 1967. The artificial fertilization and rearing of the eggs of *Coregonus clupeoides* Lacépède. *Proc. Roy. Soc. Edinb.*, B.70, (1): 82–106.

MALLOCH, P. D. H. 1910. *Life History of the Salmon, Trout and other freshwater fish*, 239 pp. London: Black.

MANN, K. H. 1955. The ecology of the British freshwater leeches. *J. Anim. Ecol.*, **24**, 1, 98–119.

MARGOLIS, L. 1963. Parasites as indicators of the geographical origin of sockeye salmon, *Oncorhynchus nerka* (Walbaum), occurring in the North Pacific ocean and adjacent seas. *International North Pacific Fisheries Commission, Bulletin* No. 11, 101–156.

MARLIER, G. 1946. Observations sur la conductivités electrique des eaux courantes de Belgique. Notes preliminaires. *Ann. Soc. zool. Belge*, **76**, 100–107.

MARR. D. H. A. 1966. Factors affecting the growth of salmon alevins and their survival and growth during the fry stage. *Association of River Authorities Year Book* 1965, 133–141.

MASTERMAN, A. T. 1913. Report on the investigations on the salmon with special reference to age determination by study of scales. Fish. Invest. Series 1, Vol. I, Part 1.

MATHISEN, O. A. and BERG, M. 1968. Growth rates of the char, *Salvelinus alpinus* (L.), in the Vardnes River, Troms, Northern Norway. *Rep. Inst. Freshw. Res., Drottningholm*, **48**, 177–186.

MAXWELL, H. 1904. *British Freshwater Fishes*, viii + 316 pp. London: Hutchinson.

MAYHEW, J. 1955. Toxicity of seven different insecticides to rainbow trout, *Salmo gairdnerii*, Richardson. *Proc. Iowa Acad. Sci.*, 62.

MAYHEW, J. K. 1962. The control of nuisance aquatic vegetation with black polythene plastic. *Proc. Iowa Acad. Sci.*, **69**, 302–307.

MENZIES, W. J. M. 1914. Further notes on the percentage of previously spawned salmon. *Fisheries, Scotland, Salmon Fish.*, **II**, 12 pp.

—— 1927. Some aspects of the growth of salmon in river and sea as observed from scale examination of Dee (Aberdeen) and Spey salmon, 1921 to 1923 inclusive. *Fisheries, Scotland, Salmon Fish.*, **VI**, 14 pp.

—— 1931. *The Salmon*, 2nd edition, pp. xiv + 213. Edinburgh: Blackwood.

—— 1949. *The stock of salmon, its migration, preservation and improvement*, 96 pp. London: Arnold.

—— 1966. Salmon fisheries and the development of hydro-electric power. Salm. Trout Assn., London conf., 1966, 15 pp.

—— 1967a. Danger ahead. *Salm. Trout Mag.*, **181**, 199–202.

—— 1967b. The past and future in salmon fisheries. *Association of River Authorities Year Book*, **199**, I–II.

MENZIES, W. J. M. and CURTIS, G. R. 1966. A new type of hatching tray. *Salm. Trout Mag.*, **178**, 221–223.

MENZIES, W. J. M. and SHEARER, W. M. 1957. Long-distance migration of salmon. *Nature*, **179**, 790.

MERCER, D. 1967. The effects of abstractions and discharges on river-water quality, 168–177. In Isaac, P. C. G. (Ed.) *River Management*, x + 258 pp. London: MacLaren.

MILLS, D. H. 1959. Salmon smolt tagging experiments at Invergarry Salmon Hatchery. *Rapp. et Proc.-Verb.*, **148,** 8–10.

—— 1962. The goosander and red-breasted merganser as predators of salmon in Scottish waters. *Freshwat. Salm. Fish. Res.*, **29,** 10 pp.

—— 1964a. The ecology of the young stages of the Atlantic salmon in the River Bran, Ross-shire. *Freshwat. Salm. Fish. Res.*, **32,** 58 pp.

—— 1964b. Report in *The Fisheries of Scotland for 1963*, Appendix vi, pp. 108–109, London: H.M.S.O.

—— 1965a. The distribution and food of the cormorant in Scottish inland waters. *Freshwat. Salm. Fish. Res.*, **35,** 16 pp.

—— 1965b. Studies of the survival of salmon fry and their application. *Rep. Challenger Soc.*, **3,** XVII, 33–34.

—— 1965c. Smolt production and hydro-electric schemes. I.C.E.S./C.M., 1965, No. 31, 3 pp.

—— 1965d. Observations on the effects of hydro-electric developments on salmon migration in a river system. I.C.E.S./C.M., 1965, No. 32, 5 pp.

—— 1966. Smolt transport. *Salm. Trout Mag.*, **177,** 138–141.

—— 1967a. Predation on fish by other animals, pp. 377–397. In Gerking, S. D. (Ed.) *The Biological Basis of Freshwater Fish Production*, Edinburgh and Oxford: Blackwell Scientific Publications.

—— 1967b. The occurrence of the fish leech (*Piscicola geometra* L.) on salmonid fish in the River Tweed and its tributaries. *Salm. Trout Mag.*, **181,** 234–235.

—— 1967c. A study of trout and young salmon populations in forest streams with a view to management. *Forestry*, **40,** (I): Supplement, 85–90.

—— 1968. Some observations on the upstream movements of adult Atlantic salmon in the River Conon and the River Meig, Ross-shire. I.C.E.S./C.M. 10, 5 pp.

—— 1969a. The survival of juvenile Atlantic salmon and brown trout in some Scottish streams, 217–228. Symposium on salmon and trout in streams. H. R. MacMillan Lectures in Fisheries, University of British Columbia.

—— 1969b. The survival of hatchery-reared salmon fry in some Scottish streams. *Freshwat. Salm. Fish. Res.*, **39,** 10 pp.

—— 1970. Preliminary observations on fish populations in some Tweed tributaries. *Annual Report to the Tweed Commissioners*, 1970, Appendix III, 16–22.

MILLS, D. H. and SHACKLEY, P. E. 1971. Salmon smolt transportation experiments on the Conon River system, Ross-shire. *Freshwat. Salm. Fish. Res.*

MINISTRY OF AGRICULTURE, FISHERIES AND FOOD. 1961. Report of Committee on Salmon and Freshwater Fisheries. Cmnd. 1350. H.M.S.O.

MINISTRY OF HOUSING AND LOCAL GOVERNMENT AND MINISTRY OF AGRICULTURE, FISHERIES AND FOOD. 1962. Water Conservation, England and Wales. Cmnd. 1693. H.M.S.O.

MONTÉN, E. 1955. Om utvandrande laxungars moj-ligheter alt oskadda passera genour kraftverksturbiner. *Vandringfiskutredningen, Meddelande* sr. 13. Stockholm.

—— 1969. Vattenfalls fiskodlingsverksamhet, 1950–1968. (Fish culturing within the Swedish State Power Board, 1950–1968). Swedish Salmon Research Institute – Report LFI Medd. 11/1969.

MORGAN, N. C. 1966. Fertilization experiments in Scottish freshwater lochs II. Sutherland, 1954, 2. Effects on the bottom fauna. *Freshwat. Salm. Fish. Res.*, **36,** 19 pp.

MORGAN, N. C. and EGGLISHAW, H. J. 1965. A survey of the bottom fauna of streams in the Scottish Highlands. Part I. Composition of the fauna. *Hydrobiologia*, xxv, 1–2, 181–211.

MORIARTY, C. I. D. 1962. Notes on some sea trout taken at sea. Appendix III, 295–296, in Went, A. E. J. Irish sea trout, a review of investigations to date. *Sci. Proc. R. Dublin Soc.* (N.S.) **10**, 265–296.

MORSE, N. H. 1965. Economic value of the Atlantic salmon fishery in Nova Scotia. Wolfville, N.S.: Acadia University Institute, 32 pp.

MOTTLEY, C. McC., RAYNER, H. J. and RAINWATER, J. H. 1938. The determination of the food grade of streams. *Trans. Amer. Fish. Soc.*, **68**, 336–343.

MOYLE, P. B. 1969. Comparative behaviour of young brook trout of wild and domestic origin. *Progve. Fish Cult.*, **30**, 144–152.

MULLEN, J. W. 1958. A compendium of the life history and ecology of the eastern brook trout *Salvelinus fontinalis* (Mitchill). *Mass. Div. Fish & Game Fish. Bull*, **23**, 38 pp.

MULLER, K. 1954. Investigations on the organic drift in North Swedish Streams. *Rep. Freshw. Res., Drottningholm*, **35**, 133–148.

MUNDIE, J. H. 1964. A sampler for catching emerging insects and drifting materials in streams. *Limnology and Oceanography*, **9**, 3, 456–459.

MUNRO, A. L. S. 1970. Ulcerative dermal necrosis, a disease of migratory salmonid fishes in the rivers of the British Isles. *Biological Conservation*, **2**, (2): 129–132.

MUNRO, J. A. and CLEMENS, W. A. 1937. The American merganser in British Columbia and its relation to the fish population. *Bull. Fish. Res. Bd. Can.*, No. 60, 50 pp.

MUNRO, W. R. 1957. The pike of Loch Choin. *Freshwat. Salm. Fish. Res.*, **16**, 16 pp.

—— 1961. The effect of mineral fertilizers on the growth of trout in some Scottish lochs. *Verh. Internat. Verein. Limnol.*, XIV, 718–721.

—— 1965a. Effects of passage through hydro-electric turbines on salmonids. I.C.E.S./C.M. 1965. No. 57, 4 pp.

—— 1965b. The use of louver screens as a means of diverting salmon smolts. I.C.E.S./C.M. 1965. No. 33, 4 pp.

—— 1965c. Observations on the migrations of salmonids in the River Tummel (Perthshire, Scotland). I.C.E.S./C.M. 1965, No. 30, 5 pp.

—— 1965d. The use of hill lochs in Scotland as rearing grounds for young salmon. Progress on the Experiment in Loch Kinardochy (Perthshire). I.C.E.S./C.M. 1965. No. 58, 5 pp.

—— 1969. The occurrence of salmon in the sea off the Faroes. *Scott. Fish. Bull.*, **32**, 11–13.

MUNRO, W. R. and BALMAIN, K. H. 1956. Observations on the spawning runs of brown trout in South Queich, Loch Leven. *Freshwat. Salm. Fish. Res.*, **13**, 17 pp.

NALL, G. H. 1933. SALMON of the River Ewe and Loch Maree. *Fisheries, Scotland, Salmon Fish.*, **II**, 14 pp.

—— 1937. Sea trout of the River Conon. *Fisheries, Scotland, Salmon Fish.*, **IV**, 31 pp.

—— 1955. Movements of salmon and sea trout, chiefly kelts, and of brown trout tagged in the Tweed between January and May 1937 and 1938. *Freshwat. Salm. Fish. Res.*, **10**, 19 pp.

NEEDHAM, P. R. and BEHUKE, R. J. 1962. The origin of hatchery rainbow trout. *Progve. Fish Cult.*, **24**, (4): 156–158.

NEESS, J. C. 1949. Development and status of pond fertilization in central Europe. *Trans. Amer. Fish. Soc.*, **76,** 335–358.

NEILL, R. M. 1938. The food and feeding of the brown trout (*Salmo trutta* L.) in relation to the organic environment. *Trans. roy. Soc. Edinb.* **59,** 481–520.

NETBOY, A. 1965. The melancholy fate of the Spanish salmon. *Salm. Trout Mag.*, **173,** 32–40.

—— 1968a. *The Atlantic Salmon a vanishing species*, 457 pp. London: Faber and Faber.

—— 1968b. Salmon in the Great Lakes. *Trout and Salmon*, **13,** 155: 23–24.

NIKOLSKY, G. V. 1963. *The Ecology of Fishes*, xv + 352 pp. London and New York: Academic Press.

—— 1969. *Theory of Fish Population Dynamics*, xvi + 323 pp. Edinburgh: Oliver and Boyd.

NILSSON, N.-A., 1955. Studies of the feeding habits of trout and char in northern Swedish lakes. *Rep. Inst. Freshw. Res., Drottningholm*, **36,** 163–225.

—— 1957. On the feeding habits of trout in a stream of northern Sweden. *Rep. Inst. Freshw. Res., Drottningholm*, **38,** 154–66.

—— 1967. Interactive segregation between fish species, pp. 295–313, in Gerking, S. D. (Ed.) *The Biological Basis of Freshwater Fish Production*, Edinburgh and Oxford: Blackwell Scientific Publications.

NYMAN, O. L. 1965. Variation of proteins in hybrids and parental species of fishes. *Swedish Salmon Research Institute Report* (LFI Medd.) **13,** 11 pp.

—— 1966. Geographic variation in Atlantic salmon (*Salmo salar* L.). *Swedish Salmon Research Institute Report* (LFI Medd.) **3,** 6 pp.

—— 1967. Protein variation in various populations of Atlantic salmon. *Swedish Salmon Research Institute Report.* (LFI Medd.) **8,** 11 pp.

OLIVER, G. C. S. 1963. XV International Congress of Limnology, Madison, U.S.A. Management of an artificial brown trout fishery in a water supply reservoir. *Salm. Trout Mag.*, **169,** 198–202.

—— 1968. The development of a trout fishery in a lowland reservoir (Eye Brook). *J. Instn. of Water Engineers*, **22,** 129–136.

ONODERA, K. 1962. Carrying capacity in a trout stream. *Bull. Freshw. Fish. Res. Lab.*, **12** (I), 41 pp.

ÖSTERDAHL, L. 1969. The smolt run of a small Swedish river, 205–215. Symposium on salmon and trout in streams, H. R. MacMillan Lectures in Fisheries, University of British Columbia.

OTTERSTRÖM, C. V. 1938. Salmon from west Jutland. *Medd. Komm. Havundersøg., kibh.*, (9), **10,** 3–20.

PALMER, C. H. 1928. *The Salmon Rivers of Newfoundland*, 271 pp. Boston: Farrington.

PATTERSON, J. H. 1903. The cause of salmon disease. Fishery Board for Scotland, Salm. Fish., 52 pp.

PEART, L. R. 1960. The value of stocking rivers with trout. Salm. Trout Assn conf. Lond., 1960, 1–13.

PENNELL, J. T. 1959. Effects on fresh water fisheries of forestry practices. In 'The effects on fresh water fisheries of man-made activities in British Columbia.' *Can. Fish Cult.*, **25,** 27–59.

PENTELOW, F. T. K. 1932. The food of the brown trout (*Salmo trutta*). *J. Anim. Ecol.* **I,** 101–107.

—— 1944. Nature of acid in soft water in relation to the growth of brown trout. *Nature*, **153,** 464.

—— 1953. *River Purification*. 63 pp. London: Arnold.

PETERSON, H. 1956. Skraken än en gang. *Svensk. Fisk-Tidskr.*, **65**, (6/7), 99–101.

—— 1968. The grayling, *Thymallus thymallus* (L.), of the Sundsvall Bay area. *Rep. Inst. Freshw. Res.*, *Drottningholm*, **38**, 70–106.

PEZON, J. 1961. Efficacité et rentabilité des diverses méthodes de repeuplement en truites. *Plaisirs de la Pêche*, Oct./Nov. 60, 61: 494–499.

PIGGINS, D. J. 1959. Investigations on predators of salmon smolts and parr. Report and Statement of Accounts, The Salmon Research Trust for Ireland Incorporated, Appendix I, 12 pp.

—— 1965. Salmon and sea trout hybrids. *Atlantic Salmon Journal*, Autumn, 3–5.

—— 1967. Analysis of recapture data from tagged sea trout kelts 1960/66. Report and Statement of Accounts, The Salmon Research Trust for Ireland Incorporated, Appendix III, 38–48.

—— 1969. Talking points in salmonid research. *Salm. Trout Mag.*, **185**, 51–65.

PIPPY, J. H. C. 1969. *Pomphorhynchus laevis* (Zoega) Müller, 1776 (Acanthocephala) in Atlantic salmon (*Salmo salar*) and its use as a biological tag. *J. Fish. Res. Bd. Can.*, **26**, (4): 909–919.

POPE, J. A., MILLS, D. H. and SHEARER, W. M. 1961. The fecundity of Atlantic salmon (*Salmo salar* Linn.). *Freshwat. Salm. Fish. Res.*, **26**, 12 pp.

POWER, G. 1966. Observations on the speckled trout (*Salvelinus fontinalis*) in Ungava. *Naturaliste Canadien*, **93**, 3, 187–199.

POWERS, E. B. 1941. Physio-chemical behaviour of waters as factors in the 'homing' of the salmon. *Ecology*, **22**, 1–16.

POWERS, E. B. and CLARK, R. T. 1943. Further evidence on the chemical factors affecting the migratory movements of fishes, especially the salmon. *Ecology*, **24**, 109–112.

PRAWOCHENSKY, R. and KOLDER, W. 1968. Synopsis of biological data on *Hucho hucho* (Linnaeus 1758). FAO Fisheries Synopsis No. 22 (Suppl.) I.

PYEFINCH, K. A. 1952. Capture of pre-grilse stage of salmon. *Scott. Nat.*, **64**, 47.

—— 1955. A review of the literature on the biology of the Atlantic salmon (*Salmo salar* Linn.). *Freshwat. Salm. Fish. Res.*, **9**, 24 pp.

—— 1960. *Trout in Scotland*. A study of brown trout research at Pitlochry. 70 pp. Her Majesty's Stationery Office.

—— 1967. Further recaptures of salmon tagged in Greenland. *Scott. Fish. Bull.*, **28**, 30.

—— 1968. Further recaptures of Greenland salmon. *Scott. Fish. Bull.*, **30**, 30.

—— 1969a. The Greenland salmon fishery. *The Salmon Net*, V, 11–19.

—— 1969b. Advisory work on freshwater fisheries. *Scott. Fish. Bull.*, **31**, 14–15.

—— 1969c. The Greenland salmon fishery. *Proc. Challenger Soc.*, IV (1): 4–12.

PYEFINCH, K. A. and WOODWARD, W. B. 1955. The movements of salmon tagged in the sea, Montrose, 1948, 1950, 1951. *Freshwat. Salm. Fish. Res.*, **8**, 15 pp.

PYEFINCH, K. A. and MILLS, D. H. 1963. Observations on the movements of Atlantic salmon (*Salmo salar* L.) in the River Conon and the River Meig, Ross-shire. I. *Freshwat. Salm. Fish. Res.*, **31**, 24 pp.

PYEFINCH, K. A. and ELSON, K. G. R. 1967. Salmon disease in Irish rivers. *Scott. Fish. Bull.*, **26**, 21–23.

QUIGLEY, J. J. 1965. Pacific salmon survive in Atlantic. *Trade News*, **17**, 6/7: 3–5.

RAE, B. B. 1960. Seals and Scottish fisheries. *Mar. Res. Scot.*, **2**, 39 pp.

—— 1968. The food of seals in Scottish waters. *Mar. Res. Scot.*, **2**, 23 pp.

RAE, B. B. and SHEARER, W. M. 1965. Seal damage to salmon fisheries. *Mar. Res. Scot.*, **2**, 39 pp.

RASMUSON, M. 1968. Populationgenetiska synpunkter på laxodling sverksamheten i Sverige. Swedish Salmon Research Institute – LFI Medd. 3/1968.

RICKER, W. E. 1954. Pacific salmon for Atlantic waters. *Can. Fish Cult.*, **16**, 6–14.

—— 1958. Handbook of computations for biological statistics of fish populations. *Bull. Fish. Res. Bd. Can.*, **119**, 1–300.

—— (Ed.) 1968. *Methods of Assessment of Fish Production in Fresh Waters.* IBP Handbook No. 3, 313 pp. Edinburgh and Oxford: Blackwell Scientific Publications.

RITCHIE, J. 1920. *The Influences of Man on Animal Life in Scotland.* xvi + 550 pp. Cambridge: University Press.

ROBERTS, R. J. 1969. The pathology of salmon disease. *Salmon Net*, V, 48–51.

ROBERTS, R. J., SHEARER, W. M. and ELSON, K. G. R. 1969. The pathology of ulcerative dermal necrosis of Scottish salmon. *J. Path.* **97** (3), 563–565.

ROBSON, D. S. and REGIER, H. A. 1968. Estimation of population number and mortality rates, in Ricker, W. E. (Ed.) *Methods for Assessment of Fish Production in Fresh Waters.* IBP Handbook No. 3. Edinburgh and Oxford: Blackwell Scientific Publications.

ROBSON, T. O. 1968. *The Control of Aquatic Weeds.* Bull. No. 194, London: H.M.S.O.

ROCHER, R. 1965. T.O.S. (Truite-Ombre-Saumon, the French National Association for the Protection of Trout, Grayling and Salmon). *Salm. Trout Mag.*, **175**, 154–163.

ROGERS, E., CRICHTON, M. and PIGGINS, D. J. 1965. Report and Statement of Accounts of the Salmon Research Trust for Ireland Incorporated, Appendix IV, 41–50.

ROSSELAND, L. 1966. The Norwegian statistics for the salmon and sea trout fishery 1876–1965 with some comments. I.C.E.S. C.M. 1966/L: 16.

ROUNSEFELL, G. A. and EVERHAUT, W. H. 1953. *Fishery Science: its methods and applications.* 444 pp. New York: Wiley.

ROYAL COMMISSION ON SEWAGE DISPOSAL. 1912. 8th Report. Vol. I. Cmnd. 6464. London: H.M.S.O.

—— 1913. 8th Report Vol. II. Appendix. Pt. II. Sect. 6, 132–140. Cmnd. 6943. London: H.M.S.O.

RUNNSTRØM, S. 1940. Age and growth of lake Vaner salmon. K. Lantbrukstyrels. *Medd.*, **18**, 1–39.

RUSSEL, A. 1864. *The Salmon.* 348 pp. Edinburgh: Edmonston and Douglas.

SALYER, J. and LAGLER, K. F. 1940. The food and habits of the American merganser during winter in Michigan, considered in relation to fish management. *J. Wildl. Mgmt.* **4**, 186–219.

SALYER, J., CLARK, H. and LAGLER, K. F. 1946. The eastern belted kingfisher, *Megaceryle alcyon alcyon* (Linnaeus) in relation to fish management. *Trans. Amer. Fish. Soc.*, **76**, 97–117.

SAUNDERS, J. W. 1966. Estuarine spawning of Atlantic salmon. *J. Fish. Res. Bd. Can.*, **23** (11), 1803–1804.

—— 1969. Mass mortalities and behaviour of brook trout and juvenile Atlantic salmon in a stream polluted by agricultural pesticides. *J. Fish. Res. Bd. Can.*, **26** (3): 695–699.

SAUNDERS, J. W. and SMITH, M. W. 1962. Physical alteration of stream habitat to improve brook trout production. *Trans. Am. Fish. Soc.*, **91** (2): 185–188.

SAUNDERS, R. L. 1966. The west Greenland salmon fishery. *Trade News*, **18** (8), 3–6.

SAUNDERS, R. L. and GEE, J. H. 1964. Movements of young Atlantic salmon in a small stream. *J. Fish. Res. Bd. Can.*, **21** (1): 27–36.

SAUNDERS, R. L., KERSWILL, C. J. and ELSON, P. F. 1965. Canadian Atlantic salmon recaptured near Greenland. *J. Fish. Res. Bd. Can.*, **22** (2): 625–629.

SCHMIDT, P. J. and BAKER, E. G. 1969. Indirect pigmentation of salmon and trout flesh with canthaxanthin. *J. Fish. Res. Bd. Can.*, **26** (2): 357–360.

SCOTT, D. 1964. The migratory trout (*Salmo trutta* L.) in New Zealand 1. The introduction of stocks. *Trans. roy. Soc. N.Z., Zool.*, **4**, 209–227.

SCOTT, M. 1968. The pathogenicity of *Aeromonas salmonicida* (Griffin) in sea and brackish waters. *J. gen. Microbiol.*, **50**, 321–327.

SCOTTISH HOME DEPARTMENT. 1957. *The Passage of smolts and kelts through fish passes.* H.M.S.O.

SCROPE, W. 1843. *Days and nights salmon fishing in the Tweed*, with a short account of the natural history and habits of salmon; instructions to sportsmen, etc. 298 pp. London: Arnold.

SEABURG, K. G. 1957. A stomach sampler for live fish. *Progve. Fish Cult.*, **19**, (3), 137–139.

SEBER, G. A. F. and LE CREN, E. D. 1967. Estimating population parameters from catches large relative to the population. *J. Anim. Ecol.*, **36**, 631–643.

SEDGWICK, D. 1960. Planting salmon. *Salm. Trout Mag.*, **160**, 204–210.

SEMPLE, G. 1967. Mythical profits of the fishing proprietors. *The Financial Scotsman*, 23rd August, p. 17.

SHEARER, W. M. 1957. The capture of sea trout at sea. *Scott. Fish. Bull.*, **6**, 13.

—— 1958. The movements of salmon tagged in the sea, Montrose, 1954, 1955. *Freshwat. Salm. Fish. Res.*, **20**, 11 pp.

—— 1959a. Sea trout transportation experiments. *Rep. Challenger Soc.*, **3**, XI, 24–25.

—— 1959b. Some notes on the efficiency of two types of tag used for tagging sea trout kelts in the River Dee, Aberdeenshire. *Rapp. et Proc.-Verb.*, **148**, 17–18.

—— 1961a. Pacific salmon in the North Sea. *New Scientist*, **10**, 184–186.

—— 1961b. Survival rate of young salmonids in streams stocked with 'green' ova. I.C.E.S./C.M., No. 98.

—— 1963. The capture of the pre-grilse stage of Atlantic salmon in freshwater. *Salm. Trout Mag.* **168**, 110–111.

—— 1965. Recaptures from releases of hatchery-reared and wild smolts in the River North Esk. I.C.E.S./C.M. 1965. No. 59, 3 pp.

SHEARER, W. M. and TREVAWAS, E. 1960. A Pacific salmon (*Oncorhynchus gorbuscha*) in Scottish waters. *Nature*, **188**, 4753: 868.

SHEARER, W. M. and BALMAIN, K. H. 1967. Greenland Salmon. *Salmon Net*, **3**, 19–24.

SHETTER, D. S., CLARK, O. H. and HAZZARD, A. S. 1946. The effects of deflectors in a section of Michigan trout stream. *Trans. Amer. Fish. Soc.*, **76**, 248–278.

SIMPSON, A. C. 1951. The fecundity of plaice. Fishery Invest., Lond., Ser. 2, **17**, 1–27.

SINHA, V. R. P. and EVANS, H. 1969. Salmon rearing in mountain tarns. The scales and growth of the fish of Llynau Dyrnogydd, Teyrn and Cilan., *J. Fish Biol.*, **1**, 285–294.

SLACK, H. D. 1955. Factors affecting the productivity of *Coregonus clupeoides* Lacépède in Loch Lomond. *Verh. Internat. Verein, Limniol*, xii, 183–186.

SLACK, H. D., GERVERS, F. W. K. and HAMILTON, J. D. 1957. The biology of the Powan. Glasg. Univ. Publ., Stud. Loch Lomond, **1**, 113–1127.

SMART, G. G. J. 1965. The practical results of increasing the accessibility of spawning grounds in the River North Esk. *The Salmon Net*, 1, 21–25.

SMITH, I. W. 1957. The occurrence of damaged sea trout on the east coast of Scotland. *Salm. Trout Mag.*, **150**, 148–150.

—— 1960. Furunculosis in salmon kelts. *Nature*, **186**, 733–734.

—— 1962. Furunculosis in kelts. *Freshwat. Salm. Fish. Res.*, **27**, 12 pp.

—— 1963. The classification of 'Bacterium salmonicida'. *J. gen. Microbiol.*, **33**, 263–274.

—— 1964. The occurrence and pathology of Dee disease. *Freshwat. Salm. Fish. Res.*, **34**, 12 pp.

SMITH, M. W. 1948. Preliminary observations upon the fertilization of Crecy Lake, New Brunswick. *Trans. Amer. Fish. Soc.*, **75**, 165–174.

SMITH, S. H. 1954. Method of producing plastic impressions of fish scales without using heat. *Progve. Fish Cult.*, **16** (2), 75–78.

SNIESZKO, S. F. and GRIFFIN, P. J. 1955. Kidney disease in brook trout and its treatment. *Progve. Fish Cult.*, **17**, 3–13.

SØMME, I. D. 1948. *Ørretboka*. Oslo, Jacob Dybwads Forlag.

SOUTHERN, R. 1932. The food and growth of brown trout. *Salm. Trout Mag.*, **67**, 168–176; **68**, 243–258; **69**, 339–344.

STEPHENS, M. 1957. The Otter Report. London: U.F.A.W.

STEWART, L. 1963. *Investigations into migratory fish propagation in the area of the Lancashire River Board*, 80 pp. Lancaster: Barber.

STEWART, L. 1965. *An investigation into the effects of electric fishing equipment on salmon and sea trout within the area of the Lancashire River Board.*

STODDART, T. T. 1831. *The Scottish Angler*. Edinburgh: The Edinburgh Printing Company.

STUART, M. R. and FULLER, H. T. 1968. Mycological aspects of diseased Atlantic salmon. *Nature*, **217**, 90–92.

STUART, T. A. 1953a. Water currents through permeable gravels and their significance to spawning salmonids, etc. *Nature*, **172**, 407–408.

—— 1953b. Spawning migration, reproduction and young stages of loch trout (*Salmo trutta* L.). *Freshwat. Salm. Fish. Res.*, **5**, 39 pp.

—— 1954. Spawning sites of trout. *Nature*, **173**, 154.

—— 1957. The migrations and homing behaviour of brown trout (*Salmo trutta* L.). *Freshwat. Salm. Fish. Res.*, **18**, 27 pp.

—— 1962. The leaping behaviour of salmon and trout at falls and obstructions. *Freshwat. Salm. Fish. Res.*, **28**, 46 pp.

SVÄRDSON, G. 1949. The Coregonid problem I. Some general aspects of the problem. *Rep. Inst. Freshwat. Res., Drottningholm*, **29**, 89–101.

—— 1950. The Coregonid problem II. Morphology of two Coregonid species in different environments. *Rep. Inst. Freshwat. Res., Drottningholm*, **31**, 151–162.

—— 1952. The Coregonid problem IV. The significance of scales and gillrakers. *Rep. Inst. Freshwat. Res., Drottningholm*, **33**, 204–232.

SWAIN, A. 1959. The efficiency of various types of tags. *Rapp. et Proc.-Verb.*, **148**, 23–25.

—— 1963. Long-distance migration of salmon. *Nature*, **197**, 923.

SWAIN, A. and HARTLEY, W. G. 1959. Movements of sea trout off the east coast of England. *Rep. Challenger Soc.*, **3**, XI, 31.

SWAIN, A., HARTLEY, W. G. and DAVIES, R. B. 1962. Long-distance migration of salmon. *Nature*, **195**, 1122.

SWIFT, D. R. 1961. The annual growth-rate cycle in brown trout (*Salmo trutta* Linn.) and its cause. *J. Exp. Biol.* (1961), **38**, 595–64.

SYMONS, P. E. K. 1968. Increase in aggression and in strength of the social hierarchy among juvenile Atlantic salmon deprived of food. *J. Fish. Res. Bd. Can.*, **25** (11): 2387–2401.

TARZWELL, C. M. 1957. Water quality criteria for aquatic life, pp. 246–272 in *Biological Problems in Water Pollution*. U.S. Dept. Health, Education and Welfare, Public Health Service, Cincinnati.

TREVAWAS, E. 1953. Sea trout and brown trout. *Salm. Trout Mag.*, **139**, 199–215.

TAYLOR, G. R. 1968. *The Biological Timebomb*. London: Thames and Hudson.

TAYLOR, J. O. 1928. *The Law Affecting River Pollution*. Edinburgh: Green.

TCHERNAVIN, V. 1938. The absorption of bones in the skull of salmon during their migration to rivers. *Fisheries, Scotl., Salmon Fish.*, **VI**, 4 pp.

TÉTREAULT, B. 1967. The salmon rivers of the province of Quebec. Swedish Salmon Research Institute Report. (LFI Medd.) **6**, 15 pp.

THOMAS, J. D. 1958. Studies on *Crepidostomum metoecus* (Braun) and *C. farionis* (Müller), parasitic in *Salmo trutta* L. and *S. salar* in Britain. *Parasitology*, **48** (3/4): 336–352.

—— 1964. Studies on the growth of trout *Salmo trutta* from four contrasting habitats. *Proc. zool. Soc. Lond.*, **142**, 459–509.

THOMPSON, W. F. 1965. Fishing treaties and salmon of the North Pacific. *Science*, **150**, No. 3705, 1786–1789.

THRING, C. F. 1959. Estuaries as seen by an industrialist. *Association of River Boards Year Book*, 1958, 1–6.

THUROW, F. 1968. On food, behaviour and population mechanisms of Baltic salmon. *Swedish Salmon Research Institute Report*. (LFI Medd.) **4**, 16 pp.

TIMMERMANS, J. A. 1960. Observations concernant les populations de truite commune (*Salmo trutta fario* L.) dans les eaux courantes. *Trav. Stat. Rech. Eaux et Forets, Groendaal*, Series D. No. 28, 36 pp.

—— 1961. Lutte contre la végétation aquatique envahissante. *Trav. Stat. Rech. Eaux et Forets, Groendaal*, Series D, No. 31, 44 pp.

TONER, E. D. 1960. Predation by pike in three Irish lakes. *Report of Irish Dept. on Sea and Inland Fisheries*, Appendix 25, 1–7.

TURING, P. 1968. The gravest threat to salmon stocks. *Trout and Salmon*, **14**, 158, 13–14.

TWOMEY, E. 1956. Fertilization of some acid or bog lakes in Ireland. *Report of Irish Dept. on Sea and Inland Fisheries*, 2–16.

VAN DUIJIN, C. 1967. *Diseases of Fishes*, 309 pp. London: Iliffe Books.

VAN SOMEREN, V. D. 1937. A preliminary investigation into the causes of scale absorption in salmon (*Salmo salar* L.). *Fish. Bd. Scotl., Salmon Fisheries*, **11**, 11 pp.

VARLEY, M. E. 1967. *British Freshwater Fishes*, 148 pp. London: Fishing News (Books) Ltd.

VIBERT, R. (Ed.) 1967. *Fishing with Electricity. Its application to biology and management.* xxviii + 276 pp. London: Fishing News (Books) Ltd.

VIK, K.-O. 1962. Fish cultivation. *Salm. Trout Mag.*, **169**, 203–208. (Reprinted from the *Flyfishers' Journal*.)

VLADYKOV, V. D. 1956. Fecundity of wild speckled trout (*Salvelinus fontinalis*) in Quebec lakes. *J. Fish. Res. Bd. Can.*, **13** (6), 799–841.

WADDEN, N. 1968. *Lamprey control in the Great Lakes*, Department of Fisheries of Canada, Ottawa.

WADDINGTON, I. 1963. Munich fish ponds. *J. Inst. Sew. Purif.*, **3**, 214–215.

WALDICHUK, M. 1962. Some water pollution problems connected with the disposal of pulp mill wastes. *Canad. Fish Cult.*, **31**, 3, 3–4.

WALLIN, O. 1957. On the growth structure and developmental physiology of the scale of fishes. *Rep. Inst. Freshwat. Fisheries, Drottningholm*, **38**, 385–447.

WARD, H. B. 1930. Some responses of sockeye salmon to environmental influence during freshwater migration. *Ann. Mag. nat. Hist.*, Ser. 10, **6**, 18–36.

WARDLE, R. A. and MACLEOD, J. A. 1952. *The Zoology of Tapeworms*, 780 pp. University of Minnesota Press.

WARREN, C. E., WALES, J. H., DAVIS, G. E. and DOUDOROFF, P. 1964. Trout production in an experimental stream enriched with sucrose. *J. Wildl. Mgmt.*, **28** (4): 617–660.

WATT, K. E. F. 1968. *Ecology and Resource Management*, London: MacGraw-Hill.

WEATHERLEY, A. and NICHOLLS, A. G. 1955. The effects of artificial enrichment of a lake. *Aust. J. Mar. Freshw. Res.*, **6**, 443–468.

WEBSTER, D. A. 1962. Artificial spawning facilities for brook trout, *Salvelinus fontinalis. Trans. Amer. Fish. Soc.*, **91**, (2): 168–174.

WENT, A. E. J. 1947. Value of the kelt, some notes on previously-spawned salmon in Ireland. *Salm. Trout Mag.*, **119**, 41–48.

—— 1949. Spring fish. Are there two types of winter salmon? *Salm. Trout Mag.* **125**, 23–26.

—— 1955. *Irish Salmon and Salmon Fisheries*. London: Arnold.

—— 1956. The Irish drift net fishery for salmon. *J. Dept. Agriculture*, Dublin, **52**, 131–145.

—— 1962. Irish sea trout, a review of investigations to date. *Sci. Proc. R. Dublin Soc.*, Ser. A, **1** (10), 265–296.

—— 1964a. The pursuit of salmon in Ireland. *Proc. Roy. Irish Acad.*, **63** (C) 6: 191–244.

—— 1964b. Irish salmon – a review of investigations up to 1963. *Sci. Proc. R. Dublin Soc.*, Ser. A, **1** (15), 365–412.

WENT, A. E. J. and PIGGINS, D. J. 1965. Long-distance migration of Atlantic salmon. *Nature*, **205**, 4972: 723.

WHEELER, A. 1969. *The Fishes of the British Isles and North West Europe*. London: Macmillan.

WHITE, H. C. 1936a. The homing of salmon in Apple River, N.S. *J. Biol. Bd. Can.*, **2** (4): 391–400.

—— 1936b. The food of kingfishers and mergansers on the Margaree River Nova Scotia. *J. Biol. Bd. Can.*, **2** (3), 227–284.

—— 1937. Local feeding of kingfishers and mergansers. *J. Biol. Bd. Can.*, **3**, (4), 323–338.

—— 1939a. Bird control to increase the Margaree River salmon. *Bull. Fish. Res. Bd. Can.*, **58**, 30 pp.

—— 1939b. The food of *Mergus serrator* on the Margaree River, N.S., *J. Fish. Res. Bd. Can.*, **4** (5): 309–311.

—— 1940a. Factors influencing the descent of Atlantic salmon smolts. *J. Fish. Res. Bd. Can.*, **4**, 323–326.

—— 1940b. Sea lice (*Lepeophtheirus*) and death of salmon. *J. Fish. Res. Bd. Can.*, **5**, 172–175.

—— 1942a. Atlantic salmon redds and artificial spawning beds. *J. Fish. Res. Bd. Can.*, **6**, 37–44.

—— 1942b. Life history of *Lepeophtheirus salmonis*. *J. Fish. Res. Bd. Can.*, **6**, 24–29.

—— 1953. The eastern belted kingfisher in the maritime provinces. *Bull. Fish. Res. Bd. Can.*, **97**, 44 pp.

—— 1957. Food and natural history of mergansers on salmon waters in the maritime provinces of Canada. *Bull. Fish. Res. Bd. Can.*, **116**, 63 pp.

WHITE, H. C. and HUNTSMAN, A. G. 1938. Is local behaviour in salmon heritable? *J. Fish. Res. Bd. Can.*, **4**, 1–18.

WHITE, H. C. and MEDCOF, J. C. 1968. Atlantic salmon scales as records of spawning history. *J. Fish. Res. Bd. Can.*, **25** (11): 2439–2441.

WILDER, D. G. 1947. A comparative study of the Atlantic salmon, *Salmo salar* Linnaeus, and the Lake salmon *Salmo salar sebago* (Girard). *Can. J. Res.*, 25 D (6): 175–189.

—— 1952. A comparative study of anadromous and freshwater populations of brook trout (*Salvelinus fontinalis* (Mitchell)). *J. Fish. Res. Bd. Can.*, **9** (4): 169–203.

WILKINS, N. P. 1967. Immunology, serology and blood group research in fishes. In: Polymorphismes biochimiques des animaux, 355–259. Inst. Natl. Rech. Agronom., Paris.

—— 1968. Multiple haemoglobins of the Atlantic salmon (*Salmo salar*). *J. Fish. Res. Bd. Can.*, **25**, (12): 2651–2653.

WILLIAMS, I. V. and GILHAUSEN, P. 1968. Lamprey parasitism on Fraser River sockeye and pink salmon during 1967. *Internat. Pacific Salmon Fish. Comm.*, Bull. 18, 22 pp.

WISBY, W. J. and HASLER, A. D. 1954. Effect of olfactory occlusion on migrating silver salmon (*O. kisutch*). *J. Fish. Res. Bd. Can.*, **11**, 472–478.

WISDOM, A. S. 1956. *The Law on the Pollution of Waters*. Shaw.

WOLF, P. 1950. *Fisheries biological investigations in the Kävlinge River*. Report to Swedish Salmon and Trout Association, Malmo.

WOLF, P. 1960a. Land drainage and its dangers as experienced in Sweden – I. *Salm. Trout Mag.*, **159**, 151–158.

—— 1960b. Land drainage and its dangers as experienced in Sweden – II. *Salm. Trout Mag.*, **160**, 176–185.

—— 1961a. Land drainage and its dangers as experienced in Sweden – III. *Salm. Trout Mag.*, **161**, 24–30.

—— 1961b. Land drainage and its dangers as experienced in Sweden – IV. *Salm. Trout Mag.*, **162**, 95–100.

—— 1961c. Land drainage and its dangers as experienced in Sweden – V. *Salm. Trout Mag.*, **163**, 145–150.

—— 1962a. Land drainage and its dangers as experienced in Sweden – VI. *Salm. Trout Mag.*, **164**, 47–54.

—— 1962b. Land drainage and its dangers as experienced in Sweden – VII. *Salm. Trout Mag.*, **165**, 102–110.

—— 1962c. Land drainage and its dangers as experienced in Sweden – VIII. *Salm. Trout Mag.*, **166**, 167–174.

WOODIWISS, F. S. 1964. The biological system of stream classification used by the Trent River Board. *Chemistry and Industry*, March 14th, pp. 443–447.

WORTHINGTON, E. B. 1940. Rainbows. A report on attempts to acclimatise rainbow trout in Britain. *Salm. Trout Mag.*, **100**, 241–260.

—— 1941. Rainbows. A report on attempts to acclimatise rainbow trout in Britain (continued). *Salm. Trout Mag.*, **101,** 62–99.

—— 1949. An experiment with populations of fish in Windermere, 1939–1948. *Proc. zool. Soc. Lond.*, 113–149.

ZARNECKI, S. 1956. Summer and winter races of salmon and sea trout from the Vistula river. I.C.E.S./C.M. 142, 3 pp.

SUBJECT INDEX